Circuits and Systems: Design and Applications

Volume I

Circuits and Systems: Design and Applications
Volume I

Edited by **Helena Walker**

LANRYE
INTERNATIONAL

New Jersey

Published by Clanrye International,
55 Van Reypen Street,
Jersey City, NJ 07306, USA
www.clanryeinternational.com

Circuits and Systems: Design and Applications
Volume I
Edited by Helena Walker

This book contains information obtained from authentic and highly regarded sources. Copyright for all individual chapters remain with the respective authors as indicated. A wide variety of references are listed. Permission and sources are indicated; for detailed attributions, please refer to the permissions page. Reasonable efforts have been made to publish reliable data and information, but the authors, editors and publisher cannot assume any responsibility for the validity of all materials or the consequences of their use.

The publisher's policy is to use permanent paper from mills that operate a sustainable forestry policy. Furthermore, the publisher ensures that the text paper and cover boards used have met acceptable environmental accreditation standards.

Trademark Notice: Registered trademark of products or corporate names are used only for explanation and identification without intent to infringe.

Printed in the United States of America.

Contents

Subthreshold Leakage Power in Standby Mode   **163**
Manish Kumar, Md. Anwar Hussain, Sajal K. Paul

Chapter 25   **Performance Evaluation of Efficient XOR Structures in Quantum-Dot**
Cellular Automata (QCA)   **171**
Mohammad Rafiq Beigh, Mohammad Mustafa, Firdous Ahmad

Chapter 26   **Graph Modeling for Static Timing Analysis at Transistor Level in**
Nano-Scale CMOS Circuits   **181**
Abdoul Rjoub, Almotasem Bellah Alajlouni, Hassan Almanasrah

Chapter 27   **A Reconfigurable Network-on-Chip Datapath for Application**
Specific Computing   **195**
Joshua Weber, Erdal Oruklu

              Permissions

              List of Contributors

Preface

At a very fundamental level, a circuit refers to an overall, complex arrangement of components such as resistors, conductors etc. which are connected in order to ensure a steady flow of current. It is only through circuits that signals or information is conveyed to the destination. Without a proper circuit system, the functional ability of any device becomes more or less redundant. The complexity and design of electronic circuits is ever increasing. Circuits are classified into analog circuits, digital circuits and mixed-signal circuits.

Circuits and systems in this book explain the handling of theory and applications of circuits and systems, signal processing, and system design methodology. The practical implementation of circuits, and application of circuit theoretic techniques to systems and to signal processing are the topics covered under this discipline. From radio astronomy to wireless communications and biomedical applications, the application of circuits and systems can be found across a varying range of subjects.

Circuits and Systems is an interesting discipline and is emerging as a coveted career option for many students. A lot of research, to develop more efficient systems is also being conducted.

I'd like to thank all the contributors for sharing their studies with us and make this book an enlightening read. I would also like to thank them for submitting their work within the set time parameters. Lastly, I wish to thank my family, whose support has been crucial for the completion of this book.

Editor

Performance Analysis of an Inverse Notch Filter and Its Application to F_0 Estimation

Yosuke Sugiura, Arata Kawamura, Youji Iiguni

Graduate School of Engineering Science, Osaka University, Osaka, Japan

ABSTRACT

In this paper, we analyze an inverse notch filter and present its application to F_0 (fundamental frequency) estimation. The inverse notch filter is a narrow band pass filter and it has an infinite impulse response. We derive the explicit forms for the impulse response and the sum of squared impulse response. Based on the analysis result, we derive a normalized inverse notch filter whose pass band area is identical to unit. As an application of the normalized inverse notch filter, we propose an F_0 estimation method for a musical sound. The F_0 estimation method is achieved by connecting the normalized inverse notch filters in parallel. Estimation results show that the proposed F_0 estimation method effectively detects F_0s for piano sounds in a mid-range.

Keywords: Band Pass Filter; Inverse Notch Filter; Impulse Response Analysis

1. Introduction

In speech processing, image processing, biomedical signal processing, and many other signal processing fields, it is important to eliminate the narrowband signal. The examples of the narrowband signal are a hum noise from the power supply, an acoustic feedback, and an interference noise, and so on. A notch filter is useful for the elimination of the narrowband signal [1-7], where the notch filter passes all frequencies expect of a stop frequency band centered on a center frequency, called as the notch frequency. The notch filter has a simple structure, and its stop bandwidth and its notch frequency are individually designed. The notch filter is used in many applications and it has been analyzed in many literatures [1,4-7].

On the other hand, an inverse notch filter is a band pass filter which has the inverse characteristics of the notch filter. In contrast to the notch filter, there are few applications of the inverse notch filter. As an example of the applications, an active noise control system for reducing a sinusoidal noise has been proposed [8]. In this system, the inverse notch filter is used to extract the sinusoidal noise. Unfortunately, the system is designed without respect to the impulse response of the inverse notch filter. Hence, the inverse notch filter cannot accurately extract the sinusoidal noise when the filter output is in the transient state. To utilize the inverse notch filter more effectively for not only the active noise control system but also many other applications, a more detail analysis of the impulse response for the inverse notch

filter needs to be required.

In this paper, we derive an explicit form for the infinite impulse response of the inverse notch filter. Additionally, we derive an explicit form for the sum of the squared impulse response. Then, we reveal the limit values of these two infinite sequences. Next, based on the analysis results, we propose a normalized notch filter whose pass band area is adjusted to unit. The normalized inverse notch filter is efficient to estimate the output power in the short time such as the frame processing. Finally, as an application of the normalized inverse notch filter, we present an F_0 estimation method for a musical sound. In the F_0 estimation method, we use multiple normalized inverse notch filters whose pass frequencies are identical to F_0s for each monophonic sound, respectively. These normalized inverse notch filters are connected in parallel. In the estimation procedure, we detect F_0 from the inverse notch filter whose output power is largest among all the inverse notch filter output powers. From the simulation results, we see that the proposed F_0 estimation method can effectively detect the F_0 both of for the monophonic sounds and the polyphonic sounds.

2. Performance Analysis of Inverse Notch Filter

In this section, we explain both of the notch filter and the inverse notch filter, where the latter filter has an inverse characteristic of the notch filter. The notch filter passes all frequencies expect of the narrow frequency band centered on the notch frequency. The stop bandwidth and the notch frequency can be individually designed [1-7]. The several structures of the notch filter have been proposed and all of them can be transformed to the inverse notch filter. In this paper, we use the structure of the notch filter proposed in [3-5], since the inverse notch filter can be simply obtained from the notch filter's transfer function. The transfer function of the notch filter $N(z)$ is given by

$$N(z) = \frac{1}{2}\left(1 + \frac{r + \alpha z^{-1} + z^{-2}}{1 + \alpha z^{-1} + rz^{-2}}\right), \tag{1}$$

where α is a parameter to design the notch frequency and $r(-1 < r < 1)$ is the stop bandwidth parameter. The notch frequency parameter is given by

$$\alpha = -(1+r)\cos\left(2\pi\frac{F}{F_S}\right), \tag{2}$$

where $F[\text{Hz}]$ denotes the notch frequency and $F_S[\text{Hz}]$ denotes the sampling frequency. When we put the stop bandwidth as $K[\text{Hz}]$, the relational expression of r and K is represented as

$$r = \frac{1 + \cos(2\pi K/F_S) - \sin(2\pi K/F_S)}{1 + \cos(2\pi K/F_S) + \sin(2\pi K/F_S)}. \tag{3}$$

From (1), we can derive the inverse notch filter represented as

$$I(z) = 1 - N(z) = \frac{1-r}{2}\frac{1 - z^{-2}}{1 + \alpha z^{-1} + rz^{-2}}, \tag{4}$$

where the $I(z)$ is the transfer function of the inverse notch filter. We see from (4) that the inverse notch filter is very easy to implement. Note that the pass bandwidth parameter r is also given as (3), where K denotes the pass bandwidth. **Figure 1** shows the structure of the inverse notch filter, where $x(n)$ is the input signal, $y(n)$ is the output signal, and $u(n)$ is the signal obtained from the IIR unit within the inverse notch filter. We see from this figure that the inverse notch filter requires only three multiplications and three additions to calculate the output signal. **Figure 2** shows the frequency amplitude response of $I(z)$ when $\alpha = 0 (F = F_S/2)$ with $r = 0.8, 0.9, 0.99$, where the vertical axis denotes the amplitude and the horizontal axis denotes the normalized frequency. We see from **Figure 2** that the amplitude at the notch frequency is 1 regardless of r, and the pass bandwidth becomes narrow with increasing r

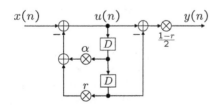

Figure 1. Structure of inverse notch filter.

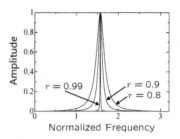

Figure 2. Power spectrum of the inverse notch filter.

toward to 1, *i.e.*, we can accurately extract a single sinusoidal signal by setting r extremely close to 1.

When filtering an input signal, one of the most important factors is the impulse response of the filter. We firstly derive the impulse response of the inverse notch filter as an explicit formulation. We see from (2) or **Figure 1** that the signal $y(n)$ and $u(n)$ are given as

$$y(n) = \frac{1-r}{2}(u(n) - u(n-2)) \tag{5}$$

with

$$u(n) = x(n) - \alpha u(n-1) - ru(n-2). \tag{6}$$

To obtain the impulse response, we put the input signal as the impulse signal represented as

$$x(n) = \delta(n), \tag{7}$$

where $\delta(n)$ is the Kronecker's delta. In this case, (6) can be represented as the following equation

$$u(n) + \alpha u(n-1) + ru(n-2) = 0, \tag{8}$$

where $n \geq 2$. Solving the above homogeneous equation with respect to $u(n)$ and introducing the initial condition that $u(0) = 1$ and $u(1) = \alpha$, we obtain the solution expressed as

$$u(n) = \frac{2}{p}r^{(n+1)/2}\sin(\theta(n+1)), \tag{9}$$

$$p = \sqrt{4r - \alpha^2}, \tag{10}$$

$$\theta = \arctan\left(\frac{p}{-\alpha}\right). \tag{11}$$

We assume that $\alpha^2 < 4r$. Note that this assumption is satisfied when $r \approx 1$. By substituting (9) into (5), we obtain the impulse response of the inverse notch filter $h(n)(n \geq 2)$ expressed as

$$y(n)\big|_{x(n) = \delta(n)} = h(n)$$
$$= \frac{1-r}{p}r^{(n-1)/2}\{r\sin(\theta n + \theta) - \sin(\theta n - \theta)\}. \tag{12}$$

From (12), we see that the impulse response becomes close to 0 with increasing n due to the term $r^{(n-1)/2}$. When $u(n) = 0, (n < 0)$, we also have $h(0)$ and $h(1)$

represented as

$$h(0) = \frac{1-r}{2}, \tag{13}$$

$$h(1) = -\alpha \frac{1-r}{2}. \tag{14}$$

Next, we formulate the sum of squared impulse response to evaluate its convergence property. Taking square of (12), the squared impulse response $h^2(n)(n \geq 2)$ is obtained as

$$h^2(n) = \frac{(1-r)^2\left\{(1-r)^2 + p^2\right\}}{2p^2} r^{n-1}$$
$$- \mathrm{Re}\left[\frac{(1-r)^2\left(1-re^{j2\theta}\right)^2}{2p^2} r^{n-1}e^{j2\theta(n-1)} \right], \tag{15}$$

where we use the following relation

$$\cos(2\theta) = 1 - p^2/2r. \tag{16}$$

The above relation is derived from (10) and (11). Using (13), (14), and (15), the sum of the squared impulse response $J(n)$ is represented as

$$J(n) = \frac{(1-r)^2}{4} + \frac{(1-r)^2\alpha^2}{4} + \sum_{m=2}^{n} h^2(m)$$
$$= \frac{1-r}{2}\left[1 - \frac{r^n}{p^2}\{q - c(n)\}\right], \tag{17}$$

where

$$q = (1+r)^2 - \alpha^2, \tag{18}$$

$$c(n) = (1-r)\left\{\cos(2\theta n) - r\cos(2\theta(n+1))\right\}. \tag{19}$$

From (17), we easily obtain the limit value of $J(n)$ with $n \to \infty$ as

$$\lim_{n \to \infty} J(n) = \frac{1-r}{2}. \tag{20}$$

The sum of the squared impulse response $J(n)$ converges to the constant which is depending on the pass bandwidth parameter r. From Parseval's theorem, we see that (20) is identical to the sum of the squared frequency response. Note that (20) also shows the pass band area of the inverse notch filter, since its frequency responses are almost zero expect of the pass band. **Figure 3** shows the actual convergence properties for the sum of the squared impulse response with $r = 0.8, 0.9, 0.99$, where the solid line denotes the sum of the squared impulse response and the dashed line denotes the theoretical limit calculated from (20). The horizontal axis denotes sample number. We see from **Figure 3** that the sum of the squared impulse response converged to each theo-

retical limit. Also we see that convergence speed becomes fast with decreasing r.

In the audio signal processing, the inverse notch filter is often utilized for measuring a narrowband frequency power which is corresponding to the inverse notch filter's output power. However, the pass band area of the inverse notch filter depends on the parameter r as shown in (20), and thus the output power also depends on r. Hence, it is difficult to evaluate the inverse notch filter's output power when there exist multiple inverse notch filters which have different r s. To solve this problem, we derive a normalized inverse notch filter whose output power is fairly available independently with r. Since the output power is actually calculated in a short frame length, we have to establish the normalized inverse notch filter by taking into account the frame length. The sum of the squared output signal is given by

$$V(L) = \sum_{n=1}^{L-1} y^2(n)$$
$$= \sum_{n=0}^{L-1}\sum_{m=0}^{n}\sum_{l=0}^{n} h(m)h(l)x(n-m)x(n-l), \tag{21}$$

where L is the frame length. Here, we consider the case that the observed signal $x(n)$ is a white noise whose mean value and variance are 0 and σ_N^2, respectively. Taking the expectation value of (21), we have

$$E[V(L)] = \sigma_N^2 \sum_{n=0}^{L-1}\sum_{m=0}^{n} h^2(m) = \sigma_N^2 \sum_{n=0}^{L-1}\sum_{m=0}^{n} J(n). \tag{22}$$

Substituting (17) into (22) gives

$$E[V(L)] = \sigma_N^2 (1-r)^2/4 \times \left[\frac{2(L-1-r)}{1-r} \right.$$
$$\left. + \alpha^2 - \frac{2r^2}{p^2}\left\{\frac{1-r^{L-2}}{(1-r)^2}q - d_L\right\} \right], \tag{23}$$

where

$$d_L = \cos(4\theta) - r^{L-2}\cos(2\theta L). \tag{24}$$

The white noise has the same magnitude for all frequencies. Thus, it is desirable that the sum of the squared

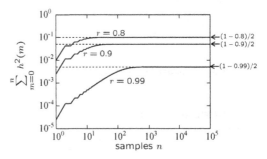

Figure 3. Convergence property for sum of squared impulse response.

output signal of the inverse notch filter is always constant regardless of the values of α, r, L. However, as shown in (23), the expectation value of $V(L)$ strongly depends on the respective values.

To solve this problem, we propose the following normalized inverse notch filter.

$$\bar{I}(z) = I(z)\Big/\sqrt{E[V(L)]} = \frac{1-r}{2\sqrt{E[V(L)]}}\frac{1-z^{-2}}{1+\alpha z^{-1}+rz^{-2}}.$$

(25)

The above normalized inverse notch filter adjusts the total pass band area in L samples to unit. **Figure 4** shows the structure of the normalized inverse notch filter, where $\bar{y}(n)$ denotes its output signal. Comparing **Figure 4** with **Figure 1**, we see that the difference is only one multiplier's value. Hence, the computational complexities of those filters are the same.

To confirm the property of the normalized inverse notch filter, we carried out a simulation. In this simulation, the capability of the normalized inverse notch filter was compared with the general inverse notch filter shown in (4). We prepared four filters which designed by different parameters. The parameter setting is summarized in **Table 1**. We used white noise as the observed signal, where its mean and variance are 0 and $\sigma_N^2 = 1$. **Figure 5** shows $E[V(L)]$ for frame length L, where "×" denotes the average value of $V(L)$ in 1000 simulations and the solid line denotes the theoretical value calculated by (23). In this figure, the horizontal axis denotes frame length. We see that the each inverse notch filter I_m gave different curves of $E[V(L)]$ due to the different parameter setting. In this case, it is not easy to evaluate the relation between filter output powers. **Figure 6** shows the result of the normalized inverse notch filter $\bar{I}_m$. We see that all the obtained $E[V(L)]$ are unit for every frame length. Hence, we can evaluate the relation between the output power regardless of the values of α, r, L.

3. Application to F_0 Estimation

In this section, as an application of the normalized inverse notch filter, we present an F_0 estimation method for musical signal. Here, we assume that the music signal consists of the F_0 frequency and its harmonics, and the amplitude of F_0 frequency is greater than other frequency amplitudes. We represent the F_0 of the music signal such as P_{ij}, where i denotes an octave number and j denotes a pitch name number, e.g., the pitch 440 Hz is represented as $P_{4,10}$. The estimating pitch range is set to $P_{3,9} - P_{5,3}$, where a piano sound in this frequency range has the maximum amplitude at its F_0 frequency. We set the notch frequency of the normalized inverse notch filter to correspond to the pitch P_{ij}. Then, the (i,j)-th normalized inverse notch filter is represented as

$$\bar{I}_{ij}(z) = \frac{1-r_{ij}}{2\sqrt{E[V(L)]}}\frac{1-z^{-2}}{1+\alpha_{ij}z^{-1}+r_{ij}z^{-2}},$$

(26)

$$\alpha_{ij} = -(1+r_{ij})\cos(2\pi P_{ij}/F_S),$$

(27)

where α_{ij} and r_{ij} are the notch frequency parameter and the pass bandwidth parameter for $I_{ij}(z)$, respectively. To eliminate overlap with the neighborhood pass bandwidth of $\bar{I}_{ij}(z)$, we design the pass bandwidth parameter r_{ij} as

$$r_{ij} = \frac{1+\cos(2\pi K_{ij}/F_S)-\sin(2\pi K_{ij}/F_S)}{1+\cos(2\pi K_{ij}/F_S)+\sin(2\pi K_{ij}/F_S)},$$

$$K_{ij} = \begin{cases} P_{ij} - P_{i-1,12}, j=1 \\ P_{i,j} - P_{i,j-1}, \text{otherwise} \end{cases}$$

(28)

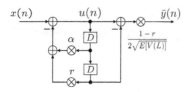

Figure 4. Structure of normalized inverse notch filter.

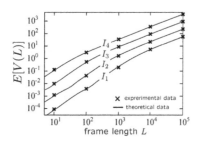

Figure 5. Sum of squared output signal of inverse notch filter output.

Table 1. Parameters for normalized inverse notch filter.

Filters		I_1, $\bar{I}_1$	I_2, $\bar{I}_2$	I_3, $\bar{I}_3$	I_4, $\bar{I}_4$
Parameters	α	−1.999	−1.989	−1.876	−0.488
	r	0.998	0.995	0.982	0.929

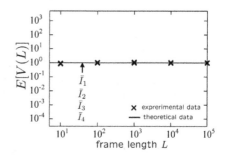

Figure 6. Sum of squared output signal of normalized inverse notch filter.

Here, we designed the pass bandwidth as the range from its notch frequency to one of the lower neighboring notch frequency. The proposed F_0 estimator is achieved by connecting the designed normalized inverse notch filters $\{\bar{I}_{ij}(z)\}$ in parallel. The F_0 estimator is shown in **Figure 7**, where $\bar{y}_{ij}(n)$ denotes the output signal of $\bar{I}_{ij}(z)$. The estimation procedure is the follows: First, we calculate $V(L)$ defined in (21) for each $\bar{I}_{ij}(z)$. We then detect the normalized inverse notch filter whose $V(L)$ is largest among all of filters. Its filter number i and j directly gives the first F_0 estimate as P_{ij}. Next, we remove the normalized inverse notch filter for $P_{ki,j}(k \in \mathrm{N})$ which is corresponding to harmonics of P_{ij}. Repeating the above estimation procedure gives the second and latter F_0 estimates. The repetition of the estimation process is finished when all the residual $V(L)$s are smaller than the threshold.

We carried out simulations to confirm the capability of the proposed F_0 estimator. In the simulations, we set the sampling frequency $F_S = 10[\mathrm{kHz}]$, and the frame length $L = 100$ (=10 [ms]). We empirically set the threshold T to 2×10^9. As the first simulation, we carried out the F_0 estimation for the monophonic sound which was played with a electronic piano. **Figure 8** shows the waveform of the input signal and the estimation result, where the true octave number i and pitch number j are displayed on the waveform as "i, j". We plotted the

estimated F_0 as the thick black line. From the result, we see that the F_0 estimation method can accurately estimate the F_0 of the observed signal, although some errors occurred in the keystroke. Additionally, we carried out the simulation for the same monophonic signal with a white noise. The estimation result shows in **Figure 9**. We see from the figure that the F_0 estimation method can robustly estimate the F_0 under the noisy environment as accurately as under the environment without noise.

As the second simulation, we carried out the F_0 estimation for the polyphonic sound. The polyphonic sound contains the octave note $\{P_{4,1}, P_{5,1}\}$ and $\{P_{4,3}, P_{5,3}\}$ which are known as a difficult combination to separately detect. **Figure 10** shows the estimation result. We see from the figure that the F_0 estimation method can estimate the F_0 although there also exist some errors at the keystroke. Especially, the proposed method can detect F_0 for the octave note. From these results, we confirmed the normalized inverse notch filter is efficiently for F_0 estimation.

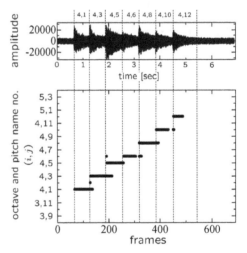

Figure 9. Simulation result for noisy monophonic sound.

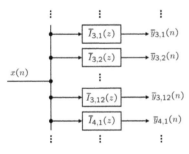

Figure 7. Structure of F_0 estimation method.

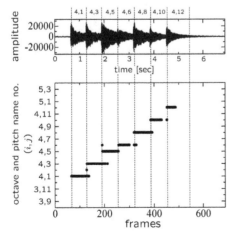

Figure 8. Simulation result for monophonic sound.

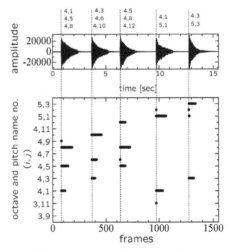

Figure 10. Simulation result for polyphonic sound.

4. Conclusion

In this paper, we analyzed the inverse notch filter and derived the explicit forms for the impulse response and the sum of squared impulse response. Based on the analysis result, we derived a normalized inverse notch filter whose pass band area is identical to unit to evaluate the output powers between the multiple inverse notch filters which have different parameters. Moreover, we established an F_0 estimator by connecting the normalized inverse notch filters in parallel. Estimation results showed that the proposed F_0 estimator effectively detects $F_0 s$ for electronic piano sound in a mid-range.

REFERENCES

[1] A. Nehorai, "A Minimal Parameter Adaptive Notch Filter with Constrained Poles and Zeros," *IEEE Transactions on Acoustics, Speech and Signal Processing*, Vol. 33, No. 4, 1985, pp. 983-996.

[2] H. C. Chong and U. L. Sang, "Adaptive Line Enhancement by Using an IIR Lattice Notch Filter," *IEEE Transactions on Acoustics, Speech and Signal Processing*, Vol. 37, No. 4, 1989, pp. 585-589.

[3] C. C. Tseng and S. C. Pei, "IIR Multiple Notch Filter Design Base on Allpass Filter," *IEEE Transactions on Circuits and Systems II: Analog and Digital Signal Processing*, Vol. 44, No. 2, 1997, pp. 133-136.

[4] S. C. Pei, W. S. Lu and C. C. Tseng, "Analytical Two-Dimensional IIR Notch Filter Design Using Outer Product Expansion," *IEEE Transactions on Circuits and Systems II: Analog and Digital Signal Processing*, Vol. 44, No. 9, 1997, pp. 765-768.

[5] Y. V. Joshi and S. C. D. Roy, "Design of IIR Multiple Notch Filters Based on All-Pass Filters," *IEEE Transactions on Circuits and Systems II: Analog and Digital Signal Processing*, Vol. 46, No. 2, 1999, pp. 134-138.

[6] M. Goto, "A Real-Time Music-Scene-Description System: Predominant-F_0 Estimation for Detecting Melody and Bass Lines in Real-World Audio Signals," *Speech Communication*, Vol. 43, No. 4, 2004, pp. 311-329.

[7] V. DeBrunner, "An Adaptive, High-Order, Notch Filter Using All Pass Sections," *IEEE International Conference on Acoustics, Speech and Signal Processing*, Vol. 3, Seattle, 12-15 May 1998, pp. 1477-1480.

[8] Y. Xiao, "A New Efficient Narrowband Active Noise Control System and Its Performance Analysis," *IEEE Transactions on Audio, Speech, and Language Processing*, Vol. 19, No. 7, 2011, pp. 1865-1874.

## 2

EMTP Induction Motor Model from Modal Measurements for Inverter Surge Analysis

Asha Shendge, Naoto Nagaoka

Department of Electrical and Electronics Engineering, Doshisha University, Kyoto, Japan

ABSTRACT

The over-voltage phenomenon is usually described using the traveling wave and reflection phenomena in variable speed drive system. A voltage pulse, initiated at the inverter, being reflected at the motor terminals due to a mismatch between the surge impedance of the motor and the cable. In this paper, resistance, inductance and capacitance of the cable and the motor windings are obtained experimentally by modal measurements and suitable models are developed to match the experimental results by considering resonance in the motor winding. This paper emphasize on Induction motor model using the theory of natural modes of propagation. The developed model validity is investigated for inverter surge application.

Keywords: Induction Motor; Modal Measurements; Inverter Surge; EMTP

1. Introduction

An induction motor (IM) is an asynchronous AC machine that consists of a stator and a rotor. An induction motor is widely used because of the rugged construction and moderate cost. Recently, the variable speed drives produced mostly consist of brushless motors and power converters. In many cases the squirrel cage induction motor is used and it is controlled by a voltage fed PWM inverter. The motor is controlled via the PWM inverter by keeping the amplitude and frequency of the reference (sinusoidal) signals constant according to the desired output speed. Thus, maintaining constant magnetic flux in the motor. For micro-surge due to reflection and refraction at motor terminal voltage peaks are developed. It is necessary to have accurate induction motor model in consideration of frequency dependent effect as motor resistance, inductance and capacitance are frequency dependent due to transient phenomena.

There are several studies carried out by different authors to simulate peak voltages at motor terminals due to inverter surge [1-5]. In this paper three phase induction motor model is developed based on natural mode measurements in steady state. The analytical calculations are carried out using theory of resonance in motor winding. The modal to phase transformation are implemented using a computational tool such as Maple, which provides template, a convenient method to analyze matrix calculations. Thus suitable induction motor model is developed for Electro-Magnetic Transient Program (EMTP). Motor peak voltage that is surge voltage is proposed as input

step waveform. The validity of model is checked by actual transient measurement of inverter surge phenomena. It is observed the model gives good agreement results for inverter surge application.

2. Experimental Set Up

A 3 phase, 2.2 Kw, 50 Hz, 200 Volts, 9.2 Amp, 1430 RPM squirrel cage induction motor is used for analysis. Motor stator is connected in Delta connection. Motor is squirrel cage means rotor winding is shorted. Steady state measurements are carried out on de-energized condition for mode-0, mode-1 and mode-2. The current distribution for all propagation modes is as shown in **Figure 1**. An impedance analyzer is used as input source (Agilent model 4294A 40 Hz - 110 MHz). Before measurements calibration is done according to the manufacture's manual.

2.1. Measured Results

Figures 2(a)-(c) are represents mode-0, mode-1 and

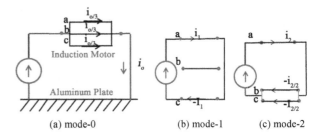

(a) mode-0   (b) mode-1   (c) mode-2

Figure 1. Current distribution of three propagation modes.

mode-2 measured impedances, respectively.

From measured waveform for mode-1 and mode-2 it is observed, the response is same as RLC parallel resonance and mode-0 response is same as discharging of capacitor.

2.2. Analytical Calculation

The analytical calculations are carried out based on well known theory of resonance. For RLC parallel circuits at t resonant condition, impedance is purely resistive *i.e.*

$$R = Z \qquad (1)$$

Resonant frequency ω in rad/sec is given by Equation (2)

$$\omega_o = 1/\sqrt{LC} \qquad (2)$$

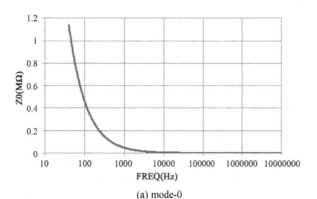

(a) mode-0

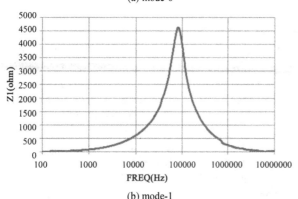

(b) mode-1

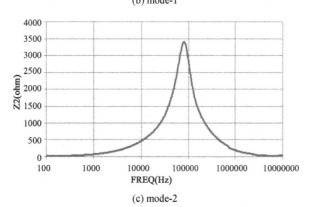

(c) mode-2

Figure 2. Measured impedance of motor.

Quality factor Q is given by Equation (4)

$$Q = R\sqrt{C/L} \qquad (3)$$

Solving Equations (2) and (3), we obtained capacitance as below

$$C = \frac{1}{\omega_o \times R} \qquad (4)$$

Once capacitance is calculated inductance can be obtained by Equation (3) as R and Q are known from measured waveform. Similarly, resonant frequency, and bandwidth B in rad/m can be calculated easily from ω_1 and ω_2.

$$B = \omega_1 - \omega_2 \qquad (5)$$

where

$$\omega_1 = 2\pi f_1 \text{ and } \omega_2 = 2\pi f_2$$

Also quality factor is given by

$$Q = \frac{\omega_o}{B} \qquad (6)$$

Using Equations (5) and (6) inductance and capacitance are calculated from measured data at resonant frequency. **Tables 1** and **2** represent the respective parameters.

From measurement of mode-0 capacitance is 3.5 nF.

The capacitance and inductance obtained in **Tables 1** and **2** and mode-0 capacitance are used to plot against total frequency range. The **Figure 3** shows the reasonable agreement some error observed due to approximation error.

2.3. Equivalent Motor Model

Figure 4 illustrates a model circuit of an induction motor obtained from modal measurements. Resistance of inductor is very small. It is approximately equal to R_{dc} therefore it is neglected. From **Figure 4** circuit it can be observed three motor winding resistance R_m, inductance

Table 1. Mode-1.

ω_0 (rad/m)	ω_1 (rad/m)	ω_2 (rad/m)	R (Ω)
509471.7	358686.8613	701894.9448	4617.94
B (rad/m)	Q	L (Henry)	C (Farad)
343208.1	1.48444	0.006106124	6.30949E−10

Table 2. Mode-2.

ω_0 (rad/m)	ω_1 (rad/m)	ω_2 (rad/m)	R (Ω)
509471.7	358686.8613	701894.9448	4617.94
B (rad/m)	Q	L (Henry)	C (Farad)
343208.1	1.48444	0.006106124	6.30949E−10

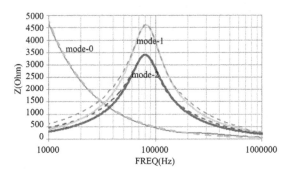

Figure 3. Comparison of measured and analytical value.

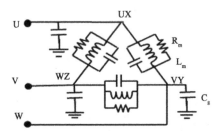

Figure 4. Simple model circuit for an induction motor.

L_m, capacitance C_m are in parallel and three motor body to ground capacitance C_g.

3. Electro Magnetic Transient Program (EMTP) Simulation [6]

Modal decomposition is given by the following matrices [7,8]

$$Z_{\text{mode}} = [T_v]^{-1} [Z_{\text{phase}}][T_i] \qquad (7)$$

$$Y_{\text{mode}} = [T_v^T] [Y_{\text{phase}}][T_v] \qquad (8)$$

$$[Z_{\text{phase}}] = [T_v] [Z_{\text{mode}}][T_i]^{-1} \qquad (9)$$

$$[Y_{\text{phase}}] = [T_i] [Z_{\text{mode}}][T_v]^{-1} \qquad (10)$$

A wave propagation characteristic of multi-phase system is determined using the theory of natural modes of propagation. Generally, a symmetrical three-phase impedance and admittance matrices are transformed using the current transformation matrix $[T_i]$ and voltage transformation matrix $[T_v]$.

$$[T_i] = \begin{bmatrix} 1/3 & 1 & 1/2 \\ 1/3 & 0 & -1 \\ 1/3 & -1 & 1/2 \end{bmatrix}, [Tv] = [T_i]_t^{-1} = \begin{bmatrix} 1 & 1/2 & 1/3 \\ 1 & 0 & -2/3 \\ 1 & -1/2 & 1/3 \end{bmatrix} \qquad (11)$$

From impedance, winding resistance and inductance can be calculated while from admittance capacitances can be calculated. R, L and C are incorporated in EMTP line constant routine. No load, resistance is converted to load condition by taking into account 6% core and mechanical loss. **Table 3** represents the R, L and C obtained in phase domain calculated using above transformation.

3.2. Motor Model Validity for Inverter Surge

Figure 5 illustrates an experimental circuit of measuring a surge in an inverter circuit connected by a cabtyre cable to a 3-phase squirrel cage induction motor (2.2 kW, 50 Hz, 200 V, 9.2 A, 1430 RPM). A 7.5 A/3.0 kVA PWM inverter (Type VFS7-2015P, Toshiba Corporation) is used as a 200 V, 60 Hz source. Terminal R, S and T represents three phase supply voltage. Converter is represented by D_1 - D_6 diodes, capacitor C is DC link and inverter transistors are represented by S_{w1} - S_{w6} switches. Measurements are carried out for investigation of peak voltage between motor phases **Figure 6** illustrates a model circuit for an EMTP simulation of an inverter surge represented in **Figure 5**. The model developed in this paper is used for inverter surge analysis. For the inverter surge simulation; the inverter is modeled by two current sources with 0.1 Ω internal resistance. A three core cabtyre cable is represented by EMTP Semlyen's distributed parameter line model [9]. The peak voltages between phases are measured.

3.3. Simulated Result

Figure 7 shows a comparison of a measured result and a simulation result by EMTP Semlyen's distributed line model including the frequency-dependent effect of the cabtyre cable. It is observed in the figure that the simulation results agree rather well with the measured result.

Table 3. Phase domain parameters.

R_m	L_m	C_m	C_g
600 Ω	9.22 mH	76.40 μF	1.04 nF

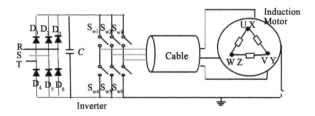

Figure 5. Experimental circuit.

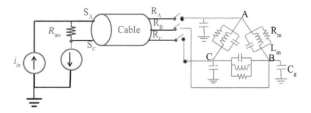

Figure 6. EMTP representation.

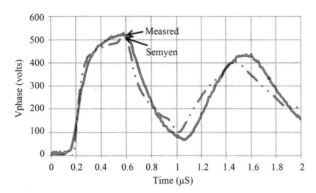

Figure 7. Surge voltage at motor terminal.

Thus, it should be clear that a transient associated with a cabtyre cable can be simulated well by proposed method in co-operation with Semlyen's line model of the EMTP.

4. Conclusion

In this paper, based on natural theory of modes measurements are carried out on induction motor in steady state condition. Based on modal measurements induction motor model is developed for it's used in Electro Magnetic Transient Program. The validity of model is investtigated by practical inverter surge measurements. It is observed using developed model the surge voltages at motor terminals can be represented accurately. This model can be used for different switching surge simulations.

5. Acknowledgements

The financial support provided by Japanese Government (MONBUKAGAKUSHO: Ministry of Education, Culture, Sports, Science and Technology—MEXT) Scholarship has made this research possible and it is greatly appreciated.

REFERENCES

[1] H. Paula, M. L. R. Chaves, D. A. Andrade, J. L. Domingos and M. A. A. Freitas, "A New Strategy for Differential over Voltages and Common Mode Currents Determination in PWM Induction Motor Drives," *IEEE International Conference on Electric Machines and Drives*, San Antonio, 15 May 2005, pp. 1075-1081,

[2] L. A. Saunders, G. L. Skibinski, S. T. Evon and D. L. Kempkes, "Riding the Reflected Wave—IGBT Drive Technology Demands New Motor and Cable Considerations," *IEEE 43rd IAS Annual Meeting*, Philadelphia, 23-25 September 1996, pp.75-84.

[3] F. Moreira, T. A. Lipo, G. Venkataramanan and S. Bernet, "High Frequency Modeling for Cable and Induction Motor Overvoltage Studies in Long Cable Drives," *IEEE Transactions on Industry Applications*, Vol. 38, No. 5, 2002, pp. 1297-1306.

[4] J. C. Oliveira, R. J. Paulsen, M. A. Amaral and D. Andrade, "Electrical Transmission System with Variable Frequency through Long Length Cable," *Offshore Technology Conference*, Houston, 6-9 May 1996.

[5] T. Makato, W. Kotaro, O. Hisashi, M. Hirataka and N. Nagaoka, "Analysis of Propagation of the Inverter Voltage and Electric Cable Surge," *Institute of Electrical Engineers Japan Transaction on Power and Energy*, Vol. 126, No. 6, 2006, pp. 771-777.

[6] W. Scott-Mayer, "EMTP Rule Book," Bonneville Power Administration, Portland, 1984.

[7] L. M. Wedepohl, "Application of Matrix Methods to the Solution of Travelling-Wave Phenomena in Polyphase Systems," *Proceedings of the Institution of Electrical Engineers*, Vol. 110, No. 12, 1963, pp. 2200-2212.

[8] A. Ametani, "A General Formulation of Impedance and Admittance," *IEEE Transactions on Power Apparatus and Systems*, Vol. 99, No. 3, 1980, pp. 902-908.

[9] A. Semlyen and A. Dabuleanu, "Fast and Accurate Switching Transients Calculations on Transmission Line with Ground Return Using Recursive Convolution," *IEEE Transactions on Power Apparatus and Systems*, Vol. 94, No. 2, 1975, pp. 561-571.

## 3

Thermal Defect Analysis on Transformer Using a RLC Network and Thermography

Geoffrey O. Asiegbu[1], Ahmed M. A. Haidar[2], Kamarul Hawari[1]
[1]Faculty of Electrical and Electronics Engineering, University Malaysia Pahang, Kuantan, Malaysia
[2]School of Electrical, Computer and Telecommunications Engineering, University of Wollongong, Wollongong, Australia

ABSTRACT

Electrical transformers are vital components found virtually in most power-operated equipments. These transformers spontaneously radiate heat in both operation and steady-state mode. Should this thermal radiation inherent in transformers rises above allowable threshold a reduction in efficiency of operation occurs. In addition, this could cause other components in the system to malfunction. The aim of this work is to detect the remote causes of this undesirable thermal rise in transformers such as oil distribution transformers and ways to control this prevailing thermal problem. Oil transformers consist of these components: windings usually made of copper or aluminum conductor, the core normally made of silicon steel, the heat radiators, and the dielectric materials such as transformer oil, cellulose insulators and other peripherals. The Resistor-Inductor-Capacitor Thermal Network (RLCTN) model at architectural level identifies with these components to have ensemble operational mode as oil transformer. The Inductor represents the windings, the Resistor representing the core and the Capacitor represents the dielectrics. Thermography of transformer under various loading conditions was analyzed base on Infrared thermal gradient. Mathematical, experimental, and simulation results gotten through RLCTN with respect to time and thermal image analysis proved that the capacitance of the dielectric is inversely proportional to the thermal rise.

Keywords: Thermal Radiation; RLC Thermal Network; Thermography; Defect Analysis

1. Introduction

Sustainability is the intermediary that runs between manufacturers of electrical equipments and her end-users. For sustainability to achieve its desired goal, electrical power facilities should be able to satisfy the demands of the users. These does not mean that faults cannot occur in equipments at any given time, however, certain electrical faults can be avoided while causes of the rest can be minimized if attention to thermal effect is considered with utmost importance. In order to throttle thermal variations in transformers within a safe-steady-state, such current dependent equipments also known as thermal producers should be monitored and assisted to function efficiently within their life span. The aim of using the Resistor-Inductor-Capacitor Thermal Network (RLCTN) is to track equipments exceeding thermal rise as early as possible by examining effects of thermal capacitance and thermal resistance on oil transformers. Secondly, to develop a mathematical model that helps in the study of thermal characteristics of oil distribution transformer components. Nearly every component gets hot before it fails [1]. Therefore, abnormal thermal rise of even minor piece of component could result to sudden failure and great setback on production. So, causes of abnormal thermal rise have to be addressed without hesitation. Hence, RLCTN model is one of the appropriate measures taken to ensure equipment durability.

Until date, many researchers have been battling with heat management in electrical equipments, which are a vital phenomenon affecting equipments performance, sustainability and overall system efficiency. Generally, increasing current $I^2 R$ that generates undesirable thermal consequence in electrical equipments mainly occur due to high current, and in some situations in the form of free convection during thermal variations in the internal and external surfaces of the current conducting parts under different electrical loads and environment conditions [2]. In many manufacturing operations, electrical power systems have been the fundamental pillars whose contributions cannot be overemphasized; adherence to IEEE thermal evaluation regulations [3] will create an enabling environment for electrical facilities to function maximally.

Obviously, most system faults were discovered when thermal variation significantly deviates from its normal thermal value(s). This can be figured out using delta T

criteria (ΔT) [4], which are of two folds first: The thermal value of equipment without thermal fault considered as reference point is compared with other ensemble equipment having similar load and similar environment condition [5]. Next is where thermal variation (ΔT) of electrical equipment is compared between equipment and its ambient temperatures [6,7]. In RLCTN, various thermal nodes will be examined and analyzed with respect to time until stability is maintained at certain thermal threshold value. The eagerness that lead to the RLCTN research came as a result of backdrops of some previous researches [8-11] on electrical defect detection where critical sustaining issues where neither properly addressed nor attended at all. Thermal fault detection is one issue and detection of remote cause of the thermal fault is another, the latter thermal problem is the focus of this paper.

At architecture design level, RLCTN will contribute to the development of mathematical algorithm to study the thermal characteristics of oil distribution transformers base on the Resistance-Inductance-Capacitance network [12]. The thermal fault model for transformers includes abnormal thermal gradient caused by failures of capacitance of dielectric property in the form of transformer oil, cellulose paper and other insulators. The second impact is in showing the application of RLCTN as a base foundation for extensive projects. To achieve the desired result and bring the proposition of this work to a logical conclusion, this model is implemented into a simulator to study the effect of thermal events on the design of abnormal thermal detection mechanism in a soft-real-time environment such as electrical power distribution substation.

Common methods of fault localization are reviewed such as digital control and advanced signal analysis algorithms-based; this concentrates on the incorporation of digital control, communications, and intelligent algorithms into power electronic devices such as direct-current-to-direct-current converters and protective switchgears. These, enables revolutionary changes in the way electrical power systems are designed, developed, configured, and integrated in aerospace vehicles and satellites [13], an active "collaboration" among modular components to improve performance and enable the use of common modules, thereby reducing costs was developed. The performance improvement goals include active current sharing, load efficiency optimization, and active power quality control. Artificial Intelligence (AI) was another method developed to monitor, predict and detect faults at an early stage in a particular section of power system. Here the detector only takes external measurements from input and output of the power system that was simulated using Artificial Neural Networks equivalent circuit developed to predict and detect fault [14]. Every electrical thermographic examination aimed at

lightly scrutinizing appropriate electrical equipment in order to pinpoint defective components and make ambient temperatures evaluations of the power distribution system. Should there be any thermal anomalies untimely detected and uncorrected, such can be potentially hazardous both to the equipment and to the user resulting to system shutdown or failure [15].

This work presents a heat management system using RLCTN algorithm for pre-fault analysis of transformers and other similar electrical equipments under various operating conditions. It was also targeted such that, the gap between system components and thermal defect monitoring against breakdown of system itself that definitely affects production is timely bridged. Hence, prevention is better than cure. The proposed work takes the advantage of using simple components comprising resistors, inductors and capacitors electrically connected to model the thermal effect on distribution transformer components such as windings, core, and dielectrics during operation and steady state. This paper is organized as follows: Section 2 presents an overview of RLCTN equivalent network and real time dynamic thermal gradient. RLCTN thermal gradient and frequency responds analysis and nodal analysis as it applies to transformer are explained in Sections 3 and 4. Section 5 is all about validation results and discussion of the proposed model while Section 6 concludes the work.

2. RLCTN Equivalent Analysis

The RLCTN analysis is derived from a simple RLC electrical network. **Table 1** shows the equivalence of concepts of the thermal RLCTN and the electrical RLC network. Taking *current* $\{I\}$ to represent *heat transfer rate* $\{H_q\}$ usually, current sources are heat producers, *Voltage* $\{V\}$ to represent *Temperature Variation* $\{T\}$, *Resistance* $\{R\}$ represents the *Thermal Resistance* $\{T_R\}$, transformer oil and other dielectrics accounts for *Thermal capacitance* $\{T_C\}$ which is the active heat absorber (storage) while the transformer radiators represents the passive heat absorber like heatsink. This analogy is possible because the same Equations apply in each model. As an example: In Ohms law $V = IR$ has an equivalent thermal Equation as $T = H_q \times T_R$.

A thermal resistance represents the difference in temperature necessary to transfer a certain amount of heat; the unit for thermal resistance is °C/Watt. Physical properties such as composition of the components in the system, shape, surface area and the volume of the components have big impacts on this value. A heat sink is designed as thermal radiators, is a passive heat absorber element that radiate heat to the ambient through the body of oil distribution transformer. This should have a minimal thermal resistance value so that it can transfer a substantial amount of heat without requiring a large difference in temperature. Because of this, the air gap or space between the radiator fins, type of material and size are importantly considered. Capacitor in this thermal analysis network plays the role of active heat absorber measured in Joule per degree centigrade, *i.e.*, J/°C. The capacitance is a measure of the amount of thermal energy that is stored or removed to increase or decrease the thermal flow within the oil distribution transformer that depends largely on the heat absorbent or storage capacity, type of materials such as oil viscosity, quality of cellulous paper and conductor insulators, then volume and size of the oil container. The above analogy describes the thermal properties as a system of linear differential equations that will be detailed in the subsequent sections of this paper; a popular technique widely adopted in most circuitries, mainly in electrical and electronic engineering designs. This very simple thermal RLCTN can analyze and predict the dynamic behavior of real-time oil distribution transformer as shown in **Figure 1** [16].

3. Thermal Gradient Analysis

RLCTN approach is used for instantaneous thermal analysis of electrical distribution substation transformer. The idea of using RLCTN for analyzing thermal effect is

Table 1. Comparison of thermal network to electrical network.

Thermal Network	Electrical Network
Temperature T (°C)	Voltage V (Volt)
Heat Transfer Rate H_q (Watt)	Current I (Ampere)
Thermal Resistance T_R (°C/Watt)	Resistance R (Ohms)
Thermal Inductance T_L	Inductance L (Henry)
Thermal Capacitance T_C (J/°C)	Capacitance C (Coulomb/Volt)
Temperature Source T_s	Voltage Source
Heat Source H_s	Current Source

not new but an analytical algorithm that describes every individual component with respect to the thermal characteristics of most current dependent or current sourcing equipment such as oil distribution transformer. In every electrical distribution substation, there exists lots of heat dissipating components comprising of instantaneous elements arranged for efficient generation of electric power. RLCTN as the name implies is reasonably less cumbersome and less complexity due to small number of components are used, which is quite imperative for on-line computation and for prediction of future thermal variations at all levels. This thermal analysis incorporates heat producers for example, transformer windings represented as inductors; core represented as resistors and heat absorbers such as transformer oil, cellulous insulators and other dielectric materials represented as capacitors.

This thermal model analysis focuses on second-order thermal networks, which are a set of component parameters that help to define the behaviors of individual components of the system (oil transformer) consisting of resistors, inductors and capacitors. By measuring the steps and thermal behaviors, the heat transfer functions can be determined. The ideology of RLCTN that depicts the thermal characteristics of oil transformer and its ambient temperature is diagrammatically illustrated in **Figure 2**.

By varying the time and capacitance values, the circuit bode plot can be generated. Referring to **Figure 2**, RLCTN consist of a resistor of thermal resistance T_R, a coil of thermal inductance T_L, a capacitor of thermal capacitance T_C and a temperature source T_S connected in series. If the quantity of heat absorbed by the capacitor is T_Q and the rate of heat flow in the thermal network is H_q, the temperatures across T_R, T_L, and T_C are;

$$H_q T_R, \quad T_L \frac{dH_q}{dt} \quad \text{and} \quad \frac{T_Q}{T_C} \text{ respectively.}$$

Using thermal equivalent of Kirchhoff's Law, the temperature difference between any two points has to be independent of the path used to travel between the two points; the Equation (1) is of the form:

$$H'_{qT_L}(t) + H_{qT_L}(t) + \frac{T_Q}{T_C}(t) = T_S(t) \qquad (1)$$

Assuming that T_R, T_L, T_C and T_S are known, this is a differential equation in two unknown quantities, H_q and T_Q. However, the two unknown quantities are

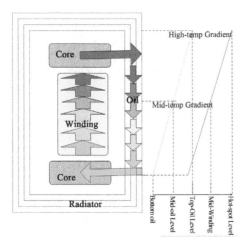

Figure 1. Dynamic thermal gradient of oil transformer.

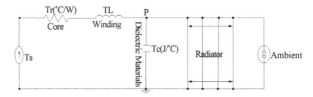

Figure 2. Ideology of RLCTN applied to transformer.

related by

$$H_q(t) = \frac{dT_Q}{dt}(t)$$

so that,

$$T_L T_Q''(t) + T_R T_Q'(t) + \frac{T_Q}{T_C}(t) = T_S(t) \tag{2}$$

or, differentiating with respect to (T_Q) and then substituting in

$$\frac{dT_Q}{dt}(t) = H_q(t),$$

$$T_L H_q''(t) + T_R H_q'(t) + \frac{H_q}{T_C}(t) = T_S(t) \tag{3}$$

For an alternating temperature source (T_S), choosing the initial time so that $T_S(0) = 0$, $T_S(t) = E_0 \sin \omega t$ and the differential equation is of the form,

$$T_L H_q''(t) + T_R H_q'(t) + \frac{H_q}{T_C}(t) = E_o \sin \omega t \tag{4}$$

Taking general solution of (4) by considering $H_q P(t) = A \sin(\omega t - \varphi)$ with the thermal rise (A) and the thermal gradient (φ) to be determined. That is, guessing that the RLCTN responds to an oscillating applied temperature source with a heat flow that oscillates with the same rate [17]. For $H_q P(t)$ to be a solution, temperature at node "P" (see **Figure 2**) has to be considered in Equation (5) as,

$$T_L H_q P(t) + T_R H_q P(t) + \frac{H_q P}{T_C}(t) = \omega E_o \cos \omega t \tag{5}$$

$$-T_L \omega^2 A \sin(\omega t - \varphi) + T_R \omega A \cos(\omega t - \varphi) + \frac{A \sin(\omega t - \varphi)}{T_C}$$

$$= \omega E_o \cos(\omega t) = \omega E_o \cos(\omega t - \varphi + \varphi) \tag{6}$$

Hence,

$$\left(\frac{1}{T_C} - T_L \omega^2\right) A \sin(\omega t - \varphi) + T_R \omega A \cos(\omega t - \varphi)$$

$$= \omega E_o \cos(\omega t - \varphi) - \omega E_o \sin \varphi \sin(\omega t - \varphi) \tag{7}$$

Matching coefficients of $\sin(\omega t - \varphi)$ and $\cos(\omega t - \varphi)$ on the left and right hand sides yields,

$$\left(T_L \omega^2 - \frac{1}{T_C}\right) A = \omega E_o \sin \varphi \tag{8}$$

$$T_R \omega A = \omega E_o \cos \varphi \tag{9}$$

Now values of φ and A can be computed which is the thermal frequency and thermal gradient in the oil transformer analyzed in the RLCTN.

Dividing Equation (8) by (9),

$$\tan \varphi = \frac{(T_L \omega^2 - 1/T_C)}{T_R \omega} \Rightarrow \varphi = \tan^{-1}\left(\frac{T_L \omega}{T_R} - \frac{1}{T_R T_C \omega}\right) \tag{10}$$

4. RLCTN Nodal Analysis

Applying nodal analysis to the RLCTN, this will make it possible to compute the heat flow rate at each junction of the RLCTN as a function of load and steady state, assuming a linear relationship between load and power dissipated with respect to time. From **Figure 3**, let t be time, $T_{m,n,o}^x$ temperatures at node m, n and o at instant x. $T_{R_{m,n,o}}$ the thermal resistance between nodes m, n, o, and $T_{C_{m,n,o}}$ the thermal capacitance at node m, n, o. $H_{T_{R_{m,n,o}}}^x$ the heat flowing through thermal resistance $T_{R_{m,n,o}}$ between node m, n, o at instant x, H_L^x the heat flowing through thermal inductance T_L at instant x and $H_{T_{C_{m,n,o}}}^x$ the heat flowing through thermal capacitance $T_{C_{m,n,o}}$ at instant x and $H_{m,n,o}$ is heat flow rate across the nodes [18].

For each node except the reference node (G), the rate at which heat is flowing $H_{m,n,o}$ in and out of each node is expressed as the algebraic sum of the heat flowing in or out of a node equals zero. (By algebraic sum, it means that the quantity of heat flowing into a node is to be considered as the same quantity negative heat flowing out of the node).

$$\sum H_{T_{C_{m,n,o}}}^x + H_{T_{C_{m,n,o}}}^x + H_{T_L}^x + H_{m,n,o} = 0 \tag{12}$$

Equation (14) represents the conservation of heat energy, it means that heat can neither be created nor destroyed rather can be converted from one form to another in a node hence heat cannot be bunched up. Expressing the heat at junction m and the entire junction o in terms of the nodal temperature at each end of the junction using Ohm's Law $(I = V/R)$ thermal equivalent $(H_q = T/T_R)$ where H_q is the Heat flow rate, T is the temperature and T_R is the thermal resistance. Equation (13) is of the form,

$$H_{q T_{R_{m,n,o}}}^x = \frac{T_{m,n,o}^x}{T_{R_{m,n,o}}} \tag{13}$$

$$\sqrt{\left[\left(T_L \omega^2 - 1/T_L\right)^2 + T_{R^2} \omega^2\right]} A = \omega E_o \Rightarrow A = \frac{\omega E_o}{\sqrt{\left(T_L \omega^2 - 1/T_C\right)^2 + T_{R^2} \omega^2}} \tag{11}$$

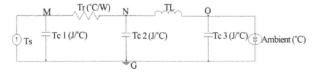

Figure 3. RLCTN nodal analysis.

As well, the resultant temperature can be computed as follows:

$$T_{m,n,o}^x = H_{T_{m,n,o}}^x T_{R_{m,n,o}} \qquad (14)$$

From Equations (13) and (14) above there is relation between the thermal resistance, temperature and heat flow rate. In other words, the rate at which heat flows downward out of node (m, n and o) for instance depends on the temperature difference $\left(T_{m,n,o}^x\right)$ and the corresponding thermal resistance $\left(T_{R_{m,n,o}}\right)$ component at each junction. Taking the first order differential Equation, the heart flowing through thermal capacitors as well as their respective dissipated temperatures are computed as shown in Equation (15). Heat flowing through capacitor at node m, n and o is,

$$H_{T_{C_{m,n,o}}}^x = T_{C_{m,n,o}} \frac{dT_{C_{m,n,o}}^x}{dt} \qquad (15)$$

Equation (16) is a discrete variable from Equation (15). Equation (16) will be used to compute the temperature at instant $x + 1$ from the temperature at instant x. Equation (16) is constantly repeated for each interval Δt, for all nodes in the system, until a threshold is reached at an instant. Equation (16) expresses the behavior and storage capacity of the energy component (capacitor) used in this model with respect to time, that is, the ability of the component to absorb heat under load and steady state. Equation (16) will be used to compute the temperature at instant $x + 1$ from the temperature at instant (x). To compute the temperature of a node, this process (Equation (16)) is constantly repeated for each interval Δt, for all nodes in the system, until a threshold is reached at an instant.

$$T_{m,n,o}^{x+1} = T_{m,n,o}^x + \frac{H_{T_{C_{m,n,o}}}^x \Delta t}{T_{C_{m,n,o}}} \qquad (16)$$

5. Results and Discussion

5.1. Experimental Validation

The experiment to validate this model involves the following: a 3-phase electrical module of purely resistive, inductive and capacitive load with the following specifications: 7 heating elements rated value 2 KW each, 7 inductors with rated value 2 KVA each and 7 capacitors with rated value 2 KVAR each (see **Figure 4**). There are 7 load steps ranging from step one to step seven, loads are increased after 300 seconds time interval. A Ti25

fluke thermal camera is used to obtain the thermal effect on the inductors and the corresponding thermal values respectively. Other numerical values such as heat flow rate and quantity of heat absorbed or removed by the dielectric (capacitance C) components are read through the external LCD on the module panel. The experimental numerical values are tabulated in **Tables 2-5** as well as the graphical bode plot in **Figures 4-9**. Often times, validation procedures suffer inconsistencies in the model, in the measurements, and in the assigned values of the constants. The mathematical model suggests that the temperature changes transiently. Corresponding bode plot are made on the collected T_R, T_L and T_C temperatures as well as the heat flow rate across nodes m, n, and o. It was observed that the graphs replicate what the mathematical model suggests. After the adjustments of the thermal capacitance parameters, the system was monitored closely with different loads, initial temperatures,

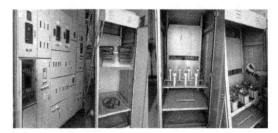

Figure 4. 3-phase electrical module of purely resistive, capacitive and inductive load.

Table 2. A RLC experimental thermal analysis result.

Time (s)	T_C (j/°C)	Quantity of Heat (J)		
		R	L	C
0	149.4	10	0	10
300	132.8	20	5	20
600	116.2	30	5	30
900	83	40	5	40
1200	66.4	45	10	50
1500	49.8	55	10	55
1800	32.2	60	10	65
2100	16.6	60	10	65

Table 3. A LC experimental thermal analysis result.

Time (s)	T_C (j/°C)	Heat Flow Rate (W)		
		m	n	o
0	149.4	20	10	20
300	132.8	30	25	30
600	116.2	40	35	40
900	83	55	55	55
1200	66.4	65	60	65
1500	49.8	80	80	80
1800	32.2	95	90	85
2100	16.6	95	90	85

Table 4. A LC experimental thermal analysis result.

Time (s)	T_C (j/°C)	Quantity of Heat (J)		
		R	L	C
0	149.4	0	0	0
300	132.8	1	10	10
600	116.2	1	10	10
900	83	1	10	10
1200	66.4	2	20	20
1500	49.8	2	20	20
1800	32.2	2	20	20
2100	16.6	3	30	20

Table 5. A RL experimental thermal analysis result.

Time (s)	T_C (j/°C)	Quantity of Heat (J)		
		R	L	C
0	149.4	20	30	3
300	132.8	40	60	5
600	116.2	90	60	8
900	83	80	120	11
1200	66.4	90	150	13
1500	49.8	110	180	15
1800	32.2	130	200	18
2100	16.6	130	200	21

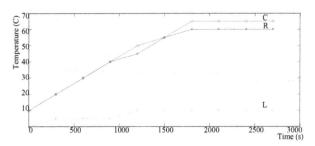

Figure 5. Effect of heat absorbed by dielectric (T_C) and core (T_R) on the winding.

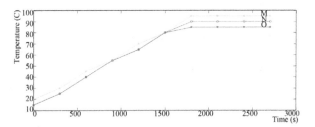

Figure 6. Heat flow rate across nodes *m*, *n*, *o* in the RLCTN.

different time intervals and different environment conditions. All the validations were much similar to the mathematical model.

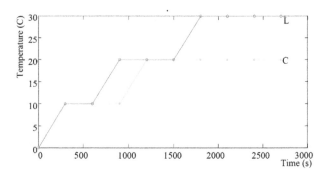

Figure 7. Effect of insufficient thermal resistance (T_R) on the winding (L).

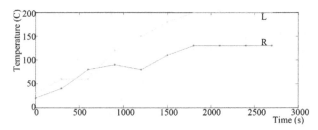

Figure 8. Effect of thermal capacitance T_C degradation on the winding (L).

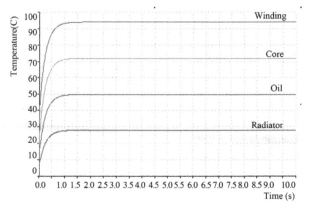

Figure 9. Thermal gradient with respect to time at $T_C = 49.8$ J/°C, $T_R = 14$ k°C/W and $T_L = 14$.

The experimental values in **Table 2** show the effect of varying the thermal capacitance on the RLC components, the higher thermal capacitance value the lower heat dissipation on the RLCTN components and vice vase. More explanation about this is graphically illustrated in **Figure 5**. This Figure shows the effect of quantity of heat absorbed by the dielectric (C) components on winding (L). As defined in Section 2, the combination of thermal components: the dielectric materials (T_C) and the core (T_R) resulted in logarithmic drop of winding temperature (T_L). Hence, more heat is been radiated to the ambient through the transformer radiator as illustrated in **Figure 2**.

The values in **Table 3** also show the effect of varying thermal capacitance on the thermal nodes (*m, n,* and *o*) as shown in **Figure 3**. This explains the higher thermal capacitance the slower heat flow rate to the node junctions and vice vase. In the case transformers, this reduces the risk of arc flash between phases or phase and neutral [19-21]. **Figure 6** replicates the nodal analysis method well defined in Section 3 and thermal equivalent of Kirchhoff's Law, stating that temperature difference between any two points has to be independent of the path used to travel between the two points. **Figure 6** graphically illustrates that the heat flow rate across the nodes were linearly increased and stabilized at about 1750 sec time interval.

In **Table 4**, it is seen that there was insufficient thermal resistance (T_R) which represent the transformer core. Here it was observed that the transformer winding (*L*) temperature increased to about 30°C irrespective of the high thermal capacitance value (T_C). **Figure 7** shows the graphical illustration.

The experimental value in **Table 5** shows the effect of thermal capacitance (T_C) degradation, which represents the dielectrics of a transformer such as oil. Here also it is seen that the transformer dielectric (T_C) materials have decreased in its heat absorption capacity causing the winding (*L*) temperature to rise so high up to 180°C at 1500 sec irrespective of the high thermal resistance value T_R. **Figure 8** graphically show the effect of thermal capacitance (T_C) degradation.

5.2. Verification of Simulation

The RLCTN was simulated with Multisim software in order to verify the results of the experiment performed in the power system laboratory using RLC electrical module and thermal imager. Comparing **Figures 9-11** it is obvious that the lager the thermal capacitance slower the transient response time that is, the rate at which temperature rises is much slower and vice vase. With reference to the model in **Figure 2**, the effect of RLC parameters used are considered with three different values of thermal capacitance at constant thermal resistance and thermal inductance values: 49.8 J/°C, 199.2 J/°C, 348.6 J/°C and 14 k°C/W and 14 T_L for thermal capacitance of transformer components for instance winding, core, oil and radiator. For this simulation, there are set initial conditions namely, the winding temperature = 38°C, the core surface temperature = 25°C, the oil temperature = 15°C and radiator temperature = 8°C. These mentioned schemes shows the rate of temperature rise of an oil transformer that means the higher the thermal capacitance the slower the rate of temperature rise. In other words, the capacity of the oil and radiators to absorb heat emitted by the winding and core depends on the dielectric property such as volume, type of material, air space, and other proper-

ties. In these scenarios, the time constant (*i.e.,* the time it takes for the transformer winding to achieve its highest stable temperature) changes from 0 second to 10 seconds as shown in **Figures 9-11**, respectively, even though the final temperature is the same. Statistically, in consumer or industrial applications, a transformer temperature rise of about 40°C to 50°C may be acceptable, resulting in a maximum internal temperature of about 100°C (transformers' temperature rise limit). However, it may be wiser to increase the capacitance as well as the core size in other to obtain reduced temperature rise and reduced losses for better power supply efficiency.

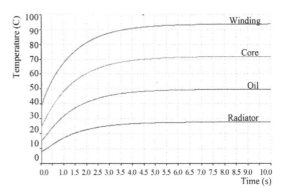

Figure 10. Thermal gradient with respect to time at
$T_C = 199.2$ **J/°C,** $T_R = 14$ **k°C/W and** $T_L = 14$.

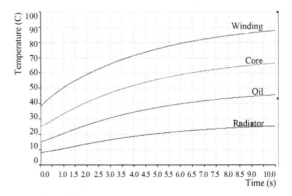

Figure 11. Thermal Gradient with respect to time at
$T_C = 348.6$ **J/°C,** $T_R = 14$ **k°C/W and** $T_L = 14$.

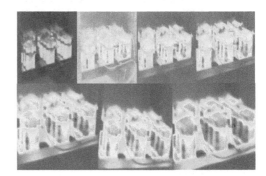

Figure 12. IRT color gradient of 7 transformers depicting

gradual degradation of dielectric materials (T_C).

5.3. Thermal Gradient

An analytical IRT thermography is characterized with a thermogram showing visible spectrum image, as indicated in **Figure 12**. As stated in Section 3, thermal images of pure inductive load were captured from real time operating transformers during validation process. This shows the effect of dielectric failure (thermal capacitance fault) on transformers. It was observed that as the thermal capacitance value is decreasing, the transformer temperature increase and vice vase. The color gradients of the IRT image in **Figure 12** depict severity of dielectric abnormal condition that is thermal capacitance fault. This also shows how suitable dielectric materials can improve efficiency transformers by removing substantial amount of heat emitted by winding and core to the ambient through the transformer radiators.

6. Conclusion

In this paper, a mathematical model capable of describeing thermal characteristics of oil transformer was presented. The model can adequately represent thermal characterristics of each component in the transformer under load, steady state operation, and abnormality in the dielectric components such as the transformer oil, cellulose insulator, and other peripherals. This model is simple, accurate and easy to be applied for measuring the thermal impact on transformer. It provides an easy way of predicting transformer's thermal status. So, it allows mechanisms like thermal throttling and load balancing to be more dynamic, rather than merely reacting to the situation when the temperature reach a critical point. Furthermore, the algorithm is efficient enough to allow dynamic recomputation of the transformer temperatures during operation. The captured thermal image brings the qualitative thermal image analysis of the model showing the thermal effect of gradual degradation of dielectric materials been represented as thermal capacitance (T_C) in the RLCTN. Within the limits of experimental errors, it was observed that the RLCTN model effectively analyzed the thermal degradation of transformer dielectrics with respect to time. Also the mathematical results replicate the simulation and experimental results, as it showed that thermal capacitance of dielectrics is inversely proportional to the transformer thermal rise.

REFERENCES

[1]   D. Susa, M. Lehtonen and H. Nordman, "Dynamic Thermal Modeling of Distribution Transformers," *IEEE Transactions on Power Delivery*, Vol. 20, No. 3, 2005, pp 1919-1929.

        http://www.ndted.org/EducationResources/CommunityCollege/Other%20Methods/IRT/IR_Applications.htm

[2]   M. Matian, A. J. Marquis and N. P. Brandon, "Application of Thermal Imaging to Validate a Heat Transfer Model for Polymer Electrolyte Fuel Cells," *International Journal of Hydrogen Energy*, Vol. 35, No. 22, 2010, pp 12308-12316.

[3]   Infraspection Institute, "Standard for Infrared Inspection of Electrical Systems & Rotating Equipment," In: Infraspection Institute, *Infrared Training and Infrared Certification*, Infraspection Institute, Burlington, 2008.

[4]   T. M. Lindquist, L. Bertling and R. Eriksson, "Estimation of Disconnectors Contact Condition for Modeling the Effect of Maintenance and Ageing," *Power Tech IEEE Conference*, St. Petersburg, 27-30 June 2005, pp. 1-7.

[5]   N. Rada, G. Triplett, S. Graham and S. Kovaleski, "High-Speed Thermal Analysis of High Power Diode Arrays," *Solid-State Electronics ISDRS*, Vol. 52, No. 10, 2008, pp. 1602-1605.

[6]   Y. Cao, X. M. Gu and Q. Jin, "Infrared Technology in the Fault Diagnosis of Substation Equipment," *China International Conference on Electricity Distribution*, Guangzhou, 10-13 December 2008, pp. 1-6.

[7]   A. M. A. Haidar, G. O. Asiegbu, K. Hawari and F. A. F. Ibrahim, "Electrical Defect Detection in Thermal Image," *Advanced Materials Research*, Vol. 433-440, 2012, pp 3366-3370.

[8]   Y. Cao, X. M. Gu and Qi Jin, "Infrared Technology in the Fault Diagnosis of Substation Equipment," *Technical Session* 1 *Distribution Network Equipment*, Shanghai Electric Power Company Shanghai Branch Southern Power, 200030, SI-17 CP1377, CICED2008.

[9]   J. G. Smith, B Venkoba Rao, V. Diwanji and S. Kamat, "Fault Diagnosis—Solation of Malfunctions in Power Transformers," *Tata Consultancy Services Limited*, Vol. 10, No. 1, 2009, pp. 1-12.

[10]   R. M. Button, "Soft-Fault Detection Technologies Developed for Electrical Power Systems," 2005. http://powerweb.grc.nasa.gov/elecsys/

[11]   Martin Technical Electrical Safety & Efficiency, "Infrared Thermography Inspection," 2012. http://www.martechnical.com/infrared_inspections/electrical_infrared_inspection_service.php

[12]   G. Biswas, R. Kapadia, D. Xu and W. Yu, "Combined Qualitative—Quantitative Steady-State Diagnosis of Continuous-Valued Systems," *IEEE Transactions on Systems, Man, and Cybernetics—Part A: Systems and Humans*, Vol. 27, No. 2, 1997, pp. 167-185.

[13]   N. Radaa, G. Tripletta and S. Graham, "High-Speed Thermal Analysis of High Power Diode Arrays," *Solid-State Electronics ISDRS*, College Park, 12-14 December 2007.

[14]   K. C. P. Wong, H. M. Ryan and J. Tindle, "Power System Fault Prediction Using Artificial Neural Networks," *International Conference on Neural Information Processing*, Hong Kong, 24-27 September 1996, Article ID: 17762.

[15] M. S. Jadin, S. Taib, S. Kabir and M. A. B. Yusof, "Image Processing Methods for Evaluating Infrared Thermographic Image of Electrical Equipment," *Progress in Electromagnetics Research Symposium Proceedings*, Marrakesh, 20-23 March 2011, p. 1299.

[16] Electric Power Engineering Center "Guide to Power Transformer Specification Issues," University of Canterbury, 2007.
http://www.scribd.com/doc/65031914/EPECentre-Guide-to-Transformer-Specification-Issues

[17] K. Harwood, "Modeling a RLC Circuit's Current with Differential Equations," 2011.
http://home2.fvcc.edu/~dhicketh/DiffEqns/Spring11proje cts/Kenny_Harwood/ACT7/KennyHarwoodFinalProject. pdf

[18] A. P. Ferreira, D. Mossé and J. C. Oh, "Thermal Faults Modeling Using a RC Model with an Application to Web Farms," 19*th Euromicro Conference on Real-Time Systems* (*ECRTS* 07), Pisa, 4-6 July 2007, pp. 113-124.

[19] M. Holt, "Understand the National Electricity Codes," Cengage Learning, Delmar, 2002.

[20] R. W. Hurst, "Electrical Safety and Arc Flash Handbook," Vol. 6, Electricity Forum, 2007.
http://www.meisterintl.com/PDFs/Electrical-Safety-Arc-F lash-Handbook-Vol-5.pdf

[21] T. Crnko and S. Dyrnes, "Arcing Flash/Blast Review with Safety Suggestions for Design and Maintenance," *Proceeding of the IEEE conference on Industry Technical*, Atlanta, 19-23 June 2000, pp. 118-126.

## 4

Behavioral Modeling and Simulation of Cascade Multibit ΣΔ Modulator for Multistandard Radio Receiver

Sonia Zouari[1], Houda Daoud[1], Mourad Loulou[1], Patrick Loumeau[2], Nouri Masmoudi[1]
[1]Information Technologies and Electronics Laboratory National Engineering School of Sfax, Sfax, Tunisia
[2]Electronics and Communications Department, Telecom ParisTech, Paris, France

ABSTRACT

In this paper, a cascade Sigma-Delta (ΣΔ) Analog to Digital Converter (ADC) for multistandard radio receiver was presented. This converter is supposed to be able to support GSM, UMTS, Wifi and WiMAX communication standards. The Sigma-Delta modulator makes use of 4 bit quantizer and Data-Weighted-Averaging (DWA) technique to attain high linearity over a wide bandwidth. A top-down design methodology was adopted to provide a reliable tool for the design of reconfigurable high-speed ΣΔMs. VHDL-AMS language was used to model the analog and mixed parts of the selected 2-1-1 cascade ΣΔ converter and to verify their reconfiguration parameters based on behavioural simulation. This multistandard architecture was high level sized to adapt the modulator performance to the different standards requirements. The effects of circuit non-idealities on the modulator performance were modeled and analyzed in VHDL-AMS to extract the required circuit parameters.

Keywords: ΔΣ ADC; Multistandard; VHDL-AMS Language; Behavioural Simulation

1. Introduction

The most significant design challenge in current and future wireless devices is to support several wireless and cellular standards in the same handheld device. The goal was to design multistandard RF terminals that are very flexible and reconfigurable with neither a decrease in the circuit performance nor an increase in power consumption or silicon area [1-4]. A high resolution high speed ADC will only allow the shifting of several RF and analog processing to the digital domain in order to provide more flexibility and increase the design complexity [5]. The use of ΔΣ modulators in multistandard receivers is suitable for several reasons among which we can cite, firstly, that ΣΔ modulators are very linear and are also less sensitive to circuit non-idealities than other types of data converters [6]. Secondly, the noise shaping and the oversampling performed by ΣΔ modulators allow to achieve high Dynamic Range (DR) for narrow bandwidths and lower DR for higher bandwidths. This characteristic is coherent with wireless standards requirements and their RF specifications which makes ΣΔ ADC suitable to perform the Analog/Digital (A/D) conversion function in a multi-standard capable RF receiver [7]. Another important advantage of ΣΔ ADC is it consumes less power than full Nyquist ADCs [8]. In this paper, the reconfigurable ΣΔ was modelled to be designed for a GSM/UMTS/WiFi/WiMAX radio receiver. **Figure 1** shows the adopted multistandard receiver architecture. The proposed architecture is a multistandard Zéro-IF receiver. It uses a multiband antenna, four RF filters for GSM/UMTS/WLAN/WiMAX selection, a multistandard low noise amplifier (LNA) and multistandard mixers for I and Q components. The A/D conversion is performed with multistandard anti Alias filter and multistandard ΣΔ Modulator (ΣΔ M). The digital processing is supported by a DSP circuit. Zero_IF architecture was chosen for its high level of integration, associated with excellent multistandard capabilities [9]. Contrary to several multistandard Zero-IF architectures proposed in literature which use channel selection in analog domain and use an automatic Gain Control (AGC) to decrease ADC dynamic requirement [10,11], in our selected multistandard receiver, channel selection is performed in the digital domain and a very high dynamic ADC is used to eliminate the need for AGC. It uses a multistandard oversampled ΔΣ M followed by a digital decimation filter as shown in **Figure 2**. This approach achieves a more programmable solution rather than an analog approach thereby, enabling such receivers to upgrade easy to multi-mode operation.

Digital channel select filtering can be made easily programmable by changing the filter coefficients in the decimation filter. However, the dynamic range of the ADC must also be made programmable to fit the RF specifications. Fortunately, Sigma-Delta modulators allow the designer to trade off bandwidth and dynamic range which make them suitable to perform the A/D conversion function in a multi-standard capable RF receiver. Relying on system specifications for various addressed RF communications standards and on chosen receiver characteristics, ADC specifications were established for each standard (**Table 1**).

The remaining of the paper is organized as follows: Section 2 shows the multistandard cascaded Sigma-Delta modulator architecture and discusses its reconfiguration. Section 3 describes the system level design of the proposed modulator using VHDL-AMS language. The simulation results modeling are presented in Section 4. Finally, we draw our conclusion in Section 5.

2. Reconfigurable ΣΔ Modulator Architecture

Given that reconfigurability must be considered to find out the optimal multistandard ΣΔ modulator architecture, the cascade ΣΔ ADC was selected as the best suited architecture (**Figure 3**) [12-14]. This fourth order cascade

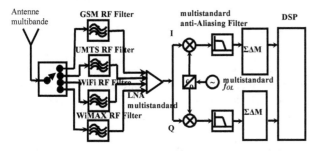

Figure 1. Proposed multistandard receiver architecture.

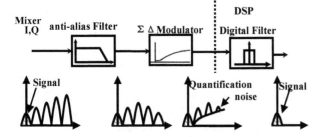

Figure 2. Channel selection with a ΔΣM and digital filter.

Table 1. DR requirements in the multistandard receiver.

Standard	Channel Bandwidth	DR (dB)
GSM	200 KHz	90 - 108
UMTS	3.84 MHz	70 - 90
Wifi	20 MHz	60 - 70
WiMAX	20 MHz	50 - 65

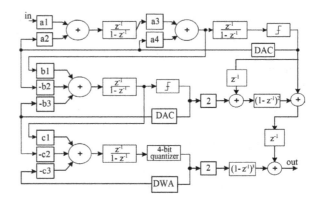

Figure 3. 2-1-1$_{4bits}$ ΔΣM linearized by DWA.

topology is a 2-1-1 architecture implemented using a cascade of second order sigma-delta loop and two first-order loops. The cascade architecture recombines the outputs of each stage in the digital domain to achieve fourth-order noise shaping. Inherently linear single-bit Digital/Analog (D/A) converters are employed in the first two stages while a four-level D/A converter is employed in the lower resolution third stage to improve the dynamic range. The proposed topology overcomes the influence of mismatch-induced errors in the multibit DAC on the 2-1-1 modulator performance of [15] by introduceing a DEM algorithm; Data Weighted Averaging (DWA) to correct the DAC mismatch non-linearity. Based on [15], the coefficients were optimized in such a way that analog coefficients could be constructed with small integer ratios in order to achieve a compact layout and good matching in the switched-capacitor (SC) implementation. The value of the integrator weights are given in **Table 2**. The presented ΣΔ modulator provides a flexible solution to the support of a large variety of specifications. It is able to operate in three distinguishable modes as in the cases of GSM, UMTS and WLAN/ WiMAX. It was considered that WLAN and WiMAX standards require the same ADC dynamic at the same bandwidth. Each mode consists of a ΣΔ topology and an over-sampling ratio (OSR) as shown in **Table 3**. A three order cascaded single bit 2-1 ΣΔM has been selected as the two first stages in order to meet the specifications of the GSM mode. The unused block in the third stage is switched off while working in the GSM mode, taking into account the design considerations like power consumption. In all the others modes, the fourth order modulator 2-1-1$_{4bits}$ cascaded is switched to operation by putting off the switch thus making it programmable. In the UMTS, this architecture operates at OSR of 16. In the WLAN/WiMAX mode, we use the same topology but at an OSR of 8. In order to validate its performance, the chosen multistandard topology was simulated using Simplorer schematic Software based on VHDL-AMS language. The obtained results are detailed in **Table 3**. **Figure 4** presents the simulated Signal-to-Noise Ratio (SNR) versus input signal amplitude, for GSM/UMTS/Wifi/WiMAX standards. Simulation results show a peak SNR of 107 dB in GSM mode, a peak SNR of 91 dB in UMTS mode, and a peak SNR of 68 dB in the Wifi/WiMAX mode. In Zero IF multiband GSM/UMTS/Wifi/WiMAX architecture, the ADC signal bandwidth is 100 KHz/1.92 MHz/10 MHz respectively.

3. ΣΔ Modulator Noise Modeling

The estimation effect of the non-ideality on the performance of the ΣΔ modulators is the main problem faced in their design. Since they have an inherent non-linearity of the modulator loop, the optimization of their performance must be done with behavioral time domain simulations. Needless to remind that the circuit level simulation is the most precise. Nevertheless, the evaluation of the effect of the circuit non-idealities and the optimization of the modulator's building blocks are quite difficult to execute because of the long simulation time required. An intermediate stage of behavioral simulations is therefore

Table 2. Coefficients Values.

a1	0.25	b2	0.5	d0	−2
a2	0.25	b3	0.5	d1	2
a3	1	c1	2	d2	0
a4	0.5	c2	1	d3	2
b1	1	c3	1		

Table 3. Performance of the multi-standard ΣΔM.

Mode	Architecture	OSR	Band (MHz)	Sampling frequency	SNRmax (dB)
GSM	2-1	64	0.1	12.8 MHz	107
UMTS	2-1-1$_{4bit}$	16	1.92	64 MHz	91
Wifi/WiMAX	2-1-1$_{4bit}$	8	10	176 MHz	68

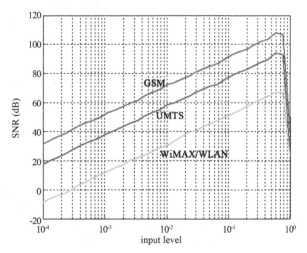

Figure 4. SNR as function of the input power.

necessary. Through multi-level abstraction models, VHDL-AMS enables us to overcome the problems. Besides, it allows a top-down design methodology. In fact, VHDL-AMS reduce simulation time and reflect circuit non-idealities phenomena through an efficient behavioral model. It also determines possible ranges of circuit specifications with reasonable design margins before the implementation of circuit components. Each block of the multistandard 2-1-1$_{4bits}$ ΣΔ modulator was modeled using Simplorer schematic models. The obtained blocks were connected in Simplorer Software environment to obtain a behavioural description of the 2-1-1 multibit architecture. The previous simulation results assume the use of ideal components and only consider the quantization noise. Nevertheless, this is not the case in practice. Then, the behavioural approach has been used to investigate the overall circuit non-idealities effects, to optimize the system parameters and establish the specifications of the analog blocks. A description level using Simplorer schematic allowing parameter setting according to the non-idealities has been performed [16]. The main non-idealities considered in this paper are finite DC gain, slew rate and gain-bandwidth limitations, capacitor mismatch, KT/C noise, clock jitter and DAC capacitor mismatch.

3.1. Operational Tranconductance Amplifier (OTA) parameters

The Switched Capacitor (SC) integrator is the most building block of ΣΔ converters and the OTA is the basic building block in a SC integrator. Therefore, behavioral simulations were carried out using VHDL-AMS environment in order to determine the specifications of the OTA for the different standards. The SC integrator model is developed using schematic level description as shown in **Figure 5**. Several non-idealities of the integrator have been included in the behavioral model: finite OTA DC gain, slew rate and gain bandwidth limitations. Using the behavioral simulations, the peak SNR was calculated as a function of each of the finite gain OTA, the gain bandwidth OTA and of slew rate OTA for the various modes. The results obtained are plotted in **Figures 6-8**, respectively. These VHDL-AMS Simulation results show that added to the proposed multistandard modulator which can tolerate an OTA dc gain of 60 dB, the OTA bandwidth needs to be at least 200 MHz and the slew rate at least 200 V/μs. These specifications have been used to select an appropriate OTA circuit topology that can meet the integrator performance requirements at minimum power dissipation. The fully differential folded cascade OTA, whose schematic is shown in **Figure 9**, has been chosen for the four integrators. This enabled us to reach the most suitable operating speed over power consumption ratio. The OTA parameters were set according to a design sample developed in [17]. The simulated parameters of the OTA are summarized in **Table 4** and reported on Simplorer OTA model.

3.2. Thermal Noise and Jitter Noise

In addition to noise from OTA, the thermal and jitter noises can also degrade the performance of the $\Sigma\Delta$ modulator. Thermal noise is mainly produced by the SC integrator finite switch resistance during the sampling and integration phases [18]. In a SC Sigma-Delta modulator, the sampling capacitor C_s is in series with a switch, which has a finite resistance R_{on}, that periodically opens.

Table 4. Proposed telescopic OTA performance.

Performance	Values
DC gain (dB)	78
GBW ($C_L = 2$ pF) (MHz)	306
Phase margin (degrees)	67
Slew rate (V/µs)	187
Power consumption (mW)	9.3
Process node/supply voltage (µm/V)	0.35/±1.3

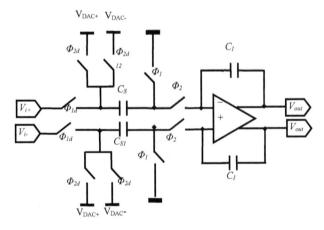

Figure 5. Switched capacitor integrator Simplorer model.

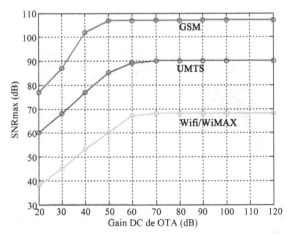

Figure 6. SNR versus OTA DC gain.

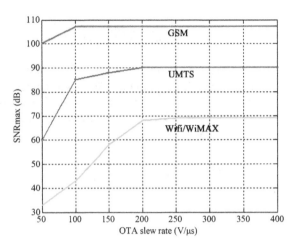

Figure 7. SNR versus OTA slew rate.

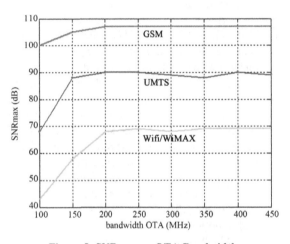

Figure 8. SNR versus OTA Bandwidth.

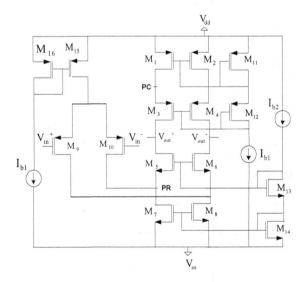

Figure 9. Fully differential folded cascode OTA topology.

Therefore it samples a noise voltage onto C_s. The total noise power can be calculate to evaluate the integral in Equation (1):

$$e_T^2 = \int_0^\alpha \frac{4KTR_{on}}{1+\left(2\pi f R_{on} C_S\right)^2} \, df = \frac{KT}{C_S} \qquad (1)$$

where K is the Boltzmann's constant, T the absolute temperature, and $4KTR_{on}$ the noise PSD associated with the switch on-resistance. The switch thermal noise voltage e_{Th} (usually called KT/C noise) appears as an additive noise to the input voltage $x(t)$ leading to:

$$y(t) = \left[x(t)+e_T(t)\right]c = \left[x(t)+\sqrt{\frac{KT}{C_S}}n(t)\right]c$$
$$= \left[x(t)+\sqrt{\frac{KT}{cC_i}}n(t)\right]c \qquad (2)$$

where $n(t)$ denotes a Gaussian random process with unity standard deviation, and c is the integrator gain and $c = C_s/C_i$. The behavior model of the switched thermal noise is shown in **Figure 10**. The clock jitter of an SC circuit can be defined as a short-term, non-cumulative variation of the switching instant of a digital clock form from its ideal position in time. It produces a non-uniform sampling time sequence and results in an error that increases the total error power quantizer output. It should be noted that when the analog signal is sampled, the clock period variation doesn't have any direct effect on the performance of the circuit. Thus, the clock jitter is introduced only by the input signal sampling, and its effect on the $\Sigma\Delta$ modulator is independent of the modulator structure or order [19]. When a sinusoidal input signal $x(t)$ with amplitude Ax and frequency fx is sampled at an instant, which is in error by a statistical non-uniform uncertainty Δt, the magnitude of this error is given by:

$$e(nT_S+\Delta t) = x(nT_S+\Delta t)-x(nT_S) = \Delta t \frac{d}{dt}x(t)\Big|_{nT_S} \quad (3)$$

Thermal and jitter noises effects have been modeled with VHDL-AMS at the behavioral level as described in **Figure 10**. Where $x(t)$ is the input signal and $r(t)$ is a random noise signal implemented with a random block, which generates a sequence of random numbers with Gaussian distribution, zero mean, and unity standard deviation. Thermal noise, called also KT/C noise, is modeled as an additive white noise source of variance KT/C

to the input signal. Jitter noise, however, is included as an additive Gaussian random process with standard deviation ΔT [20,21]. The sampling and thermal noises effect is simulated at the system level for the largest bandwidth mode WLAN/WiMAX. As shown in **Figure 11**, such noises increase the inband noise floor, which seems to degrade the modulator performance. Such degradation is not significant in the presence of jitter noise $\Delta T < 10$ ps and thermal noise $C_s > 0.2$ pF as it was proved by several simulations. Actually the total SNR of the modulator is set to be almost unchanged when each of these noises is introduced into the modulator model.

3.3. Mismatch of the Capacitor Values

In SC integrators, the gain factors are implemented using capacitors ratios. Although fabrication process can produce matching and gains that differ from their nominal values affecting the performance of the integrator. Moreover, this capacitance mismatch alters the integrator transfer function, consequently affecting the signal and quantization noise [22]. In the behavioral model integrators we assume that the mismatch error of integrator weights (capacitors) has Gaussian distribution with Standard deviation "sigma". For the behavioral simulation results in **Figure 12**, a significant degradation of SNR can be caused by a sigma value up to 0.5%.

3.4. Mismatch in Multibit DAC

The four-bit DAC in the feedback of the last stage of our multistandard 2-1-1$_{4bits}$ $\Sigma\Delta M$ can be built with 15 capacitors to determine the analog feedback signal. Due to process tolerances and variations, the values of these unit elements will deviate from the ideal weight Cu, resulting in errors in the DAC. The DWA was used to reduce the effect of such errors. Simulations were run for the UMTS

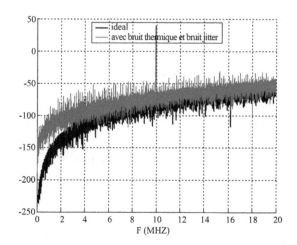

Figure 11. Power spectral density of 2-1-1$_{4bits}$ $\Sigma\Delta$ modulator with an ideal modulator and addition of thermal noise and jitter noise model ($\Delta T = 200$ ps and $C_s = 0.1$ pF).

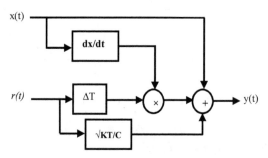

Figure 10. Thermal noise and jitter noise model.

mode of the multistandard 2-1-1$_{4bits}$ ΣΔM including DAC Integral Non Linearity (INL) of 0.5% Full Scale (FS) and 1.0% FS when the DWA was inactive and active. **Figure 13** shows the PSD for the 2-1-1$_{4bits}$ ΣΔM in UMTS mode when the DAC error is 0.0%, 0.1% and 1.0% when the DWA is inactive and active, respectively. **Figure 14** shows how the DAC mismatch decreases significantly the SNR. Moreover, it is noticeable in the same figure how the DWA algorithm eliminated the SNR degradation.

4. Simulation Results

The chosen topology was simulated using Ansoft Simplorer Software to perform a system level simulation of the proposed architecture, verifying its performance and behavior when facing analog imperfections. Based on SIMPLORER models, it was possible to include several non-idealities, such as thermal noise, jitter noise, DC gain, finite bandwidth and slew rate. **Figure 15** shows

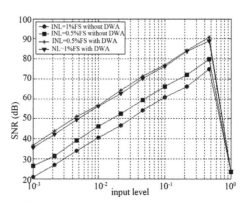

Figure 14. The SNR as function of the input power of the 2-1-1 ΣΔM (UMTS mode) using a non-ideal DAC with and without DWA.

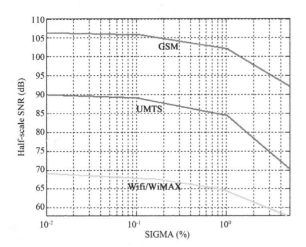

Figure 12. SNR versus capacitor mismatch.

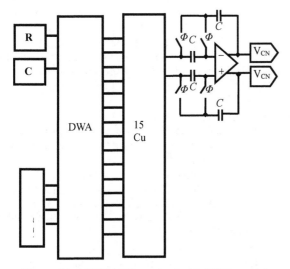

Figure 13. 4 bit DAC linearized with DWA model.

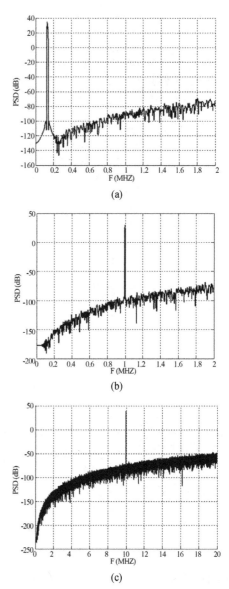

Figure 15. Power spectrum density for VHDL-AMS model validation in (a) GSM mode; (b) UMTS mode; (c) Wifi/Wi-MAX

the modulator output spectrum for GSM/UMTS/Wifi/WiMAX modes for a 0.1/1.92/10 MHz input signal at a sampling frequency of 12.8/64/176 MHz under the condition of 0.2% random capacitor mismatch, 0.5% DAC INL mismatch. Jitter and thermal noises are the other limitations assumed in this simulation with clock jitter of 10 ps and C_s equal to 0.25 pF. Taking into account the use of the real selected folded cascode OTA in the four integrators of the reconfigurable ΣΔM, these simulation results show that a high linearity can be achieved thanks to the low-distortion of the Sigma-Delta modulator. Behavioral simulation results indicate that the proposed multistandard topology achieves a peak SNR of 105/98/65 dB for GSM/WCDMA/WLAN standards respectively in the presence of these circuit non-idealities.

5. Conclusion

The major contribution of this work is the development of an accurate behavioral model of multistandard ΣΔM for GSM/UMTS/Wifi/WiMAX zero-IF receiver using VHDL-AMS as the modeling language. It takes into account at the behavioural level most of SC ΣΔ modulator non-idealities, such as DAC non-linearity, OTA parameters (finite DC gain, finite bandwidth, slew rate), thermal noise and capacitor mismatch, thus it permits to obtain a good estimation of the ΣΔ modulator performance with a short simulation time. Future works would involve the implementation of the 2-1-1 cascade ΣΔ converter using device-level simulations.

REFERENCES

[1] P.-I. Mak, U. Seng-Pan and R. P. Martins, "Transceiver Architecture Selection: Review, State-of-the-Art Survey and Case Study," *IEEE Circuits and Systems Magazine*, Vol. 7, No. 2, 2007, pp. 6-25.

[2] P. B. Kenington and L. Astier, "Power Consumption of A/D Converters for Software Radio Applications," *IEEE Transactions on Vehicular Technology*, Vol. 49, No. 2, 2000, pp. 643-650.

[3] Z. Ru, N. A. Moseley, E. Klumperink and B. Nauta, "Digitally Enhanced Software-Defined Radio Receiver Robust to Out-of-Band Interference," *IEEE Journal of Solid-State Circuits*, Vol. 44, No. 12, 2009, pp. 3359-3375.

[4] B. Razavi, "Cognitive Radio Design Challenges and Techniques," *IEEE Journal of Solid-State Circuits*, Vol. 45, No. 8, 2010, pp. 1542-1553.

[5] R. Bagheri, A. Mirzaei, M. E. Heidari, S. Chehrazi, M. Lee, M. Mikhemar, W. K. Tang and A. A. Abidi, "Software-Defined Radio Receiver: Dream to Reality," *IEEE Communications Magazine*, Vol. 44, No. 8, 2006, pp. 111-118.

[6] A. Silva, J. Guilherme and N. Horta, "Reconfigurable

[7] M. Miller and C. Petrie, "A Multibit Sigma Delta ADC for Multimode Receivers," *IEEE Journal of Solid State Circuits*, Vol. 38, No. 3, 2003, pp. 475-482.

Multi-Mode Sigma-Delta Modulator for 4G Mobile Terminals," *Integration, the VLSI Journal*, Vol. 42, No. 1, 2009, pp. 34-46.

[8] F. Medeiro, B. Pérez-Verdú and A. Rodríguez-Vázquez, "Top-Down Design of High-Performance Sigma-Delta Modulators," Kluwer Academic Publishers, Boston, 1999, p. 312.

[9] A. A. Abidi, "The Path to the Software-Defined Radio Receiver," *IEEE Journal of Solid-State Circuits*, Vol. 42, No. 5, 2007, pp. 954-966.

[10] N. Ghittori, A. Vigna, P. Malcovati, S. D'Amico and A. Baschirotto, "Analogbaseband Channel for Reconfigurable Multistandard (GSM/UMTS/WLAN/Bluetooth) Receivers," *Proceedings of the WIRTEP*, Rome, April 2006, pp. 88-92.

[11] M. Brandolini, P. Rossi, D. Manstretta and F. Svelto, "Toward Multistandard Mobile Terminals—Fully Integrated Receivers Requirements and Architectures," *IEEE Transactions on Microwave Theory and Techniques*, Vol. 53, No. 3, 2005, pp. 1026-1038.

[12] R. del Río, F. Medeiro, J. M. de la Rosa, B. Pérez-Verdú and A. Rodríguez-Vázquez, "A 2.5 V CMOS Wideband Sigma-Delta Modulator," *IEEE Instrumentation and Measurement Technology Conference*, Vail Colorado, May 2003, pp. 224-228.

[13] A. Silva, J. Guilherme and N. HortaCir, "A Reconfigurable Sigma-Delta Modulator Reconfiguration of Cascade Sigma Delta Modulators for Multistandard GSM/Bluetooth/UMTS/WLAN Transceivers," *IEEE International Symposium on Integration Circuits and Systems, ISCAS*, Island of Kos, 21-24 May 2006, pp. 1884-1887.

[14] J. Marttila, M. Allén and M. Valkama, "Design and Analysis of Multi-Stage Quadrature Sigma-Delta A/D Converter for Cognitive Radio Receivers," *Proceedings of the 16th IEEE International Workshop on Computer-Aided Modeling Analysis and Design of Communication Links and Networks*, Kyoto, 10-11 June 2011, pp. 10-11.

[15] A. Morgado, R. del Río and J. M. de la Rosa, "Design of a 130-nm CMOS Reconfigurable Cascade ΣΔ Modulator for GSM/UMTS/Bluetooth," *IEEE International Symposium on Circuits and Systems, ISCAS*, Island of Kos, 27-30 May 2007, pp. 725-728.

[16] S. zouari, *et al.*, "High Order Cascade Multibit Sigma Delta Modulator for Wide Bandwidth Applications," *International Journal of Electronic Commerce Studies*, Vol. 1, No. 1, 2007, pp. 60-66.

[17] H. Daoud, S. Bennour, S. Ben Salem and M. Loulou, "Low Power SC CMFB Folded Cascode OTA Optimiztion," *The IEEE International Conference on Electronics, Circuits, and Systems*, St. Julien, 31 August-3 September 2008, pp. 570-573.

[18] R. Schreier, J. Silva, J. Steensgaard and G. C. Temes "Design-Oriented Estimation of Thermal Noise in Switched-Capacitor Circuits," *IEEE Transactions on Circuits*

and Systems: *Regular Papers*, Vol. 52, 2005, pp. 2358-2368.

[19] Y. Yin, H. Klar and P. Wennekers, "A Cascade 3-1-1 Multibit ΣΔ Modulator with Reduced Sensitities to Non-Idealities," *The IEEE International Symposium on Circuits and Systems*, Vol. 4, 2005, pp. 3087-3090.

[20] Y. B. N. Kumar, S. Talay and F. Maloberti, "Complex Cascaded Bandpass ΣΔ ADC Design," *Proceedings of the IEEE International Symposium on Circuits and Systems*, Taipei, 24-27 May 2009, pp. 3118-3121.

[21] Van Tam, "VHDL-AMS Behavioral Modelling and Simulation of High-Pass Delta-Sigma Modulator," *IEEE Transactions on Circuits and Systems I: Fundamental Theory and Applications*, Vol. 50, No. 3, 2005, pp. 352-364.

[22] P. Malcovati, S. Brigati, F. Francesconi, F. Maloberti, P. Cusinato and A. Baschirotto, "Behavioral Modeling of Switched-Capacitor Sigma-Delta Modulators," *IEEE International Symposium on Circuits and Systems*, Vol. 50, 2003, pp. 352-364.

## 5

Electronically Controllable Fully-Uncoupled Explicit Current-Mode Quadrature Oscillator Using VDTAs and Grounded Capacitors

Dinesh Prasad[1*], Mayank Srivastava[2], Data Ram Bhaskar[1]

[1]Department of Electronics and Communication Engineering, Faculty of Engineering and Technology,
Jamia Millia Islamia, New Delhi, India
[2]Department of Electronics and Communication Engineering, Amity School of Engineering and Technology,
Amity University, Noida, India

ABSTRACT

An electronically controllable fully uncoupled explicit current-mode quadrature oscillator employing Voltage Differencing Transconductance Amplifiers (VDTAs) as active elements has been presented. The proposed configuration employs two VDTAs along with grounded capacitors and offers the following advantageous features 1) fully and electronically independent control of condition of oscillation (CO) and frequency of oscillation (FO); 2) explicit current-mode quadrature oscillations; and 3) low active and passive sensitivities. The workability of proposed configuration has been demonstrated by PSPICE simulations with TSMC CMOS 0.18 μm process parameters.

Keywords: VDTA; Quadrature Oscillator; Current-Mode Circuits

1. Introduction

Among various kinds of oscillators, the quadrature oscillators (QO) are widely used because they can provide two sinusoids with $\pi/2$ phase difference, for example, in telecommunication systems, for quadrature mixtures and single-sideband generators or for measurement purposes in vector generators or selective voltmeters [1,2]. Therefore the QO play an important role in many communication systems, instrumentation systems and signal processing see [3-11]. Recently, a CMOS realization of VDTA and its applications as 1) RF filter and 2) double tuned amplifier have been presented in [12]. In [13], an electronically controllable explicit current-output sinusoidal oscillator has been reported. Another application as a single input five output voltage-mode universal filter using VDTAs has been presented in [14]. The purpose of this communication is to introduce a new electronically controllable fully uncoupled explicit current-mode quadrature oscillator using two VDTAs and two grounded capacitors. The proposed configuration provides the advantageous features of: 1) completely and electronically independent control of condition of oscillation (CO) and

frequency of oscillation (FO); 2) explicit current-mode quadrature oscillations; and 3) low active and passive sensitivities. The workability of proposed configuration has been verified using SPICE simulation with TSMC CMOS 0.18 μm process parameters.

2. The Proposed Configurations

The symbolic notation of the VDTA is shown in **Figure 1**, where V_P and V_N are input terminals and Z, X^+ and X^- are output terminals. All terminals of VDTA exhibit high impedance values [12]. The VDTA can be described by the following set of equations:

$$\begin{bmatrix} I_Z \\ I_{X^+} \\ I_{X^-} \end{bmatrix} = \begin{bmatrix} g_{m_1} & -g_{m_1} & 0 \\ 0 & 0 & g_{m_2} \\ 0 & 0 & -g_{m_2} \end{bmatrix} \begin{bmatrix} V_{V_P} \\ V_{V_N} \\ V_Z \end{bmatrix} \qquad (1)$$

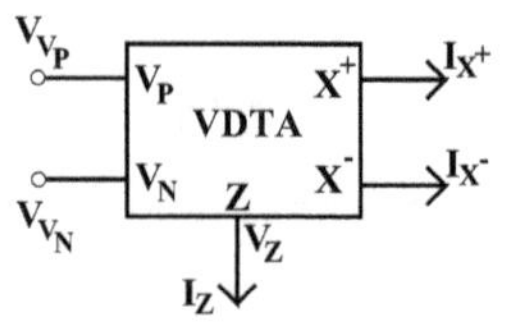

Figure 1. The symbolic notation of VDTA.

Electronically Controllable Fully-Uncoupled Explicit Current-Mode Quadrature Oscillator Using VDTAs and
Grounded Capacitors

29

The proposed configuration is shown in **Figure 2**.

Circuit analysis of **Figure 2** gives the characteristic equation (CE) as:

$$s^2 + s \frac{1}{C_2}\left(g_{m_4} - g_{m_3}\right) + \frac{g_{m_1}g_{m_2}}{C_1 C_2} = 0 \qquad (2)$$

From Equation (2), the CO and FO can be expressed as CO:

$$\left(g_{m_4} - g_{m_3}\right) \leq 0 \qquad (3)$$

and
FO:

$$\omega_0 = \sqrt{\frac{g_{m_1}g_{m_2}}{C_1 C_2}} \qquad (4)$$

Therefore, it is seen from Equations (3) and (4) that the CO and FO are completely uncoupled and electronically tunable as g_{m_i}; $i = 1 - 4$ are controlled by bias currents.

The current transfer functions obtained from **Figure 2** are given by:

$$\frac{I_{o2}(s)}{I_{o1}(s)} = \frac{g_{m_4}}{g_{m_1}g_{m_2}sC_1} \qquad (5)$$

For sinusoidal steady state, Equations (5) becomes

FO:

$$\frac{I_{o2}(j\omega)}{I_{o1}(j\omega)} = \frac{g_{m_4}}{\omega C_1 g_{m_1} g_{m_2}} e^{-j90°} \qquad (6)$$

Thus, the phase difference ϕ between (I_{o2} and I_{o1}) is $-90°$. Hence, the currents (I_{o2} and I_{o1}) are in the quadrature form.

3. Parasitic Effects and Sensitivity Analysis

By considering the various VDTA non-ideal parameters like the finite P-terminal parasitic impedance consisting of a resistance R_P in parallel with capacitance C_P, the finite N-terminal parasitic impedance consisting of a resistance R_N in parallel with capacitance C_N, the finite X-terminal parasitic impedance consisting of a resistance R_X in parallel with capacitance C_X and the parasitic impedance at the Z-terminal consisting of a resistance R_Z in parallel with capacitance C_Z then the expression of CO and FO including the influence of parasitic are given by:
CO:

$$\left\{ \frac{2C_1}{R_p} + \frac{C_1}{R_z} + \frac{2C_1}{R_x} + \frac{2C_p}{R_z} + \frac{C_2}{R_z} + \frac{C_z}{R_z} + \frac{2C_x}{R_z} + \frac{2C_z}{R_p} \right.$$
$$\left. + \frac{C_z}{R_z} + \frac{2C_z}{R_x} + C_1\left(g_{m_4} - g_{m_3}\right) + C_z\left(g_{m_4} - g_{m_3}\right) \right\} \leq 0 \qquad (7)$$

FO:

$$\omega_0 = \sqrt{\frac{\left(\dfrac{2}{R_p R_z} + \dfrac{1}{R_z^2} + \dfrac{2}{R_x R_z} + \dfrac{g_{m_4}}{R_z} - \dfrac{g_{m_3}}{R_z} + g_{m_1}g_{m_2}\right)}{\left(C_1 C_2 + 2C_1 C_p + C_1 C_z + 2C_1 C_x + 2C_p C_z + C_2 C_z + C_z^2 + 2C_x C_z\right)}} \qquad (8)$$

then the active and passive sensitivities of ω_0 can be found as:

$$S_{R_x}^{\omega_0} = \frac{-1}{R_x R_z\left(\dfrac{2}{R_p R_z} + \dfrac{1}{R_z^2} + \dfrac{2}{R_x R_z} + \dfrac{g_{m_4}}{R_z} - \dfrac{g_{m_3}}{R_z} + g_{m_1}g_{m_2}\right)}, \quad S_{R_z}^{\omega_0} = \frac{\left(-\dfrac{2}{R_p R_z} - \dfrac{2}{R_z^2} - \dfrac{2}{R_x R_z} - \dfrac{g_{m_4}}{R_z} + \dfrac{g_{m_3}}{R_z}\right)}{2\left(\dfrac{2}{R_p R_z} + \dfrac{1}{R_z^2} + \dfrac{2}{R_x R_z} + \dfrac{g_{m_4}}{R_z} - \dfrac{g_{m_3}}{R_z} + g_{m_1}g_{m_2}\right)},$$

$$S_{R_p}^{\omega_0} = \frac{-1}{R_p R_z\left(\dfrac{2}{R_p R_z} + \dfrac{1}{R_z^2} + \dfrac{2}{R_x R_z} + \dfrac{g_{m_4}}{R_z} - \dfrac{g_{m_3}}{R_z} + g_{m_1}g_{m_2}\right)}, \quad S_{g_{m_1}}^{\omega_0} = \frac{g_{m_1}g_{m_2}}{2\left(\dfrac{2}{R_p R_z} + \dfrac{1}{R_z^2} + \dfrac{2}{R_x R_z} + \dfrac{g_{m_4}}{R_z} - \dfrac{g_{m_3}}{R_z} + g_{m_1}g_{m_2}\right)} = S_{g_{m_2}}^{\omega_0},$$

$$S_{g_{m_3}}^{\omega_0} = \frac{g_{m_3}}{2R_z^2\left(\dfrac{2}{R_p R_z} + \dfrac{1}{R_z^2} + \dfrac{2}{R_x R_z} + \dfrac{g_{m_4}}{R_z} - \dfrac{g_{m_3}}{R_z} + g_{m_1}g_{m_2}\right)}, \quad S_{g_{m_4}}^{\omega_0} = \frac{-g_{m_4}}{2R_z^2\left(\dfrac{2}{R_p R_z} + \dfrac{1}{R_z^2} + \dfrac{2}{R_x R_z} + \dfrac{g_{m_4}}{R_z} - \dfrac{g_{m_3}}{R_z} + g_{m_1}g_{m_2}\right)},$$

$$S_{C_1}^{\omega_0} = \frac{-C_1\left(C_2 + 2C_p + C_z + 2C_x\right)}{2\left(C_1 C_2 + 2C_1 C_p + C_1 C_z + 2C_1 C_x + 2C_p C_z + C_2 C_z + C_z^2 + 2C_x C_z\right)},$$

$$S_{C_2}^{\omega_0} = \frac{-C_2\left(C_1 + C_z\right)}{2\left(C_1 C_2 + 2C_1 C_p + C_1 C_z + 2C_1 C_x + 2C_p C_z + C_2 C_z + C_z^2 + 2C_x C_z\right)},$$

$$S_{C_x}^{\omega_0} = \frac{-2C_x\left(C_1 + C_z\right)}{2\left(C_1C_2 + 2C_1C_p + C_1C_z + 2C_1C_x + 2C_pC_z + C_2C_z + C_z^2 + 2C_xC_z\right)},$$

$$S_{C_P}^{\omega_0} = \frac{-2C_P\left(C_1 + C_z\right)}{2\left(C_1C_2 + 2C_1C_p + C_1C_z + 2C_1C_x + 2C_pC_z + C_2C_z + C_z^2 + 2C_xC_z\right)},$$

$$S_{C_z}^{\omega_0} = \frac{-C_z\left(C_1 + 2C_p + C_2 + 2C_z + 2C_x\right)}{2\left(C_1C_2 + 2C_1C_p + C_1C_z + 2C_1C_x + 2C_pC_z + C_2C_z + C_z^2 + 2C_xC_z\right)} \tag{9}$$

For $C_1 = C_2 = 0.5$ nF, $R_p = R_z = \infty$, $C_p = C_x = C_z = 0.15$ pF, $g_{m_1} = g_{m_2} = g_{m_3} = 1.5913$ mA/V and $g_{m_4} = 1.7916$ mA/V, the sensitivities are found to be 0, 0, 0, 0.5, 0, 0, −0.899, −0.499, −2.9e−4, −2.9e−4, −1.64e−3 for Equation (9). Thus, all the active and passive sensitivities of ω_0 with respect to each active and passive elements are low.

4. Simulation Results

To verify the theoretical analysis, the proposed ECMSO was simulated using CMOS VDTA from [12]. Power supply voltages were taken as $V_{DD} = -V_{SS} = 0.9$ V and $I_{B1} = I_{B2} = I_{B3} = I_{B4} = 2$ mA (for VDTA$_1$) and $I_{B1} = I_{B2} = 2$ mA, $I_{B3} = I_{B4} = 3.687$ mA (for VDTA$_2$) biasing currents are used. The transistor aspect ratios are same as in [12]. The passive elements of the configuration were selected as $C_1 = C_2 = 0.5$ nF. The transconductances of VDTA were controlled by bias currents. PSPICE generated output waveforms indicating transient and steady state responses are shown in **Figures 3(a)** and **(b)** respectively. These results, thus, confirm the validity of the proposed configuration. The total harmonic distortion (THD) of the proposed oscillator is found to be 3.00% (**Figure 4**). From **Figure 5** it is clear that the two currents are in quadrature.

Figure 5 shows that the two currents are in quadrature and the measured value of phase shift between two waveforms is = −89.98°.

5. Concluding Remarks

In this paper, an explicit current-mode quadrature oscillator using VDTAs has been presented. The presented circuit employs two VDTAs and two grounded capaci-

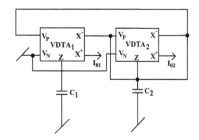

Figure 2. The proposed configuration.

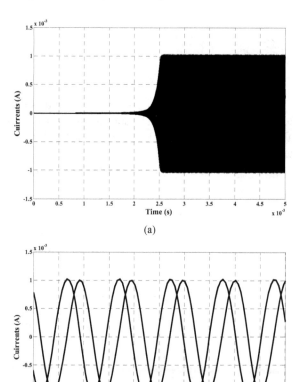

(a)

(b)

Figure 3. (a) Transient response waveform; (b) Steady state response of the quadrature outputs.

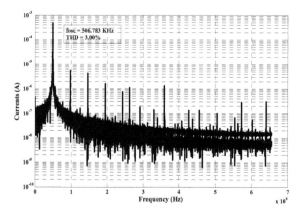

Figure 4. Simulation result of the output spectrum.

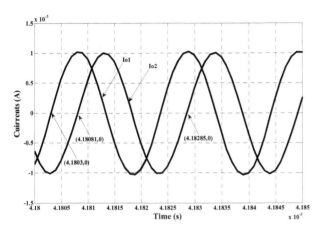

Figure 5. Steady state response of the quadrature outputs of I_{o2} and I_{o1}.

tors. The CO and FO of the proposed quadrature oscillator has the advantage of fully and electronically independent controllability. The proposed explicit current-mode quadrature oscillator also provides low active and passive sensitivities. The workability of proposed configuration has been verified using SPICE simulation.

REFERENCES

[1] J. W. Horng, "Current Conveyors Based Allpass Filters and Quadrature Oscillators Employing Grounded Capacitors and Resistors," *Computer and Electrical Engineering*, Vol. 31, No. 1, 2005, pp. 81-92.

[2] D. Prasad, D. R. Bhaskar and A. K. Singh, "Electronically Controllable Grounded Capacitor Current-Mode Quadrature Oscillator Using Single MO-CCCDTA," *Radioengineering*, Vol. 20, No. 1, 2011, pp. 354-359.

[3] W. Tangsrirat and W. Tanjaroen, "Current-Mode Sinusoidal Oscillator with Independent Control of Oscillation Frequency and Condition Using CDTAs," *Indian Journal of Pure and Applied Physics*, Vol. 48, No. 5, 2010, pp. 363-366.

[4] M. T. Abuelmatti, "New OTA-Based Sinusoidal Oscillators with Fully Uncoupled Control of Oscillation Frequency and Condition," *Frequenz: Journal of RF-Engineering and Telecommunications*, Vol. 55, No. 7-8, 2001,

pp. 224-228.

[5] M. T. Abuelmatti, "Active-Only Sinusoidal Oscillator with Electronically-Tunable Fully-Uncoupled Frequency and Condition of Oscillation," *Active and Passive Electronic Components*, Vol. 24, No. 4, 2001, pp. 233-241.

[6] M. T. Abuelmatti and H. A. Al-Zaher, "Current Mode Quadrature Sinusoidal Oscillators Using Two FTFNs," *Frequenz: Journal of RF-Engineering and Telecommunications*, Vol. 53, No. 1-2, 1999, pp. 27-30.

[7] W. Tangsrirat and S. Pisitchalermpong, "CDBA-Based Quadrature Sinusoidal Oscillator," *Frequenz: Journal of RF-Engineering and Telecommunication*, Vol. 61, No. 3-4, 2007, pp. 102-104.

[8] W. Tangsrirat, D. Prasertsoma, T. Piyatata and W. Surakampontorn, "Single-Resistance-Controlled Quadrature Oscillator Using Current Differencing Buffered Amplifiers," *International Journal of Electronics*, Vol. 95, No. 11, 2008, pp. 1119-1126.

[9] M. Kumngern and K. Dejhan, "DDCC-Based Quadrature Oscillator with Grounded Capacitors and Resistors," *Journal of Active and Passive Electronic Component*, 2009, Article ID: 987304.

[10] A. Lahiri, "Current Mode Variable Frequency Quadrature Oscillator Using Two CCs and Four Passive Component Including Grounded Capacitors," *Analog Integrated Circuits and Signal Processing*, Vol. 68, No. 1, 2011, pp. 129-131.

[11] M. T. Abuelmatti, "New Sinusoidal Oscillators with Fully Uncoupled Control of Oscillation Frequency and Condition Using Three CCII+s," *Analog Integrated Circuits and Signal Processing*, Vol. 24, No. 3, 2000, pp. 253-261.

[12] A. Yesil, F. Kacar and H. Kuntman, "New Simple CMOS Realization of Voltage Differencing Transconductance Amplifier and Its RF Filter Application," *Radioengineering*, Vol. 20, No. 3, 2011, pp. 632-637.

[13] D. Prasad and D. R. Bhaskar, "Electronically-Controllable Explicit Current Output Sinusoidal Oscillator Employing Single VDTA," *ISRN Electronics*, Vol. 2012, 2012, Article ID: 382560.

[14] J. Satansup, T. Pukkalanun and W. Tangsrirat, "Electronically Tunable Single-Input Five-Output Voltage-Mode Universal Filter Using VDTAs and Grounded Passive Elements," *Circuits, Systems and Signal Processing*, 2012.

## 6

A Synthesis of Electronically Controllable Current-Mode PI, PD and PID Controllers Employing CCCDBAs

Somchai Srisakultiew[1,2], Montree Siripruchyanun[2*]

[1]Department of Computer Engineering, Faculty of Engineering and Architecture, Rajamangala University of Technology Isan, Nakhonratsima, Thailand
[2]Department of Teacher Training in Electrical Engineering, Faculty of Technical Education, King Mongkut's University of Technology North Bangkok, Bangkok, Thailand

ABSTRACT

This paper presents a synthesis of current-mode PI, PD and PID controllers employing current controlled current differential buffer amplifiers (CCCDBAs). The features of these controllers are that: the output parameters can be electronically/independently controlled by adjusting corresponding bias currents in the proportional, integral, and deviation controllers; circuit description of the PID controller is simply formulated, it consists of four CCCDBAs cooperating with two grounded capacitors, and PI and PD controllers are composed of three CCCCDBAs and a grounded capacitor. Without any external resistor, the proposed circuits are very suitable to develop into integrated circuit architecture. The given results from the PSpice simulation agree well with the theoretical anticipation. The approximate power consumption in a closed loop control system consisting of the PI, PD and PID controller with low-pass filter passive plant are 4.03 mW, 4.85 mW and 5.71 mW, respectively, at ±1.5 V power supply voltages.

Keywords: Current-Mode; PID Controller; CCCDBA

1. Introduction

The proportional-integral-derivative (PID) controllers are the most important control devices employed in industrial process control [1]. Classical implementations of the PID controller contain several active elements to realize the transfer function. For instance, parallel structure using operational amplifiers (Op-Amp) [2] requires four sections: Proportional (P), Integral (I), Derivative (D) transfers and adder. Proportional-integral (PI), Proportional-derivative (PD) and PID controllers with adjustable parameters are implemented in various pieces of work. These controllers are used in many applications, for example, motor speed controllers, temperature controllers, fluid controllers and etc. [3,4].

For the last two decades, the attention is subsequently focused on the PID controllers using different high-performance active building blocks such as, operational transconductance amplifiers (OTAs) [5,6], current feedback op-amp (CFAs) [7,8], second generation current conveyors (CCIIs) [9-13], second generation current

controlled current conveyors (CCCIIs) [14-16], and current differencing buffered amplifiers (CDBAs) [17]. The literature surveys show that a large number of circuit realizations for PI, PD and PID controllers simulators have been reported [5-17]. Unfortunately, these reported circuits suffer from one or more of following weaknesses:

- Excessive use of the active and/or passive elements [5-17];
- Circuit requirement external resistors [5,6,7-17];
- Lack of electronic tenability [7-13,17];
- Absence of independent control of their parameters [5,7,9,14,15].

The current differencing buffered amplifier (CDBA) is a reported active component especially suitable for a class of analog signal processing [18]. The fact that the device which can operate in both current and voltage modes provides flexibility and enables a variety of circuit designs. In addition, it can offer advantageous features such as high-slew rate, free from parasitic capacitances, wide bandwidth and simple implementation [19]. However, the CDBA cannot be controlled by the parasitic

*Corresponding author.

resistances at two current input ports so when it is used in a circuit, it must unavoidably require some external passive components, especially the resistors. This makes it not appropriate for IC implementation due to occupying more chip area, higher power dissipation and cannot electronic controllable. Subsequently, Maheshwari and Khan have proposed the modified-version CDBA whose parasitic resistances at two current input ports can be controlled by an input bias current and it is newly named current controlled current differencing buffered amplifier (CCCDBA) [20].

Presently, a current-mode technique has been more popular than the voltage-mode one. This is due to operating in the low-voltage environment found portable and battery-powered equipment. Since a low-voltage operating circuit has become necessary, the current-mode technique is ideally suited for this purpose more than the voltage-mode one. Furthermore, there is a growing interest in synthesizing the current-mode circuits because of their unique potential advantages such as larger dynamic range, higher signal bandwidth, greater linearity, simpler circuitry, and lower power consumption [21].

The purpose of this paper is to introduce a synthesis of current-mode PI, PD and PID controllers employing CCCDBAs. The features of the proposed controllers are that: the output parameter can be electronically/independently controlled by adjusting corresponding bias currents in the proportional, integral, and deviation controllers: circuit description of the PID controller is very simple, consisting of four CCCDBAs cooperating with two grounded capacitors. PI and PD controller consists of three CCCDBAs cooperating with a grounded capacitor. The simulations are performed by PSpice to exhibit the performance of the developed controllers.

2. Theory and Principle

2.1. Basic Concept of Current Controlled Current Differencing Buffered Amplifier (CCCDBA)

Since the proposed circuits are based on CCCDBAs, a brief review of CCCDBA is given in this section. Basically, the CCCDBA is composed of translinear elements, mixed loops and complementary current mirrors. Generally, its properties are similar to the conventional CDBA [19], except that input voltages of CCCDBA are not zero and the CCCDBA has finite input resistances R_p and R_n at the p and n input terminals, respectively. These intrinsic resistances are equal and can be controlled by the bias current I_B as shown in the following equation

$$\begin{bmatrix} V_p \\ V_n \\ I_{z1,z2} \\ V_w \end{bmatrix} = \begin{bmatrix} R_p & 0 & 0 & 0 \\ 0 & R_n & 0 & 0 \\ 1 & -1 & 0 & 0 \\ 0 & 0 & 1 & 0 \end{bmatrix} \begin{bmatrix} I_p \\ I_n \\ V_z \\ I_w \end{bmatrix},$$ (1)

For BJT CCCDBA, the input resistances; R_p and R_n can be expressed to be

$$R_p = R_n = \frac{V_T}{2I_B}.$$ (2)

V_T and I_B are the thermal voltage and input bias current, respectively. The symbol and the equivalent circuit of the CCCDBA are illustrated in **Figures 1(a)** and **(b)**, respectively.

2.2. Synthesis of Proposed Controllers Employing CCCDBAs

2.2.1. PI Controller

PI controller is composed of a proportional and an integral term. The PI controller is sufficient when the process dynamics is an essentially first-order system. The proposed PI controller employs three CCCDBAs, a grounded capacitor as shown in **Figure 2**. Transfer function of general PI controller: $H_{PI}(s)$ can be written as (3).

$$H_{PI}(s) = \frac{I_O}{I_{in}} = K_{Pi} + \frac{1}{T_i s}.$$ (3)

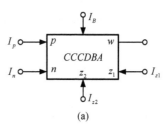

(a)

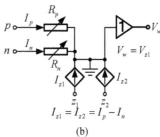

(b)

Figure 1. The CCCDBA (a) symbol (b) equivalent circuit.

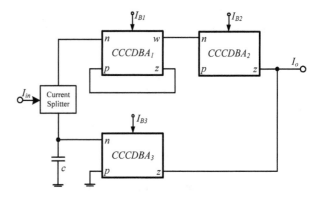

Figure 2. The proposed PI controller.

The CCCDBA based PI controller in **Figure 2** has the transfer function as

$$H_{\mathrm{PI}}\left(s\right)=\frac{I_O}{I_{in}}=\frac{I_{B2}}{2I_{B1}}-\frac{CR_n}{s}. \tag{4}$$

Substituting $R_n=\dfrac{V_T}{2I_B}$ into (4), it yields

$$H_{\mathrm{PI}}\left(s\right)=\frac{I_O}{I_{in}}=\frac{I_{B2}}{2I_{B1}}-\frac{2V_TC}{sI_{B3}}. \tag{5}$$

From (5), it is found that H_{PI} and T_i can be independently controlled by I_{B1}/I_{B2} and I_{B3}, respectively.

2.2.2. PD Controller

The PD controller is the most widely used in strategy for robot manipulators, motor speed control, and etc. Additionally, more advanced controllers often incorporate to PD algorithms in their control-loop to reach the desired configuration. The derivative term of the PD controller deals with slope of error, and it is effective in the transient-response. The derivative term has no effect if the steady-state error is constant in a corresponding time. The proposed PD controller employs three CCCDBAs, one grounded capacitor shown in **Figure 3**. The general transfer function of PD controller: $H_{\mathrm{PD}}\left(s\right)$ can be written in (6)

$$H_{\mathrm{PD}}\left(s\right)=\frac{I_O}{I_{in}}=K_{Pd}+T_ds. \tag{6}$$

The CCCDBAs based PD controller shown in **Figure 3** has the transfer function as (7)

$$H_{\mathrm{PD}}\left(s\right)=\frac{I_O}{I_{in}}=\frac{I_{B2}}{2I_{B1}}+R_nsC. \tag{7}$$

Substituting $R_n=\dfrac{V_T}{2I_B}$ into (7), it yields

$$H_{\mathrm{PD}}\left(s\right)=\frac{I_O}{I_{in}}=\frac{I_{B2}}{2I_{B1}}+\frac{V_TsC}{2I_{B3}}. \tag{8}$$

From (8), it can be seen that the K_P can be electronically controlled by either I_{B1} or I_{B2} and T_D parameter can be adjusted by adjust I_{B3} with independent each other.

2.2.3. PID Controller

Proportional-integral-derivative (PID) controllers are extensively used in industry. It is estimated that more than 90% of all control loops involve PID controllers, where the proportional term adjusts the speed response of the system, the integral term adjusts the steady-state error of the system and the derivative term adjusts the degree of stability of the system.

The proposed current-mode PID controller is shown in **Figure 4**. It consists of only four CCCDBAs and two

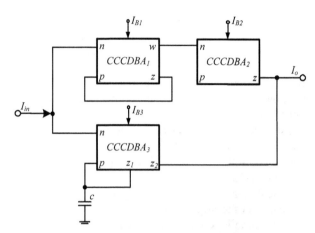

Figure 3. The proposed PD controller.

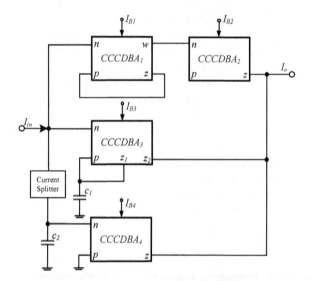

Figure 4. The proposed PID controller.

grounded capacitors. The transfer function of general analog PID controller: $H_{\mathrm{PID}}\left(s\right)$ can be written as depicted in (9), where K_p is the proportional gain, K_i is the integral time, and K_d is the derivative time parameters

$$H_{\mathrm{PID}}\left(s\right)=\frac{I_{out}\left(s\right)}{I_{in}\left(s\right)}=K_p+\frac{K_i}{s}+sK_d,$$

$$H_{\mathrm{PID}}\left(s\right)=\frac{K_ds^2+K_ps+K_i}{s}. \tag{9}$$

The transfer function of the proposed PID controller will be shown by

$$H_{\mathrm{PID}}\left(s\right)=\frac{I_O}{I_{in}}=\frac{I_{B2}}{2I_{B1}}-\frac{C_2R_{n4}}{s}+sC_1R_{n3}. \tag{10}$$

Substituting $R_{ni}=\dfrac{V_T}{2I_{Bi}}$ into (10), we obtain

$$H_{\mathrm{PID}}\left(s\right)=\frac{I_O}{I_{in}}=\frac{I_{B2}}{2I_{B1}}-\frac{V_TC_2}{s2I_{B4}}+\frac{V_TsC}{2I_{B3}}. \tag{11}$$

From (11), the PID controller's parameters can be assigned to the required values by adjusting the corresponding I_B. Additionally, it can be seen that the PID parameters (K_p, K_i and K_d) can be independently controlled by I_{B1}/I_{B2}, I_{B3} and I_{B4}, respectively.

3. Simulation Results

To prove the performances of the proposed controllers, the PSpice simulation program was used for the examinations. The PNP and NPN transistors employed in the proposed circuits were simulated by using the parameters of the PR200N and NR200N bipolar transistors of the ALA400 transistor array from AT&T [22]. **Figure 5** depicts schematic description of the CCCDBA used in the simulations. These proposed circuits were biased with corresponding input bias current I_B of the CCCDBAs with the symmetrical ±1.5 V supplies voltages.

To validate the practical application of the proposed controllers, firstly, the proposed current-mode PID controllers and passive low-pass filter were used to realize a closed-loop control system as depicted in **Figure 6**. For the current-mode low-pass filter, the circuit is shown in **Figure 7** with an additional output terminal. The current transfer function of the low-pass filter is found to be

$$H_{lp} = \frac{I_o}{I_{in}} = \frac{CR_1}{LCs^2 + (R_1 + R_2)sC + 1}. \quad (8)$$

The passive elements of the filter in **Figure 7** were determined by $R_1 = R_2 = 1$ kΩ, $L = 1$ μH and $C = 1$ μF. **Figure 8** shows frequency response of passive low-pass filter employed as a plant of closed-loop control system.

Figure 9 illustrates the simulation results of the PI controller using CCCDBAs without the plant, where $C = 1$ nF, input signal of 20 μA step waveform. A transient response of the PI controller is shown in **Figure 9(a)**. **Figure 9(b)** demonstrates that the K_{Pi} of the PI controller can be adjusted. The I_{B2} of PI controller is tuned to 13 μA, 26 μA and 52 μA where $I_{B1} = 13$ μA, $I_{B3} = 26$ μA and $C = 1$ nF. On the other hand, the integral conditions variation with I_{B3} to 13 μA, 26 μA and 52 μA is shown in **Figure 9(c)**, it can be verified that the integral conditions of the PI controller can be electronically/independently tuned by I_{B3}, as depicted in (5).

Figure 10 shows the simulation results of the proposed PD controller without a closed-loop control system, where $C = 470$ nF, $I_{B1} = 13$ μA, $I_{B2} = 26$ μA and $I_{B3} = 26$ μA, input signal of 20 μA step waveform. The simulation result as shown in **Figure 10(a)** is a transient response of the PD controller. **Figure 10(b)** demonstrates that the K_{PD} of the PD controller can be tuned. The I_{B2} of PD controller is adjusted to 26 μA, 52 μA and 104 μA, where $I_{B1} = 26$ μA, $I_{B3} = 26$ μA and $C = 470$ nF. On the other hand, the derivative condition variation with I_{B3} to 26 μA, 52 μA and 104 μA is shown in **Figure 10(c)**. It

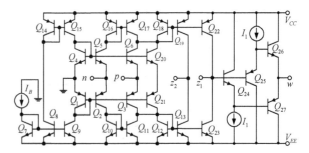

Figure 5. Internal construction of CCCDBA.

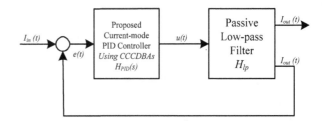

Figure 6. A closed-loop control system.

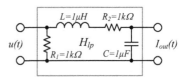

Figure 7. The passive RLC low-pass filter used as a plant.

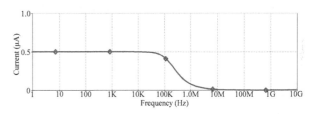

Figure 8. Frequency response of RLC low-pass filter plant.

can be verified that the differential conditions of the PD controller can be electronically/independently tuned by I_{B3}, as depicted in (8).

To obtain the proposed current-mode PID controller, whose transfer function of $K_p = 1$, $T_i = 38.46$ μs and $T_d = 235$ μs, we use the passive elements as followed: $C_1 = 1$ μF, $C_2 = 1$ nF, where $I_{B1} = 20$ μA, $I_{B2} = 40$ μA, $I_{B3} = 50$ μA and $I_{B4} = 20$ μA. We determine input signal as a step waveform of 20 μA at 1 kHz of frequency. **Figure 11(a)** shows the result of the transient response for an initial condition obtained from the closed-loop control system in **Figure 6**. Finally, **Figure 11(b)** shows the relationship between input and output signals during a steady state condition. The power consumption of the closed loop control systems is 5.71 mW.

4. Conclusion

In this study, a synthesis of novel current-mode PI, PD

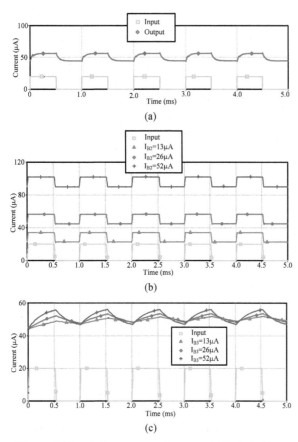

Figure 9. Simulation results of proposed PI controller.

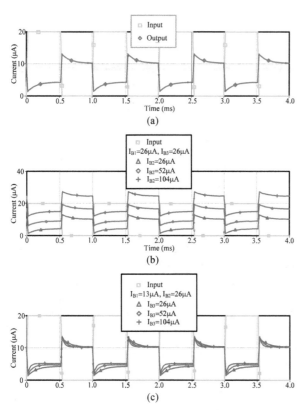

Figure 10. Simulation results of proposed PD controller.

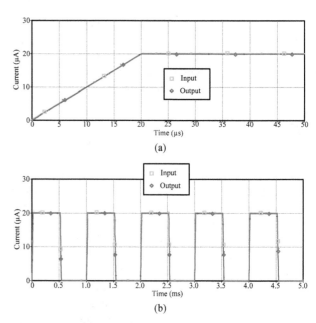

Figure 11. Input and output relationship of PID controller with closed-loop control system.

and PID controllers were realized by employing CCCDBAs. All PI, PD and PID parameters can be tuned electronically and independently by the corresponding bias currents. The circuit description of the PID controller comprises only four CCCDBAs and two grounded capacitors. PI and PD controller consists of three CCCDBAs cooperating with a grounded capacitor, without any external resistor. Simulation results confirm the theoretical analysis. It is easily modified to use in control systems using a microcontroller [20]. With mentioned features, it is very suitable to realize the proposed controllers in a monolithic chip for use in battery-powered electronic devices.

REFERENCES

[1] A. J. Michael and H. M. Mohammad, "PID Control New Identification and Design Methods," Springer, Berlin, 2005.

[2] S. Franco, "Design with Operational Amplifiers and Analog Integrated Circuits," McGraw-Hill, New York, 1997.

[3] B. C. Kuo, "Automatic Control System," Prentice-Hall, Upper Saddle River, 1997.

[4] "Designing Ultrafast Loop Response with Type-III Compensation for Current Mode Step-Down Converters," Ap. Note SLVA352, Texas Instrument, 2010. http://focus.ti.com/lit/an/slva352/slva352.pdf

[5] C. Edral, A. Toker and C. Acar, "OTA-C Based Proportional-Integral-Derivative (PID) Controller and Calculating Optimum Parameter Tolerances," *Turkish Journal of Electrical Engineering and Computer Sciences*, Vol. 9, No. 2, 2001, pp. 189-198.

[6] S. Srisakultiew, S. Lawanwisut and M. Siripruchyanun, "A Synthesis of Electronically Controllable Current-Mode PI, PD and PID Controllers Employing OTAs," *The Pro-*

ceeding of 10th *International Prince of Songkla University (PSU) Engineering Conference*, Songkhla, 14-15 May 2012.

[7] E. Cevat, "A New Current-Feedback-Amplifiers (CFAs) Based Proportional-Integral-Derivative (PID) Controller Realization and Calculating Optimum Parameter Tolerances," *Pakistan Journal of Applied Sciences*, Vol. 2, No. 1, 2002, pp. 56-59.

[8] S. Srisakultiew, S. Lawanwisut and M. Siripruchyanun, "A Synthesis of Current-Mode PI, PD and PID Controllers Employing CFAs," *The Proceeding of* 51th *Kasetsart University Annual Conference*, Bangkok, February 2013, pp. 144-151.

[9] S. Minaei, E. Yuce, S. Tokat and O. Cicekoglu, "Simple Realization of Current-Mode and Voltage-Mode PID, PI and PD Controllers," *Proceedings of the IEEE International Symposium on Industrial Electronics*, Dubrovnik, 20-23 June 2005, pp. 195-198.

[10] E. Cevat, A. Toker and C. Acar, "A New Proportional-Integral-Derivative (PID) Controller Realization by Using Current Conveyor and Calculating Optimum Parameter Tolerances," *Journal of Electrical and Electronics*, Vol. 1, 2001, pp. 267-273.

[11] J. A. Svoboda, "Current Conveyors, Operational Amplifiers and Nullors," *IEE Proceedings*, Vol. 136, No. 6, 1989, pp. 317-322.

[12] S. Minaei, E. Yuce, S. Takat and O. Cicekoglu, "Simple Realizations of Current-Mode and Voltage-Mode PID, PI and PD Controller," *Proceeding of the IEEE International Symposium on Industrial Electronics*, Vol. 1, 2005, pp. 195-198.

[13] V. Srikul, S. Srisakultiew and M. Siripruchyanun, "A Synthesis of Current-Mode PI, PD and PID Controllers Employing CCIIs," *Proceeding of Electrical Engineering Network* 2012 *of Rajamangala University of Technology*, Nong Khai, April 2012, pp. 513-516.

[14] C. Erdal, H. Kuntman and S. Kafali, "A Current Con-

trolled Conveyor Based Proportional-Integral-Derivative (PID) Controller," *Journal of Electrical & Electronics Engineering*, Vol. 4, No. 2, 2004, pp. 1248-1248.

[15] W. Naksup, V. Kiranon, J. Vongdektum and V. Sangpisit, "PID, PI and PD Controllers Based on CCCII," *Proceeding of* 31st *Electrical Engineering Conference*, Nakhonnayok, 2009, pp. 927-930.

[16] S. Srisakultiew and M. Siripruchyanun, "A Synthesis of Current-Mode PID Controller Using CCCIIs," *The Proceeding of* 3rd *National Conference on Technical Education*, 2010, pp. 63-68.

[17] A. U. Keskin, "Design of a PID Controller Circuit Employing CDBAs," *International Journal of Engineering Education*, Vol. 43, No.1, 2006, pp. 48-56.

[18] C. Acar and S. Ozoguz, "A New Versatile Building Block: Current Differ-Encing Buffered Amplifier Suitable for Analog Signal Processing Filters," *Microelectronics Journal*, Vol. 30, No. 2, 1999, pp. 157-160.

[19] S. Ozoguz, A. Toker and C. Acar, "Current-Mode Continuous-Time Fully-Integrated Universal Filter Using CDBAs," *Electronics Letters*, Vol. 35, No. 2, 1999, pp. 97-98.

[20] S. Maheshwari and I. A. Khan, "Current-Controlled Current Differencing Buffered Amplifier: Implementation and Applications," *Active and Passive Electronic Components*, Vol. 27, No. 4, 2004, pp. 219-227.

[21] C. Toumazou, F. J. Lidgey and D. G. Haigh, "Analog IC Design: The Current Approach," Peter Peregrinus, London, 1990.

[22] D. R. Frey, "Log-Domain Filtering: An Approach to Current-Mode Filtering," *IEE Proceeding Circuit Devices System*, Vol. 140, No. 6, 1993, pp. 406-416.

## 7

A Nonlinear Electrical Resonator as a Simple Touch-Sensitive Switch with Memory

Lars Q. English[1], Mauro David Lifschitz[1], Sunil Acharya[2]
[1]Department of Physics and Astronomy, Dickinson College, Carlisle, USA
[2]a.t.Q Services LLC, Carlisle, USA

ABSTRACT

We introduce a novel switching mechanism that relies on the bistability of a simple nonlinear electrical resonator which incorporates a varactor diode as its capacitive element. The switching action can be made fast and is self-contained in that no further circuitry is necessary. Unlike a flip-flop, whose state is flipped by applying a TTL pulse, this nonlinear switch can be engaged external to the circuit via magnetic, inductive or capacitive coupling; in this way, the switch becomes intrinsically touch-sensitive. Alternatively, the switching action can also be accomplished using frequency-shift-keying (FSK) modulation, which holds the promise of fast manipulation of the memory state. We demonstrate the potential application of these ideas by constructing a touch-sensitive LED lattice.

Keywords: Nonlinear Switch; Electrical Resonator; Bistability; Touch Sensitivity

1. Introduction

In digital electronics, the quintessential memory element that can be switched between two states is, of course, the flip-flop. The ubiquitous SR flip-flop, for instance, consists of two crossed NOR (or NAND) gates. When no signal is applied, the state of the flip-flop remains in its previous configuration, and in order to flip it to the other state a brief voltage signal (a TTL pulse) is applied to the respective input.

Here we propose a nonlinear electrical resonator that in some ways acts like a flip-flop. As we show, the switching between its two states is accomplished via either a driver-frequency protocol (FSK modulation), or by bringing a magnet or inductor into the vicinity of the resonator; it can also be switched by capacitive coupling. Once set, the system remembers its state until another switching action is performed. However, unlike a flip-flop, the element can be induced to switch from the outside of the circuit. Alternatively, a frequency modulation scheme can be employed for fast switching. Finally, we show the application of this idea by constructing a controllable LED array.

Since the switching action can occur in response to touch (via changing the capacitance) or proximity to a magnet or inductor, this resonator acts like touch-sensitive switch and is perhaps reminiscent of a "touch lamp". When the metal housing of such a lamp is touched, its effective capacitance is increased. There are then a num-

ber of ways to convert capacitance to a digital output [1]. Even the simplest scheme incorporates a number of integrated circuit components: a fixed-amplitude AC voltage driver charges and discharges the housing, and the charging current is increased upon touch; further circuitry senses this enhanced current and switches a flip-flop. Our nonlinear resonator, in contrast, does not require any further solid-state electronics to act like a switch; no comparators or flip-flops are needed.

Recently, enormous progress has been made in the field of capacitive coupling and sensing, and this has led to the development of touch-sensitive LCD screens. Here again, controllers and micro-processors are incorporated to compute the location of the touch on the screen [2,3]. The power of an array of nonlinear resonators proposed here (see discussion of the prototype) is that no such microprocessing is necessary—the switching action is intrinsic, relying primarily on the bistability of the nonlinear resonator.

Alternatively, fast switching can be accomplished by driving the system at a constant frequency, and then for a brief time interval (given by the FSK modulation pulse width) toggling to another nearby frequency. We show that the pulse width can be as small as two oscillation periods. In the resonator used here, the shortest switching pulse was 7 μs, but this time can be considerably reduced in principle by lowering the inductance value or employing varactor diodes of lower effective capacitance. There is little doubt that switching speeds could reach into the gigahertz range by scaling component properties and boosting the resonance frequency.

The idea of exploiting such resonance bistability is, of course, not new in general. It has been proposed and implemented in a number of physical systems, such as in optical cavities [4,5], in spin systems [6], and micromechanical oscillators [7,8]. Here we present a simple electronic oscillator that works on a similar principle.

2. The Resonance Circuit

Figure 1 depicts the basic nonlinear oscillator. It is comprised simply of an inductor and a varactor-diode in parallel. The latter is a capacitive element since charge is stored across the depletion layer of the pn-junction. As the width of this depletion layer is voltage-dependent, so is the effective capacitance of the diode. Additionally, the diode also allows current to flow through it (preferentially in one direction) and can be modeled as a resistive element with voltage-dependent resistance. The capacitive and resistive properties of the diode can be viewed from a circuit perspective as acting in parallel [9]. Here we choose radial-lead inductors of $L = 330$ mH. The NTE-618 diodes are characterized by an effective capacitance of about 800 pF at zero bias voltage, as well as a large voltage-sensitivity on capacitance; when reverse-biasing the diode this capacitance value decreases. The linear resonance frequency is computed as

$$f_0 = \frac{1}{2\pi}\sqrt{\frac{1}{LC}} \cong 310 \text{ kHz} . \qquad (1)$$

In order to excite this resonator, we couple it to a signal generator via a fairly large resistor $R_1 = 10$ kW. Note that more than one copy of this resonator could be driven in this way.

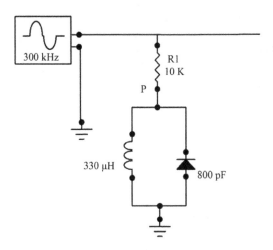

Figure 1. The basic resonance circuit consisting of an inductor and a varactor diode. The diode has effective capacitance and introduces nonlinearity into the system. The voltage response of the resonator is measured at point P.

The resonance curve for fairly large driving amplitudes is shown in **Figure 2(a)**. For low amplitudes (not shown), the resonance frequency and profile approach those expected for linear resonance, namely a symmetric near-Lorentzian profile centered at 310 kHz. The width of the curve is given by roughly 30 kHz, which yield a relatively low quality factor, $Q \approx 10$. Let us now focus on the high-amplitude trace.

At $A = 3.3$ V, the driving is strong enough to propel the resonator into its fully nonlinear regime. Thus, we clearly see that the resonator is characterized by soft nonlinearity as the resonance curve bends towards lower frequency (to the left). More importantly, we observe the generic feature of hysteresis in that the profile depends on the frequency-scan direction. The black trace corresponds to an up-scan in frequency, whereas the red trace corresponds to a down-scan. We see that both traces follow one another very closely, except within a narrow frequency window. Within this window, from roughly $f = 247$ kHz to $f = 258$ kHz, there are two stable solutions. Which one of them is actually realized by the system depends on the initial conditions, or in this case the history, of the system state.

The two solutions are depicted in time domain in **Figure 2(b)** at the driving frequency of 255 kHz (see dashed

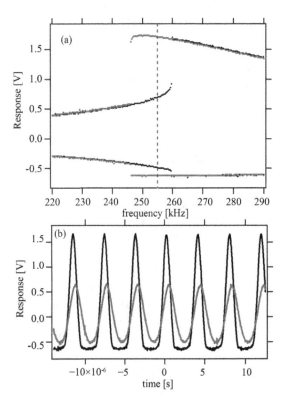

Figure 2. (a) A frequency sweep reveals the bistability region. The black trace is the response of the resonator when the frequency is slowly swept down, whereas for the red trace, it is swept up; (b) At 2 55 kHz, the time-response of the resonator in the two states is illustrated.

line in upper panel). The low-amplitude solution is fairly symmetric with an amplitude of just over 0.5 V. Not much current flows through the diode in the forward direction. The high-amplitude solution, however, is very non-symmetric. When reverse-biased, the voltage can reach up to 1.67 V, whereas in the forward direction it cannot exceed 0.64 V; beyond this value the current through the diode becomes large. This bistability between a small-amplitude and a high-amplitude solution forms the basis of the application of this resonator as a touch-sensitive switch.

In order to demonstrate this application, we use this circuit to drive an LED, as shown in **Figure 3**. The response of the resonator is connected to the base of a NPN transistor controlling the flow of current through the LED.

In this way, if the low-amplitude state is realized, the LED is not lit during any part of the cycle. This is because the base-emitter voltage of the transistor then never exceeds the necessary threshold and no current flows from collector to emitter. In contrast, when the high-amplitude state is chosen, then during parts of the cycle, the transistor is turned on allowing current to flow through the LED.

3. The Nonlinear Circuit as a Touch-Sensitive Switch

The question now is how to switch between the two states of system in the bistability region. One way to do this, of course, is to follow a driving frequency protocol, or FSK modulation. As explained in greater detail in the next section, to turn the LED on, for instance, one would for an instant move to a higher frequency. The switching time is fast due to the combination of a large resonance frequency and high Q-factor. In addition to the frequency control scheme, there exist physically more direct mechanisms.

One possible switching action relies on another interesting effect. When a magnet is brought near the radial lead inductor used in this circuit, its effective inductance

goes down. The reason is that its core consists of a paramagnetic material, a ferrite, which can be saturated by an external magnetic field.

Now when an AC magnetic field is superimposed on this strong DC field, the result is a lower AC-inductance. This effect can be easily observed qualitatively by generating spectra like the one in **Figure 2(a)** while simultaneously bringing a magnet into the inductor's vicinity—the entire spectrum then shifts to the right. To obtain quantitative data, one can use this effect to plot the linear resonance frequency, f_0, against the B-field, as shown in **Figure 4**. From this data one could also, of course, compute an effective inductance as a function of magnetic field strength.

The main lesson of **Figure 4** is that a field of roughly 100 mT is sufficient to switch the LED from an "on" to an "off"-state. Such a field easily shifts the resonance curve to the right by the minimally required 10 kHz, such that the driver at 255 kHz is no-longer situated in the bistability region but excites the lower-amplitude mode only. After the magnet is removed, the lower-amplitude state maintains itself. Thus, the LED stays off even when the magnetic field goes back to zero.

How can the LED be turned on again? It is clear that we would need an effect which increases the inductance, thus shifting the resonance curve to the left. A straightforward way of accomplishing this increase in effective inductance is via an external inductor placed in contact (or near contact) with the circuit inductor. Via the mutual inductance, the combination effectively increases the inductance, easily shifting the resonance curve to the left by at least 10 kHz. This shift, in turn, restores the high-amplitude state and switches the LED back on. The LED stays on even after the external inductor is removed.

Another physically direct method of switching modulates the capacitance in the circuit rather than the inductance. This can be most easily achieved, for instance, by driving the resonators via a capacitor instead of a resistor. When the value of that capacitor is changed, the resonance frequency in turn is altered. For example, we found that when the capacitance is changed from 580 pF

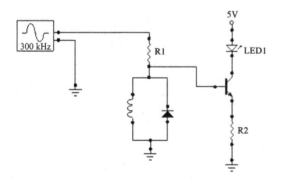

Figure 3. The nonlinear resonator can be used to control an LED in a straightforward transistor circuit.

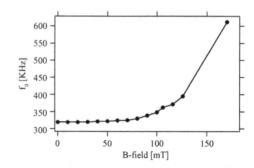

Figure 4. The dependence of the linear resonance frequency on the magnetic field strength at the inductor head. For our purposes, a 100 mT field is sufficient.

to 680 pF (keeping all other components the same), the nonlinear resonance curve shifts from 320 kHz to 306 kHz—a shift greater than the necessary 10 kHz. Thus, if we incorporate into the nonlinear resonating circuit a touch-sensitive capacitor (in place of the resistor), the switching action could be accomplished by a 15 percent increase in capacitance. Such a variation in capacitance is easily achievable, for instance, with capacitive pressure sensors [10].

4. Fast Switching

Here we demonstrate the potential of this simple non-linear resonator as a fast memory switch. Let's say that the system is driven in the bistability region and the low-amplitude state is realized. How fast can the system by switched into the high-amplitude state? As shown in **Figure 5**, the frequency is abruptly changed from $f_d = 257$ kHz to 290 kHz during a pulse of varying duration (black trace); after the pulse the frequency returns to the original value. This type of digital frequency modulation is also referred to as FSK modulation. The blue trace depicts the response of the oscillator. Note that at 260 kHz, the period is 3.8 ms. A FSK pulse of 5 ms duration is not quite long enough to allow the state to migrate to the high-amplitude solution. However, if the pulse width is lengthened to 7 ms, then the switching is accomplished.

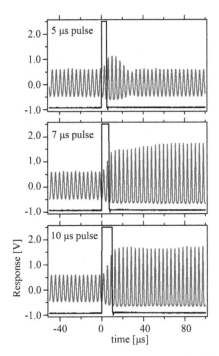

Figure 5. The system's response to FSK modulation. The pulse indicates the driving frequency: outside the pulse, $f_d = 257$ kHz, and inside the pulse 290 kHz . (a) The switch does not quite turn on at a pulse width of $t = 5$ ms; (b) For $t = 7$ ms, a state change is barely accomplished; (c) $t = 10$ ms easily propels the system into the high-amplitude state.

Thus, the pulse width is only required to be roughly two periods of oscillation.

These results suggest a way to boost switching speeds further by scaling up the frequencies. This, in turn, can be achieved by using smaller inductors, and/or by selecting varactor diodes of smaller effective capacitance values (but with sufficient nonlinearity). In order to reach industry standards for commercially-available fast flip-flops (CMOS), which feature maximum clock speeds of 80 - 200 MHz, the resonance frequency here would have to be increased by a factor of 1000. Since our test circuit currently incorporates fairly large inductance and capacitance values, we expect this to be achievable while aiding the goal of miniaturizing the resonator.

5. A Prototype System

All the pieces are now in place to construct a prototype system comprised of a number of controllable LEDs. To demonstrate the feasibility of the concept, we chose to build a three-by-three LED lattice, as illustrated in **Figure 6**. Each LED is controlled by its own resonance circuit. A two-sided pen is also shown in the figure. It consists of a magnetic tip on one side and an inductor on the other. This way, by touching a particular inductor in this array, its respective LED can be turned on and off. The effect remains robust even when a plastic cover is placed over the array (although it cannot exceed a certain thickness, otherwise the mutual inductance becomes too small). One important consideration in the design of such an array of LEDs is component uniformity. Commercially available inductors usually have a tolerance of perhaps 5 percent. This variance is too large for the purpose of this application, and so a post-selection of inductors is necessary. If this is not done, a single driver frequency will not fall into the bistability window of all resonators.

Note that any pattern of light can be induced in this LED array in a physically direct way, without the use of microprocessors. To erase a pattern and turn all LEDs off,

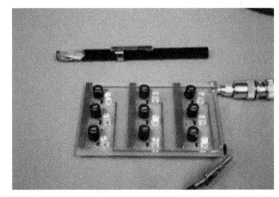

Figure 6. A 3 × 3 array of controllable LEDs. The pen at the top is used to switch the LEDs by touch.

a momentary decrease in driver frequency is all that is needed. If all LEDs are to be lit, a quick shift to larger frequency will accomplish it. In this way, this switching scheme yields flexibility and external control in a straightforward manner.

6. Conclusions

We have demonstrated a touch-sensitive switch based on a simple nonlinear electrical resonator. The bistability and hysteresis properties of the circuit provide the novel multi-mode switching functionality depending on magnetic, inductive or capacitive input. The circuit uses minimal electronic components and does not require extensive programmable logic control systems inherent to current touch-sensitive solutions. This economical design has superior response times to other current touch-sensitive solution. Furthermore, the switching time is a direct function of the resonator circuit properties, and this implies that a simple choice of resonator components can be used to "tune" the circuit response time over a range of several decades. The multi-mode switching characteristics add further dimension to these switching circuits extending the applicability to a host of new applications.

This work preludes possible applications for a more general class of nonlinear resonator networks described in literature. These topologically repeating networks allow "smart" circuit design with cheap components while using no digital programmable components. For instance, a simple local input to a node in this network can shift the resonance characteristics of the circuits causing energy to be moved between two specific nodes. This allows for a variety of power applications where arbitrary energy transfer not limited to electric is easily achieved.

We are currently prototyping several applications in illumination, signage, memory storage, and climate control applications with this general class of nonlinear resonator circuits.

7. Acknowledgements

L.Q.E. was supported by an NSF PFI/ITN Seed Assistance Grant 4437-DC-NSF-7466.

REFERENCES

[1] M. Yamada and K. Watanabe, "A Capacitive Pressure Sensor Interface Using Oversampling Delta-Sigma Demodulation Techniques," *IEEE Transactions on Instrumentation and Measurement*, Vol. 46, No. 1, 1997, pp. 3-7.

[2] M. Lee, "The Art of Capacitive Sensing," EE Times (An UBM Electronics Publication), Planet Analog Supplement, 2006.

[3] J. Schöning, *et al.*, "Multi-Touch Surfaces: A Technical Guide," Technical Report TUM-I0833, 2008.

[4] H. M. Gibbs, "Optical Bistability: Controlling Light with Light," Academic Press, New York, 1985.

[5] H. Wang, D. Goorskey and M. Xiao, "Controlling Light by Light with Three-Level Atoms Inside an Optical Cavity," *Optics Letters*, Vol. 27, No. 15, 2002, pp. 1354-1356.

[6] D. Gourier, E. Aubay and J. Guglielmi, "Bistable Switching of Nuclear Polarization States in Gallium Oxide," *Physical Review B*, Vol. 50, No. 5, 1994, pp. 2941-2952.

[7] H. B. Chan and C. Stambaugh, "Fluctuation-Enhanced Frequency Mixing in a Nonlinear Micromechanical Oscillator," *Physical Review B*, Vol. 73, No. 22, 2006, Article ID: 224301.

[8] J. Casals-Terre, A. Fargas-Marques and A. M. Shkel, "Snap-Action Bistable Micromechanisms Actuated by Nonlinear Resonance," *Journal of Microelectromechanical Systems*, Vol. 17, No. 5, 2008, pp. 1082-1093.

[9] F. Palmero, L. Q. English, J. Cuevas, R. Carretero-Gonzalez and P. G. Kevrekidis, "Discrete Breathers in a Nonlinear Electric Line: Modeling, Computation, and Experiment," *Physical Review E*, Vol. 84, No. 2, 2011, Article ID: 026605.

[10] J. Han and M. A. Shannon, "Smooth Contact Capacitive Pressure Sensors in Touch- and Peeling-Mode Operation," *IEEE Sensors Journal*, Vol. 9, No. 3, 2009, pp. 199-206.

## 8

Universal Current-Mode Biquad Filter Using a VDTA

Dinesh Prasad[1*], Data Ram Bhaskar[1], Mayank Srivastava[2]
[1]Department of Electronics and Communication Engineering, Faculty of Engineering and Technology,
Jamia Millia Islamia, New Delhi, India
[2]D/O Electronics and Communication Engineering, Amity School of Engineering and Technology,
Amity University, Noida, India

ABSTRACT

This paper presents a new current-mode single input multi output (SIMO) type biquad employing one voltage differencing transconductance amplifier (VDTA), two grounded capacitors and a single grounded resistor. The configuration realizes all basic filter functions (*i.e.* Low Pass (LP), High Pass (HP), Band Pass (BP), Notch (BR) and All Pass (AP)). The natural frequency (ω_0) and bandwidth (BW) are independently tunable. The workability of proposed configuration has been verified using SPICE simulation with TSMC CMOS 0.18 μm process parameters.

Keywords: Current Mode Filter; Voltage Differencing Transconductance Amplifier

1. Introduction

Active filters are important basic building blocks, which are frequently employed in electrical engineering applications. The current-mode approach [1] in designing active filters has become more popular due to its advantageous features such as larger dynamic range and wider bandwidth as compared to voltage-mode counterparts (particularly for the high frequency operations), simpler filtering configurations and lower power consumption. During the past few years, active filters using different current-mode/voltage-mode building blocks have been employed in which VDTA, recently introduced in [2], appears to be a useful active building block for an easy CMOS implementation of current-mode signal processing/signal generation [3-5].

Various SIMO-type active filters using different active elements are available in the literature see [6-13] and the references cited therein. In references [6-9], SIMO-type filter configurations employing 2/4 resistors and 2/3 capacitors have been presented. These proposed filter structures do not realize all the five filter responses. The configurations presented in [10] and [11] although use one resistor and two capacitors but fail to realize all the basic filter functions. Although the biquads proposed in [12] and [13] realize all the five filter functions but they use two capacitors along with 2/3 resistors. Therefore, the purpose of this communication is to propose a new SIMO-type current-mode universal biquad filter employing one VDTA, two grounded capacitors and a sin-

gle grounded resistor, which realizes all the basic filter functions *i.e.* LP, HP, BP, BR and AP. The natural frequency ω_0 and BW are independently tunable. The proposed circuit also offers low active and passive sensitivities. The workability of proposed configuration has been verified using SPICE simulation with TSMC CMOS 0.18 μm process parameters.

2. The Proposed New Configurations

The symbolic notation of the VDTA is shown in **Figure 1**, where V_P and V_N are input terminals and Z, X^+ and X^- are output terminals. All terminals of VDTA exhibit high impedance values [2]. The VDTA can be described by the following set of equations:

$$\begin{bmatrix} I_Z \\ I_{X^+} \\ I_{X^-} \end{bmatrix} = \begin{bmatrix} g_{m_1} & -g_{m_1} & 0 \\ 0 & 0 & g_{m_2} \\ 0 & 0 & -g_{m_2} \end{bmatrix} \begin{bmatrix} V_{V_P} \\ V_{V_N} \\ V_Z \end{bmatrix} \quad (1)$$

The proposed circuit configuration is shown in **Figure 2**.

A routine circuit analysis of **Figure 2** yields the following filter transfer functions:

$$T_1(s)\big|_{LP} = \frac{I_{o1}}{I_{in}} = \frac{g_{m_1} g_{m_2}}{D(s)} \quad (2)$$

$$T_2(s)\big|_{BP} = \frac{I_{o2}}{I_{in}} = -\frac{s\left(\dfrac{g_{m_1}}{C_1}\right)}{D(s)} \quad (3)$$

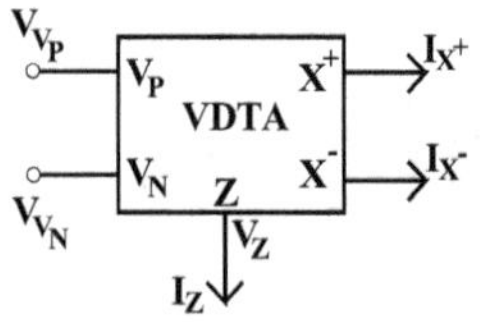

Figure 1. The symbolic notation of VDTA.

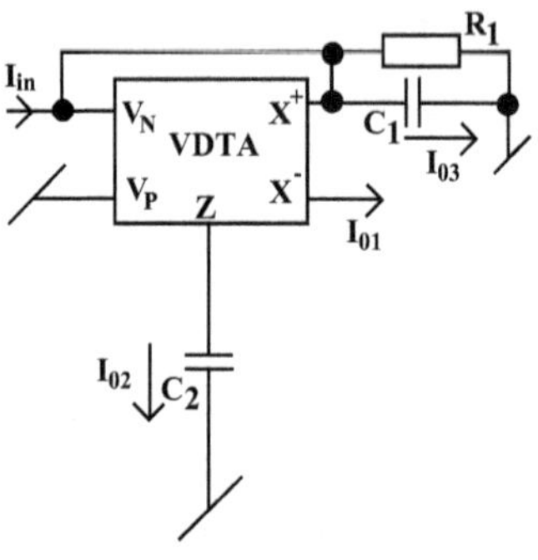

Figure 2. The proposed configuration.

$$T_3(s)\big|_{HP} = \frac{I_{o3}}{I_{in}} = \frac{s^2}{D(s)} \quad (4)$$

$$T_4(s)\big|_{NOTCH} = \frac{(I_{o3}+I_{o1})}{I_{in}} = \frac{\left(s^2 + \frac{g_{m_1} g_{m_2}}{C_1 C_2}\right)}{D(s)} \quad (5)$$

$$T_5(s)\big|_{AP} = \frac{(I_{o3}+I_{o2}+I_{o1})}{I_{in}} = \frac{\left\{s^2 - s\left(\frac{g_{m_1}}{C_1}\right) + \frac{g_{m_1} g_{m_2}}{C_1 C_2}\right\}}{D(s)} \quad (6)$$

where

$$D(s) = s^2 + s\left(\frac{1}{R_1 C_1}\right) + \frac{g_{m_1} g_{m_2}}{C_1 C_2} \quad (7)$$

The natural frequency ω_0, BW and quality factor Q_0 are given by:

$$\omega_0 = \sqrt{\frac{g_{m_1} g_{m_2}}{C_1 C_2}} \quad (8)$$

$$BW = \frac{1}{R_1 C_1} \quad (9)$$

$$Q_0 = \sqrt{\frac{g_{m_1} g_{m_2} C_1 R_1^2}{C_2}} \quad (10)$$

3. SPICE Simulation Results

To verify the theoretical analysis, the proposed configuration was simulated using CMOS VDTA from [2]. Power supply voltages were taken as $V_{DD} = -V_{SS} = 1$ V and $I_{B1} = I_{B2} = 150$ μA, $I_{B3} = I_{B4} = 42.38$ μA biasing currents are used. The passive elements of the configuration were selected as $C_1 = C_2 = 0.01$ nF and $R_1 = 1.58$ KΩ. The transconductances of VDTA were controlled by bias currents. **Figure 3** shows the simulated filter responses of LP, BP, HP, BR and AP. These results, thus, confirm the validity of the proposed configuration. A comparison with other SIMO-type current-mode biquads using a single active device is presented in **Table 1**.

4. Conclusion

A new current-mode SIMO-type biquad filter has been presented which uses only one VDTA and three grounded passive elements. The proposed filter can realize the second-order LP, BP, HP, BR and AP responses. The circuit employs all grounded passive components (which is desirable for IC implementation) and offers low active and passive sensitivities. The natural frequency (ω_0) and bandwidth (BW) are independently tunable. SPICE simulations have established the workability of the proposed formulation.

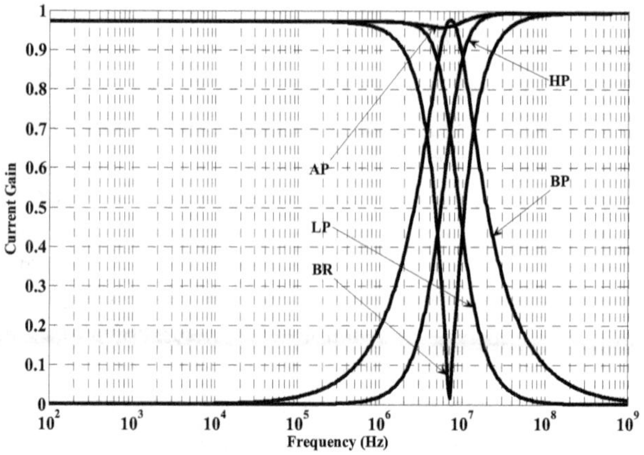

Figure 3. Frequency response.

Table 1. Comparison with other SIMO-type current-mode biquads using a single active device.

Reference	No. of active component	No. of resistors	No. of capacitors	All five filter function realized
[6]	1	4	2	NO
[7]	1	3/4	3	NO
[8]	1	2	2	NO
[9]	1	2	2	NO
[10]	1	1	2	NO
[11]	1	1	2	NO
[12]	1	3	2	YES
[13]	1	2	2	YES
Proposed	**1**	**1**	**2**	**YES**

4. Acknowledgements

This work was performed at the Advanced Analog Signal Processing Laboratory of the Department of Electronics and Communication Engineering, F/o Engineering and Technology, Jamia Millia Islamia, Jamia Nagar, New Delhi-110025, India.

REFERENCES

[1] C. Toumazau, F. J. Lidgey and D. G. Haigh, "Analogue IC Design: The Current-Mode Approach," Peter Peregrinus Limited, London, 1990.

[2] D. Biolek, R. Senani, V. Biolkova and Z. Kolka, "Active Elements for Analog Signal Processing, Classification, Review and New Proposals," *Radioengineering*, Vol. 17, No. 4, 2008, pp. 15-32.

[3] A. Yesil, F. Kacar and H. Kuntman, "New Simple CMOS Realization of Voltage Differencing Transconductance Amplifier and Its RF Filter Application," *Radioengineering*, Vol. 20, No. 3, 2011, pp. 632-637.

[4] D. Prasad and D. R. Bhaskar, "Electronically-Controllable Explicit Current Output Sinusoidal Oscillator Employing Single VDTA," *ISRN Electronics*, Vol. 2012, 2012, Article ID: 382560.

[5] J. Satansup, T. Pukkalanun and W. Tangsrirat, "Electronically Tunable Single-Input Five-Output Voltage-Mode Universal Filter Using VDTAs and Grounded Passive Elements," *Circuits, Systems, and Signal Processing*, 2012 (online).

[6] A. Fabre and J. L. Houle, "Voltage-Mode and Current-Mode Sallen-Key Implementations Based on Translinear Conveyors," *IEEE Proceedings-G: Circuits, Devices and Systems*, Vol.139, No.7, 1992, pp. 491-497.

[7] C. M. Chang, C. C. Chien and H. Y. Wang, "Universal Active Current Filters Using Single Second Generation Current Conveyor," *Electronics Letters*, Vol. 29, No. 13, 1993, pp. 1159-1160.

[8] E. Yuce, B. Metin and O. Cicekoglu, "Current-Mode Biquadratic Filters Using Single CCIII and Minimum Number of Passive Elements," *Frequenz: Journal of RF-Engineering and Telecommunications*, Vol. 58, No. 9-10, 2004, pp. 225-227.

[9] B. Chaturvedi and S. Maheshwari, "Current Mode Biquad Filter with Minimum Component Count," *Journal of Active and Passive Electronic Components*, Vol. 2011, 2011, Article ID: 391642.

[10] D. Biolek, V. Biolkova and Z. Kolka, "Current-Mode Biquad Employing Single CDTA," *Indian Journla of Pure and Applied Physics*, Vol. 47, No. 7, 2009, pp. 535-537.

[11] W. Tangsrirat, "Novel Current-Mode and Voltage-Mode Universal Biquad Filters Using Single CFTA," *Indian Journal of Engineering and Material Science*, Vol. 17, 2010, pp. 99-104.

[12] C. N. Lee and C. M. Chang, "Single FDCCII-Based Mixed-Mode Biquad Filter with Eight Outputs," *AEU: International Journal of Electronics and Communications*, Vol. 63, No. 9, 2009, pp. 736-742.

[13] D. Prasad, D. R. Bhaskar and A. K. Singh, "Universal Current-Mode Biquad Filter Using Dual Output Current Differencing Transconductance Amplifier," *AEU: International Journal of Electronics and Communications*, Vol. 63, No. 6, 2009, pp. 497-501.

Appendix: Non-Ideal Analysis

Considering the non-ideal effect of various parameters of VDTA *i.e.*, the finite *X*-terminal parasitic impedance consisting of a resistance R_X in parallel with capacitance C_X, the parasitic impedance at the *Z*-terminal consisting of a resistance R_Z in parallel with capacitance C_Z, the parasitic impedance at the V_p-terminal consisting of a resistance R_p in parallel with capacitance C_p and the parasitic impedance at the V_n-terminal consisting of a resistance R_n in parallel with capacitance C_n. The parasitic impedances belong to the circuit shown in **Figure 2** are indicated in **Figure A1**.

Considering the above parasitic impedances, the natural frequency ω_0 and quality factor Q_0 are found to be:

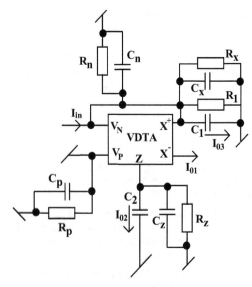

Figure A1. Parasitic impedances of VDTA affecting the circuit of Figure 2.

$$\omega_0 = \sqrt{\frac{\left(\frac{1}{R_1}+\frac{1}{R_x}+\frac{1}{R_n}\right)\frac{1}{R_z}+g_{m_1}g_{m_2}}{\left(C_1C_2+C_1C_z+C_2C_x+C_zC_x+C_2C_n+C_nC_z\right)}} \qquad (a)$$

$$Q_0 = \frac{\sqrt{\left\{\left(\frac{1}{R_1}+\frac{1}{R_x}+\frac{1}{R_n}\right)\frac{1}{R_z}+g_{m_1}g_{m_2}\right\}*\left(C_1C_2+C_1C_z+C_2C_x+C_zC_x+C_2C_n+C_nC_z\right)}}{\left(\frac{C_1}{R_z}+\frac{C_x}{R_z}+\frac{C_n}{R_z}+\frac{C_2}{R_1}+\frac{C_z}{R_1}+\frac{C_2}{R_x}+\frac{C_z}{R_x}+\frac{C_2}{R_n}+\frac{C_z}{R_n}\right)} \qquad (b)$$

The sensitivity of ω_0 and quality factor Q_0 with respect to its active and passive elements are given as:

$$S_{g_{m_1}}^{\omega_0}=S_{g_{m_2}}^{\omega_0}=\frac{g_{m_1}g_{m_2}}{2\left\{\left(\frac{1}{R_1}+\frac{1}{R_x}+\frac{1}{R_n}\right)\frac{1}{R_z}+g_{m_1}g_{m_2}\right\}}, \quad S_{R_1}^{\omega_0}=-\frac{\frac{1}{R_1R_z}}{2\left\{\left(\frac{1}{R_1}+\frac{1}{R_x}+\frac{1}{R_n}\right)\frac{1}{R_z}+g_{m_1}g_{m_2}\right\}}$$

$$S_{R_x}^{\omega_0}=-\frac{\frac{1}{R_xR_z}}{2\left\{\left(\frac{1}{R_1}+\frac{1}{R_x}+\frac{1}{R_n}\right)\frac{1}{R_z}+g_{m_1}g_{m_2}\right\}}, \quad S_{R_n}^{\omega_0}=-\frac{\frac{1}{R_nR_z}}{2\left\{\left(\frac{1}{R_1}+\frac{1}{R_x}+\frac{1}{R_n}\right)\frac{1}{R_z}+g_{m_1}g_{m_2}\right\}}$$

$$S_{R_z}^{\omega_0}=-\frac{\frac{1}{R_z}\left(\frac{1}{R_1}+\frac{1}{R_x}+\frac{1}{R_n}\right)}{2\left\{\left(\frac{1}{R_1}+\frac{1}{R_x}+\frac{1}{R_n}\right)\frac{1}{R_z}+g_{m_1}g_{m_2}\right\}}, \quad S_{C_1}^{\omega_0}=-\frac{C_1\left(C_2+C_z\right)}{2\left(C_1C_2+C_1C_z+C_2C_x+C_zC_x+C_2C_n+C_nC_z\right)}$$

$$S_{C_2}^{\omega_0}=-\frac{C_2\left(C_1+C_x+C_n\right)}{2\left(C_1C_2+C_1C_z+C_2C_x+C_zC_x+C_2C_n+C_nC_z\right)}, \quad S_{C_z}^{\omega_0}=-\frac{C_z\left(C_1+C_x+C_n\right)}{2\left(C_1C_2+C_1C_z+C_2C_x+C_zC_x+C_2C_n+C_nC_z\right)}$$

$$S_{C_x}^{\omega_0}=-\frac{C_x\left(C_2+C_z\right)}{2\left(C_1C_2+C_1C_z+C_2C_x+C_zC_x+C_2C_n+C_nC_z\right)}, \quad S_{C_n}^{\omega_0}=-\frac{C_n\left(C_2+C_z\right)}{2\left(C_1C_2+C_1C_z+C_2C_x+C_zC_x+C_2C_n+C_nC_z\right)}$$

$$S_{g_{m_1}}^{Q_0}=S_{g_{m_2}}^{Q_0}=\frac{g_{m_1}g_{m_2}}{2\left\{\left(\frac{1}{R_1}+\frac{1}{R_x}+\frac{1}{R_n}\right)\frac{1}{R_z}+g_{m_1}g_{m_2}\right\}}, \quad S_{R_1}^{Q_0}=\frac{\frac{1}{R_1}\left[-\frac{1}{2R_z}\left(D\right)+\left\{\left(\frac{1}{R_1}+\frac{1}{R_x}+\frac{1}{R_n}\right)\frac{1}{R_z}+g_{m_1}g_{m_2}\right\}\left(C_2+C_z\right)\right]}{\left(D\right)\left\{\left(\frac{1}{R_1}+\frac{1}{R_x}+\frac{1}{R_n}\right)\frac{1}{R_z}+g_{m_1}g_{m_2}\right\}}$$

$$S_{R_x}^{Q_0} = \frac{\dfrac{1}{R_x}\left[-\dfrac{1}{2R_z}(D)+\left\{\left(\dfrac{1}{R_1}+\dfrac{1}{R_x}+\dfrac{1}{R_n}\right)\dfrac{1}{R_z}+g_{m_1}g_{m_2}\right\}(C_2+C_z)\right]}{(D)\left\{\left(\dfrac{1}{R_1}+\dfrac{1}{R_x}+\dfrac{1}{R_n}\right)\dfrac{1}{R_z}+g_{m_1}g_{m_2}\right\}},$$

$$S_{R_n}^{Q_0} = \frac{\dfrac{1}{R_n}\left[-\dfrac{1}{2R_z}(D)+\left\{\left(\dfrac{1}{R_1}+\dfrac{1}{R_x}+\dfrac{1}{R_n}\right)\dfrac{1}{R_z}+g_{m_1}g_{m_2}\right\}(C_2+C_z)\right]}{(D)\left\{\left(\dfrac{1}{R_1}+\dfrac{1}{R_x}+\dfrac{1}{R_n}\right)\dfrac{1}{R_z}+g_{m_1}g_{m_2}\right\}},$$

$$S_{R_z}^{Q_0} = \frac{\dfrac{1}{R_z}\left[-\dfrac{1}{2}\left(\dfrac{1}{R_1}+\dfrac{1}{R_x}+\dfrac{1}{R_n}\right)(D)+\left\{\left(\dfrac{1}{R_1}+\dfrac{1}{R_x}+\dfrac{1}{R_n}\right)\dfrac{1}{R_z}+g_{m_1}g_{m_2}\right\}(C_1+C_x+C_n)\right]}{(D)\left\{\left(\dfrac{1}{R_1}+\dfrac{1}{R_x}+\dfrac{1}{R_n}\right)\dfrac{1}{R_z}+g_{m_1}g_{m_2}\right\}},$$

$$S_{C_1}^{Q_0} = \frac{C_1\left[\dfrac{1}{2}(C_2+C_z)(D)-(E)\dfrac{1}{R_z}\right]}{(D)(E)}, \quad S_{C_2}^{Q_0} = \frac{C_2\left[\dfrac{1}{2}(C_1+C_x+C_n)(D)-(E)\left(\dfrac{1}{R_1}+\dfrac{1}{R_x}+\dfrac{1}{R_n}\right)\right]}{(D)(E)},$$

$$S_{C_z}^{Q_0} = \frac{C_z\left[\dfrac{1}{2}(C_1+C_x+C_n)(D)-(E)\left(\dfrac{1}{R_1}+\dfrac{1}{R_x}+\dfrac{1}{R_n}\right)\right]}{(D)(E)}, \quad S_{C_x}^{Q_0} = \frac{C_x\left[\dfrac{1}{2}(C_2+C_z)(D)-(E)\dfrac{1}{R_z}\right]}{(D)(E)},$$

(c)

$$S_{C_n}^{Q_0} = \frac{C_n\left[\dfrac{1}{2}(C_2+C_z+C_p)(D)-(E)\dfrac{1}{R_z}\right]}{(D)(E)},$$

where

$$(D)=\left(\frac{C_1}{R_z}+\frac{C_x}{R_z}+\frac{C_n}{R_z}+\frac{C_2}{R_1}+\frac{C_z}{R_1}+\frac{C_2}{R_x}+\frac{C_z}{R_x}+\frac{C_2}{R_n}+\frac{C_z}{R_n}\right), \quad (E)=(C_1C_2+C_1C_z+C_2C_x+C_zC_x+C_2C_n+C_nC_z). \quad \text{(d)}$$

From the above mentioned sensitivity values, it is easy to figure out that all the active and passive sensitivities are no more than half in magnitude.

## 9

A Current Bleeding CMOS Mixer Featuring *LO* Amplification Based on Current-Reused Topology[*]

Wah Ching Lee [1,2], Kim Fung Tsang[2], Yi Shen[2], Kwok Tai Chui[2]
[1]Department of Electronic & Information Engineering, The Hong Kong Polytechnic University, Hong Kong, China
[2]Department of Electronic Engineering, City University of Hong Kong, Hong Kong, China

ABSTRACT

A double balanced Gilbert-cell class-A amplifier bleeding mixer (DBGC CAAB mixer) is proposed and implemented. The injection current is utilized to amplify the local oscillator (*LO*) signal to improve the performance of the transconductor stage. The DBGC CAAB mixer achieves a conversion gain of 17.5 dB at −14 dBm *LO* power, and the noise figure is suppressed from 45 dB to 10.7 dB. It is important to stress that the new configuration will not drain additional power in contrast to the former current bleeding mixers. This topology dramatically relieves the requirement of the *LO* power. The DBGC CAAB mixer is implemented by using 0.18-μm RFCMOS technology and operates at the 2.4 GHz ISM application with 10 MHz intermediate frequency. The power consumption is 12 mA at 1.5 V supply voltage. The DBGC CAAB mixer features the highest FOM figure within a wide range of *LO* power.

Keywords: Mixer; Gilbert-Cell; Current Bleeding; Noise; Conversion Gain; Current-Reuse; Class-A Amplifier

1. Introduction

With the rapid proliferation of modern wireless market, RF transceivers play a more and more important role in our daily lives. Mixer is one of the key blocks in the signal chain performing frequency translation before signals are further processed in the intermediate frequency circuits. The noise and the gain performance of the mixer, in general, determine the performance of the whole system at large [1]. In past decades, many research scholars made deep insights into the noise mechanism [2-5] and gain enhancement [6-8] in mixers. In order to achieve good performance including gain, noise, isolation and linearity (higher-order components), Gilbert-cell [9] is commonly used as the mixer core topology.

Amongst most factors, the conversion gain (CG) and the third-order intercept point (IP3) of the mixer are the key elements determining the mixer performance. Both CG and IP3 are proportional to the square root of the bias current (I_{b1}) of the driver stage [10,11], as shown in **Figure 1(a)**. In order to improve CG and IP3, a simple method is to increase the bias current of the driver stage M1, namely I_{b1}. However, this improvement is at the expense of other degradations. For instance, the increase of I_{b1} will also increase the currents, I_{b2} and I_{b3}, in the switch pair M2 and M3 (referred as M2-M3 thereafter).

As a result, the noise contributions from M2-M3 are also increased [12-14]. In addition, in order to keep all the transistors working in saturation region, the load resistance Z_L should be decreased to avoid too much voltage drop across them, especially in modern sub-micro CMOS technology. The load resistance reduction will in turn cause the gain compression. Hence it is concluded that increasing the bias current solely of the driver stage is not an efficient way to improve the overall performance, including gain, linearity and noise of the mixer.

In order to retain the benefits of increasing the bias current but without degrading other performances, a current bleeding topology, by applying a current source in

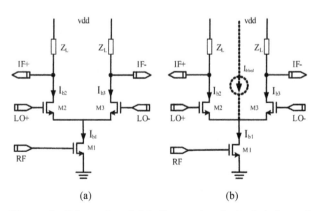

(a)   (b)

Figure 1. Schematic of (a) Conventional single-balanced mixer; (b) Single-balanced mixer with current bleeding.

[*]The work was supported by Research Grants 9220049 from City University of Hong Kong.

parallel with M2-M3, is used [15]. Analysis shows that such topology [15], [16] facilitates the quiescent current in the driver stage to be independent from M2-M3. **Figure 1(b)** shows the illustrative topology. The bleeding current source drives a higher driver stage current through the higher load resistance of M1 by virtue of the fact that part of the driver bias current is steered from M2-M3. An additional advantage of using the bleeding source is that M2-M3 can operate at a lower gate-source voltage and thus rendering a compact size. Lower gate-source voltage helps to improve the conversion efficiency as fewer charges are necessary to turn M2-M3 on and/or off.

In this paper, a double balanced Gilbert-cell class-A amplifier bleeding mixer (DBGC CAAB mixer) is developed. By inserting a class-A amplifier in parallel with M2-M3, the local oscillator (*LO*) swing is increased to drive M2-M3 into a hard switching fashion. An additional advantage is that the bias current of the class-A amplifier will enhance the bias of the driver stage of the mixer, hence improving the overall performance. The present investigation is an extension of our previous work [17] with a detailed analysis of noise reduction and gain boosting. Detailed measurement results are also provided. The paper is organized as follows: Section 2 describes the motivation of this work; Section 3 describes the topology, the design and the analysis results, Section 4 summarizes the performance of the developed mixer by including a FOM comparison and, Section 5 gives the conclusion.

2. Motivation

In the mixer analysis, the drain current of M2-M3 are presented as:

$$I_{D2} = K\left(V_{GS2} - V_T\right)^2 \quad (1)$$

$$I_{D3} = K\left(V_{GS3} - V_T\right)^2 \quad (2)$$

The voltage of Local Oscillator (*LO*), v_{LO}, is defined as:

$$v_{LO} = V_{GS2} - V_{GS3} \quad (3)$$

From KCL:

$$I_{D1} = I_{D2} + I_{D3} \quad (4)$$

and, for the differential operation of M2-M3, the output current is:

$$I_{out} = I_{D2} - I_{D3} \quad (5)$$

Based on the physics of the MOS device, Equations (1) and (2) are supported by the following relationships:

$$K = \frac{1}{2}\mu_n C_{ox}\frac{W}{L} = \frac{I_{D1}}{2V_{od}^2} \quad (6)$$

$$V_{od} = V_{GS} - V_T \quad (7)$$

In order to characterize the relationship of the output current and the performance of M2-M3, the output current is derived as a function of v_{LO}:

$$I_{out} = Kv_{LO} \cdot \sqrt{\frac{2I_{D1}}{K} - v_{LO}^2} \quad (8)$$

This formula is derived based on the condition that both M2 and M3 are at ON state. When $v_{LO} > \sqrt{2}V_{od}$, M2-M3 acts as a hard switch, and the output current, I_{out}, can be modeled as a sgn function:

$$I_{out} \approx \begin{cases} I_{D1} \cdot \sqrt{1-\left(1-\delta^2/2\right)^2}, |\delta| \le \sqrt{2} \\ I_{D1} \cdot \text{sgn}(\delta), |\delta| \gg \sqrt{2} \end{cases} \quad (9)$$

where, $\delta = v_{LO}/V_{od}$

Figure 2 shows the I-V characteristics of M2-M3 graphically. The transconductance of M2-M3, G_m, is given by:

$$G_m\left(v_{LO}\right) = 2\frac{g_{m2}\left(v_{LO}\right) \cdot g_{m3}\left(v_{LO}\right)}{g_{m2}\left(v_{LO}\right) + g_{m3}\left(v_{LO}\right)} \quad (10)$$

It will be explained in (13) that increasing v_{LO} will improve the mixer performance; hence the dependence of G_m on v_{LO} needs to be investigated. G_m is derived as a function of v_{LO}:

$$G_m\left(v_{LO}\right) = 2I_{D1}\sqrt{\frac{1}{v_{LO}^2 + \frac{2I_{D1}}{K}}} \quad (11)$$

As shown in **Figure 2**, $G_m\left(v_{LO}\right)$ reaches its maximum value as v_{LO} approaches 0. When v_{LO} increases, $G_m\left(v_{LO}\right)$ decreases and eventually approaches zero.

Noise is an important parameter in mixer design and is now discussed. In general, there are three main noise

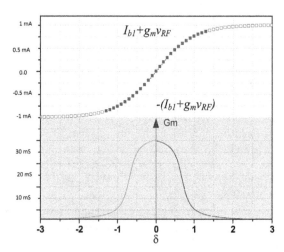

Figure 2. I-V characteristic and equivalent transconductance of M2-M3, where $\delta = v_{LO}/V_{od}$.

sources in conventional mixer circuits, namely the trans-conductor stage, the switch pair M2-M3 and the load. In Terrovitis [5] and Darabi [2] models, noise contributed to the output exactly when both switching transistors are at ON state—indicated as the switch interval Δ (will be discussed in Section 3). The noise PSD (power spectrum density), introduced within Δ is presented as:

$$PSD = 8KT\gamma G_m = 16KT\gamma \left(\frac{g_{m2} \cdot g_{m3}}{g_{m2} + g_{m3}} \right) \quad (12)$$

where K—Boltzmann's constant

　　T—Absolute temperature

　　γ—noise coefficient ($= 2/3$ for long channel device)

　　g_{m2}, g_{m3}—Trans-conductance of M2-M3

At the zero-crossing point of v_{LO}, both M2 and M3 are at ON state, thus resulting in non-zero value of g_{m2} and g_{m3}. From (11), large LO voltage swing will diminish G_m, rendering either g_{m2} or g_{m3} to vanish and thus suppressing the noise. Noise PSD can further be converted [5] to the relationship of bias current and noise contribution:

$$PSD = \frac{16KT\gamma}{\pi} \cdot \frac{I_B}{v_{LO}} \quad (13)$$

where I_B is the bias current of M2-M3. It is seen from (13) that, by increasing v_{LO}, Noise PSD is suppressed efficiently. Furthermore, by reducing I_B, PSD will also be suppressed, thus further verifying the current bleeding principle.

The other key parameter of a mixer is gain. In order to enhance the gain, the conversion gain (CG) of the mixer is also analyzed [5].

$$CG = c \cdot g_{m1} \cdot re\{Z_L\} \quad (14)$$

where the multiplier c is given by:

$$c \approx \frac{2}{\pi} \left(\frac{\sin(\pi \Delta / T_{LO})}{\pi \Delta / T_{LO}} \right) \quad (15)$$

It is seen from (15) that increasing c, and/or g_{m1}, is an efficient way to increase CG. The implementation will be discussed in Section 3.4.

Based on the above discussion, the novelties of the proposed design are:

A1) Novel bleeding source: In order to improve the gain, linearity and noise, the bias current of the driver stage should be increased. However, such a direct increase will cause other related problems, including the high noise contribution from M2-M3 as well as the excessive voltage drop on the load resistor. It is important to note that the current bleeding structure improves only the bias of the driver stage but without increasing the bias of M2-M3.

A2) *LO* amplification: Higher amplitude of V_{LO} helps to minimize the noise PSD from the M2-M3 by reducing

Δ, and at the same time, maximizing $CG \left(= 2 \cdot (g_{m1}) \cdot (Z_L) / \pi \right)$ to reach the upper limit.

In this investigation, a Gilbert-cell mixer based on the current bleeding technique is explored. Inspired from the benefit of high gain and low noise (referring to (A1) and (A2)), and taking advantage of the linearity, a class-A amplifier (referred as **Amp** thereafter), is implemented as the bleeding sources to amplify the LO signals. Hence the class-A amplifier bleeding source is employed to replace the traditional simple current source. After performing the LO amplification, the DC bias current of the class-A amplifier is steered to the driver stage of the mixer to improve the gain, noise and linearity characteristics. It will be explained that, comparing to the conventional current bleeding mixer, the CAAB structure can reuse the bleeding current more efficiently.

3. Methodology

3.1. Overall Topology

Figure 3 shows the proposed double-balanced Gilbert-cell mixer incorporating CAAB, namely DBGC CAAB mixer. As shown in **Figure 1(b)**, taking advantage of the symmetry, one half of the circuit is used for analysis. In conventional mixers, the bias current, I_{b1}, of the driver stage M1 is the sum of current of I_{b2} (of M2) and I_{b3} (of M3), *i.e.* $I_{b1} = I_{b2} + I_{b3}$. However, in a DBGC CAAB mixer, the bias current of M1 is the sum of I_{b2}, I_{b3} and I_a, *i.e.* $I_{b1} = I_{b2} + I_{b3} + I_a$. By devising component values for **Amp**, V_{LO} of M2-M3 is increased, thus reducing Δ, and rendering a noise reduction in M2-M3.

3.2. The Amp Design

The **Amp** in **Figure 3** is implemented as shown in **Figure 4**. As described in the preceding section, the bias current I_a is steered into the driver stage M1 of the mixer. Thus the provision of a uniform current (I_a) is crucial to the performance of the mixer since any potential large

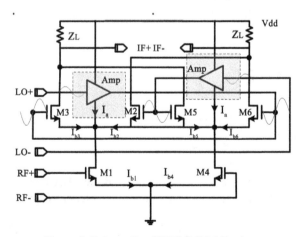

Figure 3. Schematic of DBGC CAAB mixer.

disturbance of I_a may cause gain ripples and non-linear degradations in the driver stage M1. In this case, since 0.18-μm fabrication process is used, the channel length of the transistor is small, rendering I_a more and more susceptible to the channel length modulation [18]:

$$I_a = \frac{1}{2}\mu_n C_{ox} \frac{W}{L}(V_{GS} - V_{TH})^2 (1 + \lambda V_{DS})$$ (16)

The large output voltage swing normally appearing on the drain of the transistor will change the V_{DS} dramatically and periodically. In principle, in order to avoid the channel length modulation, a cascode topology can be employed. However, this structure will limit the output voltage swing. An alternative method is to use a longer channel length. In this investigation, 0.35-μm gate length is preferred as the operating frequency is not very high (2.5 GHz).

It is important to stress that, in order to lower the inherent noise in the CAAB mixer, the **Amp** is realized as a low noise amplifier. In **Figure 4**, the components L_g, C_{gs}, C_{sr}, L_{sr} and L_s are used for noise matching [19]. In order to further analyze the amplifier, the equivalent circuit is shown in **Figure 5**. By using a large value of L_s (for isolating RF signals and *LO* signals), the impedance Z_m can be considered as open. C_{sr} is a relatively large value capacitor used for blocking the DC current but will not influence significantly on the series combination of C_{gs} and C_{sr}:

$$\frac{1}{C_{comb}} = \frac{1}{C_{gs}} + \frac{1}{C_{sr}}$$

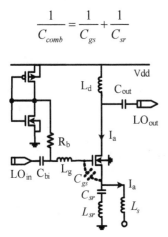

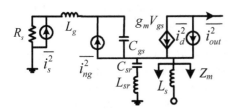

Figure 4. Topology of current bleeding source—Amp (class-A amplifier).

Figure 5. Equivalent circuits of the class-A amplifier (Amp) in Figure 4.

The input impedance Z_{in} is then degenerated to be:

$$Z_{in} \approx s(L_g + L_{sr}) + \frac{1}{sC_{comb}} + \frac{g_m}{C_{gs}}L_{sr}$$ (17)

At resonance, the imaginary part of Z_{in} vanishes, and the real part is left for 50 Ω matching [19]. The **Amp** operates at a DC bias current of 4.5 mA.

3.3. The DBGC CAAB Mixer and Implementation

The **Amp** is then designed and analyzed by SpectreRF in Cadence. Compromising the power consumption, *LO* amplification and stability, the gain of the **Amp** to be designed is chosen to be about 14 dB. The component values in **Figure 5** are optimized as:
$L_g = 8.5$ nH, $C_{gs} = 0.7$ pF, $C_{sr} = 20$ pF, $L_{sr} = 1.2$ nH.
Figure 6 shows the final characteristics of **Amp**. **Figure 7** shows the voltage waveforms at the input and the output of the **Amp** at various *LO* input power levels. An investigation of the voltage waveforms reveals that the amplitude of the *LO* signal is amplified by a factor of five (5). The achieved input 1 dB compression point ($P_{1dB,in}$) is 3 dBm, thus surpassing the traditional performance that $P_{1dB,in} < 0$ dBm.

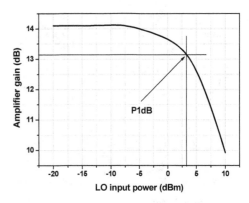

Figure 6. The simulated voltage gain of the Amp.

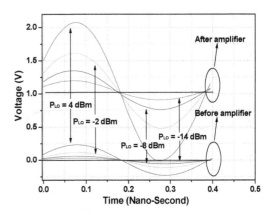

Figure 7. The voltage swing at the input and the output of Amp at varying input power level.

The DBGC CAAB mixer is realized by a 0.18-μm 1-poly 6-metal RFCMOS technology. A microphotograph of the device is shown in **Figure 8**. The chip occupies an area of 1.2×1.3 mm^2. Under nominal operation, the mixer extracts 12 mA from the 1.5 V supply. The chip was bonded to a FR4-PCB board with gold-wire for measurement. The operating frequency is 2.4 GHz with 10 MHz IF as the output frequency for testing purpose.

3.4. Noise Analysis

In essence, the LO signal is a sinusoid rather than a square wave, rendering that the current switching to approximate a soft-switch with switch interval Δ (see **Figure 9**). When $v_{LO} < V_X$, (V_X is the threshold voltage of M2-M3) both transistors of M2-M3 are "ON", and the current division ratio is biased dependently such that the total bias current of M2-M3 is constant: when M2 is biased in high level, the current flow through M2 increases, and the current in M3 decreases. When $v_{LO} > V_X$, the current will flow through one of the transistors and the other counterpart is turned off. At this point, the "ON" transistor acts as the cascode stage of the driver stage.

Figure 8. Microphotograph of the implemented DBGC CAAB mixer.

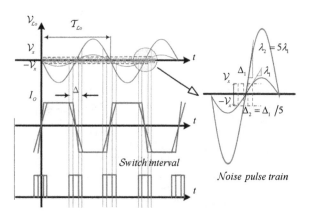

Figure 9. The influence of v_{LO} on Δ and the resulting noise contribution.

The output noise component from M2-M3 is dictated by the relationship in (10) and (12), in which g_{m2} and g_{m3} are time-varying transconductances of M2-M3 under large LO drive. When $v_{LO} > V_X$, either M2 or M3 is cutoff and g_m vanishes. Consequently, G_m, as well as PSD, also vanish. When $v_{LO} < V_X$, the non-zero G_m proliferates M2-M3 to contribute noise to the output.

Let $PSD = S_{sw,within}$ when $v_{LO} < V_X$ and $PSD = S_{sw,outside}$ when $v_{LO} > V_X$. For analysis purpose, $S_{sw,within}$ is normalized to a train of pulses [4] operating at a rate $2f_{LO}$, as shown in **Figure 9**. The width of Δ is V_X/λ, where λ is the slope of LO waveform at the zero-crossing point, and is given by:

$$\lambda = 2\pi v_{LO}/T_{LO} \qquad (18)$$

It was illustrated in Section 3.4 that by devising the **Amp**, v_{LO} has been amplified by five (5) times, thus the switch interval Δ_2 (after amplification) has been compressed to one fifth of Δ_1 (before amplification) (see **Figure 9**).

To further analyze the relationship between the noise PSD and the slope of LO waveform, λ, at the zero-crossing point, (12) is modified and derived as follows:

$$PSD = 32KT\gamma \frac{I_B}{\lambda T_{LO}} \qquad (19)$$

From (19), it is analyzed and concluded that the noise from M2-M3 is reduced by a factor of five (5). Hence it is analyzed that:

$$V_{LO} \uparrow \Rightarrow \Delta \downarrow \Rightarrow \lambda \uparrow \Rightarrow S_{sw}(f) \downarrow$$

Additional noise improvement comes from the increasing bias of the driver stage due to the current bleeding source (here, it is DC bias of the **Amp**). Based on the original 1.5 mA DC bias current, the current bleeding source feeds additional 4.5 mA DC current to the driver stage. From [18], $g_{m1} = 2I_{B1}/(V_{gs} - V_{th})$, consequently, g_{m1} is improved by a factor of 4 . For double-balanced mixer, the single-side band noise figure, NF [5], is rearranged as:

$$NF = \frac{\alpha}{c^2} + \frac{2r_{g1}\alpha + \frac{2\gamma_1\alpha}{g_{m1}} + \frac{4\gamma_3\overline{G} + 4r_{g3}\overline{G^2} + \frac{1}{R_L}}{g_{m1}^2}}{c^2 R_s} \qquad (20)$$

where γ_1 and γ_3 represent the noise coefficient of M1 and M3 respectively. The poly resistance of the gate is indicated as r_{g1} and r_{g3}. It is seen from (20) that NF is inversely proportional to g_{m1}. Thus it is seen that the current bleeding improves g_{m1} dramatically and conesquently suppresses the noise figure efficiently.

To examine the performance improvement of the DGBC CAAB mixer, an identical conventional Gilbert-quad mixer, without current bleeding—**Amp**, but having the same transistor size in both the driver stage and the switch stage, is also designed with same process. Both mixers operate at 2.4 GHz input frequency with 10 MHz IF output. **Figure 10** shows the noise comparison at *LO* power from −20 dBm to 10 dBm. It is observed that the conventional mixer presents a noise figure in the range of 13 dB to 46 dB whereas the CAAB mixer features a much lower noise figure, namely from 9 dB to 11.5 dB. The inset of **Figure 10(b)** shows the measured noise figures versus *LO* power at 10 MHz intermediate frequency. The measured *NF* varies from 12.4 dB to 8.7 dB when the *LO* power is varied from −20 dBm to 10 dBm.

3.5. Conversion Gain Analysis

In the CAAB mixer, the conversion gain is affected by the switch stage M2-M3 and the driver stage. Recapitulated from (14), a Δ decreases, $\sin(\pi\Delta/T_{LO})/\pi\Delta/T_{LO}$ approaches to unit. As a result, the CG increases until reaching the upper limit $(2/\pi)\cdot g_{m1}\cdot R_L$. **Figure 11** illustrates the switch loss, L_{sw}, versus Δ. **Figure 11(a)** shows $L_{sw,\text{lin}}$, versus Δ due to the non-ideal square wave

LO drive. **Figure 11(b)** intuitively shows the trend of $L_{sw,\text{dB}}$ (in logarithm scale) due to soft switching. **Table 1** lists the reduction of $L_{sw,\text{lin}}$ due to the *LO* amplitude amplification at four different Δ/T_{LO} cases. In the extreme case that $\Delta = 0.45$ (when *LO* voltage is very weak), the gain improvement can be as high as 3 dB. It is also seen that when Δ is one fourth of the *LO* period (T_{LO}), which is the most probably case, $L_{sw,\text{lin}}$ can be improved from $0.9\cdot(2/\pi)\cdot g_{m1}\cdot R_L$ to $0.996\cdot(2/\pi)\cdot g_{m1}\cdot R_L$. As a result, 0.88 dB CG is gained.

It is shown in Section 2 that g_{m1} is improved by a factor of 4, hence an additional 12 dB gain is obtained. Thus, it is concluded that the current bleeding structure will boost g_{m1}, provoking a higher CG.

To examine the gain performance of the DBGC CAAB mixer, a comparison with the conventional mixer and other published works is shown in **Figure 12**. For the conventional mixer, the maximum gain achieved is 11 dB when *LO* port is fed by 10 dBm signal. In contrast, a gain of 17.5 dB is achieved when −14 dBm is fed to the *LO* port of the DBGC CAAB mixer. Thus, it is con-

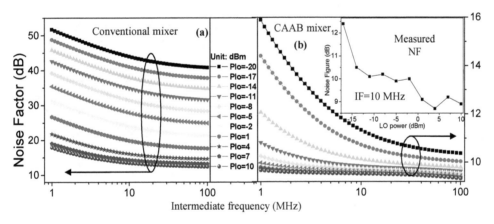

Figure 10. Noise figures at different *LO* input power. (a) Conventional mixer; (b) DBGC CAAB mixer; inset: measured *NF* at IF = 10 MHz.

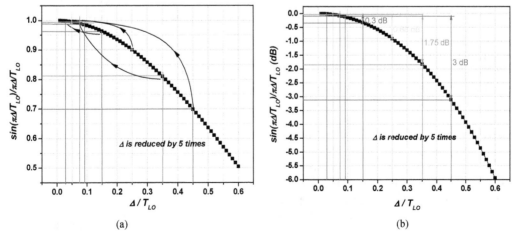

Figure 11. The switch loss reduction due to the switch interval Δ shrinkage: (a) Linear scale; (b) Logarithm scale.

Table 1. The quantized switching loss reduction due to the *LO* amplification in linear and logarithm scale.

	$\sin\left(\pi\Delta/T_{LO}\right)/\pi\Delta/T_{LO}$		$20\log\left(\dfrac{\sin\left(\pi\Delta/T_{LO}\right)}{\pi\Delta/T_{LO}}\right)$		$20\log\left(\dfrac{\sin\left(\pi\Delta/T_{LO}\right)}{\pi\Delta/T_{LO}}\right)$
	Linear scale		Logarithm scale (dB)		Logarithm (dB)
Δ/T_{LO}	Without **Amp**	With **Amp**	Without **Amp**	With **Amp**	Switching loss reduction
0.15	0.9634	0.99852	−0.3239	−0.01286	0.3
0.25	0.90032	0.99589	−0.912	−0.03574	0.88
0.35	0.81033	0.99196	−1.827	−0.07012	1.75
0.45	0.69865	0.98673	−3.115	−0.116	3

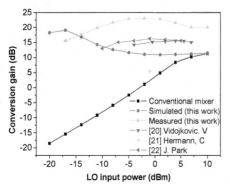

Figure 12. The conversion gain comparison between the DBGC CAAB mixer and other works.

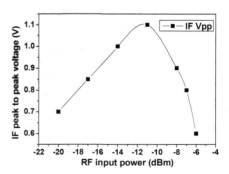

Figure 13. IF peak-to-peak voltage versus RF input power. (The result is measured with the termination of oscilloscope at IF port).

cluded that by incorporating the current bleeding *LO* **Amp**, not only the conversion gain is enhanced, but also the *LO* power requirement is relieved by more than 20 dB. The comparison with other published works [20-22] reveals that the DBGC CAAB mixer has the highest gain but requiring the lowest *LO* power requirement.

3.6. Linearity, *LO* Power Leakage and Operation Bandwidth

The output voltage swing is examined by terminating an oscilloscope at the IF (10 MHz) port. The maximum voltage swing (peak-to-peak voltage) was measured to be 1.1 V when the RF port was fed by −11 dBm input power (see **Figure 13**).

Figure 14 shows the measured third order intermodulation (IP3) of the DBGC CAAB mixer at different *LO* power levels. When the switch pair is fed with a −5 dBm *LO* power, the IIP3 obtained is 3 dBm. When the *LO* power is −17 dBm, the mixer still has an IIP3 point of −9 dBm. In the DBGC CAAB mixer, the *LO* amplitude is amplified by five (5) times. Hence, attention is drawn to the *LO* power leakage. By examining the *LO* power at RF and IF port, it is found that the *LO* to IF port leakage is smaller than −90 dBm. The *LO* to RF power leakage is measured to be less than −60 dBm (see **Figure 15**). The good *LO*-IF isolation achieved is attributed to use of the double-balanced topology.

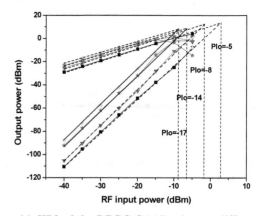

Figure 14. IIP3 of the DBGC CAAB mixer at different *LO* level.

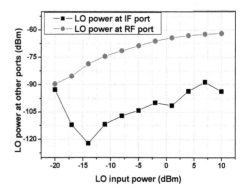

Figure 15. *LO* power leakage to RF port and IF port.

The DBGC CAAB mixer is designed for 2.4 GHz ISM band application. **Figure 16** shows the gain performance at 2.4 - 2.4835 GHz when the IF frequency is 10 MHz. In the whole band, the conversion gain of the proposed mixer varies from 19 dB to 21 dB, featuring good gain flatness.

4. Performance Summary and Comparison

Table 2 summarizes the performances of the DBGC CAAB mixer. To evaluate the mixer comprehensively, a benchmarking figure of merit, FOM, is presented:

$$FOM = 10 \cdot \log \left\{ \frac{10^{(Gain-2NF+IIP3-10-P_{LO})/20} \cdot f_0/1 \text{ KHz}}{P_{DC}/1 \text{ mW}} \right\}$$
(21)

The *FOM* takes incorporates important parameters including Gain, *NF*, *IIP3*, *LO* power, *DC* power and operating frequency into considerations. The *FOM* values are listed in **Table 2** for comparison. From the comparison, it is found that the DBGC CAAB mixer has the lowest *LO* power requirement (−17 dBm) and the highest gain (15.7 dB), while maintaining a relatively lowest noise figure of 9.7 dB.

5. Conclusion

A current bleeding with *LO* amplification mixer based on current reuse topology is designed and implemented. The developed double balanced Gilbert-cell class-A amplifier bleeding mixer (DBGC CAAB mixer) has the highest conversion gain at the lowest *LO* power when compared to mixers formerly investigated. The DBGC CAAB

mixer is implemented by using 0.18-μm CMOS technology and operates at the 2.4 GHz ISM application with 10 MHz intermediate frequency. The power consumption is 12 mA at 1.5 V supply voltage. With the novel *LO* amplification and current reuse technique, the mixer features an excellent high gain of 17.5 dB at a very low *LO* power feeding of −14 dBm. The noise performance is also good. The DBGC CAAB mixer features a noise figure of 10.7 dB, thus rendering the resulting noise to be suppressed to [8.7 dB, 12.4 dB]. In contrast, in the conventional mixer, the noise figure varies from 13 dB to 46 dB at the same *LO* feed. It is important to point out that, compared to the other mixer investigations, the DBGC CAAB mixer features the highest FOM figure within a wide range of *LO* power.

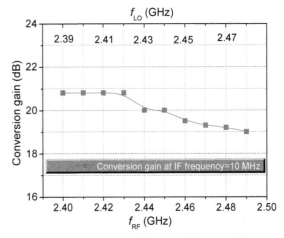

Figure 16. Conversion gain of the DBGC CAAB mixer versus frequency when IF frequency = 10 MHz.

Table 2. The performance of the DBGC CAAB mixer w.r.t. other works.

Publication	Technology	RF	VDD	P_{DC}	P_{LO}	Gain	NF	P_{1dB}	IIP_3	FOM
	CMOS	GHz	V	mW	dBm	dB	dB	dBm	dBm	dB
Darabi [5] (bleed)	0.13 μm	2	1.2	2.4	-	0.5	13.5	−1.5	10.5	-
V. Vidojkovic [20]	0.18 μm	2.4	1.8	8.1	−2	15.7	12.9	-	1	46.2
C. Hermann [21]	0.13 μm	2.5	0.6	1.6	−1	5.4	14.8	−9.2	−2.8	44
J. Park [22] (bleed)	0.18 μm	5	-	7	−1	16.2	9.8	-	−5	46.6
P. J. Sulivan [23]	0.8 μm	1.9	5	133	−3	9.7	7.8	-	−1	34.6
This work	**0.18 μm**	**2.4**	**1.5**	**18**	**−17**	**15.7**	**10.7**	**−10**	**−9**	**48.3**
This work	**0.18 μm**	**2.4**	**1.5**	**18**	**−14**	**17.5**	**10.5**	**−12**	**−8**	**48.0**
This work	**0.18 μm**	**2.4**	**1.5**	**18**	**−5**	**23**	**9.7**	**−10**	**3.5**	**47.6**

REFERENCES

[1] K. Chang, I. Bahl and V. Nair, "RF and Microwave Circuit and Component Design for Wireless Systems," Wiley-Interscience, New York, 2002.

[2] H. Darabi and A. A. Abidi, "Noise in RF CMOS Mixers: A Simple Physical Model," *IEEE Journal of Solid State Circuits*, Vol. 35, No. 1, 2000, pp. 15-25.

[3] D. Manstretta, R. Castello and F. Svelto, "Low 1/f Noise CMOS Active Mixers for Direct Conversion," *IEEE Transactions on Circuits and Systems II*, Vol. 48, 2001, pp. 846-850.

[4] H. Darabi and J. Chiu, "A Noise Cancellation Technique in Active RF-CMOS Mixers," *IEEE Journal of Solid-State Circuits*, Vol. 40, No. 12, 2005, pp. 2628-2632.

[5] M. T. Terrovitis and R. G. Meyer, "Noise in Current Commutating CMOS Mixers," *IEEE Journal of Solid-State Circuits*, Vol. 34, 1999, pp. 772-783.

[6] M. Krcmar, V. Subramanian, M. Jamal Deen and G. Boeck, "High Gain Low Noise Folded CMOS Mixer," *European Conference on Wireless Technology*, Amsterdam, 27-28 October 2008, pp. 13-16.

[7] V. Vidojkovic, J. Van der Tang, A. L. Leeuwenburgh and A. van Roermund, "A High Gain, Low Voltage Folded-Switching Mixer with Current-Reuse in 0.18 μm CMOS," *IEEE Digest of Papers. Radio Frequency Integrated Circuits (RFIC) Symposium*, Fort Worth, 6-8 June 2004, pp. 31-34.

[8] J. Harvey and R. Harjani, "Analysis and Design of an Integrated Quadrature Mixer with Improved Noise, Gain and Image Rejection," *The 2001 IEEE International Symposium on Circuits and Systems*, Vol. 4, Sydney, 6-9 May 2001, pp. 786-789.

[9] B. Gilbert, "The Micromixer: A Highly Linear Variant of the Gilbert Mixer Using a Bisymmetric Class-AB Input Stage," *IEEE Journal of Solid-State Circuits*, Vol. 32, No. 9, 1997, pp. 1412-1423.

[10] M. L. Schmatz, C. Biber and W. Baumberger, "Conversion Gain Enhancement Technique for Ultra Low Power Gilbert Cell Down Mixers," *17th Annual IEEE Gallium Arsenide Integrated Circuit (GaAs IC) Symposium*, San Diego, 29 October-1 November 1995, pp. 245-248.

[11] G. Z. Fatin, M. S. Oskooei and Z. D. K. Kanani, "A Technique to Improve Noise Figure and Conversion Gain of CMOS Mixers," *50th Midwest Symposium on Circuits and Systems*, Montreal, 5-8 August 2007, pp. 437-440.

[12] J. Yoon, H. Kim, C. Park, J. Yang, H. Song, S. Lee and B. Kim, "A New RF CMOS Gilbert Mixer with Improved Noise Figure and Linearity," *IEEE Transactions on Microwave Theory and Techniques*, Vol. 56, No. 3, 2008, pp. 626-631.

[13] J. Lerdworatawee and W. Namgoong, "Generalized Linear Periodic Time-Varying Analysis for Noise Reduction in an Active Mixer," *IEEE Journal of Solid-State Circuits*, Vol. 42, No. 6, 2007, pp. 1339-135.

[14] T. Melly, A.-S. Porret, C. C. Enz and E. A. Vittoz, "An Analysis of Flicker Noise Rejection in Low-Power and Low-Voltage CMOS Mixers," *IEEE Journal of Solid-State Circuits*, Vol. 36, No. 1, 2001, pp. 102-109.

[15] L. A. MacEachern and T. Manku, "A Charge-Injection Method for Gilbert cell Biasing," *IEEE Canidian Conference on Electrical and Computer Engingeering*, Waterloo, 24-28 May 1998, pp. 365-368.

[16] S. G. Lee and J. K. Choi, "Current-Reuse Bleeding Mixer," *Electronics Letters*, Vol. 36, No. 8, 2000, pp. 696-697.

[17] K. Xuan, K. F. Tsang, S. C. Lee and W. C. Lee, "High-Performance Current Bleeding CMOS Mixer," *Electronics Letters*, Vol. 45, No. 19, 2009, pp. 979-981.

[18] B. Razavi, "Design of Analog CMOS Integrated Circuits," McGraw-Hill, New York, 2001.

[19] D. K. Shaeffer and T. H. Lee, "A 1.5-V, 1.5-GHz CMOS Low Noise Amplifier," *IEEE Journal of Solid-State Circuits*, Vol. 32, No. 5, 1997, pp. 745-759.

[20] V. Vidojkovic, J. Van der Tang, A. Leeuwenburgh and A. H. M. Van Roermund, "A Low-Voltage Folded-Switching Mixer in 0.18-μm CMOS," *IEEE Journal of Solid-State Circuits*, Vol. 40, No. 6, 2005, pp. 1259-1264.

[21] C. Hermann, M. Tiebout and H. Klar, "A 0.6-V 1.6-mW Transformer-Based 2.5-GHz Down Conversion Mixer with +5.4-dB Gain and −2.8-dBm IIP3 in 0.13-μm CMOS," *IEEE Transactions on Microwave Theory and Techniques*, Vol. 53, No. 2, 2005, pp. 488-495.

[22] J. Park, C.-HO Lee, B.-S. Kim, and J. Laskar, "Design and Analysis of Low Flicker-Noise CMOS Mixers for Direct-Conversion Receivers," *IEEE Transactions on Microwave Theory and Techniques*, Vol. 54, No. 12, 2006, pp. 4372-4380.

[23] P. J. Sulivan, B. A. Xavier and W. H. Ku, "Low Voltage Performance of a Microwave CMOS Gilbert Cell Mixer," *IEEE Journal of Solid-State Circuits*, Vol. 32, No. 7, 1997, pp. 1151-1155.

10

Logical Function Decomposition Method for Synthesis of Digital Logical System Implemented with Programmable Logic Devices (PLD)

Mihai Grigore Timis, Alexandru Valachi, Alexandru Barleanu, Andrei Stan
Automatic Control and Computer Engineering Faculty, Technical University Gh.Asachi, Iasi, Romania

ABSTRACT

The paper consists in the use of some logical functions decomposition algorithms with application in the implementation of classical circuits like SSI, MSI and PLD. The decomposition methods use the Boolean matrix calculation. It is calculated the implementation costs emphasizing the most economical solutions. One important aspect of serial decomposition is the task of selecting "best candidate" variables for the G function. Decomposition is essentially a process of substituting two or more input variables with a lesser number of new variables. This substitutes results in the reduction of the number of rows in the truth table. Hence, we look for variables which are most likely to reduce the number of rows in the truth table as a result of decomposition. Let us consider an input variable purposely avoiding all inter-relationships among the input variables. The only available parameter to evaluate its activity is the number of "1"s or "O"s that it has in the truth table. If the variable has only "1" s or "0" s, it is the "best candidate" for decomposition, as it is practically redundant.

Keywords: Combinational Circuits; Static Hazard; Logic Design; Boolean Functions; Logical Decompositions

1. Introduction

In the implementation of logical functions we are looking to optimize some parameters such as the propagation time, cost, areas, power, etc. The decomposition problem is old, and well understood when the function to be decomposed is specified by a truth table, or has one output only. However, modern design tools handle functions with many outputs and represent them by cubes, for reasons of efficiency. We develop a comprehensive theory of serial decompositions for multiple-output, partially specified, Boolean functions. A function $f(x_1, \cdots, x_n)$ has a serial decomposition if it can be expressed as $h(u_1, \cdots, u_r, g(v_1, \cdots, v_s))$, where $U = \{u_1, \cdots, u_r\}$ and $V = \{v_1, \cdots, v_s\}$ are subsets of the set $X = \{x_1, \cdots, x_n\}$ of input variables, and g and h have fewer inputvariables than f.

It is sometimes the case that a set of Boolean functions cannot be made to fit into any single module intended for its implementation. The only solution is to decompose the problem in such a way that the requirement can be met by a network of two or more components each implementing a part of the functions. The general pro-

blem can be stated as follows. The set of functions to be implemented quires a logic block with N inputs and M outputs. The decomposition task is to design a network which will implement the function using blocks with a maximum of n inputs and m outputs, where $n < N$ or $m < M$.

(A) Initially, we will consider a decomposition algorithm of logical functions [1].

1.1. Given a Boolean function $f(x_{n-1}, \cdots, x_1, x_0)$ and p Boolean functions denoted by $\varphi_{p-1}(y_{i-1}, \cdots, y_1, y_0), \cdots, \varphi_0(y_{i-1}, \cdots, y_1, y_0)$, it is possible to decompose the function f depending on $\varphi_{p-1}, \cdots, \varphi_0$? In other words, there is a function F so that $F(\varphi_{p-1}, \cdots, \varphi_0; z_{n-1}, \cdots, z_i) = f(x_{n-1}, \cdots, x_0)$, where $Y = \{y_{i-1}, \cdots, y_0\}$ and $Z = \{z_{n-1}, \cdots, z_i\}$ are disjoint subsets of the set $X = \{x_{n-1}, \cdots, x_0\}$, that means

$$X = Y \bigcup Z \quad \text{and} \quad Y \bigcap Z = \phi \quad (1.1) \text{ (the empty set).}$$

We will call this proceeding, Type I problem.

1.2. Given a Boolean function $f(x_{n-1}, \cdots, x_1, x_0)$ there are q functions denoted by $\varphi_{q-1}(y_{i-1}, \cdots, y_1, y_0), \cdots, \varphi_0(y_{i-1}, \cdots, y_1, y_0)$ and a function F so that

$F\left(\varphi_{q-1},\cdots,\varphi_0;z_{n-1},\cdots,z_i\right)=f\left(x_{n-1},\cdots,x_0\right)$, where $Y=\{y_{i-1},\cdots,y_0\}$ and $Z=\{z_{n-1},\cdots,z_i\}$ have the same meaning as in 1.1. We will call this proceeding, the type II problem.

(B) *Matrices related to Boolean functions. The image of a logical function* [1]

It defines the image of a logical function the Boolean row array that represents the values of this function, ordered by truth table.

For example, $f\left(x_2,x_1,x_0\right)=R_1\left(0,1,3,5,7\right)$ has the following truth table:

(dec.echiv.)	x_2	x_1	x_0	f
0	0	0	0	1
1	0	0	1	1
2	0	1	0	0
3	0	1	1	1
4	1	0	0	0
5	1	0	1	1
6	1	1	0	0
7	1	1	1	1

Considering the above, we can write

$$\div f = 11010101 \tag{1.2}$$

We can verify the following properties:

$$\div(f_1\cdot f_2)=(\div f_1)\cdot(\div f_2)$$
$$\div(f_1+f_2)=(\div f_1)+(\div f_2) \tag{1.3}$$

To a function can be attached a Veitch matrix, for the previous case being:

$$x_2 \setminus x_1 x_0$$
$$E=\begin{bmatrix}1101\\0101\end{bmatrix} \tag{1.4}$$

2. The Representation of a Boolean Function Using Subfunctions. The R_{JI} Matrix

Let's consider a function G of two subfunctions f_1 and f_0 that depend on the Boolean variables x_2,x_1,x_0 and on the two variables x_4,x_3:

$$G\left(x_4,x_3,f_1,f_0\right)=f_0\cdot\overline{x_4}\cdot x_3+\overline{f_1}\cdot x_4\cdot\overline{x_3}+\overline{f_1}\cdot f_0\cdot x_4 \tag{2.1}$$

After a simple calculation is deduced the image of function G.

$$\div G = 0000010111000100 \tag{2.2}$$

We suppose that the images of the two subfunctions are:

$$\div f_1 = 01110100$$
$$\div f_0 = 01010011 \tag{2.3}$$

that means:

$$f_1 = \overline{x_2}\cdot x_1+\overline{x_1}\cdot x_0$$
$$f_0 = \overline{x_2}\cdot x_0+x_2\cdot x_1 \tag{2.4}$$

Starting from the expressions of G, f_1 and f_0 can be calculated:

$$F\left(x_4,x_3,x_2,x_1,x_0\right)$$
$$=G\left(x_4,x_3,f_1\left(x_2,x_1,x_0\right),f_0\left(x_2,x_1,x_0\right)\right)$$
$$=\overline{x_4}\cdot x_3\cdot\overline{x_2}\cdot x_0+\overline{x_4}\cdot x_3\cdot x_2\cdot x_1$$
$$+x_4\cdot\overline{x_3}\cdot x_2\cdot\overline{x_0}+x_4\cdot\overline{x_3}\cdot\overline{x_1}\cdot\overline{x_0}+x_4\cdot x_2\cdot x_1 \tag{2.5}$$

The image of function F is calculated below:

$$\div F = 00000000010100111000101100000011 \tag{2.6}$$

The Veitch tables $E'_{x_4x_3:f_1f_0}$ and $E_{x_4x_3:x_2x_1x_0}$ relating to the G and F functions are:

$$x_4x_3\setminus f_1f_0 \qquad x_4x_3\setminus x_2x_1x_0$$
$$E'=\begin{bmatrix}0000\\0101\\1100\\0100\end{bmatrix},\quad E=\begin{bmatrix}00000000\\01010011\\10001011\\00000011\end{bmatrix} \tag{2.7}$$

Note that the E' matrix has only four distinct columns that are found in E matrix.

In [1], it demonstrates that for the function F it can be attached a pseudo-unitary matrix denoted by R_{JI} in which in each column the logic digit 1 corresponds to the E' column's order number, therefore:

$$\setminus x_2x_1x_0$$
$$R_{JI}=\begin{bmatrix}10001000\\00000011\\00100100\\01010000\end{bmatrix} \tag{2.8}$$

In [1] is also demonstrated the relation:

$$E=E'\otimes R_{JI}\quad(\otimes\text{—the matrix multiplication}) \tag{2.9}$$

Therefore, the decomposition of a function in subfunctions is reduced to solving the following Boolean equations:

$X\otimes A=B$ (2.10) (the type I problem, where the E and R_{JI} matrices are known) or $A\otimes X=B$ (2.11) (the type II problem, where only the B matrix is known, $B=E$).

Considering that the columns of matrix E' are found in matrix E it deduces the matrix $A=E'$, and then the matrix R_{JI}.

Next, we present the solutions of the equations (2.10)

Logical Function Decomposition Method for Synthesis of Digital Logical System Implemented with Programmable Logic Devices (PLD)

59

and (2.11), demonstrated in [1].

A. The solution of the equation $A \otimes X = B$ [1]

a) Let's consider X a some matrix. It is valid the relation (2.12), [1].

$$X \leq \overline{t_A \otimes \overline{B}} \quad (t_A\text{-the transpose of the matrix } A) \quad (2.12)$$

b) Let's consider X a pseudo-unitary matrix. It is valid the relation (2.13) [1].

$$X \leq \overline{t_A \otimes \overline{B}} \cdot \overline{t_{\overline{A}} \otimes B} \quad (2.13)$$

B. The solution of the equation $X \otimes A = B$ [1]

a) Let's consider A a some matrix. It is assumed [1]:

$$X \leq \overline{\overline{B} \otimes t_A} \quad (2.14)$$

b) Let's consider A a pseudo-unitary matrix. It is denoted by $X_c = B \otimes t_A$ and $X_a = \overline{\overline{B} \otimes t_A}$. The sufficient condition of existence of the solution [1] is:

$$X_c = B \otimes t_A \leq X_a = \overline{\overline{B} \otimes t_A} \text{ and } X_c \leq X \leq X_a \quad (2.15)$$

If $X_c > X_a$ or $X_c \neq X_a$, there is no solution for the matrix X. In this case it is trying to solve the following equations:

$$F(x_4, \cdots, x_0)$$
$$= G_1(x_4, x_3, f_1, f_0) \quad (2.16)$$
$$+ H_1(x_4, x_3, x_2, x_1, x_0)$$

(the previous solution) or

$$F(x_4, \cdots, x_0)$$
$$= G_2(x_4, x_3, f_1, f_0) \quad (2.17)$$
$$\times H_2(x_4, x_3, x_2, x_1, x_0)$$

(the consequence solution). We will return to these problems in a future paper.

3. Examples

(A) *Let's consider the function defined by*

$$F(x_4, x_3, x_2, x_1, x_0)$$
$$= R_1(0,3,5,6,9,10,12,14,15,16,17,18,19,21,22,30) \quad (3.1)$$

Applying the Veitch-Karnaugh method [2], a minimal form is given by the expression:

$$F(x_4, x_3, x_2, x_1, x_0) = \overline{x_4} \cdot \overline{x_3} \cdot \overline{x_2} \cdot \overline{x_1} \cdot x_0$$
$$+ \overline{x_3} \cdot \overline{x_2} \cdot x_1 \cdot x_0 + \overline{x_3} \cdot x_2 \cdot x_1 \cdot x_0 + \overline{x_4} \cdot x_3 \cdot x_1 \cdot x_0$$
$$+ \overline{x_4} \cdot x_3 \cdot x_2 \cdot \overline{x_0} + x_4 \cdot x_3 \cdot x_2 \cdot x_1 + x_4 \cdot \overline{x_3} \cdot \overline{x_2} \quad (3.2)$$
$$+ x_2 \cdot x_1 \cdot \overline{x_0} + \overline{x_3} \cdot \overline{x_2} \cdot \overline{x_1} \cdot x_0$$

We define the cost of implementation as the number of

the inputs in the basic circuits, components [3]. In the previous case, by implementing with AND-OR circuits, results: $C_1(F) = (5 + 6 \cdot 4 + 2 \cdot 3) + 9 = 44$. (It is considering that the input variables are provided inverted and non-inverted, *i.e.* $x_i, \overline{x_i}$.)

Let's consider the following possible decomposition:

$$G(x_4, x_3, f_1, f_0) = F(x_4, x_3, x_2, x_1, x_0)$$

where $f_1 = f_1(x_2, x_1, x_0)$, $f_0 = f_0(x_2, x_1, x_0)$.

For the function F corresponds the following Veitch matrix, denoted by E:

$$E = \begin{bmatrix} 10010110 \\ 01101011 \\ 11110110 \\ 00000010 \end{bmatrix} \quad (3.3)$$

Matrix E having four distinct columns, a solution for E' is:

$$x_4 x_3 \setminus f_1 f_0$$
$$E' = \begin{bmatrix} 1001 \\ 0111 \\ 1101 \\ 0001 \end{bmatrix} \quad (3.4)$$

Therefore, the matrix R_{JI}, solution of the equation $E' \otimes R_{JI} = E$, is:

$$R_{JI} \leq \overline{t_{E'} \otimes \overline{E}} \cdot \overline{t_{\overline{E'}} \otimes E} = \begin{bmatrix} 10010100 \\ 01100000 \\ 00001001 \\ 00000010 \end{bmatrix} \quad (3.5)$$

From where we obtain:

$$\div f_1 = 00001011$$
$$\div f_0 = 01100010 \quad (3.6)$$

or after an elementary calculation:

$$f_1 = x_2 \cdot (x_1 + \overline{x_0})$$
$$f_0 = x_1 \cdot \overline{x_0} + \overline{x_2} \cdot \overline{x_1} \cdot x_0 \quad (3.7)$$

Using E' matrix we obtain:

$$G = \overline{f_1} \cdot \overline{f_0} \cdot \overline{x_3} + f_1 \cdot f_0 + x_4 \cdot \overline{x_3} \cdot f_0$$
$$+ \overline{x_4} \cdot x_3 \cdot f_0 + f_1 \cdot \overline{x_4} \cdot x_3 \quad (3.8)$$

with a possible implementation as in **Figure 1**.

So, we will have:

$$C(f_1) = 7 \quad C(f_0) = 8 \quad (3.9)$$

$$C(G) = (4 \times 3 + 2) + 5 = 19, \text{ so that } C(F) = 34.$$

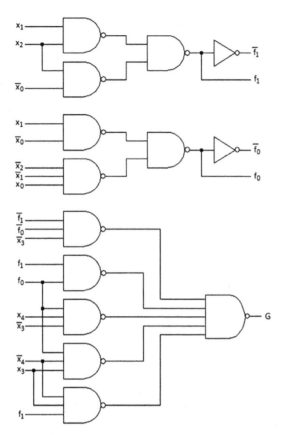

Figure 1. The implementation of the function F, using sub-functions.

(B) Implementation using programmable logic devices (PLD)

We will consider a circuit PAL10L8 [4], which has 10 inputs, 8 outputs and having an AND-OR configuration, each NOR having 2 inputs, with the structure illustrated in **Figure 2**.

Let's consider the previous function:

$$F = \sum_{i=0}^{8} m_i ,$$

where

$$m_0 = \overline{x_4} \cdot x_3 \cdot \overline{x_2} \cdot \overline{x_1} \cdot x_0$$

$$m_1 = \overline{x_3} \cdot \overline{x_2} \cdot \overline{x_1} \cdot \overline{x_0}$$

$$m_2 = x_3 \cdot \overline{x_2} \cdot x_1 \cdot x_0$$

$$m_3 = \overline{x_3} \cdot x_2 \cdot \overline{x_1} \cdot x_0$$

$$m_4 = \overline{x_4} \cdot x_3 \cdot x_1 \cdot \overline{x_0} \qquad (3.10)$$

$$m_5 = \overline{x_4} \cdot x_3 \cdot x_2 \cdot \overline{x_0}$$

$$m_6 = \overline{x_4} \cdot x_3 \cdot x_2 \cdot x_1$$

$$m_7 = x_4 \cdot \overline{x_3} \cdot \overline{x_2}$$

$$m_8 = x_2 \cdot x_1 \cdot \overline{x_0}$$

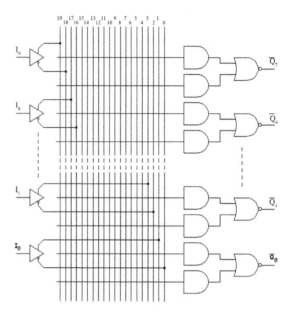

Figure 2. The circuit PAL10L8.

We will use the following algorithm:

$$Q_0 = m_0 + m_1$$

$$Q_1 = Q_0 + m_2$$

$$\vdots \qquad (3.11)$$

$$Q_7 = Q_6 + m_8 = F$$

Therefore, $Q_i = Q_{i-1} + m_{i+1}$ with $Q_{-1} = m_0$, $0 \le i \le 7$.

Will be needed: 9—product terms $(m_0 \div m_8)$, 7—Q_i terms $(0 \le i \le 6)$, so it will be used 16 product terms from maximum 20. But the number of inputs is insufficient (see **Figure 3**).

Classic, we should also use two circuits (PAL10L8), or a single circuit with greater capacity.

Let go back to the same function that uses the subfunctions f_1, f_0, which have the expressions:

$$f_1 = x_2 \cdot x_1 + x_2 \cdot \overline{x_0}$$

$$f_0 = x_1 \cdot \overline{x_0} + \overline{x_2} \cdot \overline{x_1} \cdot \overline{x_0}$$

and

$$F(x_4, x_3, x_2, x_1, x_0)$$
$$= G(x_4, x_3, f_1, f_0)$$
$$= \overline{f_1} \cdot \overline{f_0} \cdot x_3 + f_1 \cdot f_0 + x_1 \cdot \overline{x_3} \cdot f_0 \qquad (3.12)$$
$$+ \overline{x_4} \cdot x_3 \cdot f_0 + f_1 \cdot \overline{x_4} \cdot x_3$$

Therefore, after a preliminary evaluation we have: 4 product terms (f_1, f_0) and 5 product terms for function G.

Let's consider $G = (a_0 + a_1) + (a_2 + a_3) + a_4$, where a_i are the terms of the decomposed function. A PAL implementation is like in **Figures 3** and **4**.

Logical Function Decomposition Method for Synthesis of Digital Logical System Implemented with Programmable Logic Devices (PLD)

61

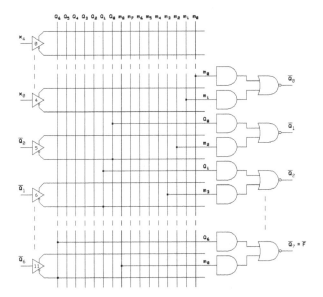

Figure 3. PAL implementation.

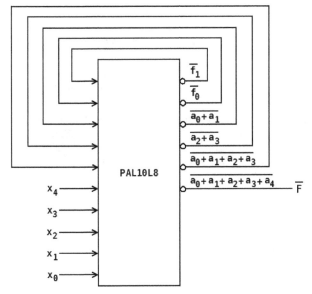

Figure 4. A possible implementation of PAL10L8 circuit.

A possible implementation would be (see **Figure 4**):

4. Decomposition into EMB Blocks

The single step of the functional decomposition replaces function F with two subfunctions [5]. This process is recursively applied to both the G and H blocks until a network is constructed where each block can be directly implemented in single logic cell of target FPGA architecture.

Logic cell can implement any function of limited input variables (typically 4 or 5). Thus the main effort of logic synthesis methods based on decomposition is to find such partition of input variables into free set and bound set that allows creating decomposition with block G not

exceeding the size of logic cell. Various methods are used, including exhaustive search since the size of logic cell is small. It should be noted that the main constraint is the number of inputs to block G and not the number of outputs. This is because block G with more outputs than in logic cell can be implemented with use of few logic cells used in parallel. Since EMB blocks can be configured to work as logic cell of many different sizes [6], approach known from methods targeted for logic cells is not efficient. The main reason is that the method must check decomposition for many different sizes of block G. The second factor is that in case of EMB the efficiency of utilization of these blocks depends on carefully selected size of block G. For example M512 RAM block of Stratix device can be configured among others as 8 input and 2 output logic cell or 7 input and 4 output logic cell. Let assume that in decomposition search following solutions are possible: block G with 8 inputs and 1 output or block G with 7 inputs and 3 outputs. From the EMB utilization point of view the second solution is better, since it utilizes 384 bits of total 512 bits available, while the first solution utilizes only 256 bits. R-admissibility is used to evaluate serial decomposition possibilities for different sizes of G block according to possible configuration of EMB blocks. Since EMB can be configured as a block of many different sizes the possible solution space is large. Using Property 1 the search can be drastically reduced. This will be explained in the following example.

Example.

R-admissibility application to serial decomposition evaluation. For function from Example 1 we have that the admissibility of single input variables $x_1, \cdots, x_6$ is accordingly 4, 4, 4, 3, 3 and 4. This means that only for $U = \{x_4\}$, $V = \{x_1, x_2, x_3, x_5, x_6\}$ and $U = \{x_5\}$, $V = \{x_1, x_2, x_3, x_4, x_6\}$ decomposition with 2 outputs from block G may exist.

When considering solutions with 4 inputs to block G, according to Property 1, [7,8] only solution with $U = \{x_4, x_5\}$, $V = \{x_1, x_2, x_3, x_6\}$ should be evaluated. We have:

$$\left(\beta_{x_4} \cdot \beta_{x_5}\right) \text{ or } \beta_F = \left\{\overline{(4)(8)}; \overline{(1)(6)}; \overline{(2)(3)}; \overline{(5)(7)}\right\}$$

$$r\left(\beta_{x_4} \cdot \beta_{x_5}\right) = 2 + e\left(\left(\beta_{x_4} \cdot \beta_{x_5}\right) \text{ or } \beta_F\right) = 2 + \lceil \log_2 2 \rceil = 3$$

$$(4.1)$$

This means that for such variable partitioning decomposition may exist with block G having 1 output. With this approach to serial decomposition, there is no difference between disjoint and non-disjoint decomposition in their calculation. Particularly, it can be concluded that for finding blanket G we can simply apply the method of calculating compatible classes of βV blocks [7] which was recently improved in [8].

5. Conclusions

The paper represents the "rediscovery" of some decomposition algorithms of Boolean logic functions, using subfunctions [1].

After a brief exposure of the decomposition methods of Boolean logical functions, the authors, through the proposed example, shows the reduction of the implementation cost using standard logical circuits.

The authors show that when using PLD circuits, the use of Boolean functions decomposition method reduces the number of circuits necessary for the implementation (see PAL10L8).

Balanced decomposition proved to be very useful in implementation of combinational functions using logic cell resources of FPGA architectures. However, results presented in this paper show that functional decomposition can be efficiently and effectively applied also to implement digital systems in embedded memory blocks. Application of r-admissibility concept makes possible fast evaluation of decompositions for different sizes of block G. This allows selecting best possible decomposition strategy.

The paper showed that the use of Boolean functions decomposition method reduces the number of circuits necessary for the implementation. However, this substitution process reduces the circuits cost by increasing the circuit complexity, which also enhances the likelihood of errors in the circuit design.

Balanced decomposition proved to be very useful in implementation of combinational functions using logic cell resources of FPGA architectures. However, results presented in this paper show that functional decomposition can be efficiently and effectively applied also to implement digital systems in embedded memory blocks.

REFERENCES

[1]   M. Denouette, J. P. Perrin and E. Daclin, "Systemès Logiques," Tome I, Dunod, Paris, 1967, pp. 4-56.

[2]   C. H. Roth, "Fundamentals of Logic Design," West Publishing Company, Eagan, 1999, pp. 148-172.

[3]   Al. Valachi, Fl. Hoza, V. Onofrei and R. Silion, "Analiza, Sinteza şi Testarea Dispozitivelor Numerice," Nord-Est, 1993, pp. 31-32; 45-53.

[4]   J. A. Brzozowski and T. Łuba, "Decomposition of Boolean Functions Specified by Cubes," *Journal of Multiple-Valued Logic and Soft Computing*, Vol. 9, 2003.

[5]   M. Rawski, "Decomposition of Boolean Function Sets," *Electronics and Telecommunications Quarterly*, Vol. 53, No. 3, 2007, pp. 231-249.

[6]   J. A. Brzozowski and T. Łuba, "Logic Decomposition Aimed at Programmable Cell Arrays," *International Conference of Microelectronics: Microelectronics*, Vol. 1783, 1992, pp. 77-88.

[7]   S. J. E. Wilton, "SMAP: Heterogeneous Technology Mapping for Area Reduction in FPGAs with Embedded Memory Arrays," *FPGA*, 1998, pp. 171-178.

[8]   "Logic Synthesis Strategy for FPGAs with Embedded Memory Blocks," Mariusz Rawski, Grzegorz Borowik, Tadeusz Łuba, Paweł Tomaszewicz, Bogdan j. Falkow- ski. Przegląd Elektrotechnic Znyelectrical Review), R. 86 NR 11a/2010.

## 11

A 0.4 V Bulk-Driven Amplifier for Low-Power Data Converter Applications

R. Rezaei[1], A. Ahmadpour[2,3*], M. N. Moghaddasi[3]

[1]Department of Electronic Engineering, Bahcesehir University, Istanbul, Turkey
[2]Department of Electronic Engineering, Islamic Azad University (Lahijan Branch), Lahijan, Iran
[3]Department of Electronic Engineering, Islamic Azad University (Science and Research Branch), Tehran, Iran

ABSTRACT

This paper presents the design of an ultra low-voltage (ULV) pseudo operational transconductance amplifier (P-OTA) that is able to operate with a single supply voltage as low as 0.4 V. The proposed circuit is based on the bulk-driven technique and use of cross-coupled self-cascode pairs that boosts the differential DC gain. The stability condition of this structure for the DC gain is considered by definition of two coefficients to cancel out a controllable percentage of the denominator. This expression for stability condition yield optimized value for the DC gain. Also, as the principle of operation of the proposed technique relies on matching conditions, Monte Carlo analyzes are considered to study of the behavior of the proposed circuit against mismatches. The designed P-OTA have a DC gain of 64 dB, 212 KHz unity gain bandwidth, 57° phase margin that is loaded by 10 pF differential capacitive loads, while consume only 16 μW. Eventually, from the proposed P-OTA, a low-power Sample and Hold (S/H) circuit with sampling frequency of 10 KS/s has been designed and simulated. The correct functionality for this configuration is verified from –30°C to 70°C. The simulated data presented is obtained using the HSPICE Environment and is valid for the 90 nm triple-well CMOS process.

Keywords: Pseudo Operational Transconductance Amplifier (P-OTA); Bulk-Input; Ultra Low-Voltage (ULV); Sample and Hold (S/H) Circuit

1. Introduction

The ultra low-voltage (ULV) supplies available in modern CMOS processes are a challenging matter for analog designers, and operation of ULV analog circuits has become inevitable due to scaling down of semiconductor technology [1-3]. This is evident from the International Technology Roadmap for Semiconductors (ITRS) [4]. This requires traditional circuit solutions to be replaced by new approaches to circuit design and more flexible structure strategies that are compatible with future standard CMOS technology trends. This is especially true for very high integration levels and very large scale integrated (VLSI) mixed-signal chips and SOCs. In mixed-signal systems, the analog circuits are combined with digital circuits in order to get the best performance with a low-voltage supply and low-power consumption. This combination should be done in an optimal way and the optimization process is application dependent. Recently, it has been possible to design circuits using power supplies as low as 1 V, and fabricated in the CMOS 90 nm

technology. So far, CMOS 22 nm technology products will be available in the year 2013 with a power supply of 0.5 V [1]. While the supply voltage applicable in deep sub-submicron design will continue to decrease and eventually fall below 1 V, the threshold voltage will remain relative stable close to 250 mV [5-7]. This problem is mangified due to the fact that the threshold voltage (V_{th}) never decreases linearly with decreases in the power supply. There are a number of techniques for ultra low-voltage circuits such as use of self-cascode MOS-FETs and cross-coupled pairs were proposed [1,2,8]. Meanwhile, self-cascode configuration connects the gates of two transistors together and provides high impedance with larger voltage headroom than the conventional cascode structure. The output resistance is roughly proportional to the transistors' dimensions and the effective voltage is the same as in a single MOSFET. Also, the bulk-input technique [9-14] shows a superior performance, which allows for operation in the moderate inversion region at supply voltages equal to the V_{th} of the technology. This technique, which uses the bulk terminal as signal input, is a promising method as it achieves enhanced performance without having to modify the exist-

---

*Corresponding author.

ing structure of the MOSFET [9-15]. Furthermore, the bulk-driven technique has better linearity and smaller power supply requirements. For a traditional MOSFET, the voltage applied to the bulk actually reduces the threshold voltage of the transistor, which increases the inversion level [16,17]. When applying this technique in circuit design, satisfactory performance can be achieved especially in ULV and low-power applications. OTAs are the key active building blocks of analog circuits. Fully differential OTAs are preferred because they provide larger signal swing, better distortion performance, better CM noise and supply noise rejection, but a CM feedback (CMFB) circuit must be added [18]. Also, fully differential OTAs work very well and can substantially improve the system's quality, especially in very unfriendly environments such as mixed-mode applications. However, at lower supply voltages, Pseudo OTAs (P-OTAs) could be used to avoid the voltage drop across the tail current source used in the fully differential structures. Various designs have been reported in the literature [1,8,16]. This paper presents the design of an ULV bulk-driven P-OTA in 90 nm triple-well CMOS technology with supply voltage as low as 0.4 V. As the principle of operation of the proposed technique relies on matching conditions, Monte Carlo analysis and Process-Voltage-Temperature (PVT) tests are considered to study of the behavior of the proposed circuit against mismatches. Eventually, from the proposed P-OTA, a low-power Sample and Hold (S/H) circuit has been designed and simulated. The design procedures of this structure are organized as follows. Sections 2.1 and 2.2 presents and analyses the small signal of the main P-OTA. In Sections 2.3 and 2.4 the bias circuit and CMFB structure are reviewed. Then S/H circuit is introduced in Section 2.5. Section 3 presents simulation results. Finally, the conclusion is given in Section 4. The Appendix gives details of the analysis.

2. Bulk-Input OTA Circuit Design

2.1. Main Amplifier Circuit

A very low-voltage bulk-input P-OTA without bias and CMFB circuits is shown in **Figure 1(a)**. Also, for small signal analysis, the AC model of this configuration is depicted in **Figure 1(b)**. In this structure, a PMOS P-OTA is implemented due to the action of M_{1x}, M_{2x}, M_{3x} and M_{4x}. The two inputs are on the bodies of PMOS transistors M_{1x} and M_{2x} and the body transconductance of these devices provides the input transconductance. These devices are loaded by the NMOS transistors M_{3x} and M_{4x}, which act as current sources. To further improve the differential gain, PMOS devices (M_{5x}, M_{6x} and M_{7x}, M_{8x}) are added. This configuration is a cross-coupled cascode pair that adds a negative resistance to the output and boosts the differential DC gain [19]. In this structure, the gate

inputs of transistors M_{5x} and M_{6x} are biased at zero due to the limitation of the power supply voltage. Also, the gate inputs of M_{7x} and M_{8x} are connected to the gates of input transistors M_{1x} and M_{2x} and biased at 100 mV, which biases them in moderate inversion. Forward biasing of the body-source junction has been applied in low-voltage digital circuits [20-23] and it is applied here to lower the V_{th} of the transistors. We typically apply a forward bias up to 400 mV of V_{DD}, which results in a lowering of the V_{th} by about 50 mV. In the context of 0.4 V operation, the risk of forward biasing the junctions is minimized since parasitic bipolar devices cannot be activated even when the full power supply is used as forward bias. In addition, to obtain adequate gain, identical gain stages can be cascaded so that a two-stage P-OTA is obtained as shown in **Figure 1(c)**. In conclusion, the P-OTA is stabilized by adding Miller compensation capacitors C_c with series resistors R_c for right half-plane zero cancellation. In the designed P-OTA, $C_c = 2.6$ pF and $R_c = 50$ kΩ are assumed, respectively.

2.2. Small Signal Analysis

The drain-to-source accurrents of an NMOS and a PMOS transistor are given by

$$i_{ds} = g_m v_{gs} + g_{mb} v_{bs} + g_{ds} v_{ds} \tag{1}$$

$$i_{sd} = g_m v_{sg} + g_{mb} v_{sb} + g_{ds} v_{sd} \tag{2}$$

where *gm*, *gmb*, and *gds* are the gate transconductance, bulk transconductance, and output conductance, respectively. Then, using (1) and (2) and considering $v_{i-} = -v_{i+}$ and $v_{o-} = -v_{o+}$, we have

$$A_v = \frac{-g_{mb1}}{\left(g_{ds1} + g_{ds4} - \alpha \cdot g_{ds7}\right)} \tag{3}$$

$$\alpha = \frac{-\left(g_{mb5} - g_{ds5}\right)}{\left(g_{m5} + g_{mb5} + g_{ds5} + g_{ds7}\right)} \tag{4}$$

As can be seen from Equation (3) the conductance of $\alpha \cdot g_{ds7}$ can be used to boost the gain of the P-OTA. Identically, we define coefficients of $\beta (0 < \beta < 1)$ and g_{margin} due to process and temperature variations so that their $\alpha \cdot g_{ds7}$ term cancels out only β percent of the denominator. According to the above statement we can obtain the first stability conditions as follows:

$$\sum g_{total} = g_{ds1} + g_{ds3} - \alpha \cdot g_{ds7} > g_{margin} > 0 \tag{5}$$

$$g_{margin} = \beta \cdot \sum g_{total}, 0 < \beta < 1 \tag{6}$$

$$\sum g_{total} > \beta \cdot \sum g_{total} \Rightarrow (1-\beta)\sum g_{total} > 0 \tag{7}$$

Then the maximum gain will be given by

$$A_{vMax} = \frac{-g_{mb1}}{\beta \cdot \sum g_{total}} = \frac{-g_{mb1}}{g_{margin}} \tag{8}$$

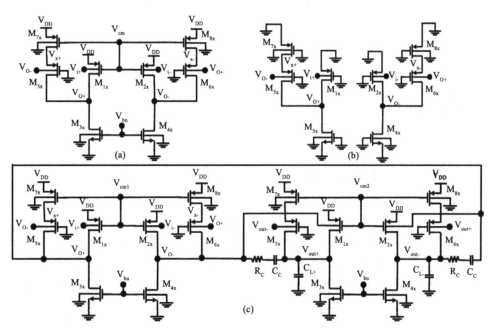

Figure 1. Proposed P-OTA: (a) One stage of the P-OTA; (b) AC model of the P-OTA; (c) Two-stage P-OTA with miller compensations.

We know that $0 < \beta < 1$; then

$$\sum g_{total} = g_{ds1} + g_{ds3} - \alpha \cdot g_{ds7} > 0 \qquad (9)$$

$$g_{ds1} + g_{ds3} - \frac{(g_{mb5} - g_{ds5})}{(g_{m5} + g_{mb5} + g_{ds5} + g_{ds7})} \cdot g_{ds7} > 0 \qquad (10)$$

We know that for boost, the gain must satisfy $\alpha < 0$. Therefore, the stability conditions for this structure can be expressed as:

$$\left\{ g_{ds1} + g_{ds3} > g_{mb5} > g_{ds5,7} \right\} \qquad (11)$$

2.3. Common-Mode Feedback Circuit

Fully differential OTAs require a Common-Mode Feedback (CMFB) circuit. This circuit should behave linearly and only respond to CM voltage. A lack of this feature causes the Total Harmonic Distortion (THD) of the circuit to increase. Furthermore, a CMFB circuit amplifies the difference between the average of V_{o+} and V_{o-}, and sends a feedback signal V_{cm} to set the bias voltage at the gates of the input transistors of the OTA. Nowadays, designing a CMFB circuit which is able to operate under a ULV supply is very difficult, mainly because of the difficulty of detecting the CM voltage. In Reference [16] a CMFB circuit was designed which operated at 0.5 V by using two resistors to sense the output CM levels. But this structure increases the die area and reduces the gain due to larger loads on the OTA. To overcome some of these problems, a CMFB circuit has been reported [8] which is used in this paper and is depicted in **Figure 2**. The CM output voltage of first stage is not coupled to the CM

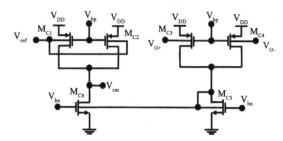

Figure 2. CMFB circuit used in reference [6] and proposed P-OTA.

output of the second stage. Therefore, two independent feedback circuits are needed to establish the CM voltage at outputs of the first and second stages. This structure uses four PMOS transistors, M_{c1} - M_{c4}, and two NMOS transistors, M_{c5} and M_{c6} in the first and second stages, respectively. The NMOS device is a bulk-input current mirror which compares the currents of the PMOS devices and then the difference between these currents is fed to the gate of the input transistors (V_{cm1} and V_{cm2}) to control the output CM voltages. This structure is able to operate with a ULV as low as 0.4 V.

2.4. Bias Circuit

A low-sensitivity reference current generator and bias circuit are illustrated in **Figure 3**. Due to limited voltage headroom, simple current mirrors are used to generate the bias voltages (V_{bn} and V_{bp}). Because the gate and source of M_{B3} and M_{B4} are common for both transistors, and the aspect ratios are equal, $I_{DM_{B3}} = I_{DM_{B4}}$.

Also, note that $V_{GSM_{B2}} = V_{GSM_{B1}} + R_B \cdot I_{DM_{B1}}$; thus

$$\sqrt{\frac{2I_{DM_{B3}}}{\mu_n \cdot C_{ox} \cdot (W/L)_{M_{B2}}}} = \sqrt{\frac{2I_{DM_{B3}}}{\mu_n \cdot C_{ox} \cdot K \cdot (W/L)_{M_{B2}}}} \\ + R_B \cdot I_{DM_{B3}} \quad (12)$$

In the above mentioned equation, K is the ratio between the aspect ratios of M_{B1} and M_{B2}. Rearranging this expression,

$$I_{DM_{B3}} = \frac{1}{R_B^2} \frac{2}{\mu_n \cdot C_{ox} \cdot K \cdot (W/L)_{M_{B2}}} \left(1 - \frac{1}{K}\right)^2 \quad (13)$$

In the target circuit, $K = 1.25$ and $R_B = 1\ k$, and thus a low sensitivity supply voltage independent reference current circuit is also designed and simulated which generates a stable 1 μA reference current for the bias circuit. As expected, the circuit is independent of the supply voltage. Transistor M_{B5} mirrors this current to generate a stable 1 μA reference current, which is used in the biasing of PMOS devices. In order to ensure that all the transistors operate in the saturation region, bias voltages V_{bn} and V_{bp} are applied to the gates of the NMOS and PMOS devices respectively in the P-OTA and CMFB circuits. These bias voltages have been tested versus temperature and power supply variations. For −30°C to 70°C temperature range and power supply variations of ±6.25%, the sensitivities of these voltages are about 0.24 mV/°C and 0.33 mV/°C, respectively.

2.5. Sample and Hold (S/H) Circuit

The in this section, the whole S/H circuit is introduced. The proposed structure has been implemented using CMOS 90 nm technology and simulated in Hspice Environment. **Figure 4** shows the entire S/H circuit. This circuit uses a two-phase, non-overlapping clock configuretion. Here, $\phi1$ and $\phi2$ are the non-overlapping clocks. The sampling frequency is 10 KS/s. During $\phi1$ the input signal is sampled differentially, while during phase $\phi2$ the P-OTA is put into a unity gain configuration.

For a power supply voltage of 0.4 V, and $V_{th} \approx 0.4$ V a transmission gate switch could possibly be used. However, the source of the switching transistor can be at a

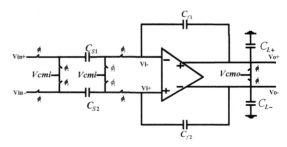

Figure 4. Sample and hold circuit.

very different voltage from the substrate, so the device threshold voltages can vary over the possible signal range [24] for typical process parameters. The well-known approach is use of Switched OTA circuits [25]. However, implementation of S/H using the switched OTA technique is impossible, while the circuits such as pipelined ADC converters require S/H operation at the input. Other approaches to overcome this problem are to use internal voltage boosting [26-32] that is used here. In voltage boosting techniques, some cases the clock voltage is doubled, and that can lead to reliability issues.

3. Simulation Results

Based on the analytical procedure described in the previous sections, a new ULV P-OTA was designed at a single supply voltage of 0.4 V from a 90 nm triple-well CMOS process and then simulated by HSPICE. The threshold voltages of this technology for NMOS and PMOS transistors are 0.42 V and −0.43 V, respectively. Then, from designed P-OTA, an ULV and low-power S/H circuit has been implemented.

3.1. Frequency and Transient Responses

The open-loop frequency response and closed-loop transient response of the P-OTA were tested. For a CM input of 200 mV, a DC gain of 64 dB, a bandwidth of 212 KHZ and a phase margin of 57° were obtained. **Figure 5** shows the frequency response of P-OTA. Also, to examine the effect of the doublet on the circuits' settling behaviors; the P-OTA was configured as closed-loop unity-gain amplifiers with 0.2 pF capacitors.

Then a 200 mV input CM voltage and a 100 mV step were applied to the P-OTA's input, and then output voltage with 1% error was observed. In this state, the output voltage settled to its final value in less than 4 μs for rising time and 3.3 μs for falling time, respectively. **Figure 6** shows the step responses of the P-OTA.

3.2. Monte Carlo Analyzes

Monte Carlo frequency and transient analyzes is considered to study of the behavior of the proposed circuit against mismatches. **Figures 7** and **8** show the Monte

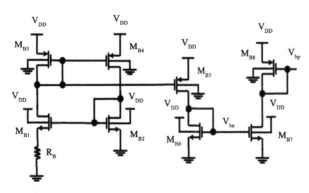

Figure 3. Reference current generator and bias circuit.

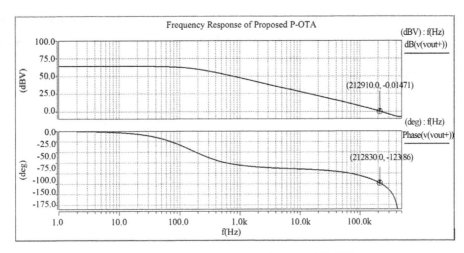

Figure 5. Frequency response of proposed P-OTA.

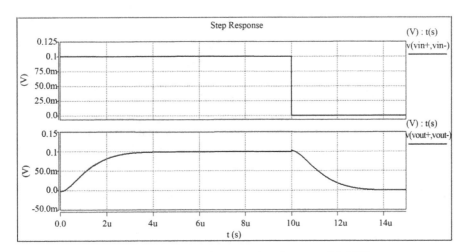

Figure 6. Settling simulated results of proposed P-OTA.

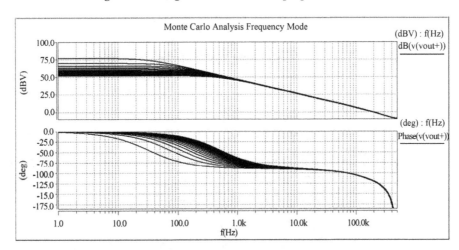

Figure 7. Monte carlo frequency analysis of proposed P-OTA.

Carlo analyzes of the P-OTA in frequency and transient modes. The result shows that the amplitude and the phase were almost independent of circuit parameters.

Also, in transient test the responses do not have any extra overshoot, because of the suitable bandwidth, phase margin and convenient CM output voltage. Also, this configuration was passed temperature variation from –30˚C to 70˚C.

3.3. Total Harmonic Distortion Response

The third obtained THD of the P-OTA, with a 200 mV amplitude and 500 Hz input frequency sampled at 10 KHz, were about 70 dB below the fundamental, as shown in **Figure 9**. It is obvious that the extra harmonics, but not the main harmonic have been eliminated. Finally, a comparison of proposed P-OTA with previous structures is summarized in **Table 1**.

3.4. Sample and Hold Output Responses

The input and output waveforms for a sinusoidal input of 200 mV peak-to-peak amplitude and 500 Hz frequency with a 10 KHz clock is depicted in **Figure 10**. To evaluate the nonlinearity, SNR and SNDR for mentioned input signal were also calculated. The result as indicated in **Figure 11** exhibits higher than 57.9 dB SNR and 56 dB SNDR that corresponds to 9 effective bits resolution. The

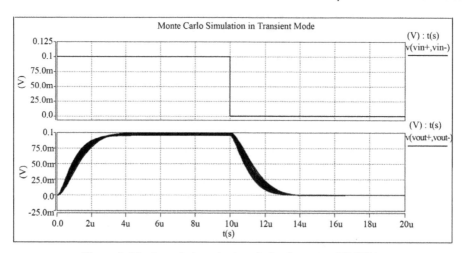

Figure 8. Monte carlo transient analysis of proposed P-OTA.

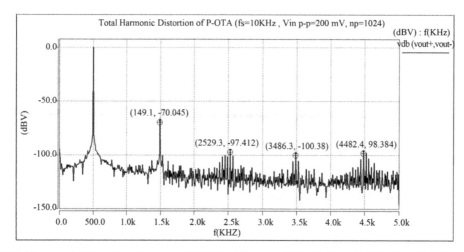

Figure 9. Total harmonic distortion of proposed P-OTA (Vinp-p = 200 mV, fin = 500 Hz, fs = 10 KS/s, n_p = 1024).

Table 1. Comparisons of characteristics of proposed P-OTAs with state-of-the-art P-OTAs.

Parameters	This work	[8]	[10]	[11]	[12]	[13]	[14]	[16]
Technology (nm)	90	180	350	350	350	350	180	180
Power supply (V)	0.4	0.5	1	1	0.6	1	0.9	0.5
DC gain (dB)	64	65	64	70.6	73.5	76.2	73.8	62
GBW (MHz)	0.212	0.55	2	4	0.01302	8.1	272	10
Phase-margin (°)	57	50	45	65	54.1	63.14	64	60
THD (%)	0.31	0.13	NA	NA	0.13	NA	NA	1
Load capacitance (PF)	10	20	1	10	15	1MΩ‖17PF	2	20
Power dissipation (μW)	16	28	130	62	0.55	358	1420	*110*

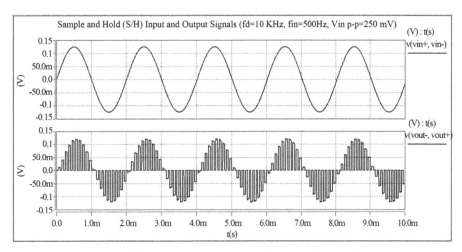

Figure 10. S/H input and output waves (fin = 500 Hz, fs = 10 KS/s).

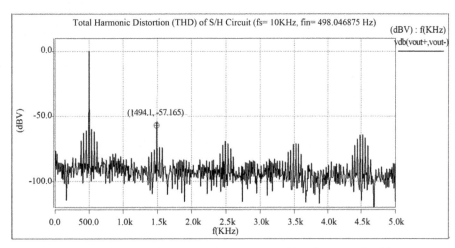

Figure 11. Total harmonic distortion of S/H (fin = 498.046875 Hz, fs = 10 KS/s, n_p = 1024).

Discrete Fourier Transform (DFT) of the data samples was also computed with the Hspice simulator. The result shows that the largest SPUR falls −57.16 dB below the RMS value of the fundamental corresponding to an SFDR of 57.16 dBc confirming the results obtained through nonlinearity evaluation.

4. Conclusion

A new bulk-driven pseudo OTA topology using of cross-coupled self-cascode pairs technique has been presented. The operation principle of proposed structure is based on modifying the effective conductance of the active loads and enhancing the effective transconductance. This structure has been simulated in the 90 nm triple-well CMOS process with a supply voltage as low as 0.4 V. The proposed cross-coupled self-cascode pairs add a negative resistance to the outputs of structure and boost the differential DC gain. Also, expression for the DC gain was given, which can be solved for the small signal analysis. Then, in this structure, the stability condition of the presented technique for the DC gain has been consid-

ered by definition of two coefficients to cancel out a controllable percentage of the denominator. This expression for stability condition yield optimized value for the DC gain. Besides, the exact expressions for the transfer function coefficients presented in the Appendix were verified for a number of different sets of component values. The transfer function coefficients were calculated using the formulas in the Appendix, the poles and zero(s) were found by factoring the numerator and denominator of the transfer function, and those results were compared to the poles and zero(s) from a HSPICE [33] pole-zero analysis of the same small-signal circuit. For future work, the optimized parameters can be found using a Genetic Algorithm (GA) to get a high performance structure in analog integrated circuits. The P-OTA provides a DC gain of 64 dB, a phase margin of 57° and an open loop unity-gain frequency of 212 KHz with a 10 pF capacitive load. The total current of the P-OTA is 40 μA. In this design, the first and second stages consume about (1/3) and (2/3) of the total power consumption. Also, an output swing of ±0.12 V was obtained for proposed structure.

Furthermore, THDs of −70 dB was given for 200 mV amplitude and 500 Hz input frequency sampled at 10 KHz. In spite of the ULV, excellent supply rejections of 71 dB at 5 KHz was obtained. Also, a reasonable CM rejection ratio of 81 dB at same frequency was achieved. However, the smaller bulk transconductance and large capacitance from the body to the substrate, limit the bandwidth of the structures. Eventually, from the proposed P-OTA, a low-power S/H circuit with sampling frequency of 10 KS/s has been designed and simulated. In addition, the preliminary simulation results demonstrate the feasibility of the P-OTA for modern ULV and low-power mixed-signal chips and SOCs.

REFERENCES

[1] S. Chatterjee, Y. Tsvidis and P. Kinget, "Ultra-Low Voltage Analog Integrated Circuits," *IEICE Transactions on Electronics*, Vol. 89, No. 6, 2006, pp. 673-680.

[2] S. Yan and E. Sanchez-Sinencio, "Low-Voltage Analog Circuit Design Techniques: A Tutorial," *IEICE Transactions on Fundamentals of Electronics, Communications and Computer*, Vol. 83, No. 2, 2000, pp. 179-196.

[3] J. Ramirez-Angulo, R. G. Carvajal and A. Torralba, "Low Supply Voltage High Performance CMOS Current Mirror with Low Input and Output Voltage Requirements," *IEEE Transactions on Circuits and Systems II: Express Briefs*, Vol. 51, No. 3, 2004, pp. 124-129.

[4] ITRS, "The International Technology Roadmap for Semiconductors," 2008. http://public.itrs.net

[5] Y. Berg and O. Mirmotahari, "Ultra Low-Voltage CMOS Current Mirrors," *Analog Integrated Circuits and Signal Processing*, Vol. 68, No. 2, 2011, pp. 83-89.

[6] A. Baschirotto, V. Chironi, G. Cocciolo, S. D'Amico, M. De Matteis and P. Delizia, "Low Power Analog Design in Scaled Technologies," *Topical Workshop on Electronics for Particle Physics*, Pairs, 21-25 September 2009, pp. 103-110.

[7] J. Pekarik, D. Greenberg, B. Jagannathan, R. Groves, J. R. Jones, R. Singh, A. Chinthakindi, X. Wang, M. Breitwisch, D. Coolbaugh, P. Cottrell, J. Florkey, G. Freeman and R. Krishnasamy, "RFCMOS Technology from 0.25 nm to 65 nm: The State of the Art," *Proceedings of the IEEE Custom Integrated Circuits Conference*, 3-6 October 2004, pp. 217-224.

[8] M. Trakimas and S. Sonkusale, "A 0.5 V Bulk-Input OTA with Improved Common-Mode Feedback for Low-Frequency Filtering Applications," *Analog Integrated Circuits and Signal Processing*, Vol. 59, No. 1, 2009, pp. 83-89.

[9] A. Guzinski, M. Bialko and J. C. Matheau, "Body-Driven Differential Amplifier for Application in Continous-Time Active-C Filter," *Proceedings of the European Conference on Circuit Theory and Design*, June 1987, pp. 315-319.

[10] G. Raikos and S. Vlassis, "Low-Voltage Bulk-Driven Input Stage with Improved Transconductance," *International Journal of Circuit Theory and Applications*, Vol. 39, No. 3, 2011, pp. 327-339.

[11] J. M. Carrillo, G. Torelli and J. F. Duque-Carrillo, "Transconductance Enhancement in Bulk-Driven Input Stages and Its Applications," *Analog Integrated Circuits and Signal Processing*, Vol. 68, No. 2, 2011, pp. 207-217.

[12] L. H. C. Ferreira, T. C. Pimenta and R. L. Moreno, "An Ultra-Low-Voltage Ultra-Low-Power CMOS Miller OTA with Rail-to-Rail Input/Output Swing," *IEEE Transactions on Circuits and Systems II: Express Briefs*, Vol. 54, No. 10, 2007, pp. 843-847.

[13] J. M. Carrillo, G. Torelli, R. Pérez-Aloe and J. F. Duque-Carrillo, "1-V Rail-to-Rail CMOS Opamp with Improved Bulk-Driven Input Stage," *IEEE Journal of Solid-State Circuits*, Vol. 42, No. 3, 2007, pp. 508-517.

[14] H. Khameh and H. Shamsi, "A Sub-1 V High-Gain Two-Stage OTA Using Bulk-Driven and Positive Feedback Techniques," *5th European Conference on Circuits and Systems for Communications*, Serbia, November 2010.

[15] Y. Tsividis, "Mixed Analog-Digital VLSI Devices and Technology," World Scientific Publishing, Singapore City, 2002.

[16] S. Chatterjee, Y. Tsvidis and P. Kinget, "0.5 V Analog Circuit Techniques and Their Application to OTA and Filter Design," *IEEE Journal of Solid State Circuits*, Vol. 40, No. 12, 2005, pp. 2373-2387.

[17] C. Duan and M. Liu, "MOSFET Modeling for Analog IC Simulation under Ultra-Deep Submicron Technologies," *Micro-Electronics Technology*, 2006, pp. 205-209.

[18] A. N. Mohieldin, "High Performance Continuous-Time Filters for Information Transfer Systems," Ph.D. Dissertation, Department of Electrical Engineering, Texas A&M University, College Station, 2003.

[19] A. Ahmadpour, "A 0.4 V Bulk-Input Pseudo Amplifier in 90 nm CMOS Technology," *Proceeding of 13th IEEE International Symposium on Design and Diagnostics of Electronic Circuits and Systems*, Vienna, 14-16 April 2010, pp. 301-304.

[20] M.-J. Chen, J.-S. Ho, T.-H. Huang, C.-H. Yang, Y.-N. Jou and T. Wu, "Back-Gate Forward Bias Method for Low-Voltage CMOS Digital Circuits," *IEEE Transactions on Electron Devices*, Vol. 43, No. 6, 1996, pp. 904-910.

[21] S. Narendra, J. Tschanz, J. Hofsheier, B. Bloechel, S. Vangal, Y. Hoskote, S. Tang, D. Somasekhar, A. Keshavarzi, V. Erraguntla, G. Dermer, N. Borkar, S. Borkar and V. De, "Ultra-Low Voltage Circuits and Processor in 180 nm to 90 nm Technologies with a Swapped-Body Biasing Technique," *IEEE International Digest of Technical Papers. Solid-State Circuits Conference*, Vol. 1, 2004, pp. 156-157.

[22] J. W. Tschanz, J. T. Kao, S. Narendra, R. Nair, D. Antoniadis and A. P. Chandrakasan, "Adaptive Body Bias for Reducing Impacts of Die-to-Die and Within-Die Parame-

ter Variations on Microprocessor Frequency and Leakage," *IEEE Journal of Solid-State Circuits*, Vol. 37, No. 11, 2002, pp. 1396-1402.

[23] V. R. Kaenel, M. D. Pardoen, E. Dijkstra and E. A. Vittoz, "Automatic Adjustment of Threshold and Supply Voltages for Minimum Power Consumption in CMOS Digital Circuits," *IEEE Symposium Digest of Technical Papers. Low Power Electronics*, San Diego, 10-12 October 1994, pp. 78-79.

[24] Q. Huang, "Low-Voltage and Low-Power Aspects of Data Converter Design," *Proceeding of the 30th European Solid-State Circuits Conference*, 21-23 September 2004, pp. 29-35.

[25] J. Crols and M. Steyaert, "Switched-Opamp: An Approach to Realize Full CMOS Switched-Capacitor Circuits at Very Low Power-Supply Voltages," *IEEE Journal of Solid-State Circuits*, Vol. 29, No. 8, 1994, pp. 936-942.

[26] T. Cho and P. Gray, "A 10 b, 20 Msample/s, 35 mW, Pipeline A/D Converter," *IEEE Journal of Solid-State Circuits*, Vol. 30, No. 3, 1995, pp. 166-172.

[27] J.-T. Wu, Y.-H. Chang and K. L. Chang, "1.2 V CMOS Switched-Capacitor Circuits," *IEEE International Digest of Technical Papers. Solid-State Circuits Conference*, San Francisco, 8-10 February 1996, pp. 388-389.

[28] T. Brooks, D. Robertson, D. Kelly, A. D. Muro and S. Harston, "A Cascaded Sigma-Delta Pipeline A/D Converter with 1.25 MHZ Signal Bandwidth and 89 dB SNR," *IEEE Journal of Solid-State Circuits*, Vol. 32, No. 12, 1997, pp. 1896-906.

[29] J. Steensgaard, "Bootstrapped Low-Voltage Analog Switches," *IEEE International Symposium on Circuits and Systems*, Vol. 2, 1999, pp. 29-32.

[30] A. Abo and P. Gray, "A 1.5-V, 10 Bit, 14.3-MS/s CMOS Pipeline Analog-to-Digital Converter," *IEEE Journal of Solid-State Circuits*, Vol. 34, No. 5, 1999, pp. 599-606.

[31] M. Dessouky and A. Kaiser, "A 1-V 1-mW Digital-Audio Modulator with 88-dB Dynamic Range Using Local Switch Bootstrapping," *Proceedings of the IEEE Custom Integrated Circuits Conference*, Orlando, 21-24 May 2000, pp. 13-16.

[32] U. Moon, G. Temes, E. Bidari, M. Keskin, L. Wu, J. Steensgaard and F. Maloberti, "Switched-Capacitor Circuit Techniques in Submicron Low-Voltage CMOS," *6th International Conference on VLSI and CAD*, Seoul, 26-27 October 1999, pp. 349-358.

[33] "Star-HSPICE Manual," Avant! Corp., Fremont, 2001.

Appendix

In addition, the transfer function and pole zero (s) analysis of the small-signal circuit in **Figure 1(c)** is analyzed here. With appropriate substitutions, the results of this analysis can be used for other related circuits in analog integrated circuit design. According to Equations of the first and second stages that is neglected here, a circuit model was obtained, which is shown in **Figure A1**. We know that the poles in this structure can be real or complex, depending upon the element values.

However, real or complex non-dominant poles can occur in practice and can be calculated using the denominators' roots from Equations in (A.12), using the exact transfer function coefficients presented in this paper.

Transfer Function Calculation

Writing KCL at the nodes $V_{x1,2}$, V_{o+} and V_{out-} for the first and second stages, yields

$$i_2' = -Y_2' \cdot v_{x2} = G_1' \cdot v_{x2} + G_2' \cdot v_{out-} \tag{A.1}$$

$$v_{x2} = \left[-G_2' / (G_1' + Y_2') \right] \cdot v_{out-} = -\alpha' \cdot v_{out-} \tag{A.2}$$

$$\alpha' = \frac{G_2'}{(G_1' + Y_2')} \tag{A.3}$$

$$i_1' = Y_1' \cdot v_{out-} \tag{A.4}$$

$$i_2' = i_1' + g_{mb2} \cdot v_{o+} + Y_c \left(v_{out-} - v_{o+} \right) \tag{A.5}$$

Substituting (A.1) and (A.4) in (A.5) result in

$$\frac{v_{out-}}{v_{o+}} = \frac{-\left(g_{mb2} - Y_c \right)}{\left[Y_1' + Y_c - \dfrac{Y_2' \cdot G_2'}{(G_1' + Y_2')} \right]} \tag{A.6}$$

In addition, for the first stage we have

$$i_2 = -Y_2 \cdot v_{x1} = G_1 \cdot v_{x1} + G_2 \cdot v_{o+} \tag{A.7}$$

$$v_{x1} = \frac{-G_2}{(G_1 + Y_2)} \cdot v_{o+} = -\alpha \cdot v_{o+} \tag{A.8}$$

$$\alpha = \frac{G_2}{(G_1 + Y_2)} \tag{A.9}$$

$$i_1 = Y_1 \cdot v_{o+} \tag{A.10}$$

$$i_2 = i_1 + g_{mb1} \cdot v_{i+} + Y_c \left(v_{o+} - v_{out-} \right) \tag{A.11}$$

Substituting (A.7) and (A.10) into (A.11) yields

$$A_v(s) = \frac{g_{mb1} \cdot \left(g_{mb2} - Y_c \right)}{\left[\left(Y_1 + Y_c - Y_{cs} \right)\left(Y_1' + Y_c - Y_{cs}' \right) + Y_c \cdot \left(g_{mb2} - Y_c \right) \right]} \tag{A.12}$$

Pole-Zero Analysis

In this Section, to perfect the design in the first and second stages of P-OTA and pole and zero(s) analysis, we assume that $\alpha = 0 \left(g_{mb5} = g_{ds5} \right)$ and $\alpha' = 0 \left(g_{mb6} = g_{ds6} \right)$. So, from Equation (A.12) we manipulate the desired P-OTA gain v_{out} / v_i. The gain transfer function is (see formula (A.13)), assuming that

$$R_C = \frac{1}{g_{mb2}} \tag{A.14}$$

$$\tau_c \cdot \tau_{o1} = R_C C_C \cdot R_{o1} C_1 = \frac{R_C C_C C_1}{(g_{ds1} + g_{ds3})} \ll 1 \tag{A.15}$$

$$\tau_c \cdot \tau_{o2} = R_C C_C \cdot R_{o2} C_1' = \frac{R_C C_C C_1'}{(g_{ds2} + g_{ds4})} \ll 1 \tag{A.16}$$

the approximate gain transfer function will be as follows

$$A_v(s) = \frac{A_0 \cdot \left(1 + \tau_c \cdot S \right)}{\left[\left(1 + \tau_1 \cdot S \right)\left(1 + \tau_2 \cdot S \right) + \dfrac{C_C \cdot A_0 \cdot S}{g_{mb1}} \right]} \tag{A.17}$$

Rewriting (A.17), we obtain

$$A_v(s) = \frac{A_0 \cdot \left(1 + \tau_c \cdot S \right)}{\left[1 + \left(\tau_1 + \tau_2 + \dfrac{C_C \cdot A_0}{g_{mb1}} \right) \cdot S + \tau_1 \tau_2 \cdot S^2 \right]} \tag{A.18}$$

Using (A.18), the poles and zero can be expressed as

$$z = \frac{-1}{\tau_c} = \frac{-1}{R_C \cdot C_C} \tag{A.19}$$

$$P_{1,2} = \frac{-\left(\tau_1 + \tau_2 + \dfrac{C_C \cdot A_0}{g_{mb1}} \right) \pm \sqrt{\left(\tau_1 + \tau_2 + \dfrac{C_C \cdot A_0}{g_{mb1}} \right)^2 - 4\tau_1 \tau_2}}{2} \tag{A.20}$$

Poles P_1 and P_2 will be real and widely spaced if

$$\left(\tau_1 + \tau_2 + \frac{C_C \cdot A_0}{g_{mb1}} \right)^2 \gg 4\tau_1 \tau_2 \tag{A.21}$$

Squaring both sides and rearranging yields

$$A_v(s) = \frac{A_0 \cdot \left(1 + \tau_c' \cdot S \right)\left(1 + \tau_c \cdot S \right)}{\left[\left(1 + \tau_1 \cdot S + \tau_c \tau_{o1} \cdot S^2 \right)\left(1 + \tau_2 \cdot S + \tau_c \tau_{o2} \cdot S^2 \right) + \dfrac{C_C \cdot A_0 \cdot S}{g_{mb1}} \left(1 + \tau_c' \cdot S \right) \right]} \tag{A.13}$$

$$\left(\sqrt{\tau_1} - \sqrt{\tau_2}\right)^2 + \frac{C_C \cdot A_0}{g_{mb1}} \gg 0 \qquad (A.22)$$

Finally, the requirements of the exact expressions for the coefficients are summarized in **Table A1**.

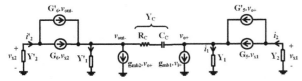

Figure A1. Circuit Model of the Proposed P-OTA.

Table A1. The exact expressions for the coefficients of the proposed P-OTA.

Parameters	Definition of parameters
Y_1	$g_{ds1} + g_{ds3} + S \cdot C_1$
Y_2	$g_{ds7} + S \cdot C_2$
C_1	$C_{db1} + C_{db3} + C_{db5}$
C_2	$C_{gs5} + C_{db7}$
Y_1'	$g_{ds2} + g_{ds4} + S \cdot C_1'$
Y_2'	$g_{ds8} + S \cdot C_2'$
C_1'	$C_{db2} + C_{db4} + C_{db6} + C_L$
C_2'	$C_{gs6} + C_{db8}$
$G_1 = G_5 = G_{6+}$	$G_1 = G_{6+} = g_{m5} + g_{mb5} + g_{ds5}$
$G_2 = G_5' = G_{5+}$	$G_2 = G_5' = g_{mb5} - g_{ds5}$
$G_1' = G_6 = G_{6-}$	$G_1' = G_6 = g_{m6} + g_{mb6} + g_{ds6}$
$G_2' = G_6' = G_{5-}$	$G_2' = G_6' = g_{mb6} - g_{ds6}$
Y_c	$\left(R_c + 1/S \cdot C_c\right)^{-1}$
α	$G_2/\left(G_1 + Y_2\right)$
α'	$G_2'/\left(G_1' + Y_2'\right)$
Y_{cs}	$\alpha \cdot Y_2$
Y_{cs}'	$\alpha' \cdot Y_2'$
A_0	$g_{mb1} \cdot g_{mb2}/\left(g_{ds1} + g_{ds3}\right)\left(g_{ds1} + g_{ds3}\right)$
τ_c'	$\left(R_c - 1/g_{mb2}\right) \cdot C_C$
τ_c	$R_c \cdot C_c$
τ_1	$\tau_c + \tau_{o1} + \tau_{c1}$
τ_{o1}	$R_{o1} \cdot C_1$
τ_{c1}	$R_{o1} \cdot C_C$
R_{o1}	$\left(g_{ds1} + g_{ds3}\right)^{-1} = r_{ds1} \| r_{ds3}$
τ_2	$\tau_c + \tau_{o2} + \tau_{c2}$
τ_{o2}	$R_{o2} \cdot C_1'$
τ_{c2}	$R_{o2} \cdot C_C$
R_{o2}	$\left(g_{ds2} + g_{ds4}\right)^{-1} = r_{ds2} \| r_{ds4}$

## 12

Voltage-Mode Universal Biquad Filter Employing Single Voltage Differencing Differential Input Buffered Amplifier

Kanhaiya Lal Pushkar[1], Data Ram Bhaskar[2*], Dinesh Prasad[2]

[1]Department of Electronics and Communication Engineering, Maharaja Agrasen Institute of Technology, New Delhi, India

[2]Department of Electronics and Communication Engineering, Faculty of Engineering and Technology, Jamia Millia Islamia, New Delhi, India

ABSTRACT

A new multi function voltage-mode universal biquadratic filter using single Voltage Differencing Differential Input Buffered Amplifier (VD-DIBA), two capacitors and one resistor is proposed. The proposed configuration has four inputs and one output and can realize all the five standard filters from the same circuit configuration. The presented biquad filter offers low active and passive sensitivities. The validity of proposed universal biquadratic filter has been verified by SPICE simulation using 0.35 μm MIETEC technology.

Keywords: Voltage Differencing Differential Input Buffered Amplifier; Analog Filter; Voltage-Mode

1. Introduction

Recently, attention has been devoted to the design of multi-input single output (MISO) or single input multi-output (SIMO) current-mode or voltage-mode universal biquadratic filters because of their versatility and flexibility for practical applications as the same circuit topology can be employed for different filter responses. Several voltage-mode/current-mode universal biquadratic filters using different types of single active building block/device have been presented in [1-8]. In reference [9] number of new active building blocks have been introduced, VD-DIBA is one of them which is emerging as a flexible and versatile active element for analog signal processing. The applications, advantages and usefulness of VD-DIBA have been recognized in [10,11]. They have been used in the realization of first order all pass filter [10], and in the realization of grounded and floating inductances as presented in [11]. The various filter configurations proposed in [1-8] and [10,11] although employ single active device/element, but use two to four capacitors and two to four resistors. Therefore, the purpose of this paper is to introduce a new voltage-mode universal biquadratic filter using single VD-DIBA, two capacitors and only one resistor. The proposed configuration has four inputs and one output and can realize all the five standard filters (low pass (LPF), high pass (HPF), band pass (BPF), band reject (BRF) and all pass (APF)) by proper selection of input

voltages from the same circuit configuration without altering the circuit topology. The active and passive sensitivities of the realized filters are low. The validity of the proposed configuration has been verified by SPICE simulation using 0.35 μm MIETC technology.

2. The Proposed Biquadratic Filter Configuration

The symbolic notation and equivalent model of the VD-DIBA (+) are shown in **Figures 1(a)** and **(b)** respectively [1]. The model includes two controlled sources: the current source controlled by differential voltage $(V_+ - V_-)$, with the transconductance g_m, and the voltage source controlled by differential voltage $(V_z - V_v)$ with the unity voltage gain.

The VD-DIBA (+) can be described by the following set of equations:

$$\begin{pmatrix} I_+ \\ I_- \\ I_z \\ I_v \\ V_w \end{pmatrix} = \begin{pmatrix} 0 & 0 & 0 & 0 & 0 \\ 0 & 0 & 0 & 0 & 0 \\ g_m & -g_m & 0 & 0 & 0 \\ 0 & 0 & 0 & 0 & 0 \\ 0 & 0 & 1 & -1 & 0 \end{pmatrix} \begin{pmatrix} V_+ \\ V_- \\ V_z \\ V_v \\ I_w \end{pmatrix} \quad (1)$$

The proposed voltage-mode universal biquadratic filter is shown in **Figure 2**.

A routine circuit analysis of **Figure 2** yields the following expression for the output voltage in terms of the input voltages

---

*Corresponding author.

$$V_o = \frac{V_1\left(\dfrac{g_m}{C_1}s + \dfrac{g_m}{R_0 C_1 C_2}\right) + V_2\left(s^2 + s\left(\dfrac{1}{R_0 C_2}\right)\right) - V_3 s^2 - V_4 s\left(\dfrac{1}{R_0 C_2}\right)}{s^2 + s\left(\dfrac{1}{R_0 C_2} + \dfrac{g_m}{C_1}\right) + \dfrac{g_m}{R_0 C_1 C_2}} \tag{2}$$

From Equation (2), various filter responses can be realized as:

1) If $V_1 = V_2 = V_4 = 0$ (grounded) and $V_3 = V_{in}$, then an inverting HPF can be realized

2) If $V_1 = V_2 = V_3 = 0$ and $V_4 = V_{in}$, then an inverting BPF can be realized

3) If $V_2 = V_3 = 0$ and $V_1 = V_4 = V_{in}$ and $C_1 = C_2$, $1/R_0 = g_m$, then a LPF can be realized

4) If $V_3 = 0$, $V_1 = V_2 = V_{in}$ and $V_4 = 2V_{in}$ and $C_1 = C_2$, $1/R_0 = g_m$, then BRF can be realized

5) If $V_3 = 0$, $V_1 = V_2 = V_{in}$ and $V_4 = 4V_{in}$ and $C_1 = C_2$, $1/R_0 = g_m$, then APF can be realized

The expressions for natural frequency (ω_0) and quality factor (Q_0) are given by

$$\omega_0 = \sqrt{\frac{g_m}{R_0 C_1 C_2}} \tag{3}$$

$$Q_0 = \frac{\sqrt{g_m R_0 C_1 C_2}}{C_1 + g_m R_0 C_2} \tag{4}$$

3. Non-Ideal Analysis and Sensitivity Performance

Let R_z and C_z denote the parasitic resistance and parasitic capacitance of the Z-terminal. Taking the non-idealities into account, namely $V_W = \left(\beta^+ V_Z - \beta^- V_V\right)$ where $\beta^+ = 1 - \varepsilon_p \left(\varepsilon_p \ll 1\right)$ and $\beta^- = 1 - \varepsilon_n \left(\varepsilon_n \ll 1\right)$ denote the voltage tracking errors, respectively, then the output voltage in terms of inputs is given by:

$$V_o = \frac{V_1\left(\dfrac{\beta^+ g_m}{C_1'}s + \dfrac{\beta^+ g_m}{R_0 C_1' C_2}\right) + V_2\left(s^2 \beta^+ + \dfrac{C_1 \beta^+}{R_0 C_1' C_2}\right) - V_3\left(s^2 \beta^- + \dfrac{\beta^-}{R_z C_1' C_2}\right) - V_4\left(s\dfrac{\beta^-}{R_0 C_2} + \dfrac{\beta^-}{R_0 R_z C_1' C_2}\right)}{s^2 + s\left(\dfrac{1}{R_0 C_2} + \dfrac{1}{R_z C_1'} + \dfrac{\beta^+ g_m}{C_1'}\right) + \dfrac{1}{R_0 R_z C_1' C_2} + \dfrac{\beta^+ g_m}{R_0 C_1' C_2}} \tag{5}$$

where $C_1' = \left(C_1 + C_z\right)$

$$\omega_0 = \sqrt{\frac{1 + R_z g_m \beta^+}{R_0 R_z \left(C_1 + C_z\right) C_2}} \tag{6}$$

$$Q_0 = \frac{\sqrt{\left(1 + R_z g_m \beta^+\right) R_0 R_z \left(C_1 + C_z\right) C_2}}{R_z \left(C_1 + C_z\right) + R_0 C_2 \left(1 + R_z g_m \beta^+\right)} \tag{7}$$

Its active and passive sensitivities can be found as:

$$S_{\beta^+}^{\omega_0} = \frac{1}{2}\frac{R_z g_m \beta^+}{\left(1 + R_z g_m \beta^+\right)} = S_{g_m}^{\omega_0}, \quad S_{R_z}^{\omega_0} = -\frac{1}{2}\frac{1}{\left(1 + R_z g_m \beta^-\right)},$$

$$S_{C_z}^{\omega_0} = -\frac{1}{2}\frac{C_z}{\left(C_1 + C_z\right)}, \quad S_{R_0}^{\omega_0} = -\frac{1}{2} = S_{C_2}^{\omega_0}, \quad S_{C_1}^{\omega_0} = -\frac{1}{2}\frac{C_1}{\left(C_1 + C_z\right)}, \quad S_{\beta^+}^{Q_0} = \frac{1}{2}\frac{R_z g_m \beta^+}{\left(1 + R_z g_m \beta^+\right)} = S_{g_m}^{Q_0} \tag{8}$$

$$S_{C_2}^{Q_0} = \frac{1}{2}\left\{\frac{\left(C_1 + C_z\right) - C_2 R_0\left(\dfrac{1}{R_z} + \beta^+ g_m\right)}{\left(C_1 + C_z\right) + C_2 R_0\left(\dfrac{1}{R_z} + \beta^+ g_m\right)}\right\} = S_{R_0}^{Q_0} = S_{R_z}^{Q_0} = -S_{C_1}^{Q_0} = -S_{C_z}^{Q_0}$$

From Equation (8), it is clearly observed that all passive and active sensitivities are no more than one half in magnitudes for the proposed multi-input single-output voltage-mode universal biquad.

4. Simulation Results

To confirm feasibility of the proposed universal biquad filter of **Figure 2**, the circuit was simulated using CMOS VD-DIBA (as shown in **Figure 3**). For simulation the passive elements of **Figure 2** were selected as $C_1 = C_2 = 0.005$ nF and $R_0 = 102$ KΩ. The transconductance of VD-DIBA was controlled through the bias voltage V_{B1}. The SPICE simulated frequency response of various proposed filters biquad is shown in **Figure 4**. **Figure 5** shows the phase plot of APF. These SPICE simulated results, thus, confirm the validity of the proposed biquad filter.

The CMOS VD-DIBA is implemented using 0.35 μm MIETEC real transistor models which are listed in **Table 1**. Aspect ratios of transistors used in **Figure 3** are given in **Table 2**. A comparison with other previously known single active element/device-based MISO-type universal biquads has been shown in **Table 3**.

5. Conclusion

A new second-order voltage-mode MISO-type universal

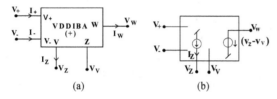

Figure 1. (a) Symbolic notation; (b) Equivalent model of VD-DIBA.

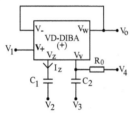

Figure 2. The proposed voltage-mode universal biquad.

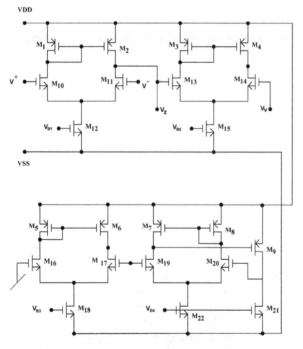

Figure 3. Proposed CMOS implementation of VD-DIBA, $V_{DD} = -V_{SS} = 2$ V, $V_{B1} = -1.45$ V, $V_{B2} = 0.52$, $V_{B3} = -0.62$ V and $V_{B4} = -0.3$ V.

Table 1. 0.35 μm MIETEC real transistor models parameters.

NMOS	PMOS
LEVEL = 3	LEVEL = 3
TOX = 7.9E−9	TOX = 7.9E−9
NSUB = 1E−17	NSUB = 1E−17
GAMMA = 0.5827871	GAMMA = 0.4083894
PHI = 0.7	PHI = 0.7
VTO = 0.5445549	VTO = −0.7140674
DELTA = 0	DELTA = 0
UO = 436.256147	UO = 212.2319801
ETA = 0	ETA = 9.999762E−4
THETA = 0.1749684	THETA = 0.2020774
KP = 2.055786E−4	KP = 6.733755E−5
VMAX = 8.309444E−4	VMAX = 1.181551E−5
KAPPA = 0.2574081	KAPPA = 1.5
RSH = 0.0559398	RSH = 30.0712458
NFS = 1E−12	NFS = 1E−12
TPG = 1	TPG = −1
XJ = 3E−7	XJ = 2E−7
LD = 3.162278E−11	LD = 5.000001E−13
WD = 7.046724E−8	WD = 1.249872E−7
CGDO = 2.82E−10	CGDO = 3.09E−10
CGSO = 2.82E−10	CGSO = 3.09E−10
CGBO = 1E−10	CGBO = 1E−10
CJ = 1E−3	CJ = 1.419508E−3
PB = 0.9758533	PB = 0.8152753
MJ = 0.3448504	MJ = 0.5
CJSW = 3.777852E−10	CJSW = 4.813504E−10
MJSW = 0.3508721	MJSW = 0.5

Table 2. Aspect ratios of transistors used in Figure 3.

Transistor	W/L (μm)
M$_1$-M$_6$	35/0.35
M$_7$-M$_9$	56/0.35
M$_{10}$-M$_{18}$	4.2/1.05
M$_{19}$-M$_{22}$	12.25/0.35

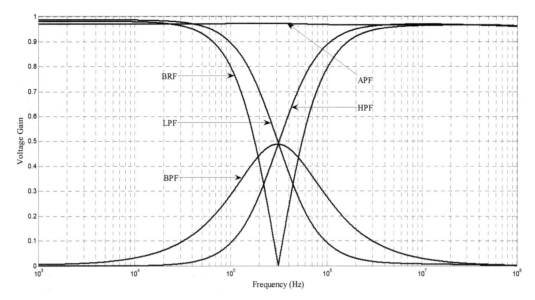

Figure 4. Frequency response.

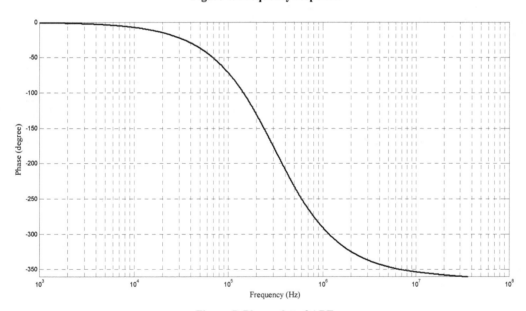

Figure 5. Phase plot of APF.

Table 3. Comparison with other previously known single active element/device-based MISO-type universal biquads.

Reference	No. of active components	No. of capacitors	No. of resistors	Requirement of matching condition(s)	Number of standard filter realized
[1]	1	2	2	Yes	Five
[2]	1	2	3	Yes	Five
[3]	1	2	2	Yes	Five
[4]	1	4	4	Yes	Five
[5]	1	2	4	Yes	Five
[6]	1	2	3	Yes	Five
[7]	1	2	2	Yes	Five
[8]	1	2	3	Yes	Five
Proposed	**1**	**2**	**1**	**YES**	**Five**

biquad filter has been presented. The proposed configuration employs single VD-DIBA with minimum number of passive elements, namely two capacitors and only one resistor. The presented biquad can yield second-order low pass, high pass, band pass, notch and all pass filter responses without altering the circuit topology. The passive and active sensitivities are low. Simulation results using 0.35 μm MIETEC technology have been presented which prove the feasibility of the proposed new biquad filter.

REFERENCES

[1]   J. Sirirat, W. Tangsrirat and W. Surakampontorn, "Voltage-Mode Electronically Tunable Universal Filter Employing Single CFTA," *International Conference on Electrical Engineering/Electronics Computer Telecommunications and Information Technology*, Chaing Mai, 19-21 May 2010, pp. 759-763.

[2]   D. Prasad, D. R. Bhaskar and A. K. Singh, "Multi-Function Biquad Using Current Differencing Transconductance Amplifier," *Analog Integrated Circuits and Signal Processing*, Vol. 61, No. 3, 2009, pp. 309-313.

[3]   J. W. Horng, "Voltage/Current-Mode Universal Biquadratic Filter Using Single CCII+," *Indian Jouranal of Pure & Applied Physics*, Vol. 48, No. 10, 2010, pp. 749-756.

[4]   A. U. Keskin, "Multi-Function Biquad Using Single CDBA," *Electrical Engineering*, Vol. 88, No. 5, 2006, pp. 353-356.

[5]   S. A. Bashir and N. A. Shah, "Voltage Mode Universal Filter Using Current Differencing Buffered Amplifier as an Active Device," *Circuits and Systems*, Vol. 3, No. 3, 2012, pp. 1-4.

[6]   N. Herencsar, J. Koton, K. Vrba and O. Cicekoglu, "Single UCC-N1B 0520 Device as a Modified CFOA and Its Application to Voltage- and Current-Mode Universal Filters," *Applied Electronics*, Pilsen, 9-10 September 2009, pp. 127-130.

[7]   N. A. Shah, M. F. Rather and S. Z. Iqbal, "A Novel Voltage-Mode Universal Filter Using A Single CFA," *Active and Passive Electronic Devices*, Vol. 1, 2005, pp. 183-188.

[8]   J. W. Horng, C. K. Chang and J. M. Chu, "Voltage-Mode Universal Biquadratic Filter Using Single Current-Feedback Amplifier," *IEICE Transactions on Fundamentals*, Vol. 85, No. 8, 2002, pp. 1970-1973.

[9]   D. Biolek, R. Senani, V. Biolkova and Z. Kolka, "Active Elements for Analog Signal Processing, Classification, Review and New Proposals," *Radioengineering*, Vol. 17, No. 4, 2008, pp. 15-32.

[10]   D. Biolek and V. Biolkova, "First-Order Voltage-Mode All-Pass Filter Employing One Active Element and One Grounded Capacitor," *Analog Integrated Circuits and Signal Processing*, Vol. 65, No. 1, 2009, pp. 123-129.

[11]   D. Prasad, D. R. Bhaskar and K. L. Pushkar, "Realization of New Electronically Controllable Grounded and Floating Simulated Inductance Circuits Using Voltage Differencing Differential Input Buffered Amplifiers," *Active and Passive Electronic Components*, Vol. 2011, 2011, Article ID: 101432.

## 13

Millimeter Wave Ring Oscillator Using Carbon Nano-Tube Field Effect Transistor in 150 GHz and Beyond

Davood Fathi[*], Baback Beig Mohammadi

School of Electrical and Computer Engineering, Tarbiat Modares University (TMU), Tehran, Iran

ABSTRACT

Carbon Nano-Tube Field Effect Transistors (CNTFETS) are the competitor of the conventional MOSFET technology due to their higher current drive capability, ballistic transport, lesser power delay product, higher thermal stability, and so on. Based on these promising properties of CNTFETs, a CNTFET-based millimeter wave ring oscillator operating around 150 GHz and beyond is introduced here in 32 nm technology node. To prevent overestimation, the CNT interconnects between transistors are also included in simulation, which are assumed to be a single layer of ballistic metallic CNTs in parallel. For the sake of simplicity in RF design, the oscillator is based on CNTFET-based inverters. The inverters with DC gain of 87.5 dB are achieved by proper design with the non-loaded delay around 0.6 ps, which is at least one order of magnitude better than the same 32 nm MOSFET-based inverters. The oscillator's average power consumption is as low as 40 µW with the fundamental harmonic amplitude of around −6.5 dB. These values are, based on our knowledge, for the first time reported in the literature in CNTFET-based oscillator designs. Also, on the average, the performance of the designed oscillator is 5 - 6 times better than MOSFET-based designs.

Keywords: CNTFET; CNT Interconnect; Millimeter Wave; Ring Oscillator

1. Introduction

Carbon nanotubes (CNTs) have shown promising electrical and mechanical performance over the conventional materials used in semiconductor industry. Electrically, CNTs are divided into two major groups: metallic and semiconducting, based on their chirality [1]. The metallic CNTs are used as interconnect in the novel integration processes [2,3] and the semiconducting ones are used in the novel semiconductor devices, beyond the conventional silicon/GaAs based technologies, like Carbon Nano-Tube Field Effect Transistors (CNTFETs) [4].

The large mean free path and hence, the ballistic transport characteristic of CNTs [5] with high current density capability, combining with extraordinary mobility [6] and very low shot noise [7], leads to CNTFETs with acceptable and outstanding electrical characteristics like high transit and maximum frequency [8] and inherent linearity [9].

Here, we present a high performance, low power CNTFET-based ring oscillator at 150 GHz and beyond with good THD. The amplitude of fundamental frequency of oscillation achieves around −6.5 dB which is to our knowledge 4 - 5 times better than the same MOSFET-based ring oscillators. The CNTFET used in this paper is a MOSFET-like CNTFET with gate length of 32 nm. In order to prevent overestimation of the ring oscillator performance, the CNT interconnects between CNTFETS are modeled and included in simulation, which have been arranged in a single layer of ballistic metallic CNTs.

This paper is organized as follow. Section II includes explanations on the CNTFET and its model used in our simulations. In Section III we discuss the modeling of metallic CNTs as interconnects. CNT-based inverter design and advantages over MOSFET-based inverters and its corresponding simulation results are represented in Section IV. Section V includes CNTFET-based ring oscillator design and simulation results. Finally, Section VI concludes this paper.

2. CNTFET and Its Modeling

There are several CNTFET models reported in literature [10-13]. The model used here is based on the [12,13].

[*]Corresponding author.

This model includes all the necessary parameters needed for simulating CMOS-like CNTFETs (*n*-type and *p*-type) up to the minimum gate length of 10 nm for both large signal and small signal simulations. These parameters are quantum confinement effects on both circumferential and axial directions, acoustic, elastic and optical scattering in the channel region, screening effects of CNTs in parallel under the gate, resistive source and drain, Schottky barrier effects and the parasitic gate capacitances [12,13].

As mentioned before, the CNTFET used here is CMOS-like CNTFET. This is due to superior device parameters and fabrication feasibility of MOSFET-like CNTFETs compared with the Schotkey barrier controlled FETs [14] which makes CMOS-like CNTFETS suitable for our purpose of operating at 150 GHz and beyond.

Figure 1 shows the CMOS-like CNTFET 3D Structure. The CNTs under the gate are intrinsic and are used in such a condition that they are semiconducting. According to the analysis reported in [1], CNTs with the chirality vector (*n*, *m*) are semiconducting when $n - m \neq 3k$ where *k* is an integer. For instance, a CNT with the chirality vector (19, 0) will behave as a semiconductor.

All the CNTs simulated in this CNTFET model are assumed to be semiconducting. Of course, this is an optimistic assumption, there are so many methods developed to purify the semiconducting CNTs from metallic types. In [1], there is a method to fabricate arrays of CNTFETs without the need to separate semiconducting CNTs from metallic types, called "constructive destruction", which is beyond our scope. The existence of metallic CNT under the gate would yield in the performance degradation through the reduction of transconductance of transistor and the increase of idle power consumption.

Despite the fact that the back-gated structure for CNTFETs is preferred to top-gate one due to simplicity in device production; we have used the top-gated topology. This is because the top-gated topology will yield higher control of gate on the channel region which enhances the transistor ability to perform better than the back-gated topology at high frequencies. Also, the structure of the circuit does not let us to utilize the back-gated topology, because the substrate that performs as the back gate is shared among all the transistors in our design.

The source and drain extensions are assumed to be made with the help of doped CNTs in parallel. This would help the device to enhance the performance of the transistor through the reduction of parasitic capacitances significantly [15]. Of course, an attention must be made that according to the lessening of mean free path of doped CNTs versus intrinsic CNTs, the length of the extended regions must be short enough in order to benefit from ballistic transport phenomena. So, there is a trade-off between parasitic capacitance reduction and ballistic transport at the extended highly doped CNT regions.

The work function of conventional CNTs with the radius of 1 - 2 nm would be around 4.5 eV which is in a good agreement with palladium [13]. So, the palladium is used as the source and drain metal contacts. Also HfO$_2$ with 4 nm thickness and relative permittivity of 16 has been used as the high-*k* gate insulator in our design.

The diameter of a CNT can be calculated from

$$d = \frac{a\sqrt{n^2 + nm + m^2}}{\pi} \qquad (1)$$

where *n* and *m* are the indices of chirality vector (*n*, *m*) and *a* is the lattice constant of CNT which is around 2.46 Å. Relation (1) suggests that for a CNT with chirality vector of (19, 0) a radius of 1.5 nm must be assumed. This radius is less than the 4 nm thickness of the gate dielectric. So, there is no need to further increasing the gate insulator thickness.

The CNTs under the gate would have screening effect on each other which would degrade the CNTFET performance with increasing the number of CNTs under the gate despite the fact that increasing the number of CNTs under the gate, at first glance, must theoretically increase the transconductance of the transistor. This phenomenon will introduce an important tradeoff between the number of the CNTs under the gate and maximum CNTFET achievable performance. As a result, a distance of 4 nm is assumed between each CNT tube pairs. Further increasing of this distance will lead to undesirable increasing of the gate width which adds up more parasitic capacitances to the circuit.

We have used Stanford University CNFET HSPICE model v. 2.2.1 in simulating CNTFETs.

3. CNT Interconnect Modeling

Due to the high frequency simulation, it is necessary to include the interconnect modeling in the design. Because of the good matching between palladium source/drain contacts' work-function and the metallic CNTs' and according to high durability of CNTs, we choose to use CNTs as interconnect material between our logic gates described in the next section.

According to [2], due to longer mean free path of single walled carbon nanotubes versus multi walled ones, it

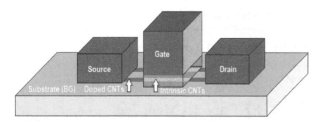

Figure 1. The three dimensional CMOS-like CNTFET structure.

is desirable to use SWCNTs as the interconnect material. For decreasing the resistance of the SWCNT, we may use single layer paralleled CNTs. **Figure 2** shows the model for parallel CNT interconnects used in our design.

The resistance of a SWCNT is divided into two parts: Quantum resistance (R_Q) and Scattering resistance (R_S) [2]. The Quantum and scattering resistances can be calculated using [16]

$$R_Q = \left(\frac{h}{4e^2}\right); \quad l < \lambda, \tag{2}$$

$$R_S = \left(\frac{h}{4e^2}\right)\left(\frac{l}{\lambda} - 1\right); \quad l > \lambda \tag{3}$$

where, λ is the mean free path, l is the length of CNT, h is the Plank's constant, and e is the electron charge.

When the length of CNT is shorter than the mean free path, the resistance is reduced to $h/4e$ which is the value of quantum resistance and remains constant at this value. This condition is maintained in our design. For longer lengths, the electron scattering increases the resistance with a linear increasing behavior.

Though the value of quantum resistance is high in ballistic CNTs; the capacitance of the CNT is significantly small, making the delay of the ballistic CNT small enough for our purpose.

The capacitance also is divided into 2 parts: The electro static capacitance (C_E) and quantum capacitance (C_Q). The electro static capacitance between a CNT with diameter of d and the ground plane at the distance of h from the center of CNT can be calculated using (4). For a typical value of h/d, this capacitance can be approximated, with the typical value of 50 aF/μm, as [3]

$$C_E = \frac{2\pi\varepsilon}{\cosh^{-1}\left(\frac{2h}{d}\right)} \approx \frac{2\pi\varepsilon}{\ln\left(\frac{h}{d}\right)}. \tag{4}$$

The quantum capacitance is in series with the electrostatic capacitance and can be calculated using [3]

$$C_Q = \frac{e^2}{\hbar\pi v_F}. \tag{5}$$

The value of this capacitance is around 100 aF/μm,

with e as the electron charge, $\hbar$ as the Plank's constant and v_F as the Fermi velocity [3]. Also, a coupling capacitance exists between each pair of CNT interconnects, which is named C_C in **Figure 2**. The coupling capacitance between two CNTs with diameters of d at the space of D can be calculated using [3]

$$C_C = \frac{\pi\varepsilon l}{\ln\left(\frac{D}{d} + \sqrt{\left(\frac{D}{d}\right)^2 + 1}\right)}. \tag{6}$$

According to the previous discussion, we have assumed 4 nm space between each pair of CNT interconnects, in order to prevent the screening effect and also to decrease the coupling capacitances significantly. The total inductance of a CNT interconnect is also divided into two parts: The kinetic inductance (L_K) and the magnetic inductance (L_M). The kinetic inductance of a CNT can be obtained using [3]

$$L_K = \frac{\hbar\pi}{e^2 v_F}. \tag{7}$$

The value of this inductance has been assumed to be 16 nH/μm in our design. In addition to the kinetic inductance, there is a magnetic inductance in the structure of a CNT interconnect model. This inductance is small in comparison with the kinetic inductance and can be approximated to have a value of about 1 nH [3]. The exact value of the magnetic inductance can be obtained using [16]

$$L_M = \frac{\mu}{2\pi}\cosh^{-1}\left(\frac{2h}{D}\right) \tag{8}$$

where μ is the carrier mobility and the other parameters in (8) are identical to those defined before. It should be noted here that, due to CNT's band structure and electron's two different spins, there are 4 conductive channels for each CNT. As a result, the effective quantum capacitance of a single CNT is four times the quantum capacitance introduced in (5). On the other hand, the effective kinetic inductance would be one quarter of the kinetic inductance in (7). So, we used $C_{Q,\,eff}$ and $L_{K,\,eff}$ in our simulations

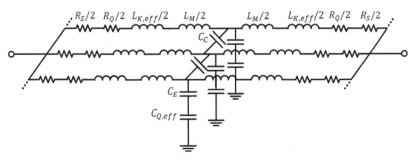

Figure 2. Parallel CNTFET interconnect model.

$$C_{Q,eff} = 4C_Q, \qquad (9)$$

$$L_{K,eff} = \frac{L_K}{4}. \qquad (10)$$

4. CNTFET-Based Inverter Design

The core of the high frequency ring oscillator is based on inverters. The higher speed inverter will lead to higher frequency ring oscillator.

The high to low and low to high delays in inverters play an important role in frequency determination of an inverter based ring oscillator. Here, the total delay is a function of several parameters like the time constant of each inverter, supply voltage and the delay introduced by interconnects and connections to other gates in a real implementation.

The delay of a CNTFET based inverter is a function of CNTFET diameter under the gate. It is shown in [13] that the FO1 delay of CNTFET based inverter would be at its minimum constant value when the diameter of the CNT is around 1.4 and beyond. So, we have chosen the diameter of CNTs to be about 1.5 nm which is obtainable by a (19, 0) CNT. It must be mentioned here that for CNTs with less than 1.3 nm diameter, the higher source/drain resistance with smaller current drive capability and hence, lower speed would be resulted [13].

There is a difference between MOSFET-based and CNTFET-based inverter design. In CMOS, there is a bulk connection for each NMOS and PMOS transistor that must be connected to proper voltages to reversely bias the p-n junctions. But here, due to physically different operational concept of CNTFETS, we have no such a connection. The back gate of the nCNTFET and pCNTFET are both the substrate and are connected to ground node in our design.

With supply voltage equal to 0.9 volts in order to prevent dielectric punch through and with proper design, the high to low and low to high delays of our CNTFET-based inverters are measured to be around 0.3 ps. The DC gain of the CNTFET-based inverter is about 87.5 dB with 5 CNTs under the gate; a value that is rarely achievable with the CMOS technology.

Figure 3 represents the voltage transfer function of a 32 nm CNTFET-based inverter and MOSFET-based inverter with different supply voltages. The significant improvement of the DC gain of the CNTFET-based inverter over MOSFET-based one is evident.

The power delay product and maximum leakage power of the CNT-based and MOSFET-based inverters are plotted versus different supply voltages and temperatures in **Figures 4** and **5** respectively.

As seen from **Figure 4**, CNTFET-based inverter has better performance by means of maximum leakage power

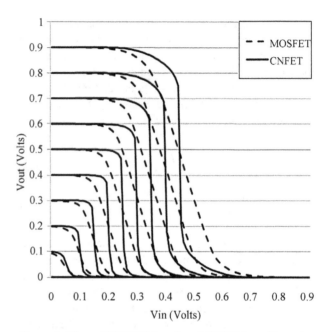

Figure 3. 32 nm CNTFET-based and CMOS based inverters' voltage trasfer function for different supply voltages [17].

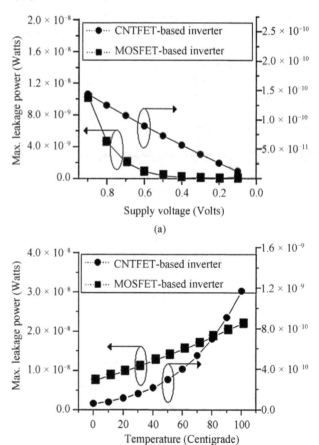

Figure 4. The maximum leakage power of CNTFET-based and MOSFET-based inverters versus (a) supply voltage and (b) temperature changes [17].

in both different supply voltages and different temperatures. On average, the overall CNTFET-based inverter's leakage power is 40 times lesser than the MOSFET-based inverter's.

Figure 5 illustrates the power delay product of CNTFET-based and MOSFET-based inverters with different supply voltages and in different temperatures. Again, the CNTFET-based inverter wins against MOSFET-based inverter.

Despite the fact that leakage power of CNTFET-based inverter increases exponentially with temperature, the overall leakage power on CNTFET-based inverter is about 25 times lesser than MOSFET-based inverter. Also, due to the strong stability of CNTs' electrical characteristics against thermal variations [17], the power delay product of CNTFET-based inverter does not change sensibly in **Figure 5(b)**.

It must be mentioned here that an overall improvement factor of at least 5 - 6 is achievable utilizing CNTFETs instead of MOSFETs by means of delay, power consumption and thermal stability [13,17].

The process variation is also important in designing and integrating reproducible electronic products. According to [17] the effective process variations in CNTFETs are different from those important in MOSFETs. The MOSFETs are 60 (26) times more sensitive to length (width) variation in gate dimensions than the CNTFETs. This is due to the fact that the current of CNTFETs is not directly related to the width and length of the channel under the gate and mostly is controlled through the number of CNTs under the gate and their chirality. Of course, this means that the purity control of CNTs under the gate is much important than dimension control in CNTFETs. It can be found that a 10% change in CNT diameter would yield a 17% change in CNTFETs current in 32 nm technology node with 0.9 V supply voltage.

5. CNTFET-Based Ring Oscillator Design

For the sake of simplicity in RF design, we have chosen the simplest inverter based ring oscillator. The ring oscillator designed here is based on the inverter-based structure including three inverters in series making a closed loop. The minimum number of three inverters is chosen to achieve the highest frequency of oscillation. The frequency of the oscillation may be predicted by

$$F = \frac{1}{2\pi N \left(\tau_{PHL} + \tau_{PLH} \right)} \quad (11)$$

where N is the number of inverter stages in ring, τ_{PHL} is the high to low delay and τ_{PLH} is the low to high delay of each inverters having all the parasitic loads at input and output nodes.

The interconnect structure between the three inverters

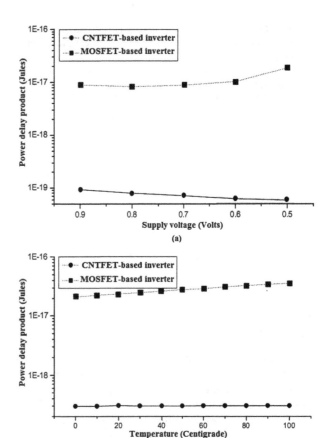

Figure 5. The power delay product of CNTFET-based and MOSFET-based inverters versus (a) supply voltage and (b) temperature changes [17].

play an important role in defining the total delay of each state and hence, the maximum achievable oscillating frequency. The interconnect modeling has been discussed previously in Section III. Our suggestion is to connect the inverters as packed as possible by stretching the palladium used in the gate while closing the loop using the CNT interconnect structure, to benefit from the fixed and noiseless conductance of metallic CNTs discussed before.

As mentioned before, there are tradeoffs between different parameters like the number of metallic CNTs in a paralleled single layer set and the parasitic capacitors, the number of CNTs under the gate and CNTFET performance and delay through screening effects and gate width which will introduce more capacitors and so on. So, we have simulated different conditions to achieve the best performance of the ring oscillator by means of higher frequency and higher fundamental harmonic amplitude with lower total harmonic distortion. All the simulations are done in HSPICE simulator environment.

Table 1 represents the simulation results for different number of metallic CNTs in the single layer interconnect structure in the closing loop of ring oscillator, as shown

Table 1. Oscillation frequency, fundamental harmonic amplitude, total harmonic distortion, average power consumption and FOM for different number of CNTs in parallel as interconnect (gate length = 32 nanometers and number of CNTs under the gate = 5).

Number of CNTs in Parallel as Interconnect	Oscillation Frequency (GHz)	Fundamental Harmonic Amplitude (dB)	THD (%)	Average Power Consumption (μW)	FOM
1	95.71	−5.98	11.49	25.46	0.164
2	125.93	−6.25	9.93	35.37	0.174
3	141.04	−5.87	14.6	40.57	0.120
4	156.15	−7.54	5.11	42.7	0.299
5	161.19	−5.95	14.98	43.48	0.125
6	166.23	−7	4.25	43.59	0.400
7	166.23	−7.33	3.47	43.73	0.471
8	171.27	−7.34	4.95	43.92	0.338
9	171.27	−6.13	13.5	44.07	0.142
10	171.27	−5.89	16.81	44.32	0.116

in **Figure 6**. Increasing the number of CNTs will increase the oscillation frequency, due to the increase of driving capability of inv. #3 and the reduction of interconnect resistance. But eventually, after achieving the required driving capability, increasing the number of CNTs will introduce more parasitic capacitances to the circuit and consequently, the oscillator performance will be degraded. As **Figure 7** shows, based on **Table 1**, the optimal condition for 32 nm technology node is achieved when 7 metallic CNTs are in parallel as interconnect. The similar result will be achieved with 5 semiconducting CNTs under the gate.

The figure of merit (FOM) in **Table 1** is calculated using

$$FOM = \frac{FHM \cdot OF}{THD \cdot APC} \quad (12)$$

where FHM is the fundamental harmonic amplitude, OF is the oscillation frequency, THD is the total harmonic distortion, and APC is the average power consumption.

As **Table 2** shows, the oscillation frequency decreases as the number of CNTs under the gate increases, due to the increase of 3 factors: the parasitic capacitances, the length of interconnect, and the screening effects which are not desired in our design.

There are very few CNTFET-based ring oscillators reported in the literature. The simulation results obtained here are far beyond the results reported previously by the others in the literature. In [18], a three stage ring oscillator has been implemented, which does not benefit from the ballistic transport. Due to very large sizes of inverters, the oscillation frequency is about 220 MHz. Also, more novel oscillators reported in [19,20], have achieved the oscillation frequencies of around 80 MHz and 500 MHz respectively.

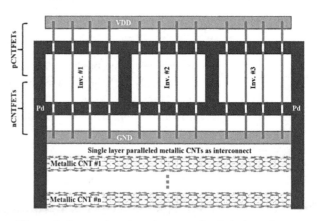

Figure 6. Connecting three inverters in chain in order to benefit from the ballistic transport phenomena in interconnect.

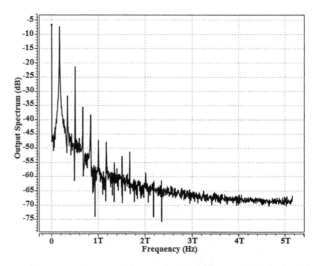

Figure 7. The output spectrum for 32 nm gate length CNTFET-based oscillator, with 5 CNTs under the gate and 7 metallic CNTs in parallel as interconnect.

Table 2. Oscillation frequency, fundamental harmonic amplitude, total harmonic distortion, average power consumption and FOM for different number of CNTs under the gate and different gate lengths (for 7 CNTs in parallel as interconnect).

Gate Length (nanometer)	Number of CNTs under the Gate	Oscillation Frequency (GHz)	Fundamental Harmonic Amplitude (dB)	THD (%)	Average Power Consumption (μW)	FOM
32	1	181.34	−7.20	6.55	10.04	1.202
32	2	186.38	−8.01	4.57	20.36	0.790
32	3	186.38	−6.46	11.39	28.02	0.279
32	4	176.30	−6.29	11.97	35.65	0.199
32	5	166.22	−7.34	3.46	43.73	0.471
32	6	161.19	−7.55	4.10	52.39	0.314
32	7	151.11	−5.59	19.5	59.83	0.067
32	8	141.04	−5.49	20.13	65.51	0.056
25	5	186.37	−6.03	12.96	42.28	0.170
25	6	176.28	−7.67	5.34	50.76	0.268
13	5	161.18	−8.80	7.62	25.14	0.305
13	6	151.10	−8.20	4.98	28.66	0.412

6. Conclusion

In this paper, we have designed and simulated a high performance millimeter wave ring oscillator, based on CNTFET-based inverters. The inverter and ring oscillator designed here have shown promising features versus MOSFET-based ones. The low-power consumption around 40 μ watts, the oscillation frequency of 150 GHz and beyond, the fundamental harmonic amplitude of about −6.5 dB with a good THD, above one order of magnitude improvement in the leakage power and also in the power delay product, and good thermal stability have been obtained. Also, different tradeoffs between several design parameters have been discussed in details. It should be noted that, the scope of this paper is to introduce the novel CNTFET technology and its significant benefits over the conventional MOSFET technology, in order to encourage electrical engineers to have a glance at this new promising technology.

REFERENCES

[1]   P. Avouris, "Carbon Nanotube Electronics," *Elsevier Chemical Physics*, Vol. 281, 2002, pp. 429-445.

[2]   D. Fathi and B. Forouzandeh, "A Novel Approach for Stability Analysis in Carbon Nanotube Interconnects," *IEEE Electron Device Letters*, Vol. 30, No. 5, 2009, pp. 475-477.

[3]   P. J. Bruke, "AC Performance of Nanoelectronics: Towards a Ballistic THz Nanotube Transistor," *Elsevier Solid-State Electronics*, Vol. 48, 2004, pp. 1981-1986.

[4]   L. Nougaret, *et al.*, "80 GHz Field-Effect Transistors Produced Using High Purity Semiconducting Single-Walled Carbon Nanotubes," *Applied Physics Letters*, Vol. 94, No. 24, 2009, Article ID: 243505.

[5]   A. Javey, *et al.*, "Self-Aligned Ballistic Molecular Transistors and Electrically Parallel Nanotube Arrays," *Nano Letters*, Vol. 4, No. 7, 2004, pp. 1319-1322.

[6]   T. Durkop, "Extraordinary Mobility in Semiconducting Carbon Nanotubes," *Nano Letters*, Vol. 4, No, 1, 2003, pp. 35-39.

[7]   P. E. Roche, *et al.*, "Very Low Shot Noise in Carbon Nanotubes," *The European Physics Journal B*, Vol. 28, No. 2, 2002, pp. 217-22.

[8]   L. C. Castro, *et al.*, "Extrapolated fmax for Carbon Nanotube Field-Effect Transistors," *IOP Nanotechnology*, Vol. 17, No. 1, 2005, pp. 300-304.

[9]   J. E. Baumgardner, *et al.*, "Inherent Linearity in Carbon Nanotube Filed-Effect Transistors," *Applied Physics Letters*, Vol. 91, 2007.

[10] S. Fregonese, *et al.*, "Computationally Efficient Physics-Based Compact CNTFET Model for Circuit Design," *IEEE Transactions on Electron Devices*, Vol. 55, No. 6, 2008, pp. 1317-1327.

[11] X. Yang, *et al.*, "Modeling and Performance Investigation of the Double-Gate Carbon-Gate Nanotube Transistor," *IEEE Electron Devices Letters*, Vol. 32, No. 3, 2011, pp. 231-233.

[12] J. Deng, *et al.*, "A Compact SPICE Model for Carbon-Nanotube Field-Effect Transistors Including Nonidealities and Its Application-Part I: Model of the Intrinsic Channel Region," *IEEE Transactions on Electron Devices*, Vol. 54, No. 12, 2007, pp. 3186-3194.

[13] J. Deng, *et al.*, "A Compact SPICE Model for Carbon-Nanotube Field-Effect Transistors Including Nonidealities and Its Application-Part II: Full Device Model and Cir-

cuit Performance Benchmarking," *IEEE Transactions on Electron Devices*, Vol. 54, No. 12, 2007, pp. 3195-3205.

[14] J. Chen, *et al.*, "Self-Aligned Carbon Nanotube Transistors with Charge Transfer Doping," *Applied Physics Letters*, Vol. 86, 2005.

[15] J. Guo, *et al.*, "Assessment of High-Frequency Performance Potential of Carbon Nanotube Transistors," *IEEE Transactions on Nanotechnology*, Vol. 4, No. 6, 2005, pp. 715-721.

[16] A. Raychowdhury, *et al.*, "A Circuit Model for Carbon Nanotube Interconnects: Comparative Study with Cu Interconnects for Scaled Technologies," *IEEE/ACM International Conference on Computer Aided Design*, January

2005, pp. 237-240.

[17] G. Cho, *et al.*, "Assessment of CNTFET Based Circuit Performance and Robustness to PVT Variations," *IEEE International Midwest Symposium on Circuits and Systems*, Cancun, 2-5 August 2009, pp. 1106-1109.

[18] A. Javey, *et al.*, "Carbon Nanotube Transistors Arrays for Multistage Complementary Logic and Ring Oscillator," *Nano Letters*, Vol. 2, No. 9, 2002, pp. 929-932.

[19] Z. Chen, *et al.*, "High Performance Carbon Nanotube Ring Oscillator," *Device Research Conference*, February 2007, pp. 171-172.

[20] A. A. Pesetski, *et al.*, "A 500 MHz Carbon Nanotube Transistor Oscillator," *Applied Physics Letters*, Vol. 93, No. 24, 2008, Article ID: 243301.

## 14

System Verification of Hardware Optimization Based on Edge Detection

Xinwei Niu, Jeffrey Fan

Department of Electrical and Computer Engineering, Florida International University, Miami, USA

ABSTRACT

Nowadays, digital camera based remote controllers are widely used in people's daily lives. It is known that the edge detection process plays an essential role in remote controlled applications. In this paper, a system verification platform of hardware optimization based on the edge detection is proposed. The Field-Programmable Gate Array (FPGA) validation is an important step in the Integrated Circuit (IC) design workflow. The Sobel edge detection algorithm is chosen and optimized through the FPGA verification platform. Hardware optimization techniques are used to create a high performance, low cost design. The Sobel edge detection operator is designed and mounted through the system Advanced High-performance Bus (AHB). Different FPGA boards are used for evaluation purposes. It is proved that with the proposed hardware optimization method, the hardware design of the Sobel edge detection operator can save 6% of on-chip resources for the Sobel core calculation and 42% for the whole frame calculation.

Keywords: IC; AHB; FPGA; Hardware Optimization; Sobel Edge Detection

1. Introduction

The technology evolves rapidly in these years. Currently, people enjoy many high-tech products such as gesture based remote controller by using digital cameras to extract valuable information. It is known that the edge detection plays an important role in the remote control process [1]. The edge detection is used to process the input data and extracts the key feature of the data for further steps. Several edge detection algorithms can be used to identify the edge of one image frame. In this paper, the Sobel edge detection is designed and verified by using the verification platform.

Integrated Circuit (IC) chip manufacture involves a variety of processes. The basic rules are the same even though there may be different kinds of design flows. In the IC design flow, Field-Programmable Gate Array (FPGA) verification is an important step. Benefited from the reconfigurabilities of the FPGA, designers can verify their design at the early stage of the IC design flow. Thus, design defects can be found and eliminated to save design cycles and costs.

The edge detection is the most commonly used approach to detect discontinuities in gray level by far. It is widely used to extract the texture of the item in one picture. There are many edge detection operators based on the gradient detection. In this research, the Sobel operator for the edge detection and a verification platform is used to test the proposed hardware design.

There are several previous researches of the edge detection design using the Sobel operator. S. Halder *et al.* designed a Sobel operator based on the optimized algorithm in [2]. However, their design used too many dividers and multipliers. Thus, too many on-chip resources are used without significant performance improvement. Besides, they did not have a complete solution for the Sobel edge detection. T. A. Abbasi *et al.* proposed an FPGA-based architecture for the Sobel edge detection operator [3]. However, they used two random-access memory (RAM) to store the data, one for the original data, and the other for the result data. Thus, the resource consumptions are too high. C. Pradabpet *et al.* proposed that they could operate the Sobel operation efficiently [4]. However, their design can only run at a very low frequency, so the efficiency is relatively low. Moreover, they still need to use two storage spaces to save the data. Another design based on Sobel operator was described in [5], the author designed a massive pipeline for algorithm calculations. This design can increase the performance significantly. However, the System-on-a-Chip (SoC) may not able to allocate enough on-chip resources for this design. Thus, the design was not a balanced one if implemented into

SoCs. V. Sanduja and R. Patial designed a complete edge detection system based on the Sobel operator, and their design had an accurate result for each pixel. However, the costs of the resources are still much higher by using two separate memory parts to store the data [6].

The rest of the paper is organized as follows. In Section 2, an overview of the IC design flow and the Sobel edge detection is presented. Section 3 explains the architecture of our hardware verification platform. In Section 4, the optimized hardware of the Sobel edge detection operator is evaluated, and then the verification platform is demonstrated. Finally, conclusions and future works are drawn in Section 5.

2. Background

Designers put different efforts in the process of making a successful IC. As shown in **Figure 1**, the most important stage in the design flow is the information acquisition stage. Designers do some researches on the aimed design including specifications, algorithms and even the architecture. With a clear understanding of the whole design, designers can go ahead for the next stage.

In the architectural design stage, designers must be familiar with all the related knowledge of the design. The selected algorithm is directly related to the structure, this is why we need to first verify and generate the most suitable algorithm form. The best architecture is the one with the fastest speed, the lowest power consumption and the minimum chip size.

Hardware designers use the hardware description language to write the source code. After that, designers must write the test bench for their design. Test bench provides simulation models for designs.

Then it goes to the Register Transfer Level (RTL) simulation, which is also called behavioral simulation. It is based on the RTL function but not timing consideration. If a designer uses an FPGA to develop the circuit, the design code can be synthesized into the FPGA netlist. The FPGA verification with the real test environment can find most of the problems.

The design code is viewed as a good one once it passes the FPGA verification stage. Then, the code is synthesized into a netlist for the chip layout. After that, designers do simulation again, which is called pre-simulation. On the pre-simulation stage, timing issues are added to the simulation, so the simulation is closer to the performance of the real chip. The timing is only added to the cells and registers, but not wires. If the pre-simulation results are not as expected, the source code should be re-designed.

After the chip layout process, another netlist is generated according to the real wires of the chip. With the consideration of the wire delay, the design goes to the post-simulation stage. If post-simulation results meet the design requirements, the design is ready for the chip fabrication.

The manufactured chip is packaged and mounted in the system to check whether it is good or not. The test pattern should have higher coverage for all the possibilities. The higher the coverage, the better of the yield of the chip. The tester uses the probe card to check the chip on the wafer. When the chip passes the chip probe stage, the wafer can be cut down for packaging. After packaging, the IC chips are tested again to make sure the chips are good. The last step in the entire workflow is to test the IC mounted on the real system.

The edge detection is the most widely used method to detect discontinuities in one image by far. An edge is a

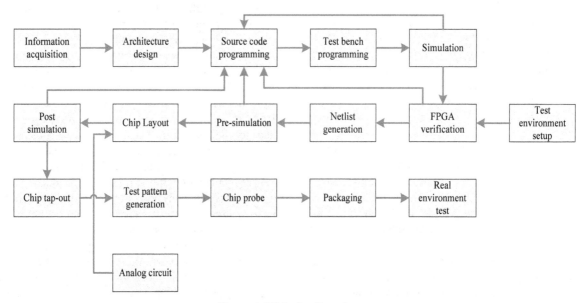

Figure 1. IC design flow chart.

number of pixels which lie on the boundary between two regions. Edges are located in the areas with strong intensity contrasts. There are many edge detection operators based on the gradient detection [1]. The Sobel operator is chosen to be used for the edge detection in this paper.

The Sobel operator is a 3 × 3 mask used to compute the gradient for the corresponding region. **Figure 2** shows pixels of the aimed image region, the Sobel operator multiplies with the image pixels to find out the gradient at the point labelled p5.

Sobel operators are as follows:

$$G_x = \begin{bmatrix} -1 & 0 & 1 \\ -2 & 0 & 2 \\ -1 & 0 & 1 \end{bmatrix} \times A \qquad (1)$$

$$G_y = \begin{bmatrix} -1 & -2 & -1 \\ 0 & 0 & 0 \\ 1 & 2 & 1 \end{bmatrix} \times A \qquad (2)$$

As shown in the Equations (1) and (2), A is the grayscale of the original images. The G_x is the row gradient and the G_y is the column gradient. An approach used frequently is to approximate the magnitude of the Sobel gradient by absolute values:

$$\nabla f \approx |G_x| + |G_y| \qquad (3)$$

After generating the value of the Equation (3), the result is compared with a threshold, which sets the final value to either black or white. The result is sent back to the image point labelled p5 for one round calculation.

3. System Architecture

In this research, the Sobel operator is used to detect the edge of a 256 × 256 grayscale image. The Sobel operation is separated into two parts, one part is a Sobel core, the other part is the Sobel full scan. The Sobel core is a single calculation of the matrix, and the Sobel full scan is used to scan the full image frame. The Sobel operator design is optimized for the hardware implementation from the following aspects:

p1	p2	p3
p4	p5	p6
p7	p8	p9

Figure 2. Image region for edge detection.

- The Sobel core needs higher frequency to finish the calculation in a pipeline design. In order to make the design run efficiently, the operation defines that one pixel is loaded to the Sobel core every clock cycle. After loading the input data, the Sobel operation can generate the output data in the following cycle. The Sobel core of this design needs two clock cycles to generate the result, so Sobel core part is connected to a clock, whose frequency is two times as the clock connected to Sobel full scan. Thus, the data can flow continuously without the latency.
- The other optimization is to put the generated data to the image pixel labelled p1 instead of p5 as shown in **Figure 3**. The design can have a higher efficiency by using this way. After the calculation of the single matrix. The Sobel mask will move to the next window, it will go through all the rows and columns in the image frame. If the generated results are sent back to p5, the Sobel mask must store the original pixel before the results are sent back. If designers want to avoid the influence of the results, they must use other storage devices to hold the results, which is a costly method. However, we store the results directly in the pixel labelled p1. The pixel labelled p1 will not be used in the future, so it has no influence for the future calculation even if the data is modified. Moreover, the designer does not need additional storage devices to keep results.

The designed hardware must be tested under the test environment, which is a system verification platform. The platform can be used to test the functionality of the design and it includes the following components:
- Test module design. The Design Under Test (DUT) module is connected to the platform as a slave.
- Verification module design. Functional simulation of the CPU is used to test the designed hardware. The memory controller and some external interface modules are designed and verified.
- Advanced Microcontroller Bus Architecture (AMBA) based protocol design. Advanced High-performance Bus (AHB) from the AMBA bus protocol is used for data transmission [7].
- Functional registers design. The hardware provides configuration registers for the software designer to design the corresponding software.

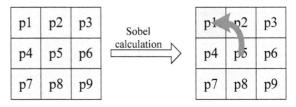

Figure 3. Optimized Sobel scheme.

Figure 4 is the system verification platform. The verification platform includes the CPU, the memory controller, the DUT, and other interfaces. The platform uses AHB as the communication bus. Each DUT must have the slave interface and the master interface for communication through the AHB bus. As the central processing unit of the system, the CPU has only the master interface to send command. As the data storage devices, memories are viewed as slaves. Thus, they only have the slave interfaces.

The master interface is used to send commands to the slave interfaces and receive the data or responses from the slave interfaces. In the system design, the CPU will initial the command to the DUT, which is the Sobel edge detection module in this project, through the DUT's slave interface. The command is used to configure the functional registers of the designed hardware intellectual property (IP). Once the designed hardware gets the command from the CPU, it extracts the information and takes further actions. The information includes the start and the stop of the DUT, the initial address of the memory or other peripherals, where the DUT can fetch data from, etc. Then, the DUT can fetch the data from memory or other peripherals through its master interface to the slave interface of the memory controller. After finishing processing, the DUT can send the results back to the memory or other peripherals if necessary.

4. Experimental Results

The Sobel edge detection design is divided into two parts: one is the single matrix calculation; the other is the full frame calculation. Because the single calculation needs time to process the data, the clock frequency of the internal single calculation is twice as the full frame calculation to make the whole data run as the pipeline. In the real case, each gate has its own timing constraint. One can only use the maximum of around six adders or subtractors together to generate the output data through combinational logics. Thus, the single matrix calculation

is separated into two RTL blocks. This can not only have the least register usage but the designed circuit can also run at a relatively higher frequency.

Compared to the single Sobel operator design in [2], they designed a single Sobel operator and mapped the design on Xilinx Spartan 3 XC3S50-5PQ208 board [8]. Their design can reach up to 190 MHz frequency. In contrast, our design can only reach up to 156 MHz on the same board. However, as for the resource costs, our design only occupies 10% of on-chip slices, while their design cost up to 16% of on-chip slices. In the System-on-a-Chip (SoC), on-chip resource costs are key factors which have great impacts on the design. The less of the resource costs, the lower of the power consumption. If a 256×256 frame needs to be processed, our design can ideally consume 0.41 ms to finish, while their design can ideally consume 0.34 ms to finish. This is still an acceptable time latency in the remote control system, especially consider the saved on-chip resources.

In another design from V. Sanduja and R. Patial [6], a 20×40 picture was processed by the Sobel edge detection design. Their design used Xilinx Virtex 4 FPGA board. The device was XC4VLX200, and the package was FF1513. Even they got the accurate result for each pixel, the design cost too much on-chip resource. **Table 1** shows the device utilization comparison. It is shown that our design uses much less resources than their design. One advantage of our design is using a single RAM to store the data, after pixels are processed by the single matrix calculation. The processed result is sent back to the position labelled p1 instead of p5. This optimization method can save a large amount of storage space and the processed picture is usable for further steps in our SoC design. The other advantage is that our design does not process the rightmost two columns and lowest two rows of the picture. This can save the processing time when the data set is huge enough. Moreover, the omitted pixels have little influence to the final results.

For the verification platform, the CPU is instantiated as a functional module, and it sends command registers to the Sobel edge detection operator. The image frame used for the experiment is a 256×256 grayscale picture, so there are 65,536 positions in the memory. The Sobel edge detection operator extracts the information from the command registers, so that the operator knows when to

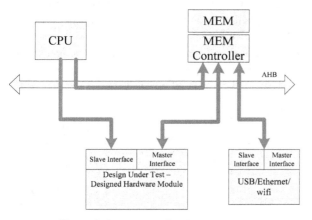

Figure 4. System verification platform.

Table 1. Device utilization comparison.

	Number of Occupied Slice	Number of Slice Flip-Flops	Number of 4-Input LUTs
Design in [6]	1987	836	3901
Proposed Design	1144	128	1400

write and read data. The Sobel edge detection operator also gets the information of where to fetch the data blocks. Then, the operator sends commands to the memory controller to fetch the data and do calculations. The system sends the results back to the memory after finishing the whole image frame calculation.

The AHB bus protocol is an industry standard, so that the platform can be used for other DUTs in the future if properly configured. The transmission on the AHB bus is 32 bit. The responses of the slaves are set to okay for easy use to ensure the communication is good for this design.

Figure 5 is the block design of the system. The system uses two synchronized clocks and one global reset signal. The Sobel core block is embedded in the Sobel_fullscan block. Two signals, which are do_fullscan and fullscan_done, are reserved for future usage. If there are more than one DUTs in the system, an arbiter will be used to accommodate different DUTs based on the AHB protocol. The Sobel operator communicates with the off-chip memory through the ddr_controller. The Sobel core IP is integrated into the sobel_fullscan IP. Figure 6 is the simulation results from Mentor Graphic Modelsim [9]. By employing the pipeline technique, the DUT runs

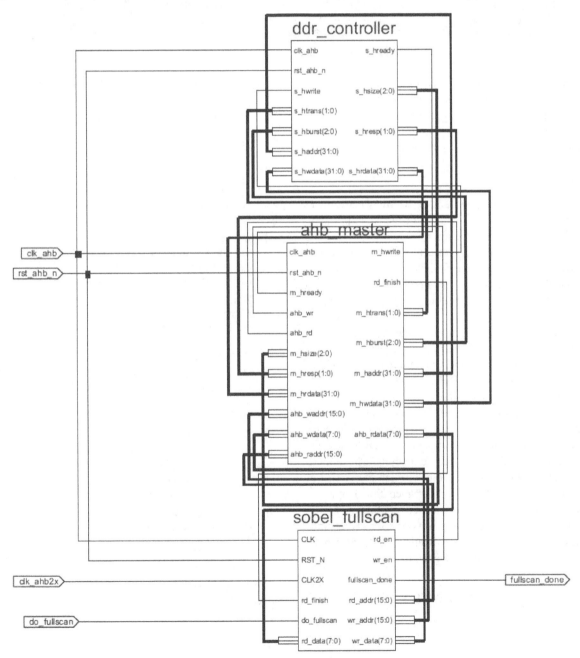

Figure 5. Schematic of Sobel operator with AHB bus.

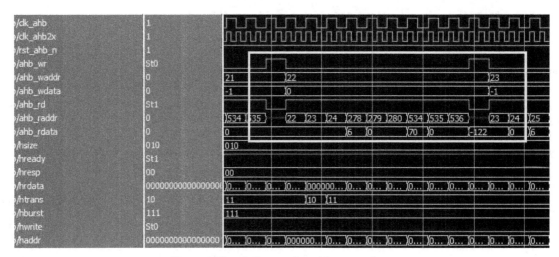

Figure 6. Simulation results with system bus.

smoothly on the verification platform. The edge detection part consumes nine clock cycles to fetch the desired pixels, then, the result can be generated in the tenth clock cycle. Thus, the design can not only have a shorter execution time but also few resource costs.

5. Conclusions

This paper introduces a system verification platform of hardware optimization based on the edge detection algorithm. The Sobel edge detection operator is designed and verified on the verification platform. The IC design flow is provided to make sure the designed chip is a good one. The Sobel edge detection operator is one of the most commonly used methods in remote controller design. In this design, the Sobel operator is separated into two parts in order to process the data more efficiently and consume fewer resources. Experimental results show that the designed Sobel edge detection operator can save 6% of on-chip resources for the Sobel core calculation and 42% for the whole frame calculation.

The system verification platform is set up to verify the designed hardware. The verification platform is composed of the functional CPU module, the DUT module, the memory module and other peripherals. These modules communicate with each other through the AHB bus protocol. It is proved that the designed Sobel operator works efficiently on this verification platform. The designed Sobel operator can be processed to the next stage to make an IC chip. The verification platform can be further used to verify other designed hardware.

REFERENCES

[1]   R. C. Gonzalez and R. E. Woods, "Digital Image Proc-

essing," 2nd Edition, Prentice Hall, Upper Saddle River, 2001.

[2]   S. Halder, D. Bhattacharjee, *et al.*, "A Fast FPGA Based Architecture for Sobel Edge Detection," *Progress in VLSI Design and Test, Lecture Notes in Computer Science*, Vol. 7373, 2012, pp. 300-306.

[3]   T. A. Abbasi and M. U. Abbasi, "A Novel FPGA-Based Architecture for Sobel Edge Detection Operator," *International Journal of Electronics*, Vol. 94, No. 9, 2007, pp. 889-896.

[4]   C. Pradabpet, N. Ravinu, *et al.*, "An Efficient Filter Structure for Multiplierless Sobel Edge Detection," *Innovative Technologies in Intelligent Systems and Industrial Applications*, 25-26 July 2009, pp. 40-44.

[5]   Z. E. M. Osman, F. A. Hussin, *et al.*, "Hardware Implementation of an Optimized Processor Architecture for Sobel Image Edge Detection Operator," 2010 *International Conference on Intelligent and Advanced Systems*, 15-17 June 2010, pp. 1-4.

[6]   V. Sanduja and R. Patial, "Sobel Edge Detection Using Parallel Architecture Based on FPGA," *International Journal of Applied Information Systems*, Vol. 4, No. 4, 2012, pp. 20-24.

[7]   AMBA Specifications. http://www.arm.com/products/system-ip/amba/amba-open-specifications.php

[8]   Xilinx Incorporated. http://www.xilinx.com

[9]   MentorGraphics Modelsim. http://www.model.com

## 15

Leakage Reduction Using DTSCL and Current Mirror SCL Logic Structures for LP-LV Circuits

Sanjeev Rai[1], Ram Awadh Mishra[1], Sudarshan Tiwari[2]

[1]Department of Electronics & Communication Engineering, Motilal Nehru National Institute of Technology Allahabad, Allahabad, India

[2]National Institute of Technology, Raipur, India

ABSTRACT

This paper presents a novel approach to design robust Source Coupled Logic (SCL) for implementing ultra low power circuits. In this paper, we propose two different source coupled logic structures and analyze the performance of these structures with STSCL (Sub-threshold SCL). The first design under consideration is DTPMOS as load device which analyses the performance of Dynamic Threshold SCL (DTSCL) Logic with previous source coupled logic for ultra low power operation. DTSCL circuits exhibit a better power-delay Performance compared with the STSCL Logic. It can be seen that the proposed circuit provides 56% reduction in power delay product. The second design under consideration uses basic current mirror active load device to provide required voltage swing. Current mirror source coupled logic (CMSCL) can be used for high speed operation. The advantage of this design is that it provides 54% reduction in power delay product over conventional STSCL. The main drawback of this design is that it provides a higher power dissipation compared to other source coupled logic structures. The proposed circuit provides lower sensitivity to temperature and power supply variation, with a superior control over power dissipation. Measurements of test structures simulated in 0.18 μm CMOS technology shows that the proposed DTSCL logic concept can be utilized successfully for bias currents as low as 1 pA. Measurements show that existing standard cell libraries offer a good solution for ultra low power SCL circuits. Cadence Virtuoso schematic editor and Spectre Simulation tools have been used.

Keywords: CMOS Integrated Circuits; CMOS Logic Circuit; Dynamic Threshold MOS (DTMOS); Power-Delay Product; Source-Coupled Logic (SCL); Sub-Threshold CMOS; Sub-Threshold SCL; Ultra-Low-Power Circuits; Weak Inversion LP-LV(Low Power-Low Voltage)

1. Introduction

The ever increasing attention on power consumption in circuit design has motivated a significant investigation of optimum design for minimizing energy or power for a given performance constraint. Technology scaling results in a significant increase in leakage current of CMOS device. Various methods and techniques, such as voltage scaling, clock gating, etc. [1-3] have been applied successfully in the medium power, medium performance region of the design spectrum for lower power consumption. Nevertheless, in some applications where ultra-low power consumption is the primary requirement and performance is of secondary importance, a more aggressive approach is warranted. Special circuit techniques have been implemented to enable operation at very low current levels and to achieve the desired performance specifications. The demand for implementing ultra-low-power digital systems in many modern applications such as mobile systems [4], sensor networks [5,6], and implanted biomedical systems [7], has increased the importance of designing logic circuits in sub-threshold regime [8].

The power dissipation is a crucial parameter in ultra-low power application. The supply voltage V_{DD} is generally reduced below the threshold voltage V_T of metal-oxide-semiconductor (MOS) devices [9]. Reducing the supply voltage or choosing high-threshold-voltage (HVT) devices results in a smaller $V_{eff} = V_{DD} - V_T$ value and, hence, less power consumption [10]. However, reducing V_{eff} results in reduction in the ratio of the ON-current of a logic gate I_{ON} to its leakage current I_{OFF}. Reduction in $\gamma = I_{ON}/I_{OFF}$ results in degradation of reliability and power efficiency of the circuit, requiring special design techniques to implement robust logic operations [9]. Sub-threshold operation (where $V_{DD} < V_T$) is currently used for some low-power applications such as watches and hearing aids. Emerging ultra-low-power applications such as distributed sensor networks are a natural fit with sub-threshold circuits. Special circuit techniques for improving robustness in deep sub-threshold have been explored [9]. In mixed mode integrated circuits the crucial parameters that affect the performance of the digital system are supply noise and substrate noise. Source coupled logic (SCL) are widely used to reduce the output voltage swing compared to CMOS logic gates for high frequency application. This paper explores performance comparison of two source coupled logic structures with previously available Sub Threshold Source Coupled Logic (STSCL) gates for implementing ultra-low-power digital systems. In this approach, the power consumption and maximum speed of operation can be adjusted linearly through the tail bias current of each gate over a very wide range [11,12], thus, efficiently decoupling the decision of output voltage swing from power dissipation and delay. To enable the operation at very low trail bias current and to achieve the desired performance, we have to use a special circuit technique for implementing very low power Source Coupled Logic circuit. In first design, the intrinsically limited output impedance of deep-submicron, dynamic threshold PMOS devices have been used to implement very high value load resistances for SCL topology. In second design an active load current mirror has been used to implement very high value of load resistance called Current Mirror Source Coupled Logic (CMSCL). Here, a more general approach with much less sensitivity to process and technology variations will be introduced [12]. This paper presents two different techniques, one for implementing Dynamic Threshold Source Coupled Logic (DTSCL) gates where the bias current of each cell can be set as low as 0.1 pA and another for implementing Current Mirror source coupled logic gates where the bias current of each cell can be set as high as 1 mA. In Section 2, after a brief review of SCL circuits, the proposed techniques for implementing different SCL gates will be introduced. Section 3 discusses about the load device concept applied to SCL circuits. Section 4 discusses about the experimental results and implementation of the proposed circuits. Section 4.4 discusses the power-delay performance of the proposed circuit configurations and comparison of different SCL logic structures, followed by conclusions in Section 4.5 and finally Acknowledgement in Section 5.

2. Different Source-Coupled Logic Structure

2.1. DTMOS Topology

In DTMOS logic, gates of transistors are tied to their substrates to achieve the same stability with direct substrate biasing without using additional control circuitry as in case of VTCMOS logic (**Figure 1**) [11]. As the substrate voltage in DTMOS logic changes with the gate input voltage, the threshold voltage is dynamically changed. In the off-state, *i.e.*, $V_{in} = 0 \left(V_{in} = V_{DD} \right)$ for NMOS (PMOS), the characteristics of DTMOS transistor is exactly the same as regular MOS transistor. Both have

the same properties, such as the same off-current, sub-threshold slope, and threshold voltage. In the on-state, however, the substrate-source voltage (V_{bs}) for NMOS (PMOS), the characteristics of DTMOS transistor is exactly the same as regular MOS transistor. When the DTMOS is in off state then it offers higher threshold voltage which in turn reduces the leakage current of the MOS device. In the on state, the substrate-source voltage (V_{bs}) increases which in turn reduces threshold voltage of the DTMOS. Reduction in threshold voltage is due to the reduction in body charge which again leads to an advantage of higher carrier mobility because the reduced body charge causes a lower effective normal field. The reduced threshold, lower normal effective electric field, and higher mobility results in higher on current drive in DTMOS than that of a simple MOS transistor.

The sub-threshold slope of DTMOS improves and approaches the ideal 60 mV/decade which makes it more efficient in sub threshold logic circuits to obtain higher gain.

2.2. Current Mirror Topology

A current mirror is a circuit designed to copy a current through one active device by controlling the current in another active device of a circuit, keeping the output current constant regardless of loading. The current being 'copied' can be, and sometimes is, a varying signal current. Conceptually, an ideal current mirror is simply an ideal current amplifier. The current mirror is used to provide bias currents and active loads to circuits. High-performance current mirrors with low input and output voltages are required as building blocks of mixed-mode VLSI systems that operate from a single supply of 1.8 V or below. High accuracy requires very high output resistance and low input resistance. Low-voltage operation requires low input and output voltages as well as low supply requirements for the control circuitry used to improve the mirror's input and output resistance. There are three main specifications that characterize a current mirror. The first is the current level it produces. The second is its AC output resistance, which determines how much the output current varies with the voltage applied to the mirror. The third specification is the minimum voltage drop across the mirror necessary to make it work properly. This minimum voltage is dictated by the need to keep the output transistor of the mirror in active mode.

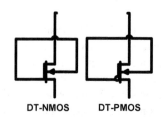

Figure 1. DT-NMOS and DT-PMOS.

The range of voltages where the mirror works is called the compliance range and the voltage marking the boundary between good and bad behavior is called the compliance voltage. There are also a number of seconddary performance issues with mirrors, for example, temperature stability.

2.3. Basic SCL Topology

The source coupled logic (SCL) topology has been a modern approach for designing of ultra low power circuits. This topology is very suitable for very low bias current operations as it provides accurate control on power consumption of each gate, where as the power dissipation of conventional static CMOS circuits is limited by their sub-threshold leakage current. Simultaneously, the gate delay in this configuration does not depend on the supply voltage and hence, there is low sensitivity to supply voltage variations.

Figure 2 shows that the switching part can be composed of a network of NMOS source-coupled pairs to implement more complex logic functions [2]. The load resistances can be implemented using PMOS devices biased in triode region.

In an SCL gate, the logic operation takes place mainly in current domain. Therefore, the speed of operation can be inherently high. The voltage swing at the output node $\left(V_{SW} = I_{SS} \cdot R_L\right)$ should be $V_{SW} > 4n_n \cdot U_T$ (n_n is the sub-threshold slope factor of NMOS differential pair devices, and U_T is the thermal voltage). To achieve the required voltage swing at very low trail bias current the load resistance should be very high, and also occupy a small area with a very good control to adjust their resistivity with respect to their trail bias current. In first design, DT-PMOS transistor can be used to provide high resistance with a relatively high voltage swing at the output, the proposed topology can operate properly as logic device. In the second design, current mirror active load is used as a load device to provide higher resistance with a relatively high voltage swing.

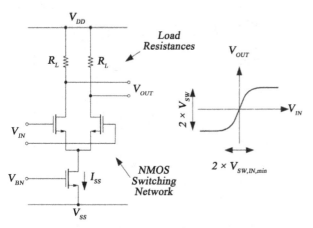

Figure 2. A conventional SCL-based inverter/buffer circuit.

In SCL topology the main leakage currents are due to the p-n junctions of the MOS devices, whereas in CMOS logic circuits the sub-threshold channel leakage current is the dominant leakage component,. The speed of operation in an SCL gate is mainly limited by the time constant at the output node which is calculated as Equation (1):

$$T_{SCL} = R_L \times C_L = V_{SW} \times CL / I_{SS} \qquad (1)$$

Based on the above, the propagation delay is inversely proportional to the tail bias current. Meanwhile, the circuit power-delay product (PDP) is independent of I_{SS} [12-14].

3. Load Device Concept

To maintain the required voltage swing at very low trail bias current it is necessary to increase the load resistance in inverse proportion to the reducing trail bias current. In sub-threshold region, the trail bias current would be in the order of few pA or even less. Therefore, to obtain a required output voltage swing, the load resistance should be of the order of few GΩ. Meanwhile, this resistance should be controlled very accurately based on the value of trail bias current I_{SS}. Hence, a well controlled high resistivity load device with a very small area is required. For this range of resistivity, conventional PMOS devices biased in triode region cannot be utilized since the required channel length of the transistor would be impractically large. Figure 3(a) shows the proposed load device, where the gate of the PMOS device is connected to its bulk where as Figure 3(b) is the conventional device. In this way, the load device provides accurate control on the resistance, which, associated with the transconductance of the differential pair will provide a controlled, limited gain and amplitude with relatively small size PMOS load device.

Figure 3(c) shows the I-V characteristics of the conventional PMOS and the proposed PMOS load device.

In the proposed load device the gate and substrate of PMOS load device are shorted. When $V_{SG} = V_{SD}$ then it will behave as conventional PMOS load device as we vary the gate voltage V_{SG} the voltage across the substrate terminal also varies as a result the threshold voltage of the device changes and also the resistance of the PMOS load device varies. In this way the proposed load device will be used as a controlled resistance.

The basic current mirror can also be implemented using MOSFET transistors, as shown in Figure 4. Transistor M_1 is operating in the saturation or active mode, and so is M_2. In this setup, the output current I_{OUT} is directly related to I_{REF}. The drain current of a MOSFET I_D is a function of both the gate-source voltage and the drain-to-gate voltage of the MOSFET given by $I_D = f\left(V_{GS}, V_{DG}\right)$, a relationship derived from the functionality of the MOSFET device. In the case of transistor

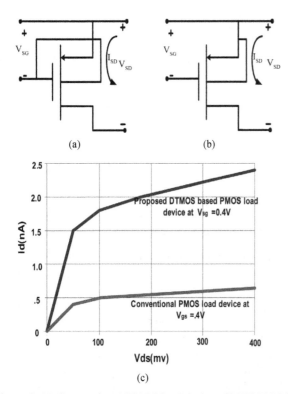

(a)   (b)

(c)

Figure 3. (a) Conventional PMOS load device; (b) DT-PMOS load device; (c) I-V characteristics of the conventional PMOS load in comparison to the proposed DT-PMOS device.

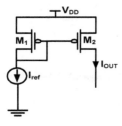

Figure 4. Basic Current Mirror Structure.

M_1 of the mirror, $I_D = I_{REF}$. Reference current I_{REF} is a known current, and can be provided by a resistor as shown, or by a "threshold-referenced" or "self-biased" current source to ensure that it is constant, independent of voltage supply variations.

Using $V_{DG} = 0$ for transistor M_1, the drain current in M_1 is $I_D = f(V_{GS}, V_{DG} = 0)$, so we find: $f(V_{GS}, 0) = I_{REF}$, implicitly determining the value of V_{GS}. Thus I_{REF} sets the value of V_{GS}. The circuit in the diagram forces the same V_{GS} to apply to transistor M_2. If M_2 also is biased with zero V_{DG} and provided transistors M_1 and M_2 have good matching of their properties, such as channel length, width, threshold voltage etc., the relationship $I_{OUT} = f(V_{GS}, V_{DG} = 0)$ applies, thus setting $I_{OUT} = I_{REF}$; that is, the output current is the same as the reference current when $V_{DG} = 0$ for the output transistor, and both transistors are matched.

The drain-to-source voltage can be expressed as $V_{DS} = V_{DG} + V_{GS}$. With this substitution, the Shichman-Hodges model Equation (2) provides an approximate form for function $f(V_{GS}, V_{DG})$:

$$I_d$$

$$= f(V_{GS}, V_{DG}) = \frac{1}{2} K_p \left(\frac{W}{L}\right)(V_{GS} - V_{th})^2 (1 + \lambda V_{DS}) \quad (2)$$

$$= \frac{1}{2} K_p \left(\frac{W}{L}\right)(V_{GS} - V_{th})^2 (1 + \lambda (V_{DG} + V_{GS}))$$

where, K_p is a technology related constant associated with the transistor, W/L is the width to length ratio of the transistor, V_{GS} is the gate-source voltage, V_{th} is the threshold voltage, λ is the channel length modulation constant, and V_{DS} is the drain source voltage. Because of channel-length modulation, the mirror has a finite output (or Norton) resistance given by the r_o Equation (3) of the output transistor, namely

$$R_N = r_o = \frac{(1/\lambda + V_{DS})}{I_D} \quad (3)$$

where λ is the channel-length modulation parameter and V_{DS} is the drain-to-source bias.

4. Proposed Implementation of DTSCL & Current Mirror SCL Gates & Results.

4.1. DTSCL Gates

The proposed DTPMOS load device can be utilized to implement an SCL gate biased in sub-threshold regime. **Figure 5** shows the basic structure of the proposed DTSCL gate. The **Figure 5** includes the replica bias circuit which is used to control the output voltage swing. Replica bias circuit consist of two major component one is op-amp and another is a current mirror circuit which

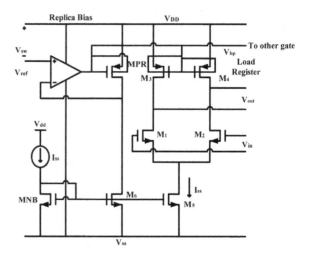

Figure 5. DTSCL gate and the replica bias circuit used to control the output voltage swing.

will maintain a constant trail bias current I_{SS}. This circuit also tracks the variations on temperature and supply voltage and, hence, compensates their effect on the circuit performance.

A simplified circuit diagram of the replica bias circuit used to control the output voltage swing is also shown. In this schematic, all devices operate in sub-threshold regime and the tail bias current can be reduced until it becomes comparable in magnitude to the leakage currents that exist in the circuit. **Figure 6(a)** illustrates the DC transfer characteristics of a DTSCL gate. The stage gain of DTSCL gate is as shown in **Figure 6(b)**. The measured stage gain of DTSCL gate is approximately 42. The measured input-output transfer characteristics of a DTSCL buffer stage at different trail bias current are shown in **Figure 6(c)**. As all the devices are operating in sub-threshold regime hence the transfer characteristic of the circuit is independent of the trail bias current.

In the plot above, the deviation from the ideal DC characteristics is mainly due to the leakage currents in the test circuit coming from electrostatic discharge (ESD) protection circuitry. To measure the DC characteristics, output voltage swing has been adjusted manually.

The variation in power dissipation and gate delay of a DTSCL gate is as shown in **Figures 7(a)** and **(b)** simultaneously. It is seen that the stabilized output of is achieved at trail bias current I_{SS} = 1 pA. At this trail bias current, DTSCL provides lowest power delay product of the order of 569.71×10^{-18} W-Sec.

The **Table 1** above describes the variation in delay with different trail bias current with subsequent power dissipation and the corresponding PDP.

4.2. Current Mirror SCL Gates

The proposed current mirror active load device can be utilized to implement an SCL gate biased in sub-threshold regime. **Figure 8** shows the basic structure of the proposed Current Mirror SCL gate.

In this schematic given below, all devices operate in sub-threshold regime and the tail bias current can be reduced until it becomes comparable in magnitude to the leakage currents that exist in the circuit.

Figure 9(a) illustrates the DC transfer characteristics of a Current Mirror SCL gate. The stage gain of Current Mirror SCL gate is as shown in **Figure 9(b)**. The measured stage gain of Current Mirror SCL gate is approximately 8.2. The measured input-output transfer characteristics of a Current Mirror SCL buffer stage at different trail bias current are shown in **Figure 9(c)**. As all the devices are operating in sub-threshold regime hence the transfer characteristic of the circuit is independent of the trail bias current.

The variation in power dissipation and gate delay of a

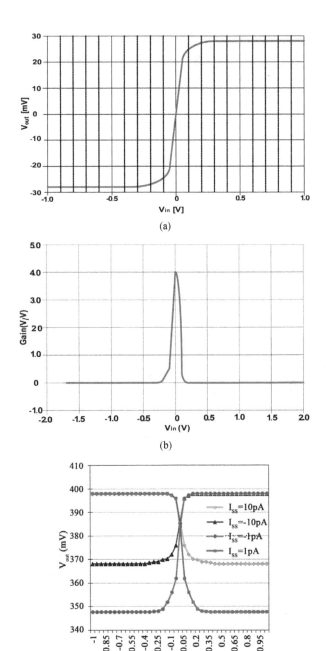

Figure 6. (a) Simulated DC transfer characteristics of a DTSCL gate biased at I_{SS} of 1 Pa; (b) DC gain of a DTSCL gate biased at I_{SS} 1 pA; (c) Measured transfer characteristics of a DTSCL buffer stage for different bias currents (I_{SS} = 1 pA, and 10 pA).

Table 1. Variation in delay with trail bias current.

Bias current I_{SS} (pA)	Power Dissipation (nW)	Delay (n sec)	PDP(10^{-18} Wsec)
1	0.1096	5200	569.71
10	1.5232	900	1370.88
100	5.23	56	2928.8

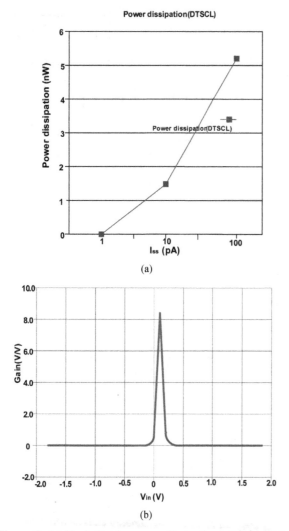

Figure 7. (a) Variation in power dissipation with trail bias current; (b) Variation in delay with trail bias current.

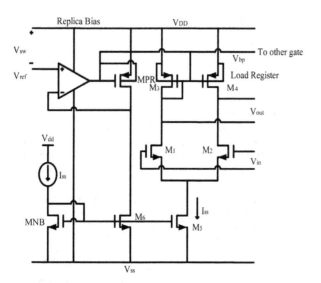

Figure 8. Current Mirror SCL gate and the replica bias circuit used to control the output voltage swing.

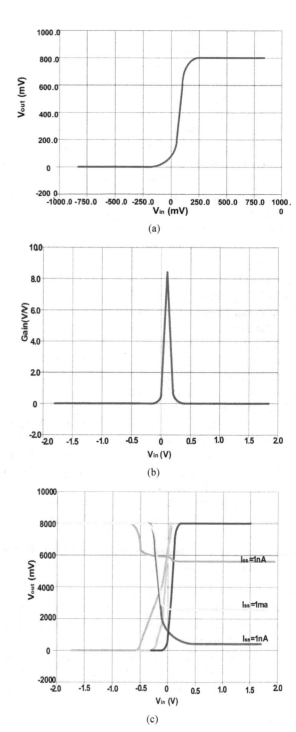

Figure 9. (a) Simulated DC transfer characteristics of a Current Mirror SCL gate biased at I_{SS} of 1 mA; (b) DC gain of a Current Mirror SCL gate biased at I_{SS} of 1 mA; (c) Measured transfer characteristics of a Current Mirror SCL buffer stage for different bias currents (I_{SS} = 1 nA, 1 µA and 1 mA).

Current Mirror SCL gate is as shown in **Figure 10(a)** and **(b)** simultaneously. It is seen that the stabilized output of is achieved at trail bias current I_{SS} = 1 mA. At this trail bias current, Current Mirror SCL provides lowest power delay product of the order of 592.238×10^{-18} W-Sec.

The **Table 2** Describes the PDP and power consumption at different trail bias currents.

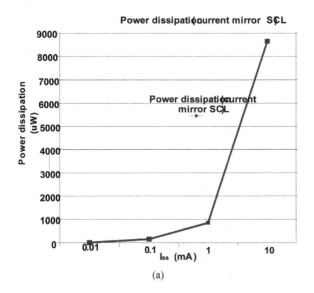

(a)

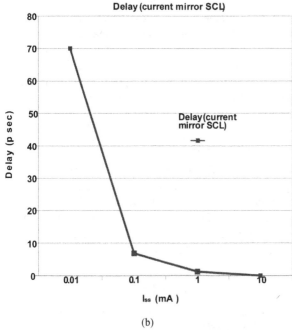

(b)

Figure 10. (a) Variation in power dissipation with trail bias current; (b) Variation in delay with trail bias current.

Table 2. Variation in delay with trail bias current.

Bias current I_{SS} (mA)	Power Dissipation (μW)	Delay (p sec)	PDP($10^\wedge$ - 18 Wsec)
0.01	16.44	70	1150.8
0.1	111.147	7.5	833.60
1.0	832.73	0.716	592.238
10	8426.12	0.0731	615.949

4.3. Voltage Swing Control

To achieve the required voltage swing at the output, a controlling circuit is used. **Figure 11** shows a simplified schematic of replica bias circuit to control the output voltage swing. The Replica bias circuit consists of a high performance current mirror circuit that can maintain a constant current I_{SS} at the output to provide accurate control on the output voltage swing. The replica bias circuit should be well matched to the SCL gates to have very low deviation in operating point. Meanwhile, amplifier should provide enough gain with a very low offset to have the desired accuracy.

In this work, a folded-cascode amplifier has been used to provide a large swing at the output node and to be able to test the SCL gates in a very wide range of bias current values. Any mismatch in the bias current of the devices of the SCL gates and RB circuit will result in variation of the desired output voltage swing.

4.4. Performance Analysis and Observation

4.4.1. Power-Speed Trade-Off in SCL Circuits
In contrast to the CMOS gates, where there is no static power consumption (neglecting the leakage current), each SCL gate draws a constant bias current of I_{SS} from a supply source (**Figure 2**). Therefore, the power consumption of each SCL gate can be calculated by Equation (4) as

$$P_{diss,SCL} = V_{DD} \times I_{SS} \qquad (4)$$

Meanwhile, the time constant at the output node of each SCL gate, is given as Equation (5) *i.e.*,

$$\tau = R_L \times C_L \approx (V_{SW}/I_{SS}) \times C_L \qquad (5)$$

is the main speed-limiting factor in this topology (C_L is the total output loading capacitance). Based on (5), one

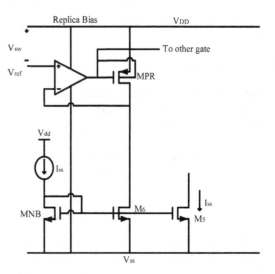

Figure 11. Replica bias circuit to control o/p voltage swing.

can choose the proper I_{SS} value to operate at the desired frequency. This circuit exhibits a very low sensitivity to the process variations because the power consumption and delay of each gate only depend on I_{SS}, which can very precisely be controlled. Meanwhile, it is not necessary to use special process options to have low threshold voltage devices, as frequently used for static CMOS [1,2,8]. Therefore, it is necessary to use the DTSCL circuits at their maximum activity rate to achieve the maximum achievable efficiency. It is also important to note that the gate delay does not depend on the supply voltage, whereas it linearly varies with the tail bias current. This property can be exploited for applications in which the supply can vary during the operation. Based on Equations (4) and (5), the power-delay product (PDP) of each gate can be approximately calculated by Equation 6 given below:

$$PDP_{DTSCL1} = \ln 2 \times V_{DD} V_{SW} C_L \qquad (6)$$

Observation 1: The delay of a logic block can be controlled without influencing PDP as the delay of DTSCL gate depends on trail bias current (I_{SS}), but not on supply voltage V_{DD}.

Observation 2: To reduce the power to frequency ratio, α should be kept as large as possible. This observation does not contradict with similar results for conventional CMOS.

4.4.2. Tabulated Comparison of Different SCL Circuit

Shown below is the comparison of the power consumption, delay and power delay product of different SCL structures (STSCL, DTSCL, Current Mirror SCL) as shown in **Table 3**. The table shows that if we wish to design a circuit with low power dissipation than proposed DTSCL is preferred over other SCL techniques and if we choose to design a circuit with higher speed than proposed Current Mirror SCL is preferred over other SCL techniques.

4.5. Conclusion

In this paper, an analytical approach for studying and comparing the performance of ultra low power STSCL, DTSCL, and Current Mirror SCL has been presented.

Table 3. Comparison of various SCL circuits.

Logic circuit	Stabilized bias current	Power dissipation	Delay	PDP (10^{-18} Wsec)
STSCL inverter	1 nA	3.136 nW	410 ns	1285.76
DTSCL inverter	10 pA	0.1523 nW	900 ns	569.71
C-M STSCL inverter	1 mA	832.73 μW	0.7 ps	592.238

While there is a tight tradeoff among the power consumption, speed of operation , and supply voltage in design of CMOS digital circuits, the SCL topology provide a more flexible deign option for ultra low power applications. In this work, two new source coupled logic design has been discussed. The first design uses a high resistance DT-PMOS load device to provide the required voltage swing at the output. The measurement result shows that the DTSCL topology provides 56% reduction in PDP compared to STSCL, using 0.18 μm CMOS technology. The second design uses basic current mirror load device to provide required voltage swing at the output. This design can be used for high speed operation at the cost of higher power dissipation. Hence this design can be used for high speed operation at the cost of power dissipation. The measurement result shows that the Current Mirror SCL provides 54% reduction in PDP compared to STSCL, using 0.18 μm CMOS technology. The trail bias current of each gate can be reduced to less than 0.1 pA, while the power delay product of the gate remains less than 1 FJ. The bias current of a SCL gate can be scaled over several decades, which makes this topology very suitable for ultra low power applications. The main advantage of this topology is that there is no effect of process and temperature variation and it can operate in a wide range of frequency. The author has used **Cadence Virtuoso** Schematic Editor [15] and **Spectre** as simulation platform. All the results and their verification has been done by using cadence tools.

5. Acknowledgements

The authors duly acknowledged with gratitude the support from ministry of communication and information technology, DIT Govt. of India, New Delhi, through special manpower Development program in VLSI and related Software's Phase-II (SMDP-II) project in ECE Department, MNNIT Allahabad-211004, India.

REFERENCES

[1] A. Tajalli and Y. Leblebici, "Leakage Current Reduction Using Sub-Threshold Source-Coupled Logic," *IEEE Transactions on Circuits and Systems—II: Express Briefs*, Vol. 56, No. 5, 2009, pp. 374-378.

[2] A. Tajalli, E. J. Brauer, Y. Leblebici and E. Vittoz, "Sub-Threshold Source-Coupled Logic Circuits for Ultra-Low Power Applications," *IEEE Journal of Solid-State Circuits*, Vol. 43, No. 7, 2008, pp. 1699-1710.

[3] D. Suvakovic and C. A. T. Salama, "A Low V_t CMOS Implantation of an LPLV Digital Filter Core for Portable Audio Applications," *Transactions on Circuits Systems, II: Analog and Digital Signal Processing*, Vol. 47, No. 11, 2000, pp. 1297-1300.

[4] G. Gielen, "Ultra-Low-Power Sensor Networks in Nano-

meter CMOS," *International Symposium on Signals, Circuits and Systems*, Vol. 1, Iasi, 13-14 July 2007, pp. 1-2.

[5]   B. A. Warneke and K. S. J. Pister, "An Ultra-Low Energy Microcontroller for Smart Dust Wireless Sensor Networks," *IEEE International Solid-State Circuits Conference*, Vol. 1, 2004, pp. 316-317.

[6]   L. S. Wong, *et al.*, "A Very Low-Power CMOS Mixed-Signal IC for Implantable Pacemaker Applications," *IEEE Journal of Solid-State Circuits*, Vol. 39, No. 12, 2004, pp. 2446-2456.

[7]   E. Vittoz, "Weak Inversion for Ultimate Low-Power Logic," In: C. Piguet, Ed., *Low-Power Electronics Design*, CRC Press, Boca Raton, 2005.

[8]   B. H. Calhoun, A. Wang and A. Chandrakasan, "Modeling and Sizing for Minimum Energy Operation in Sub-Threshold Circuits," *IEEE Journal of Solid-State Circuits*, Vol. 40, No. 9, 2005, pp. 1778-1786.

[9]   M. Anis and M. Elmasry, "Multi-Threshold CMOS Digital Circuits, Managing Leakage Power," Kluwer, Norwell, 2003.

[10] E. Brauer and Y. Leblebici, "Semiconductor Based High-Resistance Device and Logic Application," European Patent Application No. 07104895.3-1235, 2007.

[11] H. Soeleman, K. Roy and B. C. Paul, "Robust Sub-threshold Logic for Ultra Low Power Operation," *IEEE Transactions on Very Large Scale Integration (VLSI) Systems*, Vol. 9, No. 1, 2001, pp. 90-99.

[12] F. Cannillo and C. Toumazou, "Nano-Power Sub-Threshold Current-Mode Logic in Sub-100 nm Technologies," *IEEE Electronics Letters*, Vol. 41, No. 23, 2005, pp. 1268-1269.

[13] A. Tajalli, E. Vittoz, Y. Leblebici and E. J. Brauer, "Ultra Low Power Sub-Threshold MOS Current Mode Logic Circuits Using a Novel Load Device Concept," *Proceedings of the European Solid-State Circuit Conference*, Munich, September 2007, pp. 281-284.

[14] M. Horowitz, T. Indermaur, R. Gonzalez, *et al.*, "Low-Power Digital Design," *Proceedings of IEEE International Symposium on Low Power Electronics and Design*, San Diego, 10-12 October 1994, pp. 8-11.

[15] http://www.cadence.com/

## 16

An Adaptive Howling Canceller Using 2-Tap Linear Predictor

Akira Sogami, Yosuke Sugiura, Arata Kawamura[*], Youji Iiguni

Department of Systems Innovation, Graduate School of Engineering Science, Osaka University, Toyonaka, Japan

ABSTRACT

This paper proposes an adaptive howling canceller using notch filter and 2-tap linear predictor, where howling consists of a single sinusoidal signal whose magnitude is much greater than other frequency's magnitudes. The employed 2-tap linear predictor can quickly detect howling due to its high convergence speed. Although the output signal of the 2-tap linear predictor cannot be directly used as one of a howling canceller, we can obtain the frequency of howling from the filter coefficient. We utilize the filter coefficient of the 2-tap linear predictor to design a notch filter which achieves a very narrow elimination band. The designed notch filter removes only howling and retains other desired signals. Simulation results show that the proposed adaptive howling canceller can quickly detect and effectively remove howling.

Keywords: Howling Canceller; Linear Predictor; Notch Filter; Single Sinusoidal Signal; Convergence Speed

1. Introduction

Howling is an annoying and persistence problem which is mainly caused in public address system. The public address system amplifies a signal observed at a microphone and transmits the amplified signal with a loudspeaker. Then, there exists a feedback path from the loudspeaker to the microphone. This feedback path forms an acoustical closed loop. When a frequency amplitude response of the closed loop is greater than 1 and its phase response is 2π, howling is caused, *i.e.*, a single sinusoidal signal rapidly becomes large. In this case, audience cannot avoid perception of this unpleasant sound, and also it is difficult to receive a desired signal. Moreover, the public address system often breaks down due to howling. To avoid this undesired phenomenon, many approaches have been studied. One of the most famous and effective methods is an echo canceller [1]. The echo canceller adaptively estimates the acoustical impulse response from the loudspeaker to the microphone, and provides a replica of the feedback signal. When the echo canceller perfectly estimates the feedback impulse response, subtracting the replica of the feedback signal from the observed signal gives perfect suppression of the feedback signal and thus howling is not caused. Since the acoustical impulse response is time-variant, the echo canceller is required to achieve both of high estimation accuracy and high convergence speed. Unfortunately, a tread-off exists between the convergence speed and the estimation accu-

racy. Actually, in many practical environments, the echo canceller cannot work well and hence it often causes degradation of sound quality, echo, or howling. Sogami *et al.* have proposed a simple howling canceller [2-3] which estimates howling by utilizing only the distance information between the loudspeaker and the microphone. This method can estimate the frequency of howling faster than the conventional echo canceller, under the assumption that howling is depending only on the direct distance from the loudspeaker to the microphone. Although howling often depends on the direct distance, the above assumption cannot hold for howling which depends on the distance including reflections. Actually, all the distances including reflections cannot be calculated. These conventional researches imply that the occurrence of howling may not be avoided and thus we have to prepare another howling canceller which adaptively removes howling as fast as possible after it is caused.

To remove howling after its occurrence, adaptive notch filter techniques are useful [4-10]. They achieve very narrow elimination bandwidth, and automatically estimate and remove a single sinusoidal signal like howling. Unfortunately, it also has a trade-off problem between the convergence speed and the estimation accuracy. Efficient notch filters which can solve the trade-off problem have been proposed [11-13]. Their main idea is to employ two or more notch filters, where one notch filter achieves high estimation accuracy at an expense of convergence speed, and the other notch filter has high convergence speed with low estimation accuracy. In such

---

[*]Corresponding author.

techniques, addition to an increase of their computational cost, it may not achieve an accurate adaptation because the notch filter's impulse responses are long basically.

In this paper, we propose an adaptive howling canceller which achieves both of high convergence speed and high estimation accuracy to remove howling. The proposed method consists of a notch filter and a 2-tap linear predictor. Although the proposed method utilizes the additional filter, the 2-tap linear predictor updates only one filter coefficient to detect howling. With its short impulse response, the 2-tap linear predictor can quickly evaluate the prediction error signal in the steady-state for adaptation. Since the filter coefficient has the information of the frequency of howling after convergence, we easily design the notch filter whose elimination frequency is identical to the frequency of howling. Then, we can remove howling quickly and effectively. The additional computational cost of the proposed method is minimal among conventional adaptive notch filters which employ two or more additional notch filters. Simulation results show that the proposed howling canceler effectively removes howling.

2. Howling Canceller with Notch Filter

Let consider a public address system shown in **Figure 1**, where $s(n)$ denotes the source signal produced by human in general, and $y(n)$ is the feedback signal from the loudspeaker to the microphone. The observed signal is represented as

$$x(n) = s(n) + y(n). \tag{1}$$

The observed signal is amplified by the attenuator so that $\tilde{s}(n) = ax(n)$, where a is a constant. The amplified signal $\tilde{s}(n)$ is produced from the loudspeaker. The signal $\tilde{s}(n)$ is received at the microphone after passing through the unknown acoustical feedback path whose transfer function is $P(z)$. Then, the closed loop is formed as shown in **Figure 1**. When the amplitude frequency response of the closed loop is greater than 1 and the phase frequency response is 2π for a certain frequency, howling will occur at the corresponding frequency. **Figure 2** shows an example of the occurrence of howling. Here, we set the acoustical impulse response as

uniform random variables. The top panel shows the waveform of $s(n)$, and the middle panel shows the transmitted signal $\tilde{s}(n)$. In this simulation, we gradually increased a. As a result, howling occurred at around 30,000 samples. An expanded waveform is shown in the bottom panel. We see from this result that howling explosively increases and we should remove it as fast as possible.

First, we explain the standard adaptive notch filter to remove howling. The notch filter passes all frequencies expect of the narrow frequency band whose center frequency is called as the notch frequency. The elimination bandwidth and the notch frequency can be individually designed [4-10]. The transfer function of the notch filter $N(z)$ is given by [6-8]

$$N(z) = \frac{1}{2}\left(1 + \frac{r + \alpha z^{-1} + z^{-2}}{1 + \alpha z^{-1} + rz^{-2}}\right), \tag{2}$$

where α is a parameter to design the notch frequency and $r(-1 < r < 1)$ determines the elimination bandwidth. The relation between α and the notch frequency is given as

$$\alpha = -(1 + r)\cos\left(2\pi\frac{F}{F_S}\right), \tag{3}$$

where $F[\text{Hz}]$ denotes the notch frequency and $F_S[\text{Hz}]$ denotes the sampling frequency. The relation of r and the elimination bandwidth $K[\text{Hz}]$ is represented as

$$r = \frac{1 + \cos(2\pi K/F_S) - \sin(2\pi K/F_S)}{1 + \cos(2\pi K/F_S) + \sin(2\pi K/F_S)}.$$

Figure 3 shows the structure of the notch filter, where $x(n)$ is the input signal, and $\tilde{x}(n)$ is the output signal. The notch filter includes the IIR unit, and hence its impulse response is infinite. **Figure 4** shows the frequency amplitude response of the notch filter $N(z)$ when $\alpha = 0$ $(F = F_S/2)$ with $r = 0.8, 0.9, 0.99$, where the vertical axis denotes the amplitude response and the

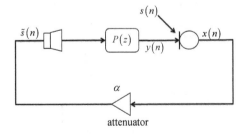

Figure 1. Public address system.

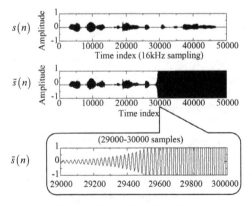

Figure 2. Example of howling.

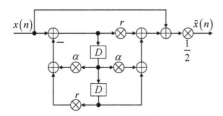

Figure 3. Structure of notch filter.

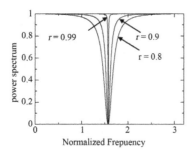

Figure 4. Frequency amplitude response of notch filter.

horizontal axis denotes the normalized frequency. We see from **Figure 4** that the elimination bandwidth becomes narrow with increasing r toward to 1. Thus, we can remove only howling when setting r close to 1.

The frequency of howling is usually unknown. Hence, we have to adaptively estimate and remove it. When the observed signal includes a sinusoidal signal whose magnitude is much greater than the other frequency's magnitudes, an adaptive notch filter can automatically estimate and remove the single sinusoidal signal when its coefficient α is updated by a gradient method [4]. The coefficient α converges so that the notch filter's output power is minimized. Since howling can be approximated such as the sinusoidal signal, the adaptive notch filter can automatically detect and remove howling.

However, the gradient method includes an annoying trade-off problem between convergence speed and estimation accuracy. To accelerate convergence speed with remaining high estimation accuracy, in many approaches, an additional adaptive notch filter is introduced [11-13], where the main notch filter has high estimation accuracy and the other notch filter has high convergence speed. Comparing their output signals, we can choose better one. This method is useful when the notch filter is appropriately updated by using the output signal in the steady state. Unfortunately, such update is difficult, because notch filter's impulse responses are generally long.

3. Howling Canceller with Notch Filter and 2-Tap Linear Predictor

In this section, we propose an adaptive howling canceller which utilizes an adaptive notch filter and an additional 2-tap linear predictor, where the proposed method

achieves both of high convergence speed and high estimation accuracy.

As mentioned above sections, howling can be approximated as a single sinusoidal signal whose magnitude is much greater than other frequency's magnitudes. Our purpose is to detect the frequency of howling as fast as possible. A linear predictor, often called as an adaptive line enhancer [1], is useful to extract a sinusoidal signal from the sinusoidal signal embedded in a wideband signal. Hence, the estimation error signal of the linear predictor does not include the sinusoid. Intuitively, we note that the estimation error signal can be utilized as the output signal of a howling canceller. Unfortunately, to accurately remove howling only, the filter length of the linear predictor must be long. In actual, the notch filter is the most effective filter to remove howling, because of its low computational complexity and steep frequency response. In the use of the adaptive notch filter, we encounter the trade-off problem again.

To solve this problem, we propose a combination method of a linear predictor and a notch filter. The employed linear predictor has the minimum impulse response which is just 2 samples (called 2-tap linear predictor) to detect the frequency of howling. The notch filter is adaptively designed from the 2-tap linear predictor's coefficient to align the notch frequency with the frequency of howling. Since the 2-tap linear predictor can achieve very short impulse response, we can quickly obtain its prediction error signal in the steady state for adaptation. It means that the 2-tap linear predictor achieves high convergence speed and we obtain the frequency of howling quickly.

Figure 5 shows the 2-tap linear predictor, where $\hat{x}(n)$ and $e(n)$ denote the predicting signal and the prediction error signal, respectively. The 2-tap linear predictor provides a replica of the present input signal by linear combination of past two input samples with two coefficients as $\hat{x}(n)=h_1(n)x(n-1)+h_2(n)x(n-2)$. Here, $h_1(n)$ and $h_2(n)$ denote the 1st and 2nd filter coefficients, respectively, and the replica has inverse phase of the present input signal. We update the 2-tap linear predictor so that the power of the following prediction error signal is minimized.

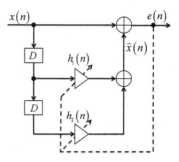

Figure 5. 2-tap linear predictor.

$$e(n) = x(n) + \hat{x}(n) = 1 + h_1(n)x(n-1) + h_2(n)x(n-2) \tag{5}$$

Under the assumption that howling can be expressed as $x(n) \approx p_1 \cos(2\pi F_1/F_S n + \theta_1)$, where F_1, p_1, θ_1 are the frequency of howling, amplitude, and phase, respectively, the 2-tap linear predictor can estimate the single sinusoidal signal by using a gradient method [3-10]. It is well known that the 2-tap linear predictor for such single sinusoidal input signal converges so that

$$h_1(n) \rightarrow -2\cos\left(2\pi \frac{F_1}{F_S}\right), h_2(n) \rightarrow 1. \tag{6}$$

Here, we note that the 1st coefficient $h_1(n)$ depends on the frequency of howling, while the 2nd coefficient $h_2(n)$ is independent with the input signal. It implies that we do not need to update the 2nd coefficient when predicting howling. Specifically, we can fix the 2nd coefficient as $h_2(n) = 1$. On the other hand, we have to update $h_1(n)$ to obtain the frequency of howling. After convergence, $h_1(n)$ is used to design the notch filter to remove howling. When the notch frequency is accurately designed, the notch filter successfully cancels howling. Comparing (3) and (6), we have the following simple relation.

$$\alpha = \frac{1+r}{2} h_1(n) \tag{7}$$

The accurate $h_1(n)$ gives the accurate α. Then, the notch filter with (7) completely cancels howling.

Figure 6 shows the proposed howling canceller, where LP denotes the 2-tap linear predictor. In the proposed system, $h_1(n)$ is updated by using the NLMS type algorithm given as

$$h_1(n+1) = h_1(n) - \mu \frac{e(n)x(n-1)}{E[x^2(n-1)]}, \tag{8}$$

where μ is the step-size for adaptation. The notch filter's coefficient α is updated with (7), where r and $h_2(n)$ are fixed.

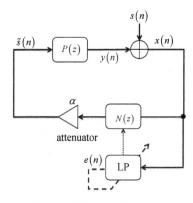

Figure 6. Proposed system.

4. Simulation

We carried out computer simulation to confirm the effectiveness of the proposed method. Here, we set feedback pass $P(z)$ as an FIR filter whose impulse response is set as a uniform random signal, where the order of the FIR filter is 50. We also set the attenuator as $\alpha = 4$ to satisfy the condition for occurrence of howling, and the step-size used in (8) as $\mu = 0.05$. The source signal was a female voice signal sampled at 16 kHz. Since the expectation value $E[x^2(n-1)]$ shown in (8) cannot be calculated, we used a time averaged value defined as

$$\overline{x^2(n-1)} = \frac{1}{M} \sum_{m=0}^{M-1} x^2(n-m), \tag{9}$$

instead of $E[x^2(n-1)]$, where we set $M = 50$. To compare the howling cancelation capability of the proposed method, we also performed the computer simulation for the conventional adaptive notch filter [4].

Figure 7 shows the results of howling cancellation, where **Figure 7(a)** shows the source signal $s(n)$, **Figure 7(b)** shows the output signal $\tilde{s}(n)$ without a howling canceller, **Figure 7(c)** denotes the output signal of the conventional adaptive notch filter, and **Figure 7(d)** shows the output signal of the proposed method. We see from **Figure 7(b)** that the waveform is explosively increasing when the howling canceller did not exist. **Figure 7(c)** shows that the conventional adaptive notch filter can remove howling. But, its convergence speed is comparatively slow, and thus we did not avoid the perception of howling. On the other hand, **Figure 7(d)** shows that the proposed method can effectively cancel howling. The difference between **Figures 7(c)** and **(d)** expresses the difference of respective convergence speeds. The proposed method removed howling faster than the conventional notch filter.

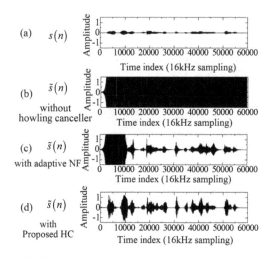

Figure 7. Waveforms of simulation result. (a) Source signal; (b) Loudspeaker output without howling canceller; (c) Loudspeaker output with conventional notch filter; (d) Loudspeaker output with proposed howling canceller.

5. Conclusion

This paper has proposed a howling canceller which employs a 2-tap linear predictor and a notch filter. The 2-tap linear predictor is for estimating the frequency of howling, and the notch filter is for eliminating howling. Since the coefficient of the 2-tap linear predictor is simply transformed to the coefficient of the notch filter, we can easily update the notch filter according to the linear predictor. The simulation result showed the effectiveness of the proposed method.

REFERENCES

[1] S. Haykin, "Introduction to Adaptive Filters," Macmillan Publishing Company, New York, 1984.

[2] A. Sogami, A. Kawamura and Y. Iiguni, "Improvement of Speech Quality in Distance-Based Howling Canceller," *IEICE Transactions on Fundamentals*, Vol. 92, No. 4, 2009, pp. 1039-1046.

[3] A. Soagami, A. Kawamura and Y. Iiguni, "A High Speech Quality Distance-Based Howling Canceller with Adaptive Cascade Notch Filter and Silent Pilot Signal," *IEICE Transactions on Fundamentals*, Vol. 94, No. 11, 2011, pp. 2306-2314.

[4] S. Nishimura, "An Improved Adaptive Notch Filter for Detection of Multiple Sinusoids," *IEICE Transactions on Fundamentals*, Vol. 77, No. 6, 1994, pp. 950-955.

[5] A. Nehorai, "A Minimal Parameter Adaptive Notch Filter with Constrained Poles and Zeros," *IEEE Transactions on Acoustics, Speech and Signal Processing*, Vol. 33, No. 4, 1985, pp. 983-996.

[6] H. C. Chong and U. L. Sang, "Adaptive Line Enhancement by Using an IIR Lattice Notch Filter," *IEEE Transactions on Acoustics, Speech and Signal Processing*, Vol. 37, No. 4, 1989, pp. 585-589.

[7] C. C. Tseng and S. C. Pei, "IIR Multiple Notch Filter Design Based on Allpass Filter," *IEEE Transactions on Circuits and Systems II: Analog and Digital Signal Processing*, Vol. 44, No. 2, 1997, pp. 133-136.

[8] S. C. Pei, W. S. Lu and C. C. Tseng, "Analytical Two-Dimensional IIR Notch Filter Design Using Outer Product Expansion," *IEEE Transactions on Circuits and Systems II: Analog and Digital Signal Processing*, Vol. 44, No. 9, 1997, pp. 765-768.

[9] Y. V. Joshi and S. C. D. Roy, "Design of IIR Multiple Notch Filters Based on All-Pass Filters," *IEEE Transactions on Circuits and Systems II: Analog and Digital Signal Processing*, Vol. 46, No. 2, 1999, pp. 134-138.

[10] V. DeBrunner, "An Adaptive, High-Order, Notch Filter Using All Pass Sections," *IEEE International Conference on Acoustics, Speech and Signal Processing*, Vol. 3, 1998, pp. 1477-1480.

[11] Y. C. Lim, Y. X. Zou and N. Zheng, "A Piloted Adaptive Notch Filter," *IEEE Transactions on Signal Processing*, Vol. 53, No. 4, 2005, pp. 1310-1323.

[12] A. Kawamura, Y. Itoh, J. Okello, M. Kobayashi and Y. Fukui, "Parallel Composition Based Adaptive Notch Filter: Performance and Analysis," *IEICE Transactions on Fundamentals*, Vol. 87, No. 7, 2004, pp. 1747-1755.

[13] A. Kawamura, Y. Iiguni and Y. Itoh, "An Adaptive Algorithm with Variable Step-Size for Parallel Notch Filter," *IEICE Transactions on Fundamentals*, Vol. 89, No. 2, 2006, pp. 511-519.

## 17

A 0.9 V Supply OTA in 0.18 μm CMOS Technology and Its Application in Realizing a Tunable Low-Pass Gm-C Filter for Wireless Sensor Networks

Soolmaz Abbasalizadeh[*], Samad Sheikhaei, Behjat Forouzandeh
School of Electrical and Computer Engineering, University of Tehran, Tehran, Iran

ABSTRACT

A low voltage low power operational transconductance amplifier (OTA) based on a bulk driven cell and its application to implement a tunable Gm-C filter is presented. The linearity of the OTA is improved by attenuation and source degeneration techniques. The attenuation technique is implemented by bulk driven cell which is used for low supply voltage circuits. The OTA is designed to operate with a 0.9 V supply voltage and consumes 58.8 μW power. A 600 mV$_{ppd}$ sine wave input signal at 1 MHz frequency shows total harmonic distortion (THD) better than −40 dB over the tuning range of the transconductance. The OTA has been used to realize a tunable Gm-C low-pass filter with gain tuning from 5 dB to 21 dB with 4 dB gain steps, which results in power consumptions of 411.6 to 646.8 μW. This low voltage filter can operate as channel select filter and variable gain amplifier (VGA) for wireless sensor network (WSN) applications. The proposed OTA and filter have been simulated in 0.18 μm CMOS technology. Corner case and temperature simulation results are also included to forecast process and temperature variation affects after fabrication.

Keywords: OTA; Low Voltage; Low Power; Bulk Driven; Gm-C Filter

1. Introduction

Due to the spreading market of portable electronic equipments, low power low voltage circuit design has become an important goal of electronic circuits industry. Many applications, like wireless sensor networks (WSNs), need low supply voltage circuits for proper operation which results in reducing their weight and increasing their battery life time. In wireless sensor networks, the voltage of battery drops over time. Since the nodes in this application cannot be easily accessed in some cases, and they should operate few months or years on a single battery, they must be designed to operate under low supply voltages to overcome voltage drop issues.

Operational transconductor amplifier (OTA) is an important building block of many analog circuits like filters, data converters, etc. This block converts input voltage to output current with a linear transformation factor. Its fast speed and bias based tunability makes this block more appropriate for analog circuits compared with conventional opamps, but it has a linearity limitation drawback. The linearity of the OTA is an important issue because the linearity of the overall system would be determined by this block. This issue becomes very challenging under

the low supply voltage and limited power consumption. Also, other specifications of the OTA would be affected by low supply voltage. So, novel circuit design techniques should be considered to improve linearity performances of the OTA and overcome the deterioration of its specifications.

In order to improve linearity of the OTA, many techniques have been reported recently, such as attenuation [1], source degeneration [2-4], nonlinear terms cancellation [5-10], and triode based transconductor [11-13]. In attenuation technique, the linearity improvement is achieved by reducing input voltage. In this technique nonlinear terms of output current is reduced by reducing input voltage. One attenuator that can be used for reducing input signal is bulk driven transistor. This cell attenuates input signal with γ factor which is the body effect coefficient and has a value between 0.2 and 0.4 [14].

In the bulk driven cell, the input signal is applied to bulk of transistor rather than its gate, and by connecting the gate to an appropriate bias voltage, the channel is formed. Since, the input signal is applied to bulk, it is not necessary to spend a part of the input voltage range to turn the transistor on and this removes the limitation that is produced by threshold voltage requirements of the transistors in low voltage designs. So, this cell can be

---
[*]Corresponding author.

used in low supply voltage circuits. In fact, the bulk driven cell can improve linearity of the OTA while operating with reduced supply voltages. In [15] and [16], two low voltage bulk driven OTAs are reported. However, these low voltage cells have some drawbacks. The bulk driven transconductance is 2 to 5 times smaller than that of the gate driven, based on the technology used. This issue leads to low DC gain, low gain bandwidth (GBW) and high input referred noise. Two transconductance enhancement techniques based on positive feedback are reported in [17] to overcome low transconductance value of the bulk driven transistor.

Source degeneration is another linearity improvement technique which is implemented by adding resistance at the source terminal of the input transistors. This technique increases noise factor of the OTA in trade off with linearity improvement. Tunablity of the source degenerated OTA is also achieved with tuning of the source degenerated resistance.

In nonlinear terms cancellation technique, linearity improvement is achieved by an appropriate sum of the nonlinear terms to cancel out nonlinearity. This technique is more suitable for low supply voltage circuits, because pseudo-differential architecture can be used easier in this technique.

In triode based transconductor, the drain-source voltage of input transistors, which is biased in triode region, is kept constant. As a result, a linear OTA with constant transconductance is achieved and tunability of the transconductance is carried out by changing the drain-source voltage of the triode transistors.

Since using these linearization techniques become very challenging under low supply voltages, some circuit design methods should be considered for low supply voltage designs. One of these methods, which is mentioned before, is the bulk driven cell. Some other low voltage circuit design methods are flipped voltage follower cell (FVF) [18], sub-threshold MOSFET [16], pseudo-differential pairs [19], and floating gate. In these methods some of the OTA's specifications such as linearity, noise, open loop DC gain, and unity gain bandwidth (UGBW) are deteriorated in trade off with reducing supply voltage. So, appropriate topology and biases should be used for getting more optimized circuits.

In this work, a low voltage low power bulk driven OTA is presented. This low voltage OTA can be used for some applications such as WSNs. The proposed OTA uses attenuation and source degeneration techniques for its linearity improvement. By using bulk driven transistors for input pairs, linearity improvement can be achieved while the OTA can operate with reduced supply voltages. The proposed OTA can operate with a 0.9 V supply voltage in a 0.18 μm CMOS n-well process. In order to overcome some drawbacks of using bulk driven

transistors, such as low DC gain, low unity gain bandwidth, and high noise, the transconductance enhancement technique, which is reported in [17], is applied to input pairs. In [17], this technique is applied to the bulk driven transistors, too. But no other linearity improvement technique is applied to input pair for further improving linearity. In the proposed OTA, this technique is applied to source degenerated bulk driven input pair and a self-cascode structure is used for increasing output impedance and so the DC gain. Also, in this work, tuning is added to the OTA for compensating the PVT variations. Tuning of the proposed OTA is achieved by varying the source degenerated resistance, which is implemented by a transistor.

As an application of the proposed low voltage low power OTA, a third-order low-pass Butterworth filter is designed. This low voltage Gm-C filter acts as a channel select filter and variable gain amplifier (VGA) for some wireless sensor network applications, such as those compliant with IEEE 802.15.4 standard, also known as Zig-Bee. The proposed filter has a gain tuning from 5 dB to 21 dB with 4 dB gain steps.

The rest of this manuscript is organized as follows. In Section 2, the proposed OTA with circuit details is discussed. Gm-C filter design and its gain tuning are described in Section 3. Section 4 shows the simulated performances of the OTA and filter. Some discussion about the circuit simulations are made in Section 5. Finally, the conclusions are drawn in Section 6.

2. Design of the Transconductance

2.1. Design of the Input Stage

In the bulk driven cell, input signal is applied to the bulk of input transistors rather than their gates. The bulk driven MOSFET cell acts similar to a JFET. The channel conductivity is varied by bulk-source voltage and, as a result, the bulk driven transistor can conduct with zero, negative, or slightly positive input voltage, similar to a depletion type device [20]. However, this low voltage cell has some disadvantages. The transconductance of the bulk driven transistor is much smaller than that of the gate driven, and this causes low DC gain, low gain bandwidth, and high input referred noise. Another disadvantage of this cell is that for an n-well process, only PMOS bulk driven MOSFETs are available. In order to use NMOS bulk driven MOSFETs, deep n-well layer is needed to achieve a twin well process. To reduce cost of circuit implementation, we have used bulk driven PMOS transistors, in this paper.

Figure 1 shows the input stage of the proposed bulk driven transconductance, which consists of the bulk driven fully-differential pair and tuning transistor. Bulk driven input transistors implement attenuation technique

A 0.9 V Supply OTA in 0.18 μm CMOS Technology and Its Application in Realizing a Tunable Low-Pass Gm-C
Filter for Wireless Sensor Networks

109

for linearity improvement of the OTA, which is appropriate for low voltage circuits. The tuning transistor, which acts as source degenerated resistance, improves linearity of the OTA and vary the transconductance value of the OTA for compensation of PVT variations. Although source degeneration technique, increases noise factor of the OTA, but, in trade off, can reduce third order harmonic distortion. When input transistors operate in strong inversion region, their drain current is expressed as follows:

$$I_D = \frac{1}{2}\mu_p C_{ox}\left(\frac{W}{L}\right)\left(V_{SG} - |V_{th}|\right)^2 \qquad (1)$$

in which, parameters have their usual meanings and the channel length modulation is ignored for simplicity. In the bulk driven transistor, threshold voltage is described by:

$$|V_{th}| = |V_{th0}| + |\gamma|\left[\sqrt{2|\phi_F| + V_{BS}} - \sqrt{2|\phi_F|}\right] \qquad (2)$$

in which, φ_F is the surface potential, γ is the body effect coefficient, and V_{th0} is threshold voltage when the bulk-source voltage is zero.

By using Equations (1) and (2), the transconductance value of the input transistors, not considering the source degenerated resistance, is given by:

$$g_{mb} = \frac{\partial I_D}{\partial V_{BS}} = \frac{|\gamma|}{2\sqrt{2|\varphi_F| + V_{BS}}} \cdot \sqrt{2\mu_p C_{ox}\frac{W}{L}I_D} \qquad (3)$$

By applying source degeneration technique to the input stage, the transconductance value is changed to:

$$g_{mb,sd} = \frac{g_{mb}}{1 + (g_{mb} \cdot R)} \qquad (4)$$

in which, R is the half of the resistance of the source degenerated transistor. From Equation (4), it is obvious that, by varying the value of R, the transconductance tuning can be achieved. Although the source degenerated technique, reduces transcondactance value by $1 + g_{mb}R$ factor, but greatly reduces the third order harmonic distortion term by factor of $(1 + g_{mb}R)^2$. The third order harmonic distortion term of the input transistors can be calculated from Equation (1) to Equation (4), as below.

$$HD_{3,saturation} = \frac{\partial^3 (I_{D,sat})}{3!\partial(V_{BS})^3}$$
$$= -\frac{\mu_p C_{ox} W \left(\gamma^2 \sqrt{2|\phi_F|} + |\gamma|\left(V_{SG} - |V_{th0}|\right)\right)}{16L\left(\sqrt{2|\phi_F| + V_{BS}}\right)\left(2|\phi_F| + V_{BS}\right)^2} \frac{1}{(1 + g_{mb}R)^2} \qquad (5)$$

As can be seen from Equation (5), the third order harmonic distortion term is attenuated by γ and $(1 + g_{mb}R)^2$ factors, which are related to the bulk driven transistors and the source degeneration transistor, respectively.

2.2. Complete Design of the Proposed Transconductance

The complete OTA is demonstrated in **Figure 2** which consists of the transconductance main stage, the common mode feedback circuit (CMFB), and the bias circuit. In this figure, all transistors with the same dimensions are labeled with the same symbols and the tuning transistor is labeled with SD (source degenerated).

In order to overcome the main bulk driven issue (low transconductance value), the transconductance enhancement technique is applied to the input pairs [17]. This technique is implemented by M_1, M_3, M_4, M_5 and M_6. A partial positive feedback which is implemented by M_3, reduces the conductance of the node A and increases $g_{mb,sd}$ by the factor η as below.

$$\eta = \frac{1}{1 - \left(g_{m,M_3}/g_{m,M_4}\right)} \qquad (6)$$

Because the overall feedback must remain negative, $g_{m,M4}$ must be larger than $g_{m,M3}$. In fact, by choosing $g_{m,M3}/g_{m,M4}$ close to unity, the circuit is very prone to instability, and linear input voltage range becomes small. So, proper sizing for M_3 and M_4 should be used to achieve a stable circuit. The flipped voltage follower current mirror is used for mirroring current to the output.

At the output stage of the OTA, self-cascode structure, which is accomplished by M_8 and M_9, is used for increasing output impedance. In low voltage circuits, it is not possible to stack transistors for increasing output impedance. Self-cascode structure is one solution, which is used in low voltage circuits to increase output impedance [21]. The self-cascode structure has much larger effective channel length and therefore much lower effective output conductance. The transistor M_9 in this structure is in linear region and acts as a resistor. For optimal operation of the structure, the dimension of M_8 should be kept larger than M_9. The self-cascode structure is more

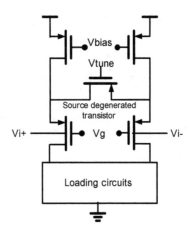

Figure 1. The input stage of the proposed bulk driven transconductance.

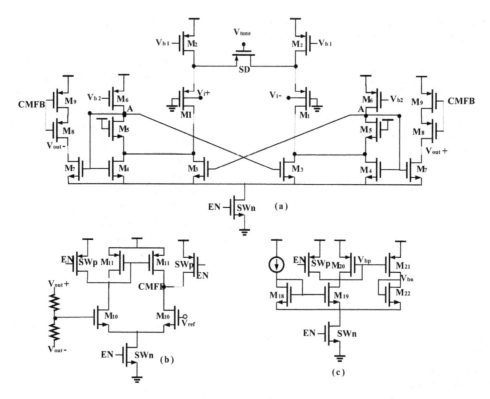

Figure 2. The complete OTA (a) The transconductance main stage; (b) The CMFB circuit; (c) The bias circuit.

suitable for low voltage circuits compared with conventional cascode, as it has high output impedance similar to that of a conventional cascode, while the output voltage requirements of the self-cascode could be similar to a single transistor.

Figure 2(b) shows the CMFB circuit, which sets the dc voltage of the output to V_{ref}. In order to achieve maximum output swing, output common mode is set to VDD/2. In the CMFB circuit, the output voltage of the OTA is averaged by resistance network and is compared with V_{ref}. The resultant signal adjusts the bias of the self-cascode structure and set the output dc voltage around V_{ref}.

The bias circuit which is used to generate the proper bias voltages of the OTA is shown in **Figure 2(c)**. In this figure, the diode connected transistors produce the fixed voltages of V_{bp} and V_{bn} for biasing of PMOS and NMOS transistors, respectively.

In **Figure 2** the transistors SWn and SWp are switches for turning on and off the OTA for gain tuning of the filter (will be described in details in Section 3). When EN

is high, the SWp and SWn switches are off and on, respectively. In this mode, the OTA is active and acts normally. For turning of the OTA, EN signal should go low. In this mode, the SWn switches are turned off and thus no current path exists to the ground. On the other hand, the SWp switches turn on and force PMOS biases to VDD. So, PMOS transistors turn off and the OTA becomes disabled.

2.3. Noise in the Proposed OTA

In this section, the noise performance of the proposed OTA is studied. Since, the major part of the voltage gain of the proposed OTA is produced by the output stage, the main part of the input referred noise is generated by the input stage. So, the noise of the output stage can be ignored. The total input referred noise of the overall OTA, which consists of flicker and thermal noise is approximated as: see Equation (7).

In the above equation, K_f is the flicker noise parameter, K is the Boltzmann constant, T is the temperature, f is the

$$\overline{V_{n,in}^2} = \left[2 \frac{8KT}{3g_{m\cdot eff}^2} \left(g_{m1} + \left(g_{mb}R/1 + g_{mb}R \right)^2 g_{m2} + g_{m3} + g_{m4} + g_{m6} \right) \right]$$

$$+ \frac{2}{c_{ox}} \frac{1}{f} \left[\left(\frac{k_{fp,sat}}{(WL)_1} \frac{g_{m1}^2}{g_{m\cdot eff}^2} \right) + \left(g_{mb}R/1 + g_{mb}R \right)^2 \left(\frac{k_{fp,sat}}{(WL)_2} \frac{g_{m2}^2}{g_{m\cdot eff}^2} \right) + \left(\frac{k_{fn,sat}}{(WL)_3} \frac{g_{m3}^2}{g_{m\cdot eff}^2} \right) + \left(\frac{k_{fn,sat}}{(WL)_4} \frac{g_{m4}^2}{g_{m\cdot eff}^2} \right) + \left(\frac{k_{fp,sat}}{(WL)_6} \frac{g_{m6}^2}{g_{m\cdot eff}^2} \right) \right] \quad (7)$$

frequency, $g_{m,eff}$ is $\eta^* g_{mb,sd}$ and other parameters have their usual meanings. The factor of 2 is considered for the two halves of the input stage.

Based on Equation (7), although the input referred noise is increased by the noise contribution of M_1 - M_4 and M_6, which is caused by the transconductance enhancement technique, the total input referred noise is reduced. In fact, by using this technique, the DC gain of the OTA enhances. Therefore, the input referred noise of the transistors not involved in this technique is reduced. Based on Equation (7), the total noise can be reduced by minimizing the gate transconductance of all transistors and the current of $M6$.

3. Gm-C Filter Design

The low voltage OTA, which is described in previously, can be used as channel selection filter and variable gain amplifier for the receiver of wireless sensor network applications. IEEE 802.15.4 or ZigBee is one standard which is introduced for wireless sensor networks. This low power standard is deigned for control applications and wireless sensing. It is also appropriate for comercial uses, industrial and home automation, personal health care appliances, and many other applications. In order to satisfy requirements of these articles, the sensors of ZigBee standard should be able to operate for several months on button cells or small batteries [22]. Therefore, the circuits of sensors used in this standard should be low voltage and low power. Considering a zero-IF architectture for the 2.4 GHz ZigBee receiver and assuming some margins in channel selection, a third order Butterworth low-pass filter with more than 2-MHz bandwidth is needed [22]. This filter provides the requirement of 0-dB

and 30-dB rejections at the adjacent channel (±5 MHz) and the alternate channel (±10 MHz), respectively [22]. In order to obtain some gain controlling based on the specifications of the receiver, the related filter should be able to operate as a variable gain amplifier, too.

Figure 3 shows the structure of the filter designed for the ZigBee standard. The filter is implemented by cascade of a first-order low-pass stage and a biquad stage for realizing a complex pole pair. This structure, which is reported in [23], is more suitable for low voltage circuits compared with the conventional structure. Because this structure can increase output swing, which is reduced due to low supply voltage. Since, the current delivered to each capacitor of the filter is the same as that of the conventional ones, the new structure does not change the cut off frequency and quality factor of the filter. Due to receiving the signal with the same amplitude and phase in both inputs of the OTA in this structure, the total voltage swing at the inputs of each transconductance is reduced compared with conventional structure and this relieves the need for a high-swing OTA.

Gain tuning of the filter can be obtained based on the fact that by increasing the number of parallel g_m blocks, the transconductance value increases linearly. In fact, by tuning the resistance of the transistor used as degeneration, and by parallelizing the first OTA of each stage in the filter by a similar OTA, gain variation is achieved.

In **Figure 3**, the switches, which are controlled by EN<i> signal, are implemented by transistors. When the cotrolling signal goes high, the related OTA is activated and increases the g_m value and also, gain of the filter. En<1-3> and EN<1-2> refer to the control of three and two OTAs that are placed in parallel, and can be turned

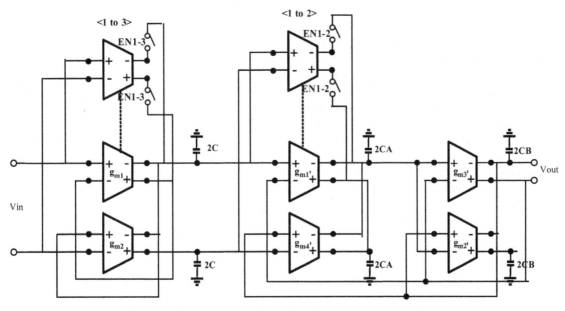

Figure 3. The implementation of the third order low-pass filter.

on and off individually to obtain the required gain value.

The frequency response of the filter is derived as: where,

$$H(S)$$

$$= \frac{g_{m1}/C}{s + g_{m2}/C} \frac{g'_{m1}g'_{m3}/C_A C_B}{s^2 + s\left(g'_{m4}/C_A\right) + g'_{m2}g'_{m3}/C_A C_B} \quad (8)$$

$$= \frac{k_1}{s + 2\pi f_c} \frac{k_2}{s^2 + s\left(\omega_0/Q\right) + \omega_0^2}$$

$$\omega_0 = 2\pi f_c \sqrt{\sigma^2 + \omega^2}, Q = \frac{\sqrt{\sigma^2 + \omega^2}}{2\sigma} \quad (9)$$

in which, σ, ω are the real and imaginary parts of the complex pole, and f_c is the cut off frequency of the filter, k_1 and k_2 are the gain values and other parameters have their usual meanings. Based on Equation (8), it is obvious that by varying the transconductance value of g_{m1} and g'_{m1}, the gain tunability of the filter can be achieved without any variation in the cut off frequency.

4. Simulation Results

4.1. Simulation Results of the OTA

The transconductor and the filter were simulated in a standard 0.18 μm CMOS n-well process with a 0.9 V power supply voltage. The OTA consumes 58.8 μW and 10.6 nW in on and off modes, respectively. The Vtune of the tuning transistor can be varied from 0 to 130 mV to obtain transconductance values of 41.5 μS to 29.7 μS. This 40% tuning can be used for compensating the PVT variations, and also at the same time for tuning the gain of the filter. The tuning of the transconductance value versus differential input voltages is demonstrated in **Figure 4**.

The simulated THD of the OTA is achieved respectively as 55.4 dB, 51.2 dB, and 47.1 dB, by applying 400 mV$_{ppd}$, 500 mV$_{ppd}$, and 600 mV$_{ppd}$ differential input signals with 1 MHz frequency. For THD simulations, the Vtune of the tuning transistor is set at 65 mV that is in the middle of the tuning range. Also, simulations show that the THD of the OTA over tuning range of the transconductance, for input amplitude of less than 600 mV$_{ppd}$, remains below −40 dB.

The input referred noise of the OTA is simulated at 1 MHz frequency and is calculated as 108 nV/√Hz for Vtune of 0 V, which increases to 148.3 nV/√Hz for Vtune of 130 mV. This noise is measured in fully-differential condition, and the large value of it, is due to the bulk driven cell and low supply voltage. In fact, this high noise value can be ignored in trade off with lowering supply voltage and power consumption. The unit of nV/√Hz comes from the dependency of noise to frequency. The noise power density is calculated in voltage

squared per hertz, and is called noise power spectral density (PSD) and its rms value is reported in V/√Hz. The common mode rejection ration (CMRR) of the OTA for Vtune of 65 mV is simulated as 139.8 dB, which is measured for a single-ended output. This CMRR will be much higher for differential outputs.

Table 1 contains a summary of the OTA performances. Corner case simulations of the OTA are summarized in **Table 2**. Process and temperature worst case performances of the proposed transconductance are shown in **Table 3**. The temperature of the OTA is varied from −40°C to 70°C. As can be seen in these tables, the OTA shows proper operation in process and temperature variations. Performance comparison of the OTA with recently published work are presented in **Table 4**. For better comparison, a figure of merit (FOM) which is defined in [10] is used. In this FOM, shown in Equation (10),

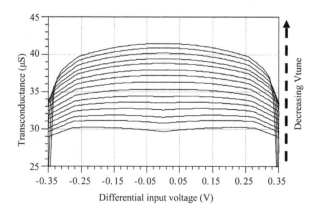

Figure 4. Transconductance tuning versus differential input voltage.

Table 1. Performance summary of the proposed OTA.

Specification	Value
Technology	Standard 0.18 μm CMOS
Power supply	0.9 V
Power consumption (μW)	On mode = 58.8 Off mode = 0.01
THD (dB)	−55.4, −51.2, −47.1[*]
Input referred noise (nV/√Hz) in tuning range	108 - 148.3@1 MHz
DC gain (dB)[**]	34.8
Unity gain bandwidth (MHz)[**]	11
CMRR (dB)[**]	139.8
PSRR+ (dB)[**]	82.7
PSRR− (dB)[**]	47.8

[*]At 400, 500 and 600 mV$_{ppd}$ input signal, respectively, @1 MHz (Vtune = 65 mV); [**]Cload = 1 pF and Vtune = 65 mV; Note: CMRR and PSRR values are reported for a single ended output. Differential output values are much higher.

Table 2. Corner case simulations of the OTA.

	TT	SS	SF	FS	FF
Power consumption (μW)	58.8 Off = 0.001	55.9 Off = 0.0006	58.7 Off = 0.0006	58.4 Off = 0.2	60.5 Off = 0.2
THD (dB) (500 mV$_{ppd}$ input signal)[*]	−51.2	−48.8	−42.8	−49.8	−44.6
Input referred noise (nV/√Hz)[*]	115	124.6	109.2	123.5	120.9

[*]@1 MHz, Vtune = 65 mV.

Table 3. Process and temperature worst case performances of the proposed OTA.

	Min	Typical	Max
Power consumption in on mode (μW)	48.8	58.8	65.2
THD (dB) for 500 mV$_{ppd}$ input signal[*]	−55.7	−51.2	−40.1
Input referred noise (nV/√Hz)[*]	111.7	115	149.4

[*]@1 MHz, Vtune = 65 mV.

Table 4. Performance summary of the OTA and comparison with recently published work.

Year	Technology/input structure	Supply voltage (V)	Input voltage range (mV$_{ppd}$)	THD of output current (dB)	Power consumption (W)	Input referred noise (nV/√Hz)	Transconductance value (μS)	FOM	FOM/VDD
2007 [5]	0.18 μm/ Gate driven	1	400	−70@1 MHz	2.5 m	13	1000	87	87
2008 [10]	0.18 μm/ Gate driven	1.5	900	−60 IM3 @40 MHz Or −69.5 THD	9.5 m	23	470	97.2	64.8
2011 [16]	0.18 μm/ Bulk driven	0.5	500	-	60 μ	80@1 MHz	-	-	-
2011 [20]	0.18 μm/ Bulk driven	1	800	−55 @1 MHz	70 μ Vtune = 0.43 V	-	5.6	75.5	75.5
This work	0.18 μm/ Bulk driven	0.9	600	−55.35, −51.2, −47.1[*]	58.8 μ	115 (Full diff)[**]	38.8	79.5	88.36

[*]At 400, 500 and 600 mVppd input signal, respectively (@1 MHz, Vtune = 65 mV); [**]@1 MHz, Vtune = 65 mV.

transconductance value, linearity performance, speed of the circuit, input swing amplitude, and power consumption are considered.

$$FOM = 10 \log \frac{G_m \times V_{id} \times THD \times f_0}{P} \qquad (10)$$

We have also included a new measure, defined as FOM/VDD, in this table to account for the effect supply voltage reduction. As can be seen, by including the effect of supply voltage, it is obvious that the proposed OTA compares well with the others.

4.2. Simulation Results of the Gm-C Filter

The filter is designed for cut off frequency of more than 1 MHz. This condition guarantees that the filter never removes desired signal power. This consideration is mentioned as the design should be able to compensate the transfer function distortion of the filter (*i.e.*, reduction of the cut off frequency). This distortion comes from truning on the parallel transconductors which leads to

reducing output impedance of the related stage.

Figure 5 shows the frequency response of the third order Butterworth low-pass filter over gain tuning of the filter. This filter has gain tuning from 5 dB to 21 dB with 4 dB gain steps. As can be seen in this figure, the cut off frequency of the filter is more than 1 MHz in complete range of the gain tuning. The proposed filter achieves attenuation of 32.1 dB and 50.2 dB at 5 MHz and 10 MHz, respectively for a 5 dB gain of the filter. The proposed filter consumes 411.6 μW to 646.8 μW powers for 5 dB to 21 dB gains of the filter.

The input referred noise of the filter is simulated as 67 nV/√Hz at maximum gain of the filter, which is increased to 167.1 nV/√Hz at minimum gain. This noise value seems good for bulk driven filter with low supply voltage. The simulated in-band IIP_3 of the filter is shown in **Figure 6** which is 10.75 dBm at a 5 dB gain. This IIP_3 value is measured with two input tones of 0.99 MHz and 1.01 MHz. The simulations show that the IIP_3 is reduced to −7 dBm at 21 dB gain of the filter.

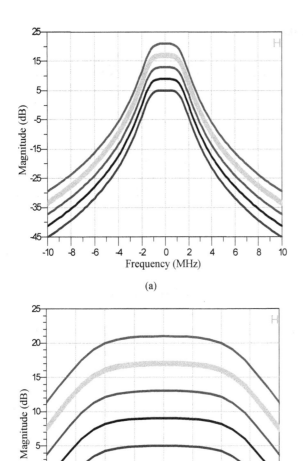

(a)

(b)

Figure 5. Frequency response of the third order low-pass filter. (a) Total response; (b) Zoom in on the pass band of the frequency response

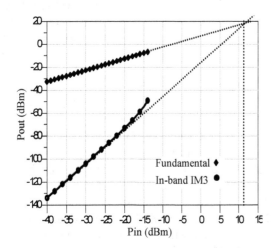

Figure 6. In-band *IIP*₃ calculation for a 5 dB gain of the filter.

The simulated performances of the filter are listed in **Table 5**. Corner case simulations of the filter are presented in **Table 6**. Corner cases and temperature variations from −40°C to 70°C are simulated as well, and show *IIP*₃ better than 7 dBm, cut off frequency better than 1.2 MHz, attenuation at 5 MHz better than 31 dB and attenuation at 10 MHz better than 49.2 dB, in worst cases, for 5 dB gain of the filter. These values show that the filter operates properly in process and temperature variations. In order to compensate corner case and temperature variations, the Vtune of the tuning transistor is adjusted to obtain appropriate gain of filter and cut off frequency more than 1 MHz. The performance comparison of the filter with recently published work is included in **Table 7**. Performances of the proposed filter are calculated at 5 dB gain of the filter. For better comparison, a figure of merit (FOM) is used as follows [24]:

$$FOM = \frac{\left(\dfrac{P_C}{N}\right)}{f_c SFDR N^{4/3}}, \quad SFDR = \left(\frac{IIP_3}{P_N}\right)^{2/3} \quad (11)$$

in which, P_c is the power consumption of the filter, N is the number of poles and zeros, f_c is the cutoff frequency

Table 5. Performance summary of the proposed filter.

Specification	Value
Technology	0.18 μm CMOS
Power supply	0.9 V
Filter type	3rd order low-pass Butterworth
Cut off frequency (MHz)	More than 1
Gain tuning (dB)	5 to 21
Attenuation (dB)	32.1@5 MHz* 50.2@10 MHz*
Power consumption (μW)	411.6, 646.8**
Differential output swing (V)	0.86*
*IIP*₃ (dBm)	10.75, −7**
Input referred noise @1 MHz (nV/√ Hz)	67, 167.1**

*At 5 dB gain of the filter; **At 5 dB and 21 dB gain of filter, respectively.

Table 6. Corner case simulation results of the filter (Vtune is adjusted per corner case to obtain gain = 5 dB and fc > 1 MHz).

Performances at 5 dB gain of the filter	TT	SS	SF	FS	FF
*IIP*₃ (dBm)	10.75	9.5	11.5	11	11.5
Noise figure (dB)	45.2	46	45.7	45.8	45.26
Cut off frequency (MHz)	1.4	1.3	1.3	1.3	1.3
Attenuation (dB) @5 MHz	32.1	34.3	32.7	34.4	32.7
Attenuation(dB) @10 MHz	50.2	52.4	50.8	52.4	50.9

A 0.9 V Supply OTA in 0.18 μm CMOS Technology and Its Application in Realizing a Tunable Low-Pass Gm-C
Filter for Wireless Sensor Networks

115

Table 7. Performance summary of the filter and comparison with recently published work.

Year	Technology/ input structure	VDD (V)	Power consumption (W)	IIP_3 (dBm)	Input referred noise (nV/√Hz)	Order of low-pass filter	Cut off frequency (MHz)	FOM (fJ)	FOM* VDD
2011 [24]	90 nm/gate driven	1	4.35 m	21.7 - 22.1	(Diff) 75	6	8.1 - 13.5	0.02*	0.02*
2009 [25]	0.18 μm/gate driven	1.2	4.1 m - 11.1 m	19 - 22.3	12 - 425	3	0.5 - 20	1.54*	1.85*
2011 [16]	0.18 μm/bulk driven	0.5	326 μ	-	171 (@1 MHz)	3	1.4 - 6	-	-
This work	0.18 μm/bulk driven	0.9	411.6 μ**	10.75**	(Diff) 167.1@1 MHz**	3	1	0.41**	0.37**

*Average of FOM, **@5 dB gain.

and the $SFDR.N^{4/3}$ expression is the normalized spurious free dynamic range [24]. For a better comparison of the designs, the average of the FOM is used for filters with cut off frequency tuning. In contrast with the FOM defined for the OTA in Equation (10), the lower FOM in Equation (11) shows a better design. Therefore, for taking effects of supply voltage into account, FOM*VDD is included also in **Table 7**. This table shows that the proposed filter compares favorably with others.

5. Discussion/Analysis

In this paper, a 0.9 V supply transconductance with bulk driven input pairs is represented. A range of 40% tuning of the transconductance value is achieved by varying the source degeneration resistance, which is also used for further improving linearity. This tuning can be used for compensating PVT variations and achieving gain tuning for a third order Butterworth low-pass filter. Further gain tuning of the filter is achieved by parallelizing of transconductor blocks. Using these two methods the gain of the filter can be tuned from 5 dB to 21 dB.

The OTA and filter are simulated in a standard 0.18 μm CMOS technology. The OTA consumes 58.8 μW and filter consumes 411.6 μW to 646.8 μW powers for 5 dB to 21 dB gains. The OTA shows input reffered noise of 108 nV/√Hz to 148.3 nV/√Hz over tuning range of the transconductance value, which is due to the resistance variation of the tuning transistor. The filter shows 167.1 nV/√Hz input reffered noise and 10.75 dBm $IIP3$ at 5 dB gain, too. Process corners and temperature variations from −40°C to 70°C are also studied in the paper to forecast the operation of the OTA and filter after fabrication. The simulations show good stability in all process corners and temperatures.

6. Conclusions

A low supply transconductance with bulk driven input pair is proposed in this work. Linearity improvement of the OTA is done by attenuation and source degeneration techniques. Attenuation is implemented by a bulk driven

cell, which is used to overcome the threshold voltage limitations of the transistor in low supply voltage circuits. A transconductance enhancement technique is applied to the input pairs of the transconductor to ovecome some drawbacks of the bulk diven cell, including low transconductance value, low DC gain, and high noise. The high noise drawback of the bulk driven cell could be further reduced by some noise cancellation technique. A self cascode structure is also applied to the output stage of the transconductor for further enhancing the DC gain.

As an application of the proposed low voltage OTA, a third order low-pass filter is implemented. The gain of the filter can be tuned. This tunable filter can be used as a channel select filter and variable gain amplifier for wireless sensor network (WSN) applications. The simulation results prove that the proposed design satisfies the required performance of the ZigBee standard, used for wireless sensor network applications.

REFERENCES

[1] A. El Mourabit, G. Lu and P. Pittet, "Wide-Linear-Range Subthreshold OTA for Low-Power, Low-Voltage, and Low-Frequency Applications," *IEEE Transactions on Circuits and Systems I*, Vol. 52, No. 8, 2005, pp. 1481-1488.

[2] A. Worapishet and C. Naphaphan, "Current-Feedback Source-Degenerated CMOS Transconductor with Very High Linearity," *Electronics Letters*, Vol. 39, No. 7, 2003, pp. 17-18.

[3] A. J. López-Martín, J. Ramirez-Angulo, C. Durbha and R. G. Carvajal, "A CMOS Transconductor with Multidecade Tuning Using Balanced Current Scaling in Moderate Inversion," *IEEE Journal of Solid-State Circuits*, Vol. 40, No. 5, 2005, pp.

[4] F. A. P. Barúqui and A. Petraglia, "Linearly Tunable CMOS OTA with Constant Dynamic Range Using Source-Degenerated Current Mirrors," *IEEE Transactions on Circuits and Systems II*, Vol. 53, No. 9, 2006, pp. 791-801.

[5] T.-Y. Lo and C.-C. Hung, "A 1-V 50-MHz Pseudodifferential OTA with Compensation of the Mobility Reduction," *IEEE Transactions on Circuits and Systems II*, Vol.

54, No. 12, 2007, pp. 1047-1051.

[6] K. Kwon, H.-T. Kim and K. Lee, "A 50 - 300-MHz Highly Linear and Low-Noise CMOS Gm-C Filter Adopting Multiple Gated Transistors for Digital TV Tuner ICs," *IEEE Transactions on Microwave Theory and Techniques*, Vol. 57, No. 2, 2009, pp. 306-313.

[7] H. Le-Thai, H.-H. Nguyen, H.-N. Nguyen, H.-S. Cho, J.-S. Lee, *et al.*, "An IF Bandpass Filter Based on a Low Distortion Transconductor," *IEEE Journal of Solid-State Circuits*, Vol. 45, No. 11, 2010, pp. 2250-2261.

[8] A. Lewinski and J. S. Martinez, "OTA Linearity Enhancement Technique for High Frequency Applications With IM3 Below −65 dB," *IEEE Transactions on Circuits and Systems II*, Vol. 51, No. 10, 2004, pp. 542-548.

[9] S. Ouzounov, E. Roza, J. A. (Hans) Hegt, G. Weide and A. H. M. van Roermund, "A CMOS V-I Converter with 75-dB SFDR and 360-μW Power Consumption," *IEEE Journal of Solid-State Circuits*, Vol. 40, No. 7, 2005, pp. 1527-1532.

[10] T.-Y. Lo and C.-C. Hung, "A 40-MHz Double Differential-Pair CMOS OTA with −60-dB IM3," *IEEE Transactions on Circuits and Systems I*, Vol. 55, No. 1, 2008, pp. 258-265.

[11] C. I. Luján-Martinez, R. G. Carvajal, A. Torralba, A. J. Lopez-Martin, J. Ramirez-Angulo, *et al.*, "Low-Power Baseband Filter for Zero-Intermediate Frequency Digital Video Broadcasting Terrestrial/Handheld Receivers," *IET Circuits, Devices and Systems*, Vol. 3, No. 5, 2009, pp. 291-301.

[12] U. Yodprasit and C. C. Enz, "A 1.5-V 75-dB Dynamic Range Third-Order Gm-C Filter Integrated in a 0.18-μm Standard Digital CMOS Process," *IEEE Journal of Solid-State Circuits*, Vol. 38, No. 7, 2003, pp. 1189-1197.

[13] S. Han, "A Novel Tunable Transconductance Amplifier Based on Voltage-Controlled Resistance by MOS Transistors," *IEEE Transactions on Circuits and Systems II*, Vol. 53, No. 8, 2006, pp. 662-666.

[14] E. Sánchez-Sinencio and J. Silva-Martinez, "CMOS Transconductance Amplifiers, Architectures and Active Filters: A Tutorial," *IEEE Proceedings Circuits, Devices and Systems*, Vol. 147, No. 1, 2000, pp. 3-12.

[15] J. M. Carrillo ,G. Torelli, R. P. Aloe, J. M. Valverde and J. F. Duque-Carrillo, "Single-Pair Bulk-Driven CMOS Input Stage: A Compact Low-Voltage Analog Cell for

Scaled Technologies," *Integration, the VLSI journal*, Vol. 43, No. 3, 2010, pp. 251-257.

[16] F. Rezaei and S. J. Azhari, "Ultra Low Voltage, High Performance Operational Transconductance Amplifier and Its Application in A Tunable Gm-C Filter," *Microelectronics Journal*, Vol. 42, No. 6, 2011, pp. 827-836.

[17] J. M. Carrillo, G. Torelli and J. F. Duque-Carrillo, "Transconductance Enhancement in Bulk-Driven Input Stages and Its Applications," *Analog Integrated Circuits and Signal Processing*, Vol. 68, No. 2, 2011, pp. 207-217.

[18] R. G. Carvajal, J. R. Angulo, A. J. López-Martín, A. Torralba, J. Antonio Gómez Galán, *et al.*, "The Flipped Voltage Follower: A Useful Cell for Low-Voltage Low-Power Circuit Design," *IEEE Transactions on Circuits and Systems I*, Vol. 52, No. 7, 2005, pp. 1276-1291.

[19] T.-Y. Lo and C.-C. Hung, "A 250 MHz Low Voltage Low-Pass Gm-C Filter," *Analog Integrated Circuits and Signal Processing*, Vol. 71, No. 3, 2012, pp. 465-472.

[20] Y. H. Kong, H. Yang, M. Jiang, S. Z. Xu and H. Z. Yang, "Low-Voltage Transconductor with Wide Input Range and Large Tuning Capability," *Tsinghua Science and Technology*, Vol. 16, No. 1, 2011, pp. 106-112.

[21] S. S. Rajput and S. S. Jamuar, "Low Voltage Analog Circuit Design Techniques," *IEEE Circuits and Systems Magazine*, Vol. 2, No. 1, 2002, pp. 24-42.

[22] N.-J. Oh and S.-G. Lee, "Building a 2.4-GHz Radio Transceiver Using IEEE 802.15.4," *IEEE Circuits & Devices Magazine*, Vol. 21, No. 6, 2005, pp. 43-51.

[23] A. Tajalli and Y. Leblebici, "Linearity Improvement in Biquadratic Transconductor-C Filters," *Electronics Letters*, Vol. 43, No. 24, 2007, pp. 1360-1362.

[24] M. S. Oskooei, N. Masoumi, M. Kamarei and H. Sjöland, "A CMOS 4.35-mW + 22-dBm IIP_3 Continuously Tunable Channel Select Filter for WLAN/WiMAX Receivers," *IEEE Journal of Solid-State Circuits*, Vol. 46, No. 6, 2011, pp. 1382-1391.

[25] T.-Y. Lo, C.-C. Hung and M. Ismail, "A Wide Tuning Range Gm-C Filter for Multi-Mode CMOS Direct-Conversion Wireless Receivers," *IEEE Journal of Solid-State Circuits*, Vol. 44, No. 9, 2009, pp. 2515-2524.

## 18

A New Design Technique of CMOS Current Feed Back Operational Amplifier (CFOA)

Hassan Jassim

Department of Electrical Engineering, College of Engineering, Babylon University, Babylon, Iraq

ABSTRACT

A new design technique employing CMOS Current Feedback Operational Amplifier (CFOA) is presented. This design approach applies CFA OTA as input stage cascaded with class AB cross-coupled buffer stage. The performance parameters of CMOS CFOA such as bandwidth, slew rate, settling time are extensively improved compared with conventional CFOA. These parameters are very important in high frequency applications that use CMOS CFOA as an active building block such as A/D converters, and active filters. Also the DC input offset voltage and harmonic distortion (HD) are very low values compared with the conventional CMOS CFOA are obtained. P-Spice simulation results using 0.35 μm MI-ETEC CMOS process parameters shows considerable improvement over existing CMOS CFOA simulated model. Some of the performance parameters for example are DC gain of 67.2 dB, open-loop gain bandwidth product of 104 MHz, slew rate (SR+) of +91.3 V/μS, THD of −67 dB and DC input offset voltage of −0.2 mV.

Keywords: Synthesis CFA OTA and CMOS CFOA; Cross Coupled Buffer Stage; High Performance CFOA; Low Input Offset Voltage CFOA; Low Distortion CFOA

1. Introduction

The role of analog integrated circuits in modern electronic systems remains important, even though digital circuits dominate the market for VLSI solutions. Analog systems have always played an essential role in interfacing digital electronics to the real world in applications such as analog signal processing and conditioning, industrial process, motion control and biomedical measurements [1]. However, the conventional CMOS CFOA design is still facing certain problems, first, the offset voltage on the current feedback can not be made zero. CFOA usually adopts an analog buffer as the input stage. As a result, the non-inverting input has very high impedance, while the inverting input has very low impedance. Hence, the CFOAs offset is higher than folded cascade voltage amplifier (VFA) Design. Second, the constant bandwidth feature of the CFOA is only approximate if the inverting input impedance is not small enough [2,3]. The low-input offset voltage is considered as an important aspect of the performance of an amplifier especially when signals are in the range of few hundred micro volts [4]. Several CMOS realizations for the CFOA have been reported in the literature [5-12]. The design still suffers from many drawbacks such as high distortion, high noise, high consumption of power and complex circuitry. The CFOA has been always seen as an extension of the CCII, therefore, the design approach was cascade with CCII+ with a voltage follower to realize a complete circuit. The obtained bandwidth was always the degraded version of CCII+.

The current feedback operational amplifier (CFOA), a two-port (four-terminal) network. The CFOA could be realized by using second generation current conveyor CCII+ cascaded with a voltage follower [13].

This paper describes an alternative approach to CMOS CFOA design which provides symmetrical high impedances (infinite for DC) inputs together with high performance parameters in high frequency operation. This design approach applies CFA OTA as input stage cascaded with class AB cross-coupled buffer as output stage. The symmetrical input stage of CFA OTA will reduce the DC offset voltage of CMOS CFOA with improvement of high frequency parameters. Moreover, class AB cross coupled buffer stage provide high current drive capability. P-Spice simulation results confirm the theoretical calculations.

2. Theoretical Background of CFB OTA

The two output terminals are not seen as one port each, but as four independent terminals that can have different impedance levels. As a consequence, hybrid stages appear, namely a H input stage and a H output stage. The H input stage, which has become well known through the CFB opamp, can also be understood as an extended input stage whose analogue ground voltage is not fixed, but can be set through an additional terminal. The V output can also be extended to a hybrid stage. It copies the current flowing into the voltage output terminal to an additional current output terminal. This technique, which is called output current sensing or supply current sensing, has played an important role in the development of new opamps, e.g. the current-feedback opamp [14], or its extension, the operational floating conveyor (OFC) which has both a H input and H output.

All operational amplifiers are already known, with exception of hybrid input (e.g. current and voltage) to output current (*H-I amplifier*). *We decided to call it current-feedback OTA (CFB OTA)*, although it is a current amplifier with an additional voltage input [14]. The mean idea behind this decision was to maintain the symmetry in the classification.

It should be mentioned here that the same functionality can also be described from a completely different theoretical back-ground. *One can show that the so-called infinite-gain second-generation current conveyor (CCII∞) from [15] is essentially the same as the CFB OTA.* The background from which it came is, however, different, the *CCII∞* was developed on the transistor level in order to optimize the trade-off between speed and distortion in current amplifiers. The CFB OTA shown in **Figure 1** is described by:

$$i_1 = 0, v_2 = v_1, i_3 = -A_i i_2, i_4 = A_i i_2, A_i = \infty . \quad (1)$$

3. Proposed of CMOS CFOA

Our design technique of CMOS CFOA consists of two stages, the first stage is the CFB OTA cascading with class AB cross-coupled buffer as second stage as shown in **Figure 2** to provide high current drive capability as mention in Section 1. We start by designing fully differential folded cascade OTA using Gm/Id technique in strong inversion region [16]. The current equation of OTA signifies that the transconductance of OTA strongly depends on the bias current [16] and is given by

$$Id = G_m \{Vin(+) - Vin(-)\} \quad (2)$$

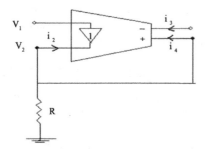

Figure 1. Block diagram of current feedback operational transconductancxe amplifier (CBA OTA).

The operation of folded cascode OTA consists of one differential pair consisting of NMOS transistors M_1 and M_2. MOS transistors M_{12} and M_{13} provide the DC bias voltage to M_{11} transistor. The folded cascode OTA characterized by performance such as high DC voltage gain, wide gain bandwidth product, low noise and consumption power [17]. The gain of the folded cascode OTA is given by:

$$V_O/V_{in} = G_{m1} R_O \quad (3)$$

and the gain bandwidth product is given by:

$$GBW = G_{m1}/C_L \quad (4)$$

where G_{m1} is the transconductance of transistor M_1 and R_O (output resistance) =(R_O looking into drain of M_4)//(R looking into transistor into drain of M_8). After applying the design strategy clarified previously, the design parameters in strong inversion region, the gate-dimensions, biasing currents, and overdrive voltages of MOS transistors are summarized in **Table 1**.

4. Simulation Results

A new alternative CMOS CFOA with high performance operation, very low input offset voltage and low distortion is proposed in this paper. Since, the high frequency parameters such as voltage gain, (–3 dB) bandwidth, slew rate (SR), settling time (t_s) and gain bandwidth product (GBW) are improved. **Figure 3** clarifies the improvement in the open loop voltage gain and gain bandwidth product (GBW) of the proposed CMOS CFOA. In addition, the magnitude curve shows the frequency response (variation of frequency against the voltage gain and phase curve show the variation of frequency against the phase shift between input and output voltage. The value of output impedance of buffer stage is decreased drastically due to using cross-coupled buffer stag we note

Table 1. Gate dimensions and biasing currents of MOS transistors of proposed CMOS CFOA.

Transistors no.	Gate dimensions and biasing currents		
	W (μm)	L (μm)	Biasing current (μA)
M_1, M_2	12.0	0.35	50.0
M_3, M_4	16.1	0.35	50.0
M_5, M_6	11.59	0.35	100.0
M_7, M_8, M_9, M_{10}	6.21	0.35	50.0
M_{11}, M_{12}	2.51	0.35	100.0
M_{15}	9.5	0.35	100
M_{16}	2.0	0.35	100
M_{17}	23.8	0.35	100
M_{18}	6.0	0.35	100

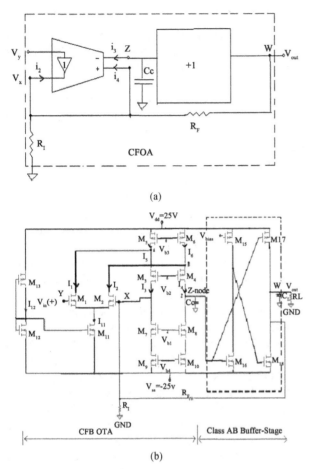

(a)

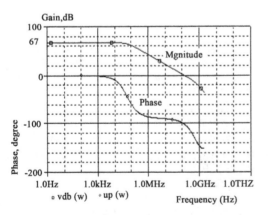

(b)

Figure 2. (a) Block diagram of proposed CMOS CFOA; (b) Schematic of proposed CMOS CFOA.

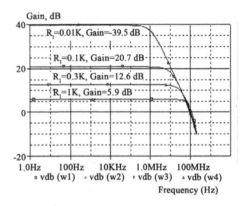

Figure 3. Open-loop frequency response of the proposed CMOS CFOA.

that in **Figure 4**. **Figure 5** indicates that the improvement in closed loop (–dB band width) of the proposed CMOS CFOA, since the values of (–dB bandwidth) is 104 MHz compared with 36.2 MHz with introduce the closed loop resistors are R_F = 1 KΩ and R_I = 1 KΩ. The value of voltage gain will increased with decreasing in the (–3 db) bandwidth due to change the value of R_I and keep the

value of R_F is constant. The slew rate of CMOS CFOA are measured from **Figure 6**. DC characteristics of CMOS CFOA is shown in **Figure 7**, we note that there is a large enhancement in linearity of DC characteristics of the CMOS CFOA due to the symmetry in operation of the fully differential input stage of CFA OTA. Moreover, we note that the value of input offset voltage is –0.2 mV due to the symmetry in input stage (inverting and non inverting inputs) of the proposed CMOS CFOA. **Table 2** shows the effect of varies input resistors R_I value on the feedback loop gain and CMOS CFOA, closed loop voltage gain (Av), gain bandwidth product (GBW), (–3 dB) bandwidth, phase margin (PM), and total harmonic distortion (HD). Simulation results of proposed CMOS

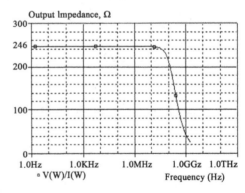

Figure 4. Closed-loop frequency response of the proposed CMOS CFOA with different values of R_I.

Figure 5. Output impedance of the proposed CMOS CFOA.

Table 2. Performance parameters of proposed CFOA with variation of Feedback resistance R_I.

Feedback resistance (R_I) KΩ	Performance parameters			
	–3 dB B.W MHz	GBW MHz	PM deg.	THD dB	Av dB
1	79.6	104	49.9°	–67.0	5.9
0.3	32.7	89.2	48.6°	–65.0	12.5
0.1	10.7	81.8	46.0°	–41.7	20.4
0.01	1.0	78.6	45.0°	–41.0	39.1

CFOA confirmed the theoretical concepts in previous sections.

Table 3 Summarizes the comparison between several previous works and the proposed CFOA, we note there are a considerable improvement of performance parameters of proposed CFOA compared with previous works. Specially high frequency parameters, harmonic distortion and input offset voltage.

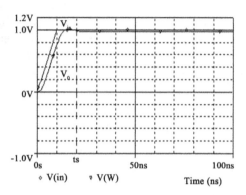

Figure 6. 1V Step response of the CMOS CFOA using (C_L) = 10 PF.

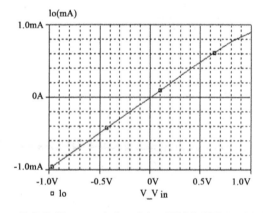

Figure 7. DC Characteristics of the CMOS CFOA with R_L = 1 KΩ.

Table 3. Summarize the comparison between several works.

Reference	[1]	[2]	[13]	Proposed CFOA
VDD, −VSS	1.5 V	3.3 V	0.75 V	2.5
Power dissipation	0.45 mW	5.3 mW	0..456 mW	5.5 mW
GBW	120 MHz	58 MHz	120 MHz	104 MHz
Input offset voltage	<20 mV	1.3 mV	<20 mV	0.2 mV
DC gain	-	74 dB	-	67 dB
Input voltage dynamic range	−0.65 V to +0.65 V	-	−0.65 V to +0.65 V	−1 V to +1V
THD	-	−83 dB	-	−67 dB
Technology	0.25 μm	0.35 μm	0.25 μm	0.35 μm

5. Conclusion

A new design technique of the CMOS CFOA with attractive features for high frequency, low offset voltage and low distortion is proposed in this paper. The proposed design based on cross-coupled buffer stage that connected as output stage of the CMOS CFOA. Since this technique operates on logic transition concept which gives the high speed, symmetry operation of the output signal and high current drive capability of proposed CMO CFOA. The high speed operation improved high performance parameters such as gain bandwidth (GBW), (−3 dB) bandwidth, slew rate (SR) and settling time (t_s) with ensure the phase margin (PM) in acceptable value that keep the stability of operation. Moreover, the symmetry of input differential of folded cacode CFA OTA technique decreased the distortion in output signal and improved (DC) characteristics of CMOS CFOA. In addition to that using folded cascode OTA (FC-OTA) as the input stage of CMOS CFOA make the symmetry of inverting and non inverting inputs that reduce input offset voltage. The trans-impedance node (Z) of the CMOS CFOA gained high value due to cascoding transistors of CFA OTA. This feature is very important for design CMOS CFOA with high gain. We can summarize our conclusion by saying that the proposed CMOS CFOA with symmetry of the input stage and symmetry of the output stage will gain CMOS CFOA attractive features for many high frequency, low distortion, low input offset voltage applications such as (A/D) converters, switched capacitor filters, active filters.

REFERENCES

[1] A. H. Madian, S. A. Mahmoud and A. M. Soliman, "Configurable Analog Block Based on CFOA and Its Application," *WSEAS Transactions on Electronics*, Vol. 5, No. 6, 2008, pp. 220-225.

[2] S. Pennisi, "High-Performance CMOS Current Feedback Operational Amplifier," *IEEE International Symposium on Circuits and Systems*, Vol. 2, 2005, pp. 1573-1576.

[3] H. L. Chao and D. S. Ma, "CMOS Variable-Gain Wide-Bandwidth CMFB-Free Differential Current Feedback Amplifier for Ultrasound Diagnostic Applications," *IEEE International Symposium on Circuits and Systems*, Island of Kos, 21-24 May 2006, pp. 649-652.

[4] G. Giustolisi, G. Palmisano, G. Palumbo and S. Pennisi, "High-Drive CMOS Current-Feedback Opamp," *IEEE International Symposium on Circuits and Systems*, Sacramento, 3-6 August 1997, pp. 229-232.

[5] J. Mahattanakul and C. Toumazou, "A Theoretical Study of the Stability of High Frequency Current Feedback Op-Amp Integrators," *IEEE Transactions on Circuits and Systems*, Vol. 43, No.1, 1996, pp. 1-12.

[6] G. Di Cataldo, A. D. Grasso and S. Pennisi, "Two CMOS Current Feedback Operational Amplifiers," *IEEE Trans-*

actions on Circuits and Systems, Vol. 54, No. 11, 2007, pp. 1-5.

[7] A. Assi, M. Sawan and J. Zhu, "An Offset Compensated and High-Gain CMOS Current-Feedback Op-Amp," *IEEE Transaction on Circuits and Systems*, Vol. 45, No. 1, 1998. pp. 85-90.

[8] A. M. Ismail and A. M. Soliman, "Novel CMOS Current Feedback Op-Amp Realization Suitable for High Frequency Applications," *IEEE Transaction on Circuits and Systems*, Vol. 47, No. 6, 2000, pp. 918-921.

[9] S. Selvanayagam and F. J. Lidgey, "Wide Bandwidth CMOS Current Feedback Op-Amp for Inverting Applications," *IEEE Electronics Letters Journal*, London, 10 May 1996, pp. 1-4.

[10] J. Y. Zhu, M. Sawan and K. Arabi, "An Offset Compensated CMOS Current-Feedback Operational Amplifier," *IEEE International Symposium on Circuits and Systems*, Seattle, 30 April-3 May1995, pp. 1552-1555.

[11] G. Palumbo and S. Pennisi, "Current-Feedback Amplifiers versus Voltage Operational Amplifiers," *IEEE Transaction on Circuits and Systems*, Vol. 48, No. 5, 2001, pp. 617-623.

[12] M. Djebbi, A. Assi and M. Sawan, "An Offset-Compensated Wide-Bandwidth CMOS Current-Feedback Operational Amplifier," *IEEE International Symposium on Circuits and Systems*, Vol. 1, 2003, pp. 73-76.

[13] S. A. Mahmoud, A. H. Madian and A. M. Soliman, "Low-Voltage CMOS Current Feedback Operational Amplifier and Its Applications," *ETRI Journal*, Vol. 29, No. 2, 2007, pp. 655-658.

[14] H. Schmid, "The Current-Feedback OTA," *IEEE International Symposium on Circuits and Systems*, Sydney, 6-9 May 2001, pp. 655-658.

[15] K. Koli, "CMOS Current Amplifiers: Speed versus Nonlinearity," Ph.D. Thesis, Dissertation in Department of Electrical and Communication Engineering, Helsiniki University of Technology, Espoo, 2000.

[16] P. E. Allen and D. R. Holberg, "CMOS Analog Circuit Design," 2nd Edition, Oxford University Press, New York, 2004.

[17] T. Singh, M. Kaur and G. Singh, "Design and Analysis of CMOS Folded-Cascode OTA Using G_m/I_d Tecghnique," *International Journal of Electronics and Computer Science Engineering*, Vol. 1, No. 2, 2012, pp. 727-733.

## 19

Universal Current-Mode Biquad Employing Dual Output Current Conveyors and MO-CCCA with Grounded Passive Elements

Kasim Karam Abdalla

Department of Electrical Engineering, Engineering Collage, University of Babylon, Hilla, Iraq

ABSTRACT

A new universal multiple input multiple output (MIMO) type current-mode biquad employing two dual output current conveyors (DOCCII), one multiple output current controlled current amplifier (MOCCCA) and four passive grounded elements is proposed which can realize all the five basic filtering functions namely, low-pass (LP), high-pass (HP), band-pass (BP), band-stop (BR) and all-pass (AP) in current mode from the same configuration. The centre frequency ω_o can be set by the passive elements of the circuit and the quality factor Q_o is electronically tunable through bias currents of the MOCCCA. Therefore, the biquad filter has independent tenability for the ω_o and Q_o. The active and passive sensitivities of Q_o and ω_o are low. The workability of the new configuration has been demonstrated by PSPICE simulation results based upon a CMOS CCII in 0.35 μm technology.

Keywords: Current-Mode Filters; Current Conveyors; Analog Circuit Design; CMOS Circuits

1. Introduction

Recently, Chunhua, Hiaguang and Yan presented two new universal multiple input single output (MISO) current-mode (CM) biquadatic filters using one MOCCCA, two grounded capacitors (GC) and two grounded resistors (GR) and realize all the five generic filter responses in CM (*i.e.* with current as input and current as output) [1].

The purpose of this paper is to introduce a new configuration which although uses exactly same number of active and passive components but in contrast to the circuit of reference [1] realizes a MIMO-type biquad and hence, does not require any additional hardware to duplicate/invert current inputs which is required in case of MISO-type filters of [1].

In the literature there are SIMO-type filter circuits which have three active devices but suffer from the independent tunability as in [2-5] or have more passive or active elements as in [4-9]. The circuits in [10-12] need double inputs and outputs to realize all five generic filters. The circuit in [13] has two MO-CCCIIs and one DO-CCCII, the draw back of this circuit is the control currents $I_{oi}, i=1,2,3$ are temperature dependent. The circuit in [14] has two MO-CCCIIs and one MOCCCA but realizes only SIMO-type biquad.

2. The Proposed Configuration

The proposed configuration is shown in **Figure 1**.

Assuming the CCIIs to be characterized by

$$\begin{bmatrix} I_Y \\ V_X \\ I_Z \end{bmatrix} = \begin{bmatrix} 0 & 0 & 0 \\ 1 & 0 & 0 \\ 0 & \pm 1 & 0 \end{bmatrix} \begin{bmatrix} V_Y \\ I_X \\ V_Z \end{bmatrix} \qquad (1)$$

The symbolic notation of MO-CCCA is given in **Figure 2(a)**, where i represent input, $(I_{o1} - I_{on})$ are n outputs respectively, and I_A and I_B denote DC bias currents. **Figure 2(b)** is a CMOS realization of MO-CCCA. Here I_i denotes the input signal; I_{o1}, I_{o2}, I_{o3} are the three output currents, respectively.

If the channel lengths of M_5-M_8 are all n times of that of M_4, and the channel size of M_{17} is n times that of M_{18}, namely

$$(W/L)_{M_5} \big/ (W/L)_{M_4}$$
$$= (W/L)_{M_6} \big/ (W/L)_{M_4} = (W/L)_{M_7} \big/ (W/L)_{M_4}$$
$$= (W/L)_{M_8} \big/ (W/L)_{M_4} = (W/L)_{M_{17}} \big/ (W/L)_{M_{18}} = n,$$

the output current expressions can be obtained as

$$I_{o1} = I_{o2} = \cdots = I_{on} = \frac{nI_B}{2I_A} = KI_i \qquad (2)$$

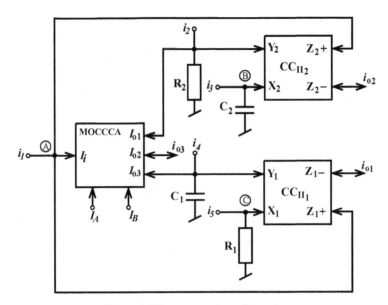

Figure 1. The proposed configuration.

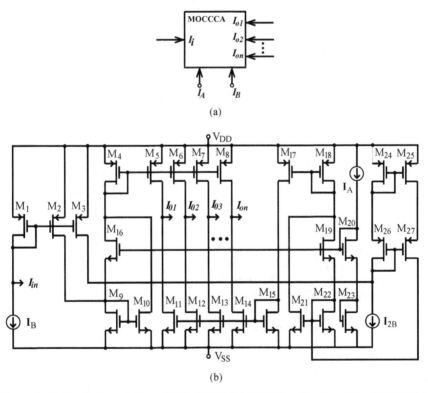

(a)

(b)

Figure 2. (a) Symbolic notation of MO-CCCA (b) CMOS realization of the MO-CCCA.

where K represents the current gain. It is clear from Equation (2) that the value of K can be set by I_B and I_A.

Consider now the following special cases:

2.1. MISO Type:

When i_1, i_2, i_3, i_4 and i_5 are input currents and taking i_{03} as output current, then a routine analysis of the circuit reveals the following expression of the output current

i_{03} in terms of the five input currents i_1, i_2, i_3, i_4 and i_5:

$$i_{03} = \frac{1}{\Delta}\left[i_2 s^2 C_1 C_2 + i_4 G_1 G_2 + (i_1 - i_3 - i_5) s C_1 G_2\right] \quad (3)$$

where $\Delta = s^2 C_1 C_2 + \frac{1}{K} s C_1 G_2 + G_1 G_2,$, $G_1 = 1/R_1$ and $G_2 = 1/R_2$.

Then, the various filter responses can be realized from

the circuit are:

LPF: when $i_4 = i_{in}$ (non-inv.) and $i_1 = i_2 = i_3 = i_5 = 0$.

HPF: when $i_2 = i_{in}$ and $i_1 = i_3 = i_4 = i_5 = 0$.

BPF: when $i_1 = i_{in}$ and $i_2 = i_3 = i_4 = i_5 = 0$ or $i_3 = i_{in}$ and $i_1 = i_2 = i_4 = i_5 = 0$ or $i_5 = i_{in}$ and $i_1 = i_2 = i_3 = i_4 = 0$.

Notch: when $i_2 = i_4 = i_{in}$ and $i_1 = i_3 = i_5 = 0$.

APF: when $i_2 = i_3 = i_4 = i_{in}$ and $i_1 = i_5 = 0$ or $i_2 = i_4 = i_5 = i_{in}$ and $i_1 = i_3 = 0$.

2.2. SIMO Type

If i_1 is input current, $i_2 = i_3 = i_4 = i_5 = 0$ (open circuited) then, the various filter responses realized are given by:

$$\text{LPF: } \frac{i_{01}}{i_1} = \frac{-1}{\Delta}\left[G_1 G_2\right] \qquad (4)$$

$$\text{HPF: } \frac{i_{02}}{i_1} = \frac{-1}{\Delta}\left[s^2 C_1 C_2\right] \qquad (5)$$

$$\text{BPF: } \frac{i_{03}}{i_1} = \frac{1}{\Delta}\left[s C_1 G_2\right] \qquad (6)$$

$$\text{Notch: } \frac{i_{01}+i_{02}}{i_1} = \frac{-1}{\Delta}\left[s^2 C_1 C_2 + G_1 G_2\right] \qquad (7)$$

$$\text{APF: } \frac{i_{01}+i_{02}+i_{03}}{i_1} = \frac{-1}{\Delta}\left[s^2 C_1 C_2 - s C_1 G_1 + G_1 G_2\right] \qquad (8)$$

The various parameters of the realized filters are given by

$$\omega_o = \sqrt{\frac{1}{C_1 C_2 R_1 R_2}}, BW = \frac{1}{KC_2 R_2}, Q_o = K\sqrt{\frac{C_2 R_2}{C_1 R_1}} \qquad (9)$$

From Equation (9), the centre frequency ω_o can be set by varying R_1 without disturbing ω_o/Q_o. The Q_o can also be set by I_B and I_A without disturbing ω_o. Therefore, the biquad filter has independent tenability for the ω_o and Q_o.

From the above, the active and passive sensitivities of the transfer function are given as

$$S_{C_1}^{\omega_o} = S_{C_2}^{\omega_o} = S_{R_1}^{\omega_o} = S_{R_2}^{\omega_o} = -\frac{1}{2}, S_{C_2}^{Q_o} = S_{R_2}^{Q_o} = \frac{1}{2}$$

$$S_{C_1}^{Q_o} = S_{R_1}^{Q_o} = -\frac{1}{2}, S_K^{Q_o} = 1 \qquad (10)$$

The active and passive sensitivities of ω_o and Q_o are found to be in the range $-\frac{1}{2} \leq S_x^F \leq 1$, and the circuit, thus, enjoys low sensitivities.

3. Simulation Results

To verify the validity of the various modes of operation of the proposed configuration, circuit simulation of the current mode filters (MISO and SIMO) have been carried out using the CMOS CCII implementation with multiple outputs shown in **Figure 3** (as in [15], modified from [16]).

The model parameters of n-channel and p-channel MOSFETs are given in [17], whereas aspect ratios of the CCII MOSFETs are shown in **Table 1**, and aspect ratios of the MO-CCCA MOSFETs are shown in **Table 2**.

The CMOS CCII was biased with DC power supply voltages $V_{DD} = +1.5$ V, $V_{SS} = -1.5$ V, $V_1 = -0.5$ V, and $V_2 = -0.9$ V.

To achieve the MISO type filters with $f_o = 1$ MHz and quality factor of $Q_o = 1$, the component values were selected $K = 1(n = 1, I_A = 50$ μA, $I_B = 100$ μA$)$, $R_1 = R_2 = 1$ kΩ and $C_1 = C_2 = 159$ pF. The frequency responses of LPF, BPF, HPF, Notch and APF (theoretical and simulation) are shown in **Figure 4**.

To test the input dynamic range of the proposed filters, the simulation of the band-pass filter as an example has

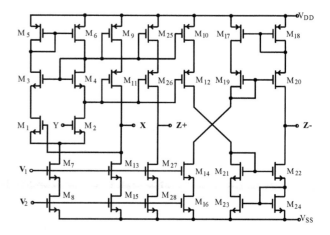

Figure 3. CMOS realization of the CCII.

Table 1. Aspect ratios of CCII MOSFETs.

MOS transistors	W/L
M_1 - M_4	10/0.35
M_5, M_6	16/0.35
M_7, M_8 , M_{13} - M_{16}, M_{21} - M_{24}, M_{27}, M_{28}	16/0.35
M_9 - M_{12}, M_{17} - M_{20}, M_{25}, M_{26}	30/0.35

Table 2. Aspect ratios of MO-CCCA MOSFETs.

MOS transistors	W/L
M_1 - M_3	9.5/0.55
M_4 - M_8, M_{17}, M_{18}, M_{24} - M_{27}	27.5/1.5
M_{10} - M_{15}, M_{21} - M_{23}	9.5/1.35
M_{16}, M_{19}, M_{20}	4.5/0.7

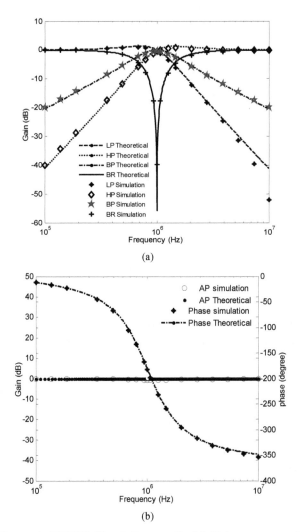

(a)

(b)

**Figure 4. PSPICE Simulation results (a) Gain response of
LPF, BPF, HPF and Notch; (b) Gain and Phase response of
APF.**

been done for a sinusoidal input signal at $f_o = 1\,\text{MHz}$.
Figure 5 shows that the input dynamic range of the filter
response extends up to amplitude of 105 μA without significant distortion. The dependence of the output harmonic distortion on the input signal amplitude is illustrated in **Figure 6**. For input signal amplitudes lower
than 110 μA, the total harmonic distortion (THD) is of
the order of less than 1% after that rapidly increasing is
occurred. The obtained results show that the circuit operates properly even at signal amplitudes of about 120 μA
and THD less than 4%.

To achieve the SIMO type filters with $f_o = 1$ MHz
and quality factor of $Q_o = 2$, the component values were
selected $K = 2\left(n = 1, I_A = 25\,\mu\text{A}, I_B = 100\,\mu\text{A}\right)$,
$R_1 = R_2 = 1\,\text{k}\Omega$ and $C_1 = C_2 = 159\,\text{pF}$. The circuit realizes LP, HP, and BP responses, respectively, at $i_{01}; i_{02}$
and i_{03} simultaneously. The frequency responses of
Notch and AP can be realized by, respectively,
$\left(i_{01} + i_{02}\right)$ and $\left(i_{01} + i_{02} + i_{03}\right)$. Four filter responses are

shown in **Figure 7**.

Figure 8 shows the simulation results for control of Q_o
while keeping f_o fixed (1MHz) with $C_1 = C_2 = 159$ pF
for different values of Q_o as shown in **Table 3**. **Figure 9**
shows the simulation results for control of f_o while keeping $Q_o = 1$ with $C_1 = C_2 = 53$ pF for different values of
f_o as shown in **Table 3**. The current mode band pass filter

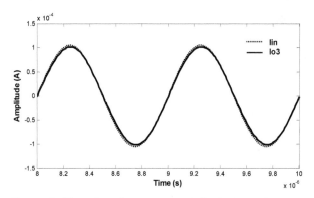

**Figure 5. Time domain response of the input and output
waveforms of the band-pass filter of the proposed circuit
for 1 MHz sinusoidal input current of 105 μA.**

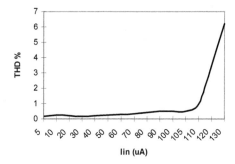

**Figure 6. Dependence of output current harmonic distor-
tion on input current amplitude of the band-pass filter of
proposed circuit.**

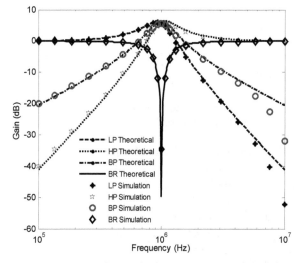

**Figure 7. PSPICE Simulated gain responses of LP, BP, HP
and Notch for SIMO type filter.**

Table 3. The R_1 and R_2 values for controlling of Q_o and C_1 and C_2 values for controlling f_o.

	Fixed f_o			Fixed Q_o	
Q_o	R_1 kΩ	R_2 kΩ	f_o MHz	R_1 kΩ	R_2 kΩ
1	1	1	1	3	3
2	0.7	1.43	2	1.5	1.5
4	0.5	2	3	1	1

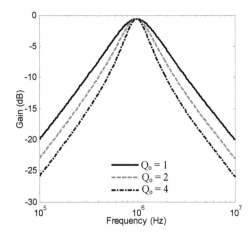

Figure 8. Simulation results for control of Q_o while keeping f_o fixed (1 MHz) for band pass filter.

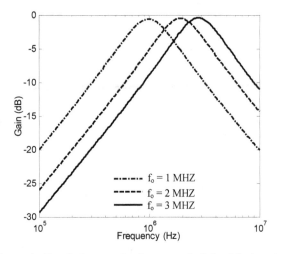

Figure 9. Simulation results for control of f_o while keeping Q_o (=1) fixed for band pass filter.

is tested for gain and quality factor tuning while keeping pole frequency constant at 1 MHz. $R_1 = R_2 = 1\,\text{k}\Omega$, $C_1 = C_2 = 159\,\text{pF}$ and $K = 1, 2, 4$ are taken for gain = quality factor $= 1, 2, 4$, respectively. The simulated results are shown in **Figure 10**.

A very good correspondence between design values and values determined from PSPICE simulations is observed, which confirms the workability of the current mode filters realized from the proposed configuration.

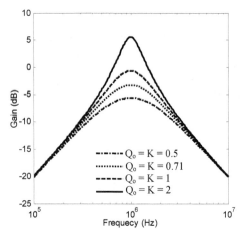

Figure 10. Simulation results for control of Q_o and gain while keeping $f_o = 1$ MHz fixed for band pass filter.

4. Concluding Remarks

A new universal MISO/SIMO type current-mode biquad employing two DOCCII, one MOCCCA and four passive grounded elements is proposed in this paper. The purpose of this paper as to introduce a new configuration which although uses exactly same number of active and passive components but in contrast to the circuit of reference [1] realizes a MIMO-type biquad and hence, does not require any additional hardware duplicate/invert current inputs which is required in case of MISO-type filters of [1]. The centre frequency ω_o can be set by the passive elements of the circuit and the quality factor Q_o is electronically tunable through bias currents of the MOCCCA. Therefore, the biquad filter has independent tenability for the ω_o and Q_o. The active and passive sensitivities Q_o and ω_o are low.

The workability of the new configuration has been demonstrated by PSPICE simulation results based upon a CMOS CCII in 0.35 μm technology

REFERENCES

[1] W. Chunbua, L. Haiguang and Z. Yan, "Universal Current-Mode Filter with Multiple Inputs and One Output Using MOCCII and MO-CCCA," *International Journal of Electronics and Communications (AEU)*, Vol. 63, No. 6, 2009, pp. 448-453.

[2] R. Senani and A. K. Singh, "A New Universal Current-Mode Biquad Filter," *Frequenz: Journal of Tele-Communications*, Vol. 56, No. 1-2, 2002, pp. 55-59.

[3] R. Senani, V. K. Singh, A. K. Singh and D. R. Bhaskar, "Tunable Current-Mode Universal Biquads Employing Only Three MOCCs and All Grounded Passive Elements: Additional New Realizations," *Frequenz: Journal of Tele-Communications*, Vol. 59, No. 7-8, 2005, pp. 220-224.

[4] R. Senani, A. K. Singh, V. K. Singh, "New Tunable SIMO-Type Current-Mode Universal Biquad Using Only Three MOCCs and All Grounded Passive Elements,"

Frequenz: *Journal of Tele-Communications*, Vol. 57, No. 7-8, 2003, pp. 160-161.

[5] H. Y. Wang and C. T. Lee, "Versatile Insensitive Current Mode Universal Biquad Implementation Using Current Conveyors," *IEEE Transactions on CAS-II. Analog and Digital Signal Processing*, Vol. 48, No. 4, 2001, pp. 409-413.

[6] W. Chunhua, Z. Yan, Z. Qiujing and D. U. Sichun, "A New Current Mode SIMO-Type Universal Biquad Employing Multi-Output Current Conveyors (MOCCIIs)," *Radioengineering*, Vol. 18, No.1, 2009, pp. 83-88.

[7] J. W. Horng, C. L. Hou, C. M. Chang, J. Y. Shie and C. H. Chang, "Universal Current Filter with Single Input and Three Outputs Using MOCCIIs," *International Journal of Electronics*, Vol. 94, No. 4, 2004, pp. 191-197.

[8] M. Siripruchyanun and W. Jaikla, "Cascadable Current-Mode Biquad Filter and Quadrature Oscillator Using DO-CCCIIs and OTA," *Circuits Systems and Signal Processing*, Vol. 28, No. 1, 2009, pp. 99-110.

[9] R. Senani, "New Universal Current Mode Biquad Employing All Grounded Passive Components but Only Two DOCCs," *Journal of Active and Passive Electronic Devices*, Vol. 1, No. 3-4, 2006, pp. 281-288.

[10] M. Kumngern, W. Jongchanachavawat and K. Dejhan, "New Electronically Tunable Current-Mode Universal Biquad Filter Using Translinear Current Conveyors," *International Journal of Electronics*, Vol. 97, No. 5, 2010, pp. 511-523.

[11] T. Tsukutani, Y. Sumi and N. Yabuki, "Versatile Current-Mode Biquadratic Circuit Using Only Plus Type DO-DVCCs and Grounded Passive Capacitors," *International Journal of Electronics*, Vol. 94, No. 12, 2007, pp. 1147-1156.

[12] T. Tsukutani, Y. Sumi and N. Yabuki, "Novel Current-Mode Biquadratic Circuit Using Only Plus Type DO-DVCCs and Grounded Passive Components," *International Journal of Electronics*, Vol. 94, No. 12, 2007, pp. 1137-1146.

[13] H. P. Chen and P. L. Chu, "Versatile Universal Electronically Tunable Current-Mode Filter Using CCCIIs," *IEICE Electronics Express*, Vol. 6, No. 2, 2009, pp. 122-128.

[14] C. H. Wang, J. Xu, A. Ü. Keskin, S. C. Du and Q. J. Zhang, "A New Current-Mode Current-Controlled SIMO-Type Universal Filter," *International Journal of Electronics and Communications (AEU)*, Vol. 65, No. 3, 2011, pp. 231-234.

[15] V. K. Singh, A. K. Singh and R. Senani, "Dual Function Capability of Recently Proposed Four-Current Conveyor-Based VM Biquad," *Journal of Circuits, Systems and Computers*, Vol. 14, No. 1, 2005, pp. 51-56.

[16] S. I. Liu, H. W. Tsao and J. Wu, "CCII-Based Continuous-Time Filters with Reduced Gain Bandwidth Sensitivity," *IEEE Proceedings of Circuits, Devices & Systems*, Vol. 139, No. 2, 1991, pp. 210-216.

[17] E. Yuce, S. Minaei and O. Cicekoglu, "A Novel Grounded Inductor Realization Using a Minimum Number of Active and Passive Components," *ETRI Journal*, Vol. 27, No. 4, 2005, pp. 427-432.

## 20

A Novel Time Domain Noise Model for Voltage Controlled Oscillators

Li Ke, Peter Wilson, Reuben Wilcock
Electronics and Computer Science, University of Southampton, Southampton, UK

ABSTRACT

This paper describes a novel time domain noise model for voltage controlled oscillators that accurately and efficiently predicts both tuning behavior and phase noise performance. The proposed method is based on device level flicker and thermal noise models that have been developed in Simulink and although the case study is a multiple feedback four delay cell architecture it could easily be extended to any similar topology. The strength of the approach is verified through comparison with post layout simulation results from a commercial simulator and measured results from a 120 nm fabricated prototype chip. Furthermore, the effect of control voltage flicker noise on oscillator output phase noise is also investigated as an example application of the model. Transient simulation based noise analysis has the strong advantage that noise performance of higher level systems such as phase locked loops can be easily determined over a realistic acquisition and locking process yielding more accurate and reliable results.

Keywords: Voltage Controlled Oscillators; Noise Model; Simulation

1. Introduction

Low jitter reference frequency generation is a key requirement for high performance analogue and mixed-signal integrated circuits and is usually achieved using a stable reference crystal and phase locked loop (PLL). An important trade-off exists between PLL phase noise and loop bandwidth and it is vital to explore this balance, particularly when targeting low output jitter [1]. At the heart of every PLL is a voltage controlled oscillator (VCO) which greatly influences the performance of the PLL itself and is typically the biggest noise contributor in the system [2]. In order facilitate PLL noise analysis, therefore, a VCO noise model is required which will accurately predict noise performance under realistic closed loop conditions whilst maintaining simulation efficiency.

It is widely agreed that time domain transistor level simulations provide the most reliable and accurate means to examine the performance of closed loop PLLs [3]. One approach for noise analysis is to include noise behavior for each transistor within the transient simulation, in a technique known as transient noise analysis. Unfortunately, however, few commercial simulators include support for noise as part of a transient simulation, focusing on less accurate linearized approaches instead. Indeed, transient noise analysis tends to be impractical for realistic circuit designs due to the huge simulation resources required [3]. To address this problem, a number

of alternative approaches have been proposed in the literature based on a variety of design platforms including Matlab-Simulink [3-4], C [5], and VHDL [6]. All these methods extract behavioral model parameters from transistor level simulations first, which can lead to inaccuracy since the parameters are only valid for limited operating conditions. With the decrease in technology node size this problem is exacerbated as devices are becoming increasingly difficult to characterize.

In this paper, a novel time domain VCO noise model is proposed, which incorporates transistor level noise behavior whilst maintaining simulation efficiency. In order to accurately define true dynamic behavior the VCO model accepts an instantaneous control voltage input and dynamically generates the correct output waveform, whilst incorporating the relevant noise sources to ensure an accurate representation of the phase noise performance. Further post processing of the VCO output waveform then provides both the oscillation frequency and signal purity. A careful balance is struck between accuracy and complexity to ensure meaningful results yet manageable simulation times. Section 2 introduces the VCO structure used in this work and derives the combined VCO tuning behavior and noise performance model. Section 3 presents a case study complete with transistor level simulations and measurements from a prototype chip to demonstrate the work on a realistic example. Finally, Section 4 discusses the significance of the work, with some concluding remarks.

2. VCO Architecture and Tuning Model

A high performance VCO architecture is at the core of this approach and is detailed in this section. Both the frequency tuning behavior and noise performance characteristics are considered and combined into a complete time domain model that facilitates accurate and efficient system simulation.

2.1. VCO Tuning Model

Passive inductor and capacitor (LC) based VCO structures offer excellent phase noise performance yet can be difficult and expensive to integrate on deep sub-micron CMOS processes due to their large physical size and additional processing requirements. Conversely, inverter based oscillators (also referred to as RC or ring oscillators) are easily integrated onto standard CMOS processes but generally suffer from inferior phase noise performance [7]. Despite this, their compact size and additional advantages of wider tuning range and direct quadrature output has led to great interest in RC oscillators. Recent research has focused on achieving phase noise performance in RC oscillators that is close to equivalent LC based designs [1]. Given the importance of modeling the phase noise of RC oscillator accurately, they are a suitable candidate for the development of an improved model, as described in this paper.

The oscillator architecture employed in this work is shown in **Figure 1** and is based on a multiple feedback four delay cell topology in order to achieve a wide tuning range [8]. Within each delay cell, the two internal transistors, $Mp1$ and $Mn1$, operate as an inverter and the two current control transistors, $Mp2$ and $Mn2$, in each stage are responsible for frequency control. Transistors $Mp3$ and $Mp4$ form a secondary feedback loop to increase the oscillator frequency. Since the on-resistance ($Ronn$ and $Ronp$) and lumped gate capacitance C of the two inverting transistors ($Mp1$ and $Mn1$) are independent of the frequency of oscillation, they can be modeled as fixed values defined by Equations (1)-(3) [9].

$$Ronn = \frac{V_{DS}}{I_{DS}} = V_{DS} \bigg/ \left(\frac{1}{2} \mu_n C_{ox} (Wni/Lni)(V_{GS} - V_{th})^2 \right) \quad (2)$$

$$Ronp = \frac{V_{DS}}{I_{DS}} = V_{DS} \bigg/ \left(\frac{1}{2} \mu_n C_{ox} (Wpi/Lpi)(V_{GS} - V_{th})^2 \right) \quad (3)$$

where C_{ox} is the unit-area gate oxide capacitance, C_{gdo} is

the gate-drain overlap capacitance per unit-length, μ_n is the mobility parameter and V_{th} is the transistor threshold voltage, Wni/Lni and Wpi/Lpi are the transistor dimensions for NMOS and PMOS inverter transistors respectively. V_{DS} and V_{GS} are the effective drain-source and gate-source voltage difference for each transistor. Defining V_{DS} and V_{GS} within Equations (2) and (3) is difficult since the voltages at the gate and drain nodes of the device dynamically change within each oscillation cycle. The gate and drain voltages of Mni increase from $V_{DD}/2$ to V_{DD} and decrease from V_{DD} to $V_{DD}/2$ respectively within each propagation delay. For simplicity, therefore, it is assumed that both drain and gate nodes are fixed at $3V_{DD}/4$ within the propagation delay, ensuring that Mni stays in saturation. The two control transistors, Mpc and Mnc, are modeled as variable resistors R_{ctp} and R_{ctn} with values defined by the external control voltage, and the linearity of this relationship governs the linearity of the VCO's tuning function. The resistance relationship depends on the operating region of the transistor and for Mnc is given by Equations (4) and (5) for the saturation and deep triode regions respectively. Equations (6) and (7) give the corresponding equations for Mpc.

$$Rctn\_sat = \frac{Vct}{\frac{1}{2} \mu_n C_{ox} \frac{Wnc}{Lnc} (Vct - V_{th})^2} \quad (4)$$

$$Rctn\_tri = \frac{Vct}{I_D} = \frac{1}{\mu_n C_{ox} \frac{Wnc}{Lnc} (Vct - V_{th})} \quad (5)$$

$$Rctp\_sat = \frac{Vct}{\frac{1}{2} \mu_n C_{ox} \frac{Wpc}{Lpc} (Vct - V_{th})^2} \quad (6)$$

$$Rctp\_tri = \frac{Vct}{I_D} = \frac{1}{\mu_n C_{ox} \frac{Wpc}{Lpc} (Vct - V_{th})} \quad (7)$$

As illustrated in **Figure 1**, Wnc/Lnc and Wpc/Lpc are the dimensions of the current controlling transistors. During each period of oscillation the drain source voltage of the control transistors Mpc and Mnc can vary by several hundred mV and so the region of operation is difficult to define. A good compromise is to assume that the effective ON resistance of the control transistor Mnc is a combination of Equations (4) and (5) (or (6) and (7) for transistor Mpc). The combination is determined linearly by the instantaneous control voltage, Vct, and is given by Equation (8) for $Rctn$ and Equation (9) for $Rctp$.

$$C = 2 \left(C_{gdo} \cdot Wni + C_{gdo} \cdot Wpi \right) + \frac{3}{2} \left(Wni \cdot Lni \cdot C_{ox} + Wpi \cdot Lpi \cdot C_{ox} \right) + 2 \left(C_{gdo} \cdot Wni + C_{gdo} \cdot Wpi \right) \quad (1)$$

with the braces above labeled C_{out} (over the first term) and C_{in} (over the remaining terms).

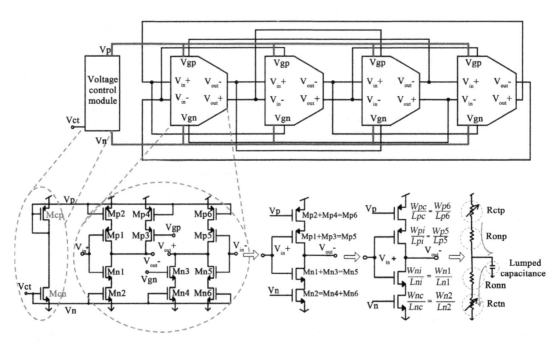

Figure 1. Modeling of effective RC delay for a VCO delay cell.

$$Rctn = Rctn\_sat\left(\frac{V_{DD}-Vct}{V_{DD}}\right) + Rctn\_tri\left(\frac{Vct}{V_{DD}}\right) \quad (8)$$

$$Rctp = Rctp\_sat\left(\frac{V_{DD}-Vct}{V_{DD}}\right) + Rctp\_tri\left(\frac{Vct}{V_{DD}}\right) \quad (9)$$

Now that the effective capacitive and resistive components have been modelled, the corresponding propagation delays, t_{d_push} and t_{d_pull}, can be obtained directly from Equations (10) and (11). The time constant is obtained from the product of the effective resistance $\left(R_{eff}\right)$ and capacitance $\left(C_{eff}\right)$ in each case

$$t_{d\_push} = R_{eff}C_{eff} = \frac{V_{DD}}{2I}C = \frac{V_{DD}/2}{I/C} = \frac{\left(V_{DD}/2\right)}{\left(\dfrac{V_{DD}}{Rctn+Ronn}\right)\Big/C}$$
$$(10)$$

$$t_{d\_pull} = R_{eff}C_{eff} = \frac{V_{DD}}{2I}C = \frac{V_{DD}/2}{I/C} = \frac{\left(V_{DD}/2\right)}{\left(\dfrac{V_{DD}}{Rctp+Ronp}\right)\Big/C}$$
$$(11)$$

As the pull-up path uses the same principle and structure as the push-down path for the dual inverter based ring oscillator, it is straightforward to combine 2N stages (as it is a dual feedback loop structure) of push delay $\left(t_{d\_push}\right)$ and 2N stages of pull delay $\left(t_{d\_pull}\right)$ to obtain the nominal oscillation cycle, T_o which is given in Equation (12). **Figure 2** illustrates the complete tuning model, which has been implemented in Simulink.

$$T_0 = 2N\left(t_{d\_pull} + t_{d\_push}\right) \quad (12)$$

To verify the accuracy of the tuning model, its behaviour has been compared with schematic level transistor simulations using standard foundry models. This comparison is shown in **Figure 3**, where the correlation across the range of *Vct* of the oscillation frequency is good between the proposed model and the more detailed transistor level circuit.

In practice, the circuit will also suffer from layout parasitics, which will typically result in a reduced oscillation frequency. Realistic estimation of the performance with parasitic components taken into account can be achieved through post layout extraction simulations. A simple extension to the model can be included to correctly predict the performance reduction, in the form of a parasitic delay factor that can be added to the overall oscillation period as shown in Equation (13). The value of parasitic delay can be quickly obtained from simple dc analyses, and the more accurate model used for later noise analysis, increasing confidence in the noise results. The effect of the parasitic delay can be seen in **Figure 4**, where the extracted simulation results are compared with the revised model and a clear reduction in the maximum oscillation frequency from over 1 GHz to 840 Mhz was observed.

$$T_0 = 2N\left(t_{d\_pull} + t_{d\_push}\right) + parasitic\_delay \quad (13)$$

2.2. Transistor Level Noise Model

Thermal noise and flicker noise dominate a transistor's noise spectrum and can be summarised by Equation (14) where $S_{in\_thermal}$ and $S_{in\_flicker}$ are the drain current noise power spectral density (PSD) for thermal and flicker

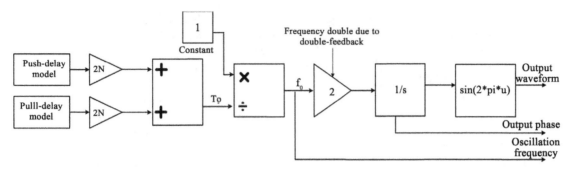

Figure 2. Complete VCO tuning model.

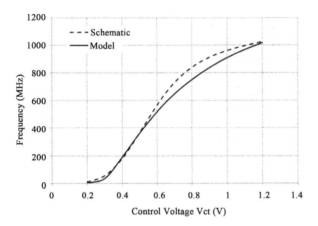

Figure 1. Comparison of transistor level schematic and model simulation results.

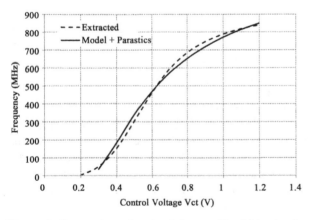

Figure 4. Comparison of extracted parasitic delay simulation and model including *parasitic delay*.

noise, k is the Boltzmann constant, T is the absolute temperature in Kelvin and g_m is the device transconductance. The flicker noise coefficient K_f is a process independent parameter of the order of 10^{-24} and γ is a bias-dependent factor which may be set at 2/3 for long channel transistors and must be replaced by a larger value for submicron MOSEFTs. The point of intersection between the flicker noise and thermal noise contributions is referred to as the device's corner frequency, f_c, and is given in Equation (15). Above the corner frequency, the noise level is dominated by thermal noise, whereas below the corner frequency flicker noise dominates with an increasing factor of 20 dB/decade [9,10].

$$\overline{V_{n,\text{out}}^2} = \left(S_{i_n\text{-thermal}} + S_{i_n\text{-flicker}}\right)R^2$$
$$= \left(4kT\gamma g_m + \frac{K_f}{C_{OX}W_{eff}L_{eff}f}g_m^2\right)R^2 \quad (14)$$

MATLAB code has been made available in the literature [11] to model this relationship and is used as a starting point in this work. Firstly, the thermal noise is created by a random number generator based on a variance given in Equation (16), which is determined by both the absolute thermal noise level, $S_{in\text{-thermal}}$, and the system sampling time, *systs*.

$$\text{Variance} = \frac{S_{in\text{-thermal}}}{2systs} = \frac{4kT\gamma g_m}{2systs} \quad (16)$$

Secondly, using the mathematical functions proposed in [11], a bank of single-pole low pass filters was created to produce a noise-shaping filter, which can approximately generate the correct flicker noise response. The transfer function of this noise-shaping filter is given by Equation (17).

$$H(s) = 1 + \sum_{n=0}^{K+1} \frac{1 \times 10^{-0.5n}}{\sqrt{2}} \frac{2\pi f_c}{s + 2\pi \times 10^{-n}f_c} \quad (17)$$

where f_c is the device's corner frequency, given in Equation (15), and a K value of approximately 10 is required for correct modelling of the flicker noise. The model realization of this noise-shaping filter is illustrated in **Figure 5(a)**. Separate output ports are used for the thermal and flicker noise contributions to allow a better understanding of how these different noise types affect the

$$4kT\gamma g_m = \frac{K_f}{C_{ox}W_{eff}L_{eff}f}g_m^2 \Rightarrow f_{\text{corner}} = f_c = \frac{K_f g_m}{C_{ox}W_{eff}L_{eff}} \cdot \frac{1}{4kT\gamma} \quad (15)$$

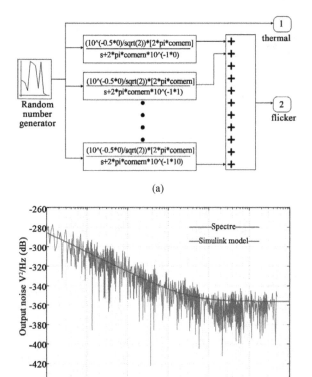

(a)

(b)

Figure 5. Simulink model of thermal and flicker noise sources (a) and PFD of single device noise (b).

VCO noise as a whole. A power spectral density comparison of the single device noise model and a simulation in Spectre is shown together in **Figure 5(b)**, confirming correct operation of the model at this level.

Combined VCO Noise and Tuning Model

Having developed both the VCO level tuning model and device level noise model the final stage is to combine both aspects in a model which will predict both the tuning and noise performance of the VCO. The first challenge in achieving this is to relate the noise quantity, currently in the form of current (A) to the VCO time domain jitter (s) and frequency domain phase noise (dBc/Hz@offset). The jitter, Δt_d occurring within a single propagation delay can be calculated by integrating the noise current, $i_n(t)$, over the time interval t_d and dividing by the pull-up/push-down current, I, as described by Equations (18) and (19) [10]. The propagation delay and pull-up/push-down current can be obtained directly from the model in **Figure 2**.

$$v_n = \frac{1}{C}\int_0^{t_d} i_n(t)\,\mathrm{d}t \qquad (18)$$

$$\Delta t_d = \frac{v_n}{I}C = \frac{1}{I}\int_0^{t_d} i_n(t)\,\mathrm{d}t \qquad (19)$$

It is possible at this stage to combine 4N noise generators from the previous section for an N stage VCO model where each delay cell has four transistors ($Mn1$, $Mn2$, $Mp5$, $Mp6$). However, with each noise block requiring 11 transfer functions for flicker noise generation, the total of 44 transfer functions would degrade the simulation efficiency. Furthermore, having to adjust the model structure as the number of stages changes is undesirable, so instead N should be an input variable. For this reason, three simplifications are performed on the model to improve efficiency. First, it is possible to combine pairs of noise contributors into one lumped transistor by making the reasonable assumption that the inverting and control transistors share the same dimensions. This halves the number of noise generators, which greatly enhances the efficiency of the model. Secondly, assumeing a lumped transistor noise model it is important to establish the relationship between the control voltage and the trans-conductance of the lumped transistor as this will have an impact on its noise characteristics. As a result of this, the altered noise profile of this lumped transistor can be determined by Equations (20) and (21) where g_{m_lump} is its trans-conductance.

$$g_{m\_lump} \approx \mu_n C_{ox}\frac{Wni}{Lni}(Vct - V_{th}) \qquad (20)$$

$$f_c = \frac{K_f g_{m\_lump}}{C_{ox}Wni\cdot Lni}\cdot\frac{1}{4kT\gamma} \qquad (21)$$

Thirdly, for short t_d time intervals it can be assumed that the noise current stays at a constant value within the interval meaning that Equation (19) can be reduced to Equation (22). If the change in noise current within the time interval is noticeable, however, this so-called jitter amplitude spread is known to be proportional to the length of the time interval and trans-conductance, but inversely proportional to the load capacitance [10]. Furthermore, it is known that the jitter amplitude spread is proportional with the order of device's corner frequency allowing Equation (22) to be extended to the more general case of Equation (23).

$$\Delta t_d = \frac{1}{I}\int_0^{t_d} i_n(t)\,\mathrm{d}t = \frac{i_n}{I}t_d \qquad (22)$$

$$\Delta t_d(t) = \frac{i_n(t)}{I}t_d\cdot\frac{t_d\cdot g_{m\_lump}\cdot(\log10(fc))}{C\cdot} \qquad (23)$$

Based on the above refinement the proposed jitter generator is shown in **Figure 6** which is a combination of the propagation delay generator and the noise generator. The accuracy of this model can be attributed to the noise current, the push current and the length of the propagation delay all being a function of the control voltage, rather than assuming independence from this important circuit parameter. The resulting full VCO model results in 2N PMOS and 2N NMOS based noise generators for an N stage oscillator. Summing all squares of the noise contributors gives the total noise which is then transformed into the jitter value. In order to determine the phase noise, the instantaneous oscillation frequency and output phase is also available at the model output. The phase noise, which is the parameter of ultimate interest, can be approximated by the power spectral density (PSD) function of extra phase.

3. Results

In this section the novel VCO noise model is tested and compared to results from an industry standard simulator. A case study circuit was designed for this purpose with the dimensions given in **Table 1**, which refer to the schematic of **Figure 1**.

Phase Noise Simulations

Figure 7(a) shows the developed model phase noise results using the case study circuit dimensions based on just flicker noise. Here the new model is shown to agree

well with post layout simulations of the fully extracted circuit. Both curves have a roll-off factor of 30 dB/decade, which demonstrates that the device flicker noise is being modeled correctly. For further analysis the noise source in the model was changed from flicker to thermal, which correctly resulted in a shallower roll-off factor of 20 dB/decade [10] as shown in **Figure 7(b)**. The behavioral models in both cases took 1 minutes and 45 seconds to generate, whereas the transistor level simulations took from 3 - 4 minutes. Although this demonstrates an efficiency saving of 50% - 60%, it is important to point out, as discussed in Section 1, that the real benefit of the proposed model is its suitability for simulating the noise of complex systems such as PLLs, due to its time domain nature.

It is well known that flicker noise in the VCO control voltage plays a more significant role than any other noise source in the oscillator circuit [10] which makes it an interesting aspect to investigate with the proposed model. Within the current mirror structure that generates the control voltage, the diode connected transistor is the major noise contributor and can be modeled by another instance of the device noise model. In order to translate the

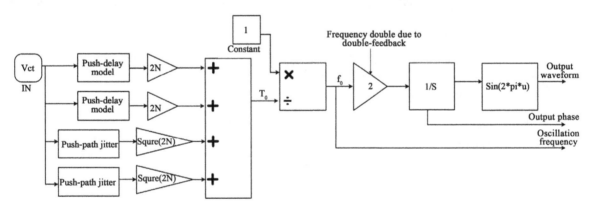

Figure 6. Combination of the noise generator with the VCO behavioral model.

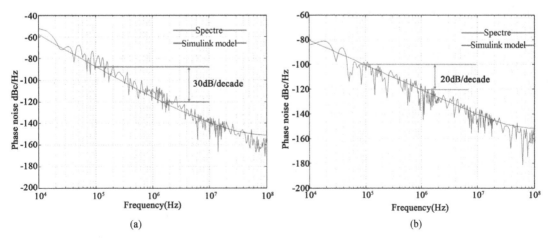

(a)   (b)

Figure 7. Comparison between the proposed Simulink model and Spectre based results for flicker noise (a) and thermal noise (b) induced phase noise.

current noise of the device model to control voltage noise is it multiplied by the transistor's output resistance which is obtained through a simple DC simulation.

Table 2 shows four example designs where the current mirror transistors are varied, keeping all other design parameters the same. For the purposes of fair comparison, the differential control voltages generated from the control module were designed to be almost identical ($V_{ct} = 1.2$ V), resulting in almost identical oscillation frequencies. However, a significant difference is apparent for the phase noise performances of these four design examples, which are shown in **Figure 8**. As in the previous design example, both the circuit simulator based post layout simulation results and the proposed model results were obtained. The phase noise results obtained from these two methods agree strongly for these four analytical design cases, confirming the accuracy of the proposed VCO model.

As expected, the results clearly show that lowering the transistor output resistance through a greater W/L ratio is an essential requirement for reducing the VCO output phase noise, highlighting the well-known trade-off between power and noise performance. In this example the proposed model has allowed accurate analysis of the

VCO output phase noise without paying a penalty in simulation time. The recommended design going forward would be Design 3 which achieves excellent phase noise without the compromise of a large transistor area and correspondingly large gate capacitance, which could cause stability problems in a larger system.

4. Prototype Chip

To verify the proposed VCO model further, the VCO design example of the previous section with the recommended control module sizing of Design 3 was realized with a prototype chip fabricated on a standard 120 nm 1.2 V CMOS process. **Figure 9(a)** shows the layout view of the chip with the VCO highlighted, and **Figure 9(b)** shows the die being probed on a high speed wafer probing station. Bench tests used an Agilent E4443A 3 Hz-6.7 GHz spectrum analyser and gave the phase noise plot in **Figure 10**. A battery was used for the power source to ensure very low noise from the supply.

The phase noise spectrum shows a roll off of −30 dBc/Hz/decade, indicating that flicker noise is dominant in the design. The results shown in **Figure 10** are consistent with the modeling results and simulation results

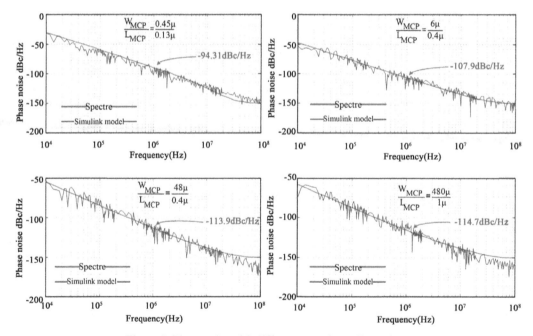

Figure 8. Phase noise with different transistor dimensions.

Table 1. Transistor dimensions of design example.

Transistor:	W/L (mm):	Transistor:	W/L (mm):
$Mp1$, $Mp2$	100/0.4	$Mn1$, $Mn2$	64/0.4
$Mp3$, $Mp4$	100/0.4	$Mn3$, $Mn4$	32/0.4
$Mp5$, $Mp6$	199/0.4	$Mn5$, $Mn6$	32/0.4

Table 2. Varying the control current mirror transistors in four design examples.

Device	Design 1	Design 2	Design 3	Design 4
M_{cn}	0.15 μm/0.13 μm	2 μm/0.4 μm	16 μm/0.4 μm	160 μm/1 μm
M_{cp}	0.45 μm/0.13 μm	6 μm/0.4 μm	48 μm/0.4 μm	480 μm/1 μm
g_{ds} of M_{cp}	23 μ	44.77 μ	374.4 μ	849.2 μ

shown in **Figure 7(a)**. It is important to investigate the phase noise with different tuning voltages and measured results for this parameter are summarized within **Table 3** along with the predicted results from the developed model.

The results are very encouraging, given the difficulty in accurately measuring noise in practice. The discrepancies at 100 kHz offset and the ramp in the spectrum under 100 kHz are attributed to the noise of the DC voltage source, which was not included in the model. The discrepancy towards the lower end of the frequency range with 10 MHz offset is due to the noise floor of the testing platform. Elsewhere, the variations of phase noise between the simulated and measurement are generally less than 5 dB.

5. Conclusion

One of the most challenging problems when simulating PLLs is obtaining accurate jitter and phase noise performance from transient simulations. VCOs largely dominate the noise performance of PLLs and this paper presents a novel VCO noise model to address this challenge, which facilitates efficient analysis of phase noise and tuning performance from time domain simulations. The key advantage of this approach is its application in higher level PLL system simulations since commercial software seldom supports transient noise analysis, however there is also the benefit of increased simulation efficiency with reduced simulation times. The accuracy of the predicted phase noise performance using the proposed model has been extensively validated through comparison with both extracted layout simulations and measured results from a 120 nm CMOS prototype chip. To demonstrate an application of the model, the effect of control voltage flicker noise on VCO output phase noise has been investigated and guidelines for the voltage control module proposed as a result. Compared with alternative approaches, the proposed model enables circuit de-

signers to correctly and efficiently predict true time domain noise performance in VCOs allowing them to make informed decisions about transistor sizing as a result.

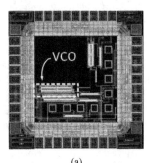

(a)

(b)

Figure 9. Prototype chip layout view (a) and probe station setup (b).

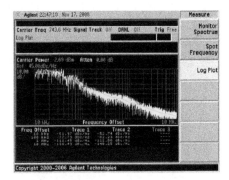

Figure 10. Measured phase noise at 744 MHz.

Table 3. Measured and simulated phase noise over the full tuning range.

Effective control voltage (V)	Oscillation frequency (MHz)	Measured/simulated phase noise (dBc/Hz)		
		100 kHz offset	1 MHz offset	10 MHz offset
1.2	743.6	−82.23/−**80.09**	−112.8/−**110.91**	−140.25/−**140.36**
1.06	721.7	−73.1/−**81.02**	−112.25/−**111.34**	−140.06/−**141.78**
0.93	685.2	−69.38/−**82.82**	−112.55/−**112.92**	−139.38/−**142.48**
0.8155	646.1	−87.24/−**83.31**	−112.26/−**113.19**	−139.66/−**142.51**
0.7157	569.8	−75.56/−**84.55**	−109.14/−**113.43**	−137.81/−**143.01**
0.619	455.7	−78.27/−**84.78**	−109.45/−**114.39**	−136.00/−**144.32**
0.5	288.9	−79.42/−**85.37**	−107.35/−**114.71**	−134.75/−**145.8**
0.414	164.9	−81.8/−**86.91**	−109.32/−**115.85**	−135.28/−**145.2**
0.353	97.55	−83.17/−**87.32**	−110.66/−**116.32**	−136.6/−**145.19**

REFERENCES

[1]   Z. H. Gao, Y. C. Li and S. L. Yan, "A 0.4 ps-RMS-Jitter 1 - 3 GHz Ring Oscillator PLL Using Phase-Noise Pre-amplification," *IEEE Journal of Solid-State Circuits*, Vol. 43, No. 9, 2008, pp. 2079-2089.

[2]   G. Manganaro, S. UngKwak, S. H. Cho and A. Pulin-cherry, "A Behavioral Modelling Approach to the Design a Low Jitter Clock Source," *IEEE Transactions on Circuit and Systems II*, Vol. 50, No. 11, 2003, pp. 804-814.

[3]   L. Bizjak, N. Da Dalt, P. Thurner, R. Nonis, P. Paletri and L. Selmi, "Comprehensive Behavioral Modeling of Conventional and Dual-Tunig PLLs," *IEEE Transactions on Circuit and System I*, Vol. 55, No. 6, 2008, pp. 1628-1638.

[4]   S. Brigati, F. Francesconi, A. Malvasi, A. Pesucci and M. Polerri, "Modeling of Franctional-N Division Frequency Synthesizers with Simulink and Matlab," *The 8th IEEE International Conference on Electronics, Circuits and Systems*, Vol. 2, 2001, pp. 1081-1084.

[5]   M. H. Perrott, "Fast and Accurate Behaviotal Simulation of Fractional-N Frequency Synthesizers and Other PLL/DLL Circuits," *Proceedings of the 39th annual Design Automation Conference*, New York, 10-14 June 2002, pp. 498-503.

[6]   R. B. Staszewski, C. Fernando and P. T. Balsara, "Event-Driven Simulation and Modeling of Phase Noise of an RF Oscillator," *IEEE Transactions on Circuit and Systems I*, Vol. 52, No. 4, 2005, pp. 723-733.

[7]   D. A. Badillo and S. Kiaei, "A Low Phase Noise 2.0 V 900 MHz CMOS Voltage Controlled Ring Oscillator," *Proceedings of the 2004 International Symposium on Circuits and Systems*, Vol. 4, 2004, p. 533

[8]   K. Li, R. Wilcock and P. Wilson, "Improved 6.7 GHz CMOS VCO Delay Cell with up to Seven Octave Tuning Range," *IEEE International Symposium on Circuits and Systems*, Seattle, 18-21 May 2008, pp. 444-447.

[9]   R. J. Baker, "CMOS Circuit Design, Layout and Simulation," 2nd Edition, IEEE Press, Wiley, Hoboken, 2008.

[10] A. A. Abidi, "Phase Noise and Jitter in CMOS Ring Oscillators," *IEEE Journal of Solid-State Circuits*, Vol. 41, No. 8, 2006, pp. 1803-1816.

[11] S. C. Terry, J. Blalock, J. M. Rochelle, M. N. Ericson and S. D. Caylor, "Time-Domain Noise Analysis of Lineat Time-Invariant and Linear Time-Variant Systems Using MATLAB and HSPICE," *IEEE Transactions on Nuclear Science*, Vol. 52, No. 3, 2005, pp. 1418-1422.

## 21

Performance Prospects of Fully-Depleted SOI MOSFET-Based Diodes Applied to Schenkel Circuit for RF-ID Chips

Yasuhisa Omura, Yukio Iida

Department of Electric, Electronics and Informatics, Kansai University, Suita, Japan

ABSTRACT

The feasibility of using the SOI-MOSFET as a quasi-diode to replace the Schottky-barrier diode in the Schenkel circuit is examined by device simulations primarily and experiments partly. Practical expressions of boost-up efficiency for *d. c.* condition and *a. c.* condition are proposed and are examined by simulations. It is shown that the SOI-MOSFET-based quasi-diode is a promising device for the Schenkel circuit because high boost-up efficiency can be gained easily. An *a. c.* analysis indicates that the fully-depleted condition should hold to suppress the floating-body effect for GHz-level RF applications of a quasi-diode.

Keywords: RF-ID; Schenkel Circuit; SOI-MOSFET; Quasi-Diode; Low-Power

1. Introduction

Since RF-ID chips have no internal power supply, they need a way of using the received signal as an energy source; a common approach is the Schenkel circuit [1,2]. The basic Schenkel circuit is shown in **Figure 1**. It usually consists of capacitors and pn diodes (PND's) or Schottky-barrier diodes (SBD's). Modern RF applications such as RF-ID chips often use Schottky-barrier diode (SBD) in this circuit [2-4]. Unfortunately, generally speaking, the reverse-biased current (I_R) of an SBD is not significantly lower than the forward-biased current (I_F) because the requirement for high drive currents results in a low barrier height. The reverse-biased current should be extremely low because the *a. c.* signal voltage received is very small in RF-ID systems. Overall, generally speaking, Schenkel circuits that use SBD's fail to offer high boost-up efficiency, resulting in many stages of boost-up circuit block.

Recently, RF-ID chips are applied to various systems without limitation of production costs because applications to social security including living safe attract attention [5]. In these cases, performance and reliability are primarily important. So, a new market of RF-ID chips is growing up.

On the other hand, SOI MOSFET is one of promising devices that can be applied to RF circuit applications [6]

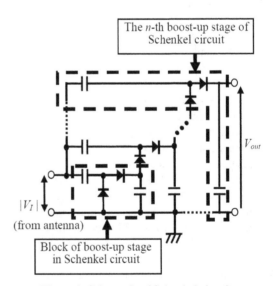

Figure 1. Schematic of Schenkel circuit.

because high-resistivity substrate can be easily introduced [7]. Since the high-resistivity substrate presents not only a low-loss transmission of RF signal [7], but also a low cross-talk in digital circuits [8], various applications are already reported [9,10].

In this paper, we discuss using the SOI-MOSFET-based quasi-diode (SOI-QD) to replace that SBD in Schenkel circuits. First we propose the expression of boost-up efficiency for a low-frequency range using experimental *d. c.* characteristics of SOI-QD made from various SOI MOSFET's, and *a. c.* analyses of SOI-QD are conducted using a two-dimensional (2D) device simulator (ISE *DESISS* [11]) to investigate operation stability in the RF band. We also define another expression of boost-up efficiency in the RF band, and examined its availability on the basis of *a. c.* simulation results. RF-band potential of SOI-MOSFET-based quasi-diode is addressed from the viewpoint of future RF applications.

2. Remaining Issues of Conventional Schenkel Circuit and an Advanced Proposal

At first, we used the circuit simulator PSPICE [12,13] to examine the performance of a Schenkel circuit that used Schottky barrier diode (SBD), pn-junction diode (PND) or conventional bulk MOSFET-based quasi-diode (CB-QD); in the CB-QD variant, the gate terminal and the drain terminal are connected and the source terminal and the substrate terminal are connected. We assumed that the SBD and PND had a junction area of 46.1 μm^2, and that the gate width and the gate length of the bulk MOSFET were 20.6 μm and 0.32 μm. All devices had identical active areas; the junction area of bulk MOSFET is 39.5 μm^2. The circuit simulations employed the empirical model (Level = 3) for simplicity [12]. To acquire realistic device performance from the PND and SBD variants, we introduced the minority carrier lifetime model shown in Appendix A.

Figure 2 shows simulated rectifier characteristics of the various diodes in a low voltage range of input anode voltage (V_A). We can see that SBD with the barrier height (ϕ_b) of 0.15 eV has the largest driving current among the three diodes, but it has the highest reverse-biased current (4.43 μA). **Figure 3** shows the performance of 5-stage Schenkel circuits that use the three different diodes for an input voltage $|V_I|$ of 100 mV. It is shown that the conventional bulk-MOSFET-based quasi-diode (CB-QD) successfully boosts the input signal from a very low level to an acceptable level, while SBD and pn-junction diode fail to do so. SBD failed to match this despite its large driving current; since current SBD designs have a high I_R value, almost identical to I_F, in the low voltage range of 100 mV, the high leakage current (I_R) degrades the signal boost process. On the other hand, the I_F and I_R values of CB-QD are much smaller than those of SBD. However, CB-QD offers an acceptable level of boost. The main reason is that I_F of CB-QD is larger than own I_R, which means that the effective boost efficiency (η) of a Schenkel circuit should not be determined by the direct value of driving current, but by the ratio of I_F to I_R defined as

$$\eta = I_F / \left(I_F + |I_R| \right). \tag{1}$$

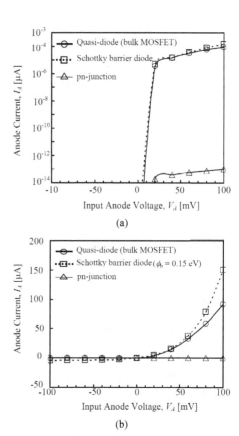

Figure 2. Forward and reverse characteristics of various diodes (Pspice simulation results). (a) Log scale plot; (b) Linear scale plot.

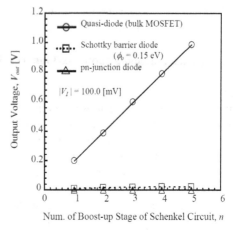

Figure 3. Boost-up performance of Schenkel circuit with various diodes (Pspice simulation results).

In mechanism of voltage boost-up, a large I_R value loses a part of charge stored in a capacitor connected in series. So, the above definition of boost-up efficiency is available independently of the number of boost stages on low-frequency conditions where non-local effects are negligibly small. In addition, the voltage across the capacitor rises when the capacitance of the rectifier is larger that of the capacitor connected in series; however, this results in a low-level current source in contrast to the purpose. Therefore, we have to optimize the capacitance of the capacitor so as to fit the performance request.

Unfortunately, we can not apply the above CB-QD to a practical Schenkel circuit as is because it has a crucial drawback; a CB-QD made on an n-channel bulk MOS-FET has a parasitic pn-junction diode between the drain and the substrate that can work when the drain is negatively biased. This effective reverse current I_R of CB-QD that passes through the parasitic pn-junction diode degrades the η value.

Our solution is to base the quasi-diode on an SOI MOSFET instead of a bulk MOSFET to raise the η value. **Figure 4** shows the device structure assumed here and the terminal nodes of an SOI-MOSFET-based quasi-diode (SOI-QD). The n-channel fully-depleted (FD)-SOI MOSFET's used here for evaluation of device performance had channel lengths (L) of 0.32 and 1.0 μm (see **Table 1**); these devices are used only for a feasibility test and they are not well tempered for the present purpose. Later we perform *a. c.* simulations for SOI-QD. In this case, it is anticipated that the gate-to-source capacitance and the gate-to-drain capacitance play important roles in the *a. c.* analyses because they yield various parasitic

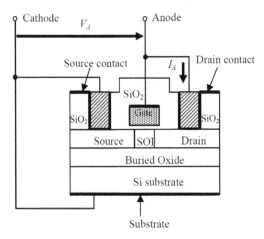

Figure 4. SOI-MOSFET and terminal nodes for quasi-diode operation. Device structure is also assumed for *a. c.* analyses. Device parameters are carefully designed to take account of practical evaluate gate overlap capacitance, S/D parasitic resistance, fringing capacitance, and other parasitic effects in the device.

Table 1. Device parameters used in experiments.

Parameters	Values [Units]
L	0.32 (or 1.0) [μm]
W	20.6 [μm]
t_{SOI}	50.0 [nm]
t_{BOX}	80.0 [nm]
t_{OX}	7.0 [nm]
$N_{a,ch}$	3.0×10^{17} [cm^{-3}]

capacitances including fringing capacitances [14]. So, we consider a realistic device structure to get reliable *a. c.* simulation results. All physical parameters to draw the cross-section of device are determined on the basis of 0.4-μm CMOS design rule [15]; they are identical to those of the device used in the present experiments. In simulations described later, the doping level of the SOI layer, $N_{a,ch}$, was changed from 6.0×10^{16} cm^{-3} to 3.0×10^{17} cm^{-3} to adjust the threshold voltage.

Figure 5 shows the I_D-V_G characteristics of the FD-SOI MOSFET's ($L = 0.32$ and 1.0 μm) measured at $V_D = 50$ mV; the substrate bias was 0 V. The subthreshold swing (S) values of the two devices are quite different. It can be seen that, because of short channel effects, the S value is larger at $L = 0.32$ μm than at $L = 1.0$ μm.

Since it is anticipated that the device characteristics are sensitive to substrate bias (V_{SUB}) because of the thin buried oxide layer, we can produce SOI-QD's with various rectification characteristics by modifying the substrate bias (V_{SUB}) applied to the FD-SOI MOSFET. It should be noted that this technique is introduced to examine how the threshold voltage of FD-SOI MOSFET modulates the η value through the change of I_F and I_R. By the substrate bias, we can easily vary the S value and the current level as well as the threshold voltage. As a result, we can find the best solution of the SOI-QD's rectification characteristics to be tuned. In practical applications, we cannot assume the substrate bias to the device because the assumed RF-ID chip has not a voltage supplier; at the stage of device design, the threshold voltage must be tuned by positive voltage parameter if possible. In this paper, as an attempt, we apply a negative, zero or a positive V_{SUB} value to the device; these conditions are labeled by "A", "B" or "C" (see **Table 2**), respectively. It should be noted that V_{SUB} value at different L value is not identical when the threshold voltage (V_{TH}) is adjusted to be the same. **Figure 6** shows the I_A-V_A characteristics of SOI-QD "A", "B" and "C".

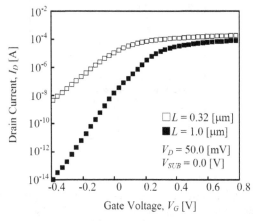

Figure 5. I_D-V_G characteristics of fully-depleted SOI MOS-FET (experimental results).

Table 2. I_F, I_R, R_{ch}, and η values of SOI-QD at various operation conditions (*Amplitude of input signal is 100 mV).

$L = 0.32$ [μm]	S [mV/dec.]/V_{th} [V]	Forward bias		Reverse bias		η [%]*
		I_F [μA]	R_{ch} [kΩ]	I_R [μA]	R_{ch} [kΩ]	
A $V_{BS} = 0.25$[V]	211/0.01	90.0	1.1	−47.0	2.2	64.4
B $V_{BS} = 0.0$ [V]	142/0.1	2.1	47.0	−0.89	110	70.7
C $V_{BS} = -1.5$ [V]	132/0.27	1.2	81.0	−0.55	180	69.3

$L = 1.0$ [μm]	S [mV/dec.]/V_{th} [V]	Forward bias		Reverse bias		η [%]*
		I_F [μA]	R_{ch} [kΩ]	I_R [μA]	R_{ch} [MΩ]	
A $V_{BS} = 3.0$ [V]	169/0.01	29.0	3.4	−11.0	8.8e−3	72.0
B $V_{BS} = 0.0$ [V]	71.8/0.20	0.25	401.0	−0.016	6.2	94.0
C $V_{BS} = -3.0$ [V]	71.5/0.92	7.2e−3	1.39e4	−2.6e−4	3.9e3	96.6

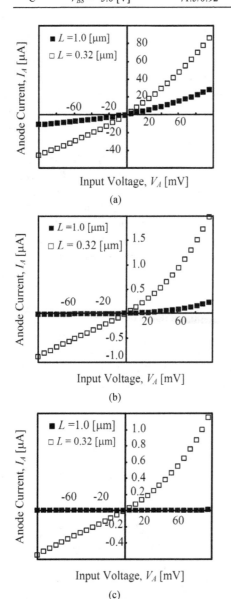

Figure 6. Rectifier *I-V* **characteristics of SOI-QD (experimental results). (a) Operation condition "A"** ($V_{SUB} > 0$); **(b) Operation condition "B"** ($V_{SUB} = 0$ V); **(c) Operation condition "C"** ($V_{SUB} < 0$).

At first, we consider the impact of L value as shown in **Figure 6**. In condition "A", the SOI-QD works near the threshold voltage (V_{TH}) because V_{SUB} is positive. S value is large in condition "A" than in condition "B", resulting in a smaller ratio of I_F/I_R and thus a smaller η value (see **Table 2**, and **Figures 6(a)** and **(b)**). In condition "A", however, since the channel resistance (R_{ch}) is reduced due to the lowering of the threshold voltage (V_{TH}), the driving current of the device increases. In contrast, in condition "C", the device works in the subthreshold region because of the negative substrate bias (V_{SUB}). The S value is smaller in condition "C" than in condition "B"; the channel resistance (R_{ch}) in condition "C" increases due to the raising of the threshold voltage (V_{TH}), resulting in a lower drive current, but identical η value to that seen in condition "B" (see **Figure 6(c)**).

Next we compare the performance of the two devices ($L = 1.0$ and 0.32 μm) shown in **Figure 6**. As mentioned above, the S value with $L = 1.0$ μm is smaller than that with $L = 0.32$ μm. Accordingly, I_F/I_R is larger with $L = 1.0$ μm than that with $L = 0.32$ μm, and the η value with $L = 1.0$ μm is larger than that with $L = 0.32$ μm as shown in **Table 2**. It should be noted that the difference in forward current level (I_F) at the same bias comes from not only the different W/L value but also the different S value. This means that we must take account of the trade-off between η and I_F; that is, it is necessary to select the most suitable operation bias condition and to reduce the S value. **Table 2** suggests that the S value should be less than 75 mV/dec to reduce I_R value and threshold voltage should be ranging from 0.1 V to 0.2 V to simultaneously gain a high η value.

Finally, we briefly compare the performance of SBD, pn-junction diode and SOI-QD; **Table 2** shows I_F, I_R and η of SOI-QD at various operation conditions when the input signal amplitude ($|V_A|$) is 100 mV. According to a recent report [3], when $V_A = 100$ mV, the SBD has an I_F value of about 1.0 nA and the pn-junction diode has an I_F value of about 0.1 pA; this indicates that the SOI-QD has identical I_F to the other devices or has larger I_F at all conditions for the two L values examined. In addition, since the SOI MOSFET has lower leakage current than the SBD and subthreshold characteristic of well-tempered SOI MOSFET is excellent, a high boost efficiency can be expected when the SOI-QD is used.

3. Simulation-Based Consideration of RF Performance of SOI-QD

In order to investigate of the feasibility of using SOI-QD's in RF applications [16], we conducted extensive *a. c.* analyses using a 2D device simulator [11]. **Figure 7** shows the simulated rectifier characteristics of the SOI-QD for various $N_{a,ch}$ values. Since the threshold voltage (V_{th}) rises sharply with the increase in doping level of the SOI layer ($N_{a,ch}$), the forward-biased anode current (I_F) decreases greatly and the reverse-biased anode current (I_R) also decreases. However, η increases on the basis of Equation (1) as $N_{a,ch}$ increases because the reduction of I_R overwhelms that of I_F, which is as is expected. A simple estimation method of η value of SOI MOSFET is shown in Appendix B.

When a high-frequency operation is considered, *a. c.* response to applied signal amplitude should be evaluated; this is very important in SOI MOSFET because it is anticipated that the floating-body effect delays the current response to the applied signal [17]. We think that anode conductance g_A ($=dI_A/dV_A$) successfully traces response capability of SOI MOSFET because g_A is extracted from a small signal analysis; we think a large signal analysis is not always required because Fourier transformation results of signals are effectively considered. Then we define the boost-up efficiency to *a. c.* signals as

$$\eta = \frac{\left\{\Delta I_{AF}\left(f\right)/\Delta V_{A}\left(f\right)\right\}}{\left\{\Delta I_{AF}\left(f\right)/\Delta V_{A}\left(f\right)+\Delta I_{AR}\left(f\right)/\Delta V_{A}\left(f\right)\right\}},\quad (2)$$
$$= g_{AF}\left(f\right)/\left\{g_{AF}\left(f\right)+\left|g_{AR}\left(f\right)\right|\right\}$$

where g_{AF} and g_{AR} mean the anode conductance at the forward and the backward bias conditions, respectively;

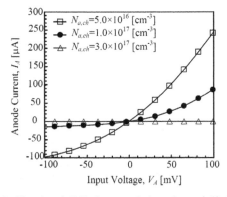

Figure 7. Simulated *I-V* characteristics of quasi-diodes (device simulations).

I_{AF} and I_{AR} are the anode current at the forward and the backward bias conditions, respectively. Some **Figure 8** shows the simulated g_A-V_A curves for various $N_{a,ch}$ values, where g_A ($=dI_A/dV_A$). **Figure 8(a)** is for $N_{a,ch} = 5 \times 10^{16}$ cm^{-3}, **Figure 8(b)** for $N_{a,ch} = 1 \times 10^{17}$ cm^{-3}, and **Figure 8(c)** for $N_{a,ch} = 3 \times 10^{17}$ cm^{-3}. Frequency f was changed from 1 Hz to 10 GHz. In the case of $N_{a,ch} = 5.0 \times 10^{16}$ cm^{-3} (see **Figure 8(a)**), the g_A-V_A characteristic is not sensitive to frequency (1 Hz to 10 GHz). In the cases of $N_{a,ch} = 1.0 \times 10^{17}$ cm^{-3} (see **Figure 8(b)**) and 3.0×10^{17} cm^{-3} (see **Figure 8(c)**), however, the g_A-V_A characteristic is sensitive to frequency. In particular, for $N_{a,ch} = 3.0 \times 10^{17}$ cm^{-3}, the g_A-V_A characteristic reacts strongly to frequency.

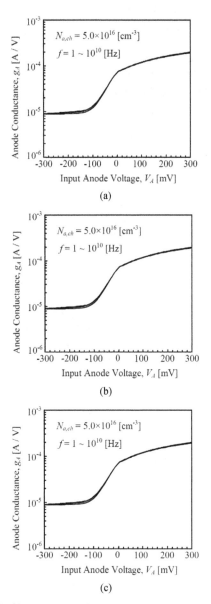

Figure 8. Simulated g_A-V_A characteristics (device simulations). (a) $N_{a,ch} = 5.0 \times 10^{16}$ [cm^{-3}]; (b) $N_{a,ch} = 1.0 \times 10^{17}$ [cm^{-3}]; (c) $N_{a,ch} = 3.0 \times 10^{17}$ [cm^{-3}].

Since the SOI layer is 50 nm thick, the fully-depleted condition is satisfied in two cases (**Figures 8(a)** and **(b)**) [18]. Majority carriers (holes) are basically not responsible for device operation, and so the parasitic bipolar action is not expected at the bias condition used ($|V_A| < 0.3$ V). Since the threshold voltage is very low (~0 V), electrons in the inversion layer rule device operation; in this case, the frequency dependence of the dielectric response of electrons ("majority carriers" near the surface) limits the g_A-V_A characteristic. The limit of the frequency response of electrons in Si is higher than 100 GHz [16], so the simulation results shown in **Figures 8(a)** and **(b)** are acceptable. The smaller variation in g_A-V_A characteristics seen in **Figure 8(b)** is related to the remaining hole density near the bottom of SOI layer, which should be higher than that in **Figure 8(a)**.

We note that the fully-depleted condition is not satisfied in the case of $N_{a,ch} = 3.0 \times 10^{17}$ cm^{-3} [18]. That is, the majority carriers (holes), remaining near the SOI/ buried oxide interface, play an important role in determining device operation, which corresponds to the typical floating body effect [17]. Since the g_A-V_A characteristics at frequencies above 10 MHz differ from those below 10 MHz as seen in **Figure 8(c)**; in other words, the g_A-V_A characteristics at frequencies above 10 MHz are not normal. In the present case, it is easily anticipated that the generation process of majority carriers (holes) (around the junction and inside the depleted body) rules the dynamic operation of SOI-QD. Since the generation-recombination time constant is about 0.1 μsec in the present simulations (see Appendix A), the hole generation process does not respond at frequencies above 10 MHz, resulting in the body floating effect [17].

Figure 9 shows the simulated $\eta - f$ characteristics of the SOI-QD from $f = 1$ Hz to 1 THz with the parameter of $N_{a,ch}$, although the simulated value of η is not reliable for $f > 100$ GHz because physical models for devices in the device simulator [11] are not proposed for such a high frequency; we simply focus on the behavior of η. η values shown in **Figure 9** are calculated by Equation (2).

In **Figure 9**, it should be noted that η values calculated by g_A (Equation (2)) at low frequency region are almost identical to η values calculated from *d. c.* current (experimental results) for $L = 1.0$ μm by Equation (1). So this suggests that η value can be estimated using Equation (2) at RF region. In **Figure 9**, we can see that the η value remains higher than 90% independently of $N_{a,ch}$ up to 10 MHz; this is supported by the fact that S value in the active range of I_A of SOI-QD is sufficiently small. However, when f is higher than 100 MHz, especially when $N_{a,ch} = 3.0 \times 10^{17}$ cm^{-3}, η falls to 60%. This comes from the body-floating effect as mentioned previously. On the other hand, at $N_{a,ch} = 5.0 \times 10^{16}$ cm^{-3} and 1.0×10^{17} cm^{-3}, η remains high up to 10 GHz. As a result, SOI-QD's with $N_{a,ch} = 5.0 \times 10^{16}$ cm^{-3} and 1.0×10^{17} cm^{-3} can be used in RF applications; when $N_{a,ch} = 3.0 \times 10^{17}$ cm^{-3}, the SOI-QD is no longer suitable because of the significant body floating effect.

Figure 10 shows the simulated η-$N_{a,ch}$ characteristics of the SOI-QD at 1 MHz and 4 GHz. In the low frequency range (~1 MHz) η slightly increases with $N_{a,ch}$ because of the reduction of S at the driving point, and finally reaches its upper limit when the reduction in S value ceases. Since $N_{a,ch}$ increases, driving current (I_A) decreases because the threshold voltage of FD-SOI MOSFET rises. Thus, the doping level of the SOI layer of SOI-QD must be optimized to realize a high performance Schenkel circuit. In the radio frequency range (~4 GHz), η peaks because of the floating body effect mentioned above. This strongly suggests that the value of $N_{a,ch}$ must be selected so as to hold the SOI layer in the fully-depleted condition of the SOI layer. As for the present simulation, $N_{a,ch} = 1.0 \times 10^{17}$ cm^{-3} yields the best SOI-QD performance in RF applications up to 100 GHz; when SOI layer is thinned to a range of sub-50 nm, $N_{a,ch}$ value higher than 1×10^{17} cm^{-3} can be applied to devices [19].

In the above simulations, we assumed $V_A = 0.1$ V because we considered the case of short-distance communications. Since the above simulations show that the pro-

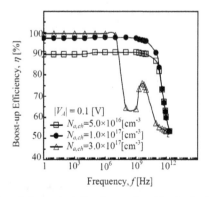

Figure 9. η-f characteristics for various body doping levels (device simulations).

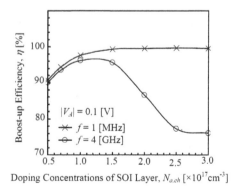

Figure 10. η-$N_{a,ch}$ characteristics for various frequencies (device simulations).

posed SOI-QD produces almost identical performance at $V_A < 0.1$ V, we think that Schenkel circuits with SOI-QD's are also applicable to long-distance communications.

4. Conclusion

The feasibility replacing SBD's in the Schenkel circuit with SOI-MOSFET's as quasi-diodes was examined by experiments and simulations. The reverse-biased current (I_R) of the SOI-QD is much lower than its forward-biased current (I_F) and the driving current (I_F) is high because of the excellent S value provided by the SOI-MOSFET arrangement; we noted that the trade-off between boost efficiency (η) and I_F should be taken into account. In addition, *a. c.* analyses using a two-dimensional device simulator showed that the body doping concentration ($N_{a,ch}$) of the SOI layer should be optimized so as to hold the fully-depleted condition for RF applications up to 100 GHz.

5. Acknowledgements

This study is financially supported by Kansai University research grants, Grant-in-Aid for Joint Research (2004-2005). The authors wish to express their thanks to Mr. Takuta Tamura, Mr. Yuki Tahara, and Mr. S. Namura for their technical support on device simulations.

REFERENCES

[1]   U. Karthaus and M. Fischer, "Fully Integrated Passive UHF RFID Transponder IC with 16.7-μW Minimum RF Input Power," *IEEE Journal of Solid-State Circuits*, Vol. 38, No. 10, 2003, pp.1602-1608.

[2]   M. Usami and M. Ohki, "The μ-Chip: Ultra-Small 2.45 GHz RFID Chip for Ubiquitous Recognition Applications," *IEICE Transactions on Electronics*, Vol. E86-C, No. 4, 2003, pp.521-528.

[3]   W. Jeon, T. M. Firestone, J. C. Rodgers and J. Melngailis, "Design and Fabrication of Schottky Diode, On-Chip RF Power Detector," *Solid-State Electronics*, Vol. 48, No. 10-11, 2004, pp. 2089-2093.

[4]   B. Strassner and K. Chang, "Passive 5.8-GHz Radio-Frequency Identification Tag for Monitoring Oil Drill Pipe," *IEEE Transactions on Microwave Theory and Techniques*, Vol. 51, No. 2, 2003, pp. 356-363.

[5]   K. Ahsan, H. Shah and P. Kingston, "RFID Applications: An Introductory and Exploratory Study," *International Journal of Computer Science Issues*, Vol. 7, No. 1, 2010, pp. 1-7.

[6]   Y. Kado, M. Suzuki, K. Koike, Y. Omura and K. Izumi, "A 1 GHz/0.9 mW CMOS/SIMOX Divide-by-128/129 Dual-Modulus Prescaler Using a Divide-by-2/3 Synchronous Counter," *IEEE Journal of Solid-State Circuits*, Vol. 28, No. 4, 1993, pp. 513-517.

[7]   O. Rozeau, J. Jomaah, J. Boussey and Y. Omura, "Comparison between High- and Low-Dose Separation by Implanted Oxygen MOS Transistors for Low-Power Radio-Frequency Applications," *Japanese Journal of Applied Physics*, Vol. 39, No. 4B, 2000, pp. 2264-2267.

[8]   J. P. Raskin, A. Viviani, D. Flandre and J.-P. Colinge, "Substrate Crosstalk Reduction Using SOI Technology," *IEEE Transactions on Electron Devices*, Vol. 44, No. 12, 1997, pp. 2252-2261.

[9]   Y. Omura, "Negative Conductance Properties in Extremely Thin Silicon-on-Insulator Insulated-Gate pn-Junction Devices (Silicon-on-Insulator Surface Tunnel Transistor)," *Japanese Journal of Applied Physics*, Vol. 35, No. 11A, 1996, pp. L1401-L1403.

[10] Y. Omura and T. Tochio, "Significant Aspects of Minority Carrier Injection in Dynamic-Threshold SOI MOSFET at Low Temperature," *Cryogenics*, Vol. 49, No. 11, 2009, pp. 611-614.

[11] Synopsys Inc., "TCAD-*DESSIS*/GENESISe Operation Manual," ver. 7.5. http://www.sysnopsys.com/

[12] Microsim Corp., "PSpice Reference Manual." http://www.microsimcom.com/

[13] K. Takahashi, S. Y. Wang and M. Mizunuma, "Complementary Charge Pump Booster," *Electronics and Communications in Japan Part II-Electronics*, Vol. 82, No. 6, 1999, pp. 73-81.

[14] Y. Taur and T. H. Ning, "Fundamentals of Modern VLSI Devices," Cambridge University Press, Cambridge, 1998.

[15] Y. Kado, M. Suzuki, K. Koike, Y. Omura and K. Izumi, "An Experimental Full-CMOS Multi-gigahertz PLL LSI Using 0.4-μm Gate Ultrathin-Film SIMOX Technology," *IEICE Transactions on Electronics*, Vol. E76-C, No. 4, 1993, pp. 562-571.

[16] C. Wann, F. Assaderaghi, L. Shi, K. Chan, S. Cohen, H. Hovel, K. Jenkins, Y. Lee, D. Sadana, R. Viswanathan, S. Wind and Y. Taur, "High-Performance 0.07-μm CMOS with 9.3-ps Gate Delay and 150 GHz f_T," *IEEE Electron Devices Letters*, Vol. 18, No. 12, 1997, pp. 625-627.

[17] J.-P. Colinge, "Silicon-on-Insulator: Materials to VLSI," 3rd Edition, Kluwer Academic Publishing, Dordrecht, 2004.

[18] Y. Omura, S. Nakashima and K. Izumi, "Investigation on High-Speed Performance of 0.1-μm-Gate, Ultrathin-Film CMOS/SIMOX," *IEICE Transactions on Electronics*, Vol. E75-C, No. 12, 1992, pp. 1491-1497.

[19] Y. Omura, S. Nakashima, K. Izumi and T. Ishii, "0.1-μm-Gate, Ultrathin-Film CMOS Devices Using SIMOX Substrate with 80-nm-Thick Buried Oxide Layer," *IEEE Transactions on Electron Devices*, Vol. 40, No. 5, 1993, pp. 1019-1022.

[20] J. R. Brews, "A Charge-Sheet Model for the MOSFET," *Solid State Electronics*, Vol. 21, No. 2, 1978, pp. 345-355.

[21] Y. Sakurai, A. Matsuzawa and T. Dozeki, Eds., "Fully-Depleted SOI CMOS Circuits and Technology for Ultralow-Power Applications," Springer, Berlin, 2006.

Appendix A: Simulation Model for Minority Carrier Lifetime

Here we introduce the model for minority carrier lifetimes [11] used in **PSPICE** simulations to ensure consistency with **DESSIS** simulation results.

$$\tau = \tau_{max} + \frac{\tau_{max} - \tau_{min}}{1 + \left(N/N_{ref} \right)^{\gamma}}, \qquad (A1)$$

where N is the doping density, N_{ref} is the doping parameter, γ is the fitting parameter, τ_{max} and τ_{min} are lifetime parameters. Parameter values used here are summarized in **Table 3**.

Appendix B: On the Design Guideline of SOI-QD's

We rewrite the expression of boost-up efficiency given by Equation (1).

$$\eta = I_F \big/ \left(I_F + |I_R| \right), \qquad (B1)$$

When no short-channel effect is assumed, I_F and I_R can be expressed approximately as

$$I_F = \left(\frac{W}{2(1+\alpha)L} \right) \mu_n C_{ox} (V_A - V_{TH})^2 + I_{TH} \quad (V_A > V_{TH}), (B2)$$

$$I_R = I_{TH} 10^{\frac{V_A - V_{TH}}{S}} \quad (V_A < V_{TH}), \qquad (B3)$$

where most of notations are conventional, and S stands for the subthreshold swing for the fully-depleted SOI MOSFET [17]. Parameters α and I_{TH} (threshold current) are given by

$$\alpha = \frac{C_{SOI} C_{BOX}}{C_{ox} \left(C_{SOI} + C_{BOX} \right)}, \qquad (B4)$$

$$I_{TH} = \mu_n \left(\frac{W}{L} \right) q N_A \left(\frac{kT}{q} \right)^2 \frac{1}{E_S}, \qquad (B5)$$

where C_{SOI} is the SOI layer capacitance [17], C_{BOX} is the buried oxide layer capacitance [17], and E_s is the surface electric field. The derivation of α is given in [17], and that of I_{TH} is given in [20,21].

Table 3. Physical parameters assumed in device simulations (DESSIS).

Parameters	Values [units]	Comments
τ_{max}	1.0×10^{-5} [s]/3.0×10^{-5} [s]	Electrons/Holes
τ_{min}	0.0 [s]/0.0 [s]	Electrons/Holes
N_{ref}	1.0×10^{16} [cm^{-3}]	-
γ	1.0	-

## 22

Classic Linear Methods Provisos Verification for Oscillator Design Using NDF and Its Use as Oscillators Design Tool

Angel Parra-Cerrada, Vicente González-Posadas, José Luis Jiménez-Martín, Alvaro Blanco

Department Ingeniería Audiovisual y Comunicaciones, Universidad Politécnica de Madrid, Madrid, Spain

ABSTRACT

The purpose of this paper is to show the conditions that must be verified before use any of the classic linear analysis methods for oscillator design. If the required conditions are not verified, the classic methods can provide wrong solutions, and even when the conditions are verified each classic method can provide a different solution. It is necessary to use the Normalized Determinant Function (NDF) in order to perform the verification of the required conditions of the classic methods. The direct use of the NDF as a direct and stand-alone tool for linear oscillator design is proposed. The NDF method has the main advantages of not require any additional condition, be suitable for any topology and provide a unique solution for a circuit with independence of the representation and virtual ground position. The Transpose Return Relations (RR_T) can be used to calculate the NDF of any circuit and this is the approach used to calculate the NDF on this paper. Several classic topologies of microwave oscillators are used to illustrate the problems that the classic methods present when their required conditions are not verified. Finally, these oscillators are used to illustrate the use and advantages of the NDF method.

Keywords: Oscillator; Provisos; NDF; RR; RR_T

1. Introduction

The oscillators are one of the most important circuit types on nowadays for communication systems and, due to its non-linearity, they are one of the circuits that have more problems on their design and optimization process. The linear simulation of these circuits is really important due to it is suitable for circuit optimization [1-3] and it needs less computational resources than the non-linear simulation. In any case, even if the designer is going to use a non-linear simulation, it is necessary to perform a linear simulation to have a good approximation of oscillation frequency before starting the non-linear simulation. But to be sure that the linear methods provide good solutions, there are some provisos that must be verified.

2. Classic Methods Provisos

The classic methods for linear analysis of oscillators can be classified into two groups: reference plane methods [1,4] and the gain-loop method [5]. The provisos for each group of methods are described in the following sections.

This paper describes the main conclusions and the necessary provisos for the proper use of the classic methods; they are defined and justified in detail by the authors [6-8].

2.1. Reference Plane Methods

Any oscillator may be analyzed using Z, Y or Γ network functions (**Figure 1**), in some cases it is more convenient to use a specific method, but any of the reference plane methods can be used. It is important to remember that all the system poles are included on any network function; however all the poles are not always included on general transfer functions. The necessary condition for a circuit to be a proper oscillator is that it must only have a pair of complex conjugated poles in the Right Half Plane (RHP).

The traditional drawing way is conditioned in order to

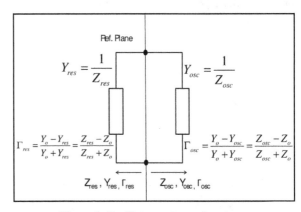

Figure 1. Oscillator as two subsystems.

find the resonant structure as a dipole isolated from the negative $Z/Y/\Gamma$ generator. The reference plane can be any (**Figure 1**), without being a real division between resonator and generator; it is possible thanks to the denominator of any network function has all the information about the system poles. But using one of the traditional divisions simplifies the necessary conditions to assure a correct linear analysis. These classic methods are really the application of the Nyquist's criteria for resolving the location of poles in the RHP of the network functions.

2.2. Negative Conductance Analysis (Impedance Network Function)

Figure 2 presents the conceptual diagram for a negative conductance analysis. The impedance network function is defined by Equation (1), where I_g is the external current; V is the circuit response; and Z is the inverse of the sum of the admittances of **Figure 2**. The circuit is a proper oscillator if the network function has only a pair of conjugated complex poles in the RHP. The poles of the network function are defined by the zeros of Equation (2), which is the characteristic function of the circuit. Then, Equation (2) is analysed with the Nyquist criteria.

$$V = Z \cdot I_g \qquad (1)$$

where:

$$\begin{aligned} Z &= 1/(Y_{res} + Y_{osc}) \\ Y_T &= Y_{res} + Y_{osc} = 0 \end{aligned} \qquad (2)$$

The classic oscillator start-up condition,
$\Im(Y_T) = \Im(Y_{res} + Y_{osc}) = 0$ and
$\Re(Y_T) = \Re(Y_{res} + Y_{osc}) < 0$ is a simplification of the Nyquist analysis to a condition for a single frequency, but it is not sufficient condition to guarantee the start-up of the oscillator [6]. The additional condition before analyzing an oscillator with the negative conductance method (Impedance Network Function) is to assure that Y_{osc} does not have any poles (visible or hidden) in the RHP. This verification uses the Normalized Determinant Function (NDF) [9] of a network built with the active sub-circuit terminated with a short-circuit, as it is de-

scribed by Jackson based on Platzker and Ohtomo papers [9-11]. Each clockwise turning circle around the origin of the NDF analysis, for positive frequencies, confirms the existence of a pair of conjugated poles. As NDF has an asymptotic response with frequency to +1, the upper analysis frequency is easily determined. So, the Nyquist analysis of the NDF of the active subnetwork loaded with a short-circuit must not encircle the origin, then the negative conductance analysis of the oscillator can be performed with guarantee. With this condition the Nyquist analysis of the Equation (2) will predict the oscillation if it has a unique encircle of the origin.

The NDF can be calculated by means of the Return Relations (RR) as it was described by Platzker and in a most suitable way using the Transpose Return Relations (RR_T) [7], Equation (3). The formulation of the NDF which uses the RR_T is the one used by the authors to analyze the examples. To use the RR_T, it is necessary to replace the active devices with their linear models, then the RR_{Ti} term is the Transpose Return Relation for the i-depending generator while previous i-1 ones have been disabled.

$$NDF = \frac{\Delta(s)}{\Delta_0} = \prod_{i=0}^{n}(RR_i + 1) = \prod_{i=0}^{n}(1 - RR_{T_i}) \qquad (3)$$

Negative Impedance Analysis (Admittance Network Function).

The oscillators to be analyzed with the Y network function must also guarantee an additional proviso in the same way as the ones to be analyzed with the Z network function. This proviso also makes use of the NDF analysis. The Y network function is analyzed by means of the Z characteristic function, then the Nyquist analysis of the NDF of the active sub-circuit loaded with an open-circuit must not encircle the origin. With this condition the Nyquist analysis of the Equation (4) will predict the oscillation if it has a unique encircle of the origin [6].

$$Z_T = Z_{res} + Z_{osc} = 0 \qquad (4)$$

Negative Conductance Analysis (Impedance Network Function).

The Γ network function must satisfy that the Nyquist analysis of the NDF of the Z_o loaded active sub-circuit must not encircle the origin.

Then, the oscillation condition can be determined by the analysis of the Equation (5), so the oscillation is satisfied if the Nyquist analysis of $1 - \Gamma_{res} \cdot \Gamma_{osc}$ encircles clockwise the 0 or if the Nyquist analysis of $\Gamma_{res} \cdot \Gamma_{osc}$ encircles clockwise the +1 [6].

$$\Gamma_T = 1 - \Gamma_{res} \cdot \Gamma_{osc} = 0 \qquad (5)$$

2.3. Loop-Gain Method

When the feedback path of the circuit can be identified, the Loop-Gain is commonly used [3]. When it is possible

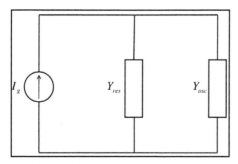

Figure 2. Negative conductance method conceptual diagram.

to define the feedback path, this method is preferred by the designers because it is more intuitive and it can provide more useful information about the circuit. The start point for the loop-gain analysis is the general function of a loopback system (**Figure 3**), and the most important equation used nowadays is the one defined by Randall and Hock (Equation (6)) [5].

$$G_L = \frac{Z_{21} - Z_{12}}{Z_{11} + Z_{22} - 2Z_{12}} = \frac{S_{21} - S_{12}}{1 - S_{11}S_{22} + S_{12}S_{21} - 2S_{12}} \quad (6)$$

The Nyquist analysis of the loop-gain (G_L) must search for +1 clockwise encirclement to assure a proper oscillation condition, but the poles of the system must be only from the zeros of $1 - G_L$. To guarantee that the poles of the system only come from the zeros of $1 - G_L$ it is necessary that [7]:

None of the S parameters can have any poles in the RHP. This condition can be verified with the Nyquist analysis of the NDF of the open-loop circuit loaded with Z_o in both ports.

"Test function" $TF = 1 - S_{11}S_{22} + S_{12}S_{21} - 2S_{12}$ must not have any zeros in the RHP. This condition is verified with the Nyquist analysis of TF when the condition of the previous point has been satisfied.

3. Calculus Using the RR_T

The NDF can be easily calculated with the RR_T of each active device using the Equation 3 as it was described by Platzker [9]. The first step for the RR_T simulation of a transistor is to have a linear model of the device. If this linear model is not available for the transistor the parameters can be extracted with an "annotate" from the spice model with the AWR simulation software.

Once the linear model of the transistor is available, the next step is to calculate its RR_T. It can be calculated by making the transistor work as an independent AC Cur-

rent Source (ACCS) with a constant value for all frequencies and with a voltage meter that measures the voltage at the control point of the real linear transistor model, **Figure 4**.

The same process must be performed for each transistor, but the ACCS of the already analyzed ones must be disabled before starting the simulation of the RR_T of the next one.

Some commercial simulation software, as for example AWR, provides NDF function, but it is also possible to calculate RR_T with any simulator. RR_T is $-RR$ and it is "the true loop gain". The authors did not use the AWR NDF function for the simulations presented in this paper, but they used a general function based on the simulation of the RR_T of each transistor.

4. NDF as Oscillators Design Tool

The main conclusion that can be obtained from the study of provisos for the classic linear oscillator design methods is that it is necessary to use the NDF to guarantee the applicability of any method. So, as it is described by the authors [8] the NDF is itself an interesting linear design method for oscillators design.

The NDF is the quotient of the network determinant and the normalized network determinant, Equation (3). The normalized network determinant is obtained by disabling all the active devices of the network, but it is easily solved by using the RR_T, as it has been described in the previous section.

The Nyquist plot analysis of the NDF determines in a single step the number of poles in the RHP of a network. Each clockwise encirclement of the origin for positive frequencies indicates the existence of a pair of conjugated complex poles in the RHP. So, the total phase evolution for a proper oscillator of the NDF for positive frequencies from 0 Hz up to ∞ Hz must be −360 deg. The

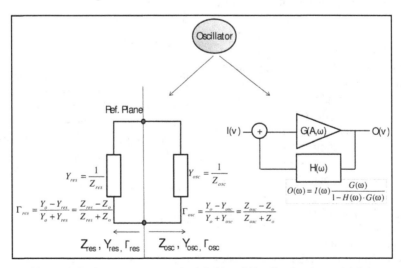

Figure 3. Reference plane method (left) and Feedback scheme (right).

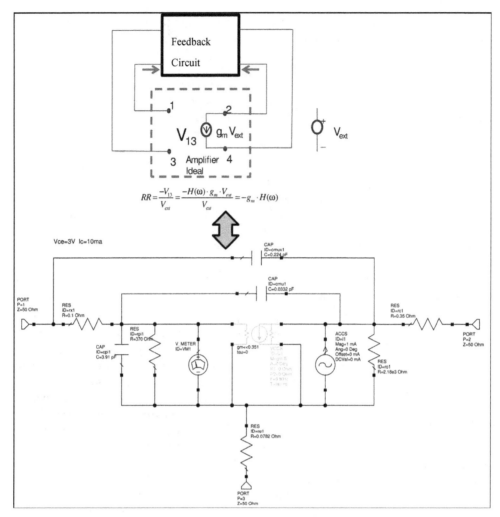

$$RR = \frac{-V_{13}}{V_{ext}} = \frac{-H(\omega) \cdot g_m \cdot V_{ext}}{V_{ext}} = -g_m \cdot H(\omega)$$

Figure 4. Simulation of the RR_T of a transistor.

NDF has an asymptotic behavior towards +1 which is useful for determining the analysis upper frequency limit without ambiguity. As the NDF can be applied to any oscillator topology, it is a universal tool for analyzing oscillators on a single step.

Other useful characteristics of the NDF are that it can predict the oscillation frequency without transistor compression (g_m) for Kurokawa's first harmonic approximation; and that it is suitable for the calculus of the Q_L of the circuit because it is directly related with the RR_T [8]. These characteristics make it suitable to use it as an optimization tool for low noise oscillators [12]. In the same way it is also suitable for estimating the start-up time. These two parameters, phase-noise and start-up time, are proper to the loop-gain method, but also to the NDF method. This way the NDF method makes available for any oscillator topology the parameters that until now were only available for the topologies that can be analysed with the loop-gain method, and on a single step and without ambiguity. This method is suitable for calculateing the real Q_L factor of the circuit and the gain margin,

so it is possible to estimate the start-up time and the phase noise of any oscillator without dependence with its topology.

5. Examples

Two examples are presented on this paper, one oscillator circuit which is usually analyzed with a reference plane method and another that is usually analyzed with the loop-gain method. These two examples have been chosen to illustrate the importance of the verification of the provisos and the advantage of using the NDF as an oscillator linear design tool. The circuits use as active device a BFR360F transistor biased with $I_C = 10$ mA and $V_{CE} = 3$ V. The AWR software has been used for all the simulations shown in this paper.

5.1. Example A

The common collector oscillators, **Figure 5**, are usually analyzed by negative resistance, due it has the behaviour of a negative resistance generator for its first harmonic approximation response. The Nyquist representations of the total impedance and admittance of the example circuit are shown in **Figures 6(a)** and **(b)**.

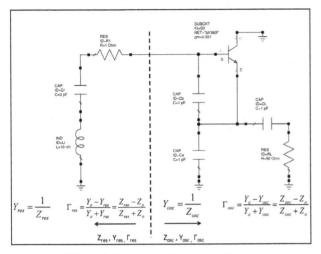

Figure 5. Common collector oscillator.

The Nyquist analysis of Z_T, **Figure 6(a)**, predicts an oscillation frequency of 1887 MHz, but the Nyquist analysis of Y_T, **Figure 6(b)**, does not predict any oscillation condition. It can be explained because Y_{osc} has a conjugated pair of poles in the RHP that hide the zeros on the Nyquist analysis of Y_T. This discrepancy points out the importance of the verification of the provisos before performing any classic analysis to an oscillator.

The Nyquist plot of the NDF of the active sub-circuit loaded with an open-circuit, **Figure 7(a)**, does not encircle the origin, so it is possible to analyze this oscillator using the Y network function (Nyquist analysis of the Z_T). But the NDF of the short-circuit loaded active sub-circuit, **Figure 7(b)**, encircles the origin, Y_{osc} has a pair of poles that will hide the zeros when the Nyquist criteria is used with the Y_T. Then the oscillator cannot be analyzed by the Z network function (admittance analysis).

As an example of the use of the NDF, the NDF analysis of this circuit, **Figure 8** encircles the origin and predicts an oscillation at 1474 MHz. The difference of os-

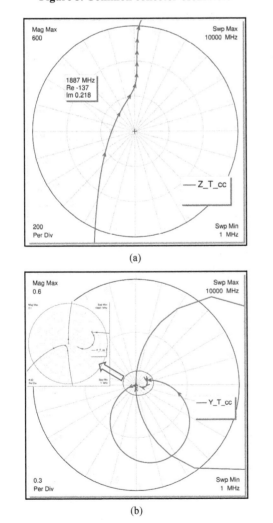

(a)

(b)

Figure 6. (a) Common collector oscillator total impedance and (b) total admittance.

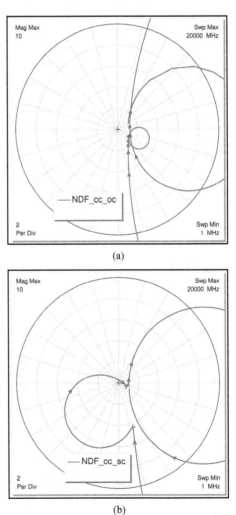

(a)

(b)

Figure 7. NDF of the (a) open-circuit and (b) short-circuit of

the active sub-circuit.

cillation frequency is caused because the Z_T method does not provided the first harmonic approximation but the NDF solves the first harmonic approximation without transistor compression. If the transistor is compressed to $g_m = 0.0125$ then the Z_T solution is the same that the NDF one, **Figure 9**.

As it has been shown with this example, an important advantage of using the NDF method is that it can be used with all oscillator topologies. In this example an oscillator that is usually analyzed with a reference plane method has been presented, so the main parameters that the reference plane methods cannot provide are now. The NDF is a "loop-gain concept" and it provides the first harmonic approximation without transistor compression. The Q_L of the oscillator obtained with Equation (7) [12] is 9.3, **Figure 10**, and the gain margin is defined by the real part of NDF at the crossing point of the encircle of the origin. The big difference between the frequency ob-

$g_m = 0.0125$.

tained by the Z_T without compression and the one obtained by the NDF is due to the low Q_L of the oscillator.

$$Q_L = -\frac{\omega}{2} \cdot \frac{\partial}{\partial \omega} Arg\left(RR_T(\omega)\right) \qquad (7)$$

5.2. Example B

An oscillator, **Figure 11(a)**, to which different virtual ground points [13] are applied, is used for this example. Some resulting possibilities of this example are the well-known classic topologies: common collector (also named Colpitts), common emitter (also named Pierce) and common base. Using virtual ground concept, it is demonstrated that there is a unique oscillator topology and, as it will be explained throughout this example that the NDF/RR_T is the best tool to analyze it. The circuits in **Figure 11** include the parasites of the package of all devices, but these parasites have not been represented for readability.

The open-loop analysis, **Figure 12**, predicts that only the common emitter topology will oscillate, but "How can it be possible if the three schematics represent the same circuit?". The problem appears due to the Nyquist analysis of G_L expression is not valid for common collector and common base topologies. In these two cases the denominators of G_L have two hidden zeros which make Nyquist analysis not encircle +1. It is interesting to point out that the G_L analysis of the common base circuit complies the Barkhausen criteria at two different frequencies, 1131 MHz and 3825 MHz. The first one crosses from a positive to a negative phase, but the second one crosses from a negative to a positive phase. The +1 is not encircled on the common collector example, neither on the common base, so they can be considered as complementary to Nguyen examples [14].

On the other hand, the NDF (or the RR_T), analyses have a unique solution for the three schematics, **Figure 13**. As all the NDF analyses are identical and they predict a unique complex pair of poles in the RHP, so the required condition for proper oscillation is satisfied for the

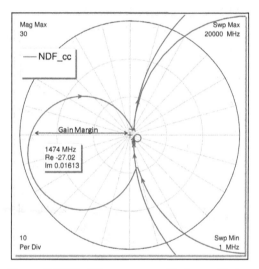

Figure 8. NDF of the common collector oscillator.

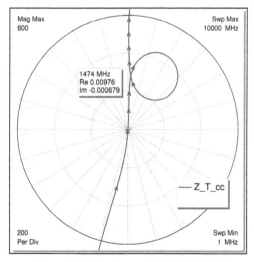

Figure 9. Common collector oscillator total impedance with

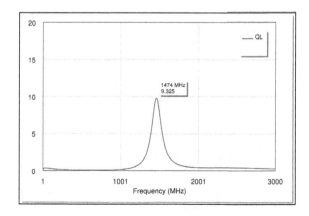

Figure 10. Q_L of the common collector oscillator.

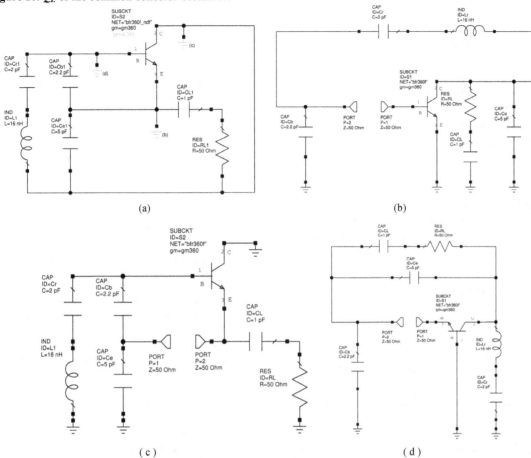

(a)   (b)

(c)   (d)

Figure 11. (a) Ground-less oscillator; (b) Common emitter oscillator; (c) Common collector oscillator; (d) Common base oscillator.

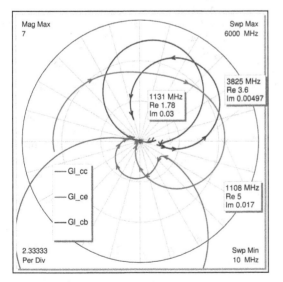

Figure 12. G_L Nyquist plot for common emitter, common collector and common base.

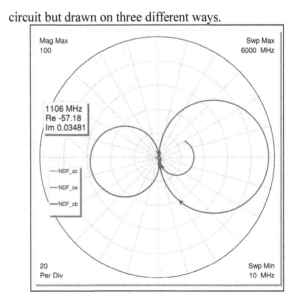

circuit but drawn on three different ways.

Figure 13. NDF Nyquist plot for the three circuit topologies.

three schematics. As it is expected, the solution for the three examples is the same, because they are the same

6. Conclusions

The NDF method is a suitable tool for direct analysis of oscillators and it does not require any additional proviso or conditions before using it. Another advantage of this NDF method is that all oscillator topologies can be analyzed with a "loop-gain concept" and the main parameters that the reference plane methods cannot provide are now available for any oscillator topology.

The NDF solution is independent of the virtual ground position and it provides the oscillation frequency at first harmonic approximation without requiring transistor g_m compression. This NDF independence is based on its relation with the Return Relations (and RR_T), as they provide the "true open-loop-gain". To sum up, the NDF/RR_T method is an optimum tool for the quasi-lineal oscillator analysis in a single step; it does not require any additional proviso or verification; and it is suitable for any oscillator topology.

REFERENCES

[1]   D. J. Esdale and M. J. Howes, "A Reflection Coefficient Approach to the Design of One Port Negative Impedance Oscillators," *IEEE Transactions on Microwave Theory and Techniques*, Vol. 29, No. 8, 1981, pp. 770-776.
http://ieeexplore.ieee.org/xpl/articleDetails.jsp?arnumber=1130445

[2]   S. Alechno, "Advancing the Analysis of Microwave Oscillators," *Microwaves RF*, Vol. 39, No. 6, 2000, pp. 55-67.

[3]   R. W. Rhea, "Discrete Oscillator Design: Linear, Nonlinear, Transient, and Noise Domains," Artech House Publishers, New York, 2010.

[4]   R. W. Jackson, "Criteria for the on Set of Oscillation in Microwave Circuits," *IEEE Transactions on Microwave Theory and Techniques*, Vol. 40, No. 3, 1992, pp. 566-569.
http://ieeexplore.ieee.org/xpl/articleDetails.jsp?arnumber=121734

[5]   M. Randall and M. J. Hock, "General Oscillator Characterization Using Linear Open-Loop S-Parameters," *IEEE Transactions on Microwave Theory and Techniques*, Vol. 49, No. 6, 2001, pp. 1094-1100.

[6]   V. González-Posadas, J. L. Jiménez Martín, A. Parra-Cerrada, D. Segovia-Vargas and L. E. García-Muñoz, "Oscillator Accurate Linear Analysis and Design. Classic Linear Methods Review and Comments," *Progress in*

Electromagnetics Research PIER, Vol. 118, 2011, pp. 89-116.
http://www.jpier.org/PIER/pier.php?paper=11041403

[7]   J. L. Jiménez-Martín, V. González-Posadas, A. Parra-Cerrada, L. E. García-Muñoz and D. Segovia-Vargas, "Comments and Remarks over Classic Loop-Gain Linear Method for Oscillators Design and Analysis. New Proposed Method Based on NDF/RRT," Radioengineering, Vol. 21, No. 1, 2012, pp. 478-491.

[8]   J. L. Jiménez-Martín, V. González-Posadas, A. Parra-Cerrada, L. E. García-Muñoz and D. Segovia-Vargas, "Provisos for Classic Linear Oscillator Design Methods. New Linear Oscillator Design Based on the NDF/RRT," *Progress in Electromagnetics Research PIER*, Vol. 126, 2012, pp. 17-48.
http://www.jpier.org/PIER/pier.php?paper=11112308

[9]   A. Platzker and W. Struble, "Rigorous Determination of the Stability of Linear N-Node Circuits from Network Determinants and the Appropriate Role of the Stability Factor K of Their Reduced Two-Ports," *3rd International Workshop on Integrated Nonlinear Microwave and Millimeterwave Circuits*, 1994, pp. 93-107.
http://ieeexplore.ieee.org/xpl/articleDetails.jsp?arnumber=512515

[10] R. W. Jackson, "Rollett Proviso in the Stability of Linear Microwave Circuits-a Tutorial," *IEEE Transactions on Microwave Theory and Techniques*, Vol. 54, No. 3, 2006, pp. 993-1000.
http://ieeexplore.ieee.org/xpl/articleDetails.jsp?arnumber=1603843

[11] M. Ohtomo, "Proviso on the Unconditional Stability Criteria for Linear Twoport," *IEEE Transactions on Microwave Theory Tech*, Vol. 43, No. 5, 1995, pp. 1197-1200.

[12] J. L. Jiménez Martín, V. González-Posadas, A. Parra-Cerrada, A. Blanco-del-Campo and D. Segovia-Vargas, "Transpose Return Relation Method for Designing Low Noise Oscillators," *Progress in Electromagnetics Research PIER*, Vol. 127, 2012, pp. 297-318.
http://www.jpier.org/PIER/pier.php?paper=12022305

[13] S. Alechno, "The Virtual Ground in Oscillator Design—A Practical Example," *Applied Microwave & Wireless*, Vol. 39, No. 7, 1999, pp. 44-53.

[14] N. M. Nguyen and R. G. Meyer, "Start-Up and Frequency Stability in High-Frequency Oscillators," *IEEE Journal of Solid-State Circuits*, Vol. 27, No. 5, 1992, pp. 810-820.

## 23

Design of Secure Microsystems Using Current-to-Data Dependency Analysis

Haleh Vahedi[1], Radu Muresan[2], Stefano Gregori[2]
[1]The Edwards S. Rogers Sr. Department of Electrical and Computer Engineering, University of Toronto, Toronto, Canada
[2]School of Engineering, University of Guelph, Guelph, Canada

ABSTRACT

This paper presents a method for designing a class of countermeasures for DPA attacks based on attenuation of current variations. In this class of countermeasures, designers aim at decreasing the dynamic current variations to reduce the information that can be extracted from the current consumption of secure microsystems. The proposed method is based on a novel formula that calculates the number of current traces required for a successful DPA attack using the characteristics of the microsystem current signal and the external noise of the measurement setup. The different stages of the proposed method are illustrated through designing an example current flattening circuit. Meanwhile validity and applicability of the proposed formula is verified by comparing theoretical results with those obtained experimentally for the example circuit. The proposed formula not only estimates the required level of attenuation for a target level of robustness defined by design requirements, it also predicts the effectiveness of a countermeasure using simulation results therefore dramatically reducing the time to design of secure microsystems.

Keywords: Secure Microsystems; Differential Power Analysis Attack; Countermeasure; Current Flattening Circuit

1. Introduction

Microsystems such as smart cards are at the heart of applications where security is a major concern. In secure microsystems, generally the secret key cannot be accessed directly because of its embedded nature, however, it can be revealed through side-channel attacks that use information extracted from the physical implementation. The most effective side-channel attacks are differential power analysis (DPA) attacks, which use statistical analyses for extracting information from variations of the power-supply current of a cryptographic device [1].

Countermeasures against DPA attacks [2-4] are either software-based or hardware-based, which, in turn, are based on circuit-level or system-level solutions [5]. Typically, system-level solutions assume that attenuating the variations of the power-supply current makes DPA attacks more difficult [5-7]. The number of current traces required for a successful DPA attack (hereafter NCT-DPA) is used to evaluate the robustness of a secure microsystem against DPA attacks or the effectiveness of a countermeasure. In the existing literature, such number of traces is found experimentally by running DPA attacks on an increasing number of current traces and repeating

the process until the attack is successful.

In this paper a formula is introduced for calculating NCT-DPA of secure microsystems. Here, the NCT-DPA is presented by the characteristics of the current variations of the microsystem while executing a cryptography algorithm and the external noise of the current measurement setup in DPA attacks (*i.e.* the ac rms value of these two signals). In [8] (p. 54), a formula has been extracted that shows the relationship of the signal to noise ratio, SNR, and NCT-DPA. However, there is an unspecified parameter in the formula (related to the algorithmic noise). Also in [9] (p. 147), a formula has been suggested for the relationship between the SNR and NCT-DPA. In this paper, there will be a cross check between our formula and the relationship suggested by authors of [9].

The proposed formula is used to develop a method for designing countermeasures that aim at attenuating dynamic current variations of microsystems. The resulting method has two main benefits: 1) it allows designers to estimate the required level of current attenuation for a certain level of protection, therefore it can be used as a starting point of design for any countermeasure based on the current variations reduction; 2) it can be used for assessing the robustness of countermeasures in the simulation stage therefore significantly reducing the time to design of secure microsystems.

The remainder of this paper is organized as follows: Section II focuses on deriving the formula for calculating NCT-DPA. In Section III, the attenuation level is estimated by using a specific countermeasure requirement. Section IV briefly discusses a countermeasure circuit as an example for validation of the method. In Section V, the robustness of the proposed design and the credibility of the proposed formula are demonstrated. Section VI discusses the effect of noise on the efficiency of the example circuit and shows the role of the proposed formula in revealing the efficiency of the circuit in conditions where experimental methods are not possible. Concluding remarks appear in Section VII.

2. Deriving a Formula for Calculating NCT-DPA

In a ciphertext-based DPA attack targeting a data encryption standard (DES) algorithm, for each guessed sub-key, e.g. the n-th sub-key, the collected current traces are partitioned into two groups G_1 and G_0 (using the target bit of a given selection function D). The averages of the partitioned current traces are calculated and their difference gives the differential current trace

$$DT_n = \overline{T}_1 - \overline{T}_0, \tag{1}$$

where $\overline{T}_1$ and $\overline{T}_0$ are the averages of the current traces partitioned in groups G_1 and G_0 respectively. For example, if a 6-bit sub-key of a DES encryption is chosen, there are 64 possible sub-key guesses, which form a set of differential current traces $DT = \{DT_1, DT_2, \cdots, DT_{64}\}$. The correct guessed sub-key is the one that corresponds to the differential trace with the maximum peak [1].

As a figure of merit for evaluating the robustness of a cryptographic device, the difference between the maximum peak of the differential trace for the correct key (i_{pc}) and the maximum peak appearing on the differential traces for the wrong keys (i_{pw}) is called success value indicator [10]

$$SVI = i_{pc} - i_{pw}. \tag{2}$$

In a DPA attack with a small number of current traces, some spikes of differential traces corresponding to wrong sub-keys may be higher than the spike of the differential trace for the right sub-key; in this case SVI < 0 and the correct sub-key cannot be guessed. By increasing the number of current traces, the spike of the trace corresponding to the right sub-key increases and those corresponding to wrong sub-keys decrease and eventually, when SVI > 0, the right sub-key can be guessed correctly. The minimum number of traces NCT-DPA for which the value of the maximum peak of the differential trace cor-

responding to the right sub-key is equal to the highest peak value of the differential traces corresponding to wrong sub-keys gives a quantitative indication of the time required by a DPA attack to be successful.

Obviously, in order to identify the correct sub-key with acceptable confidence, the spike in the differential trace for the correct sub-key must be bigger than the spikes in the differential traces for the wrong sub-keys. To quantify how much bigger it should be, the probability distributions of the spikes and their dependency on electric noise have to be considered.

The sources of noise are modelled as algorithmic and non-algorithmic [8] (p. 53). The algorithmic noise depends on the type of DPA attack being executed and on the number of bits exploited [8] (p. 57), [9] (p. 75). The non-algorithmic noise includes external noise, intrinsic noise, and quantization noise. The external noise is generated by power supply, clock generator, and interference with other parts of a microsystem [9] (p. 55). The intrinsic noise is due to the fundamental properties of electronic devices and it includes thermal, shot, and flicker noise. The quantization noise depends on the quality of the analog-to-digital converter used for sampling the current traces. The dominant non-algorithmic noise is typically the external noise since intrinsic noise is controlled at the design stage and quantization noise is minimized with an appropriate measurement setup [9].

The deviation of the spikes of the differential traces for wrong sub-keys is mainly due to external noise, which can be modelled with a normal distribution [9] (p. 65). The deviation of the spikes of the differential traces for the correct sub-key is mainly due to external noise and algorithmic noise. The algorithmic noise depends on the probability distribution of data, which is binomial and can be modelled as a normal distribution for large number of events. Since algorithmic noise and external noise are independent, their variances can be added up. **Figure 1** represents the spike of the differential trace corresponding to the correct sub-key, i_{pc}, and the maximum spike of the differential traces for wrong sub-keys, i_{pw},

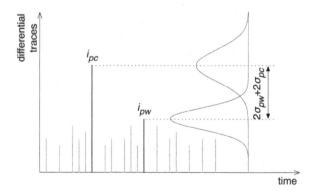

Figure 1. Probability distributions of the spikes of differential traces for the correct sub-key and for wrong sub-keys.

and their distributions. The confidence on revealing the correct sub-key depends on the spacing of the two distributions. As an example, assuming that the standard deviation of the spike of the correct key is much larger than the standard deviation of the spike of the wrong keys are the same, *i.e.* $\sigma_{pc} \gg \sigma_{pw}$, if the difference of the two mean values is

$$i_{pc} - i_{pw} = 2\sigma_{pc} + 2\sigma_{pw} \qquad (3)$$

then the probability of revealing the correct sub-key is over 97%.

If a DPA attack is run for N number of traces, when N is large enough, one can assume that for half of these traces the target bit of the selection function D is equal to 1 and for the other half the target bit is equal to zero. Therefore, if σ^2 is the variance of a current trace, the variance of each group of $\overline{T}_0$ and $\overline{T}_1$ is approximated to $\dfrac{\sigma^2}{N/2}$ and the variance of the differential trace will be the sum of the variances of these two independent groups, that is $\dfrac{4\sigma^2}{N}$ [8] (p. 55). Therefore, (3) can be rewritten as:

$$i_{pc} - 2\sqrt{\frac{4\sigma_{pc}^2}{N}} = i_{pw} + 2\sqrt{\frac{4\sigma_{pw}^2}{N}}. \qquad (4)$$

As mentioned earlier, the variance of the spike of the correct key is due to the external noise and the algorithmic noise (which are independent) and the variance of the spike of the wrong keys is due to the external noise. Therefore:

$$i_{pc} - 4\frac{\sqrt{\left(\sigma_{alg.}\right)^2 + \left(\sigma_{ext.}\right)^2}}{\sqrt{N}} = i_{pw} + 4\frac{\sigma_{ext.}}{\sqrt{N}} \qquad (5)$$

where $\sigma_{alg.}$ and $\sigma_{ext.}$ are the standard deviations of the algorithmic noise and the external noise, respectively.

The values in (5) should be related to the characteristics of the current traces and noise. Comparing the rms value of the population of x with N samples, $x_{rms} = \sqrt{\dfrac{\sum x^2}{N}}$, with the standard deviation of the population x with the mean value μ, $\sigma = \sqrt{\dfrac{\sum(x-\mu)^2}{N}}$, shows that if the mean value is zero, then the rms value and the standard deviation are the same. In other words, the standard deviation is obtained by removing the DC component and measuring the ac rms value. This property is used to measure the standard deviation of the algorithmic noise and the external noise. If in the cryptographic algorithm an n-bit word is processed and the number of collected current traces are large enough, it can be assumed that the deviation of the microsystem

current signal is due to n bit transitions. In DPA attacks, if the changes of m bits are exploited, the changes of the remaining $n - m$ bits are considered the algorithmic noise. Therefore, the variance of the algorithmic noise is $(n - m)/n$ times of the variance of the current signal. If the variance is expressed in terms of the standard deviation, and hence in terms of the ac rms value, (5) can be rewritten as:

$$i_{pc} - 4\frac{\sqrt{\frac{(n-m)}{n}\cdot(i_s)^2 + (i_{ext.})^2}}{\sqrt{N}} = i_{pw} + 4\frac{i_{ext.}}{\sqrt{N}} \qquad (6)$$

where i_s and $i_{ext.}$ are the ac rms values of the microsystem current signal and the external noise respectively. The required number of traces, N, can be derived by solving (6) to obtain:

$$N = \left(4\frac{\sqrt{\frac{(n-m)}{n}\cdot(i_s)^2 + (i_{ext.})^2} + i_{ext.}}{i_{pc} - i_{pw}}\right)^2. \qquad (7)$$

For the DPA attack used in this research, the variations of one bit of a 6-bit word are exploited. Hence, (7) reduces to:

$$N = \left(4\frac{\sqrt{\frac{5}{6}\cdot(i_s)^2 + (i_{ext.})^2} + i_{ext.}}{i_{pc} - i_{pw}}\right)^2. \qquad (8)$$

Assuming that the $i_{pc} - i_{pw}$ term is proportional to the rms value of the microsystem current signal (see Section V-B), (8) can be rewritten as:

$$N = \left(4\frac{\sqrt{\frac{5}{6}\cdot(i_s)^2 + (i_{ext.})^2} + i_{ext.}}{k_1 \cdot i_s}\right)^2 \qquad (9)$$

where k_1, i_s and $i_{ext.}$ are parameters determined by the characteristics of the current signal of a microsystem and the DPA attack measurement setup. In this paper we use (9) to estimate the required level of attenuation for obtaining a certain level of robustness (expressed in terms of NCT-DPA) for a specific microsystem. To that end, we should measure $i_{ext.}$ and k_1 for the *microsystem*. Finding k_1 requires measuring NCT-DPA for the unprotected microsystem. Finding $i_{ext.}$, requires measuring the external noise of the DPA attack measurement setup. The following sub-sections will discuss these measurements.

2.1. Measurement of NCT-DPA for a Specific Unprotected Microsystem

First a set of current traces were measured at the supply

pin of an unprotected microsystem while the microsystem was executing DES encryptions. The chosen microsystem device was an 8-bit AVR microcontroller (ATmega16, from ATMEL) operating at 4 MHz clock frequency with a 3.3-V power supply voltage [11]. This is a typical microcontroller used in smart card applications. While the ATmega16 microcontroller was executing DES encryptions on randomly generated plaintexts, 1000 current traces of the microcontroller were collected at the supply pin. The setup for the measurement is shown in **Figure 2**. It consists of a resistor (R), high frequency differential probes, a signal generator for providing the clock signal, a high-precision power supply, and a high-speed digital sampling oscilloscope for collecting the current traces.

A ciphertext-based DPA attack for a DES algorithm [1] was performed over the collected current traces. For the unprotected microcontroller, the correct sub-key was revealed within 400 traces. This result was obtained by measuring the Success Value Indicator (SVI). **Figure 3** shows the SVI graph for DPA attacks with different number of current traces. When SVI (on y axis) is less than zero, the peak value of the differential trace of the correct sub-key is less than the peak value of the differential traces corresponding to the remaining sub-keys; hence, the correct sub-key can not be distinguished. As shown in **Figure 3**, for the number of traces less than 400, SVI is less than zero. When the number of traces is

greater than 400, SVI is greater than zero and the correct sub-key may be revealed. This number will be used later for calculating k_1.

2.2. Measurement of the External Noise of the Microcontroller Setup

In order to find out the characteristics of the external noise influencing the setup, a DES algorithm was executed over a fixed plaintext for 1000 times. Since the operation and the data were not changed, one would expect that the collected current traces would remain the same. However, because of the external noise, the current traces were not exactly the same. The mean of these 1000 traces was measured and then the external noise was obtained by subtracting the mean from one of the signals. This experiment was performed 5 times and the least noise was chosen. **Figure 4** shows the external noise and the mean of the current traces. The rms value of the external noise was 2.015×10^{-4} A and the rms value of the current signal was 8.5×10^{-4} A.

2.3. Deriving k_1 for the ATmega Microcontroller

By substituting N, i_s and $i_{\text{ext.}}$ (from previous sub-sections) into (9), we obtain k_1:

$$400 = \left(4 \frac{\sqrt{\frac{5}{6} \times \left(8.5 \times 10^{-4}\right)^2 + \left(2 \times 10^{-4}\right)^2} + 2 \times 10^{-4}}{k_1 \cdot 8.5 \times 10^{-4}} \right)^2 \quad (10)$$

$$k_1 = \left(4 \frac{9.9}{20 \times 8.5} \right) = 0.23.$$

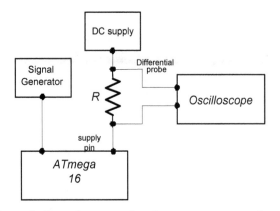

Figure 2. Setup for measuring the current consumption of ATmega16 microcontroller.

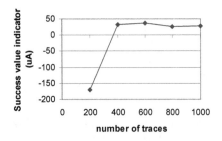

Figure 3. SVI versus the number of current traces for the unprotected microcontroller.

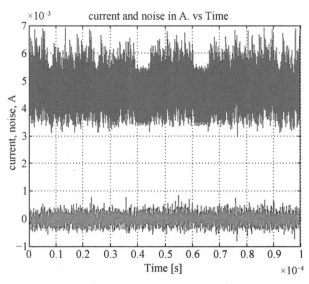

Figure 4. The mean of th e ATmega current trace and the external noise of the setup used for collecting current traces of ATmega microcontroller.

By substituting this value of k_1 in (9), a formula is obtained for NCT-DPA that is only based on the ac rms values of the current signal and the external noise (for ATmega16).

$$N = \left(4 \frac{\sqrt{\frac{5}{6} \cdot (i_s)^2 + (i_{ext.})^2} + i_{ext.}}{0.23 \cdot i_s} \right)^2 . \qquad (11)$$

This formula can be derived for any type of microsystems and will be used as a starting-point of a design methodology discussed in the next sections.

3. Estimating the Required Attenuation Level

As an example, let us consider the design of a countermeasure to protect the ATmega16 microcontroller so that the DPA attack is not successful for less than 10,000 current traces. The rms value of the external noise is assumed to be 2×10^{-4} A (*i.e.*, the least value of noise seen in the experiment). The required rms value of the current traces can be calculated using (11):

$$10000 = \left(4 \frac{\sqrt{\frac{5}{6} \cdot (i_s)^2 + (2 \times 10^{-4})^2} + 2 \times 10^{-4}}{0.23 \cdot i_s} \right)^2 .$$

$$i_s = 8 \times 10^{-5} \text{ A} .$$

This current can be translated to a level of attenuation of:

$$\frac{(8.5 \times 10^{-4} - 8 \times 10^{-5})}{8.5 \times 10^{-4}} \times 100 = 91\%$$

where 8.5×10^{-4} A is the ac rms value of the current of the unprotected microcontroller while running a DES algorithm.

Having this number in mind, we designed a current flattening circuit that attenuates the dynamic current variations with more than 90% [12]. In the next sections, this example circuit will be introduced briefly, and its efficiency will be investigated and compared with what was expected through the proposed formula (8).

4. Designing a Countermeasure for the Required Level of Attenuation

Figure 5 shows the block diagram of the example circuit. We wish to keep the current through the supply pin (V_{DD}) at a constant level by using a current injection technique.

In **Figure 5**, the current sensor measures I_S at V_{DD}. The output of the sensor, I'_S, an attenuated version of I_S, is subtracted from I'_R, an attenuated version of reference

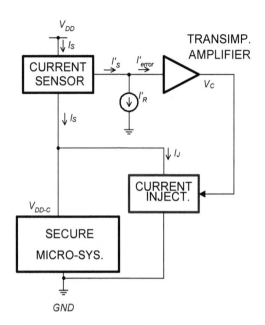

Figure 5. Block diagram of the current flattening circuit.

current (I_R); the resultant is fed to a transimpedance amplifier. The output of the amplifier V_C controls the current injection block. When $I_S < I_R$, this block absorbs an extra current I_J and maintains I_S close to I_R.

Figure 6 shows the schematic of this circuit. The current sensor is a customized current mirror (M1 and M2) which produces I'_S, an attenuated version of the current of the secure microsystem. The current I'_{error}, the difference between I'_S and I'_R, is fed to a transimpedance amplifier. I'_{error} is amplified and converted to the voltage V_C, the output of the amplifier. This voltage is used for controlling transistor M6, which implements the current injection. This circuit is the design described in [12] and its functionality in reducing the dynamic current variations was verified through extensive simulations and testing the fabricated chip.

5. Investigation of the Robustness of the Example Circuit

To see how robust the example circuit is, NCT-DPA was calculated for different levels of the current attenuation using both the experimental method and the formula (8). This can be considered as a third stage of the design method. In addition, this will be used as a solid experiment for investigating the credibility of the proposed formula.

5.1. NCT-DPA for the Example Circuit

In order to investigate the robustness of the example circuit and also observe the relationship between the current attenuation and NCT-DPA, the current traces collected from the unprotected ATmega16 microcontroller (Section II-A) were imported into the Cadence environment.

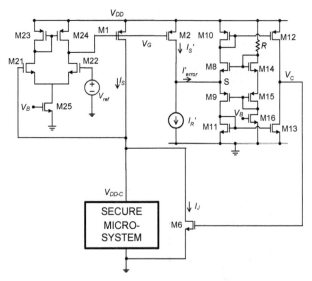

Figure 6. Schematic diagram of the current flattening circuit.

These current traces were applied as the input signal to the current flattening circuit in order to emulate the current variations of a smart card microcontroller performing a DES encryption. Setting the reference input of the current injection loop, the original current traces were flattened with different levels of attenuation. **Table 1** summarizes the simulation results. As seen in **Table 1**, the simulation was run for five different current reference values and five sets of current traces with different level of attenuations were obtained. The attenuation of each set was calculated in terms of the rms value of the current signal.

Next, DPA attacks were run over each set of current traces. **Figure 7** and the last column of **Table 1** show how the flattened signals with different levels of attenuation responded to a DPA attack. The y axis in **Figure 7** is SVI for the DPA attack. One can see that by reducing the ac rms value of the flattened current signal, NCT-DPA increases. When the rms value of the flattened current is 6.3×10^{-6} A, which is translated to 99.26% attenuation, NCT-DPA reaches 9600.

Since the experiments were performed over the noise-free output of the simulator, our experimental results show different attenuation value compared to the attenuation obtained through the formula in Section III; that is 99.26% attenuation required for a NCT-DPA of 9600 in the experimental method compared to 91% attenuation estimated for a NCT-DPA of 10,000 in the first stage of the design. Repeating the calculation presented in Section III and using (11) with only the attenuated external noise added to the input signal, 4×10^{-6} A, i_s will be equal to 1.4×10^{-6} A. This value can be translated to 99.8% expected attenuation, which is close to what was obtained through the Cadence experiment. Hence the

Table 1. Rms value, attenuation, and NCT-DPA for signals with different levels of attenuation.

Current traces	rms value (A)	Percentage of attenuation	NCT-DPA
original	8.5×10^{-4}	None	400
Set 1	1.4×10^{-5}	98.35	600
Set 2	1.06×10^{-5}	98.75	1200
Set 3	9.11×10^{-6}	98.93	2400
Set 4	8.26×10^{-6}	99.03	4600
Set 5	6.3×10^{-6}	99.26	9600

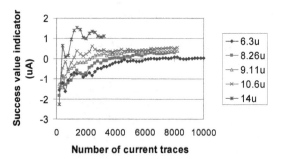

Figure 7. SVI versus number of current traces for flattened currents with different rms values.

validity of the estimation in the previous section is verified.

For verifying the validity of the formula (8), the NCT-DPA values for the 5 sets introduced in **Table 1** were calculated by using this formula. For this purpose, the spike values of the differential current traces for the correct sub-key and wrong sub-keys were obtained by running a DPA attack with 10,000 traces. The spike values and their corresponding current rms values are shown in **Table 2**. Since simulation results are used here, the external noise can be considered zero. By substituting the values i_s, i_{pc}, and i_{pw} from this table into the formula (8), the NCT-DPA is obtained as shown in the 4-th column of **Table 2**. The NCT-DPA obtained experimentally (**Table 1**) is repeated in the 5-th column of this table. Comparing these two columns shows that the NCT-DPA obtained through these two methods are very close to each other, which verifies the credibility of (8).

The difference in the last two columns can be quantified by comparing (2) and (3), which are repeated here:

$$\text{SVI} = i_{pc} - i_{pw} .$$

$$i_{pc} - 2\sigma_{pc} = i_{pw} + 2\sigma_{pw} .$$

Decision point for the experimental method is the point where SVI is equal to zero:

$$i_{pc} - i_{pw} = 0 \qquad (12)$$

and the decision point for the formula is where:

$$i_{pc} - i_{pw} = 2\sigma_{pc} + 2\sigma_{pw} . \qquad (13)$$

Table 2. NCT-DPA using the formula and the experimental method for the flattened current traces with different rms values.

i_s (A)	i_{pc} (A)	i_{pw} (A)	NCT-DPA (formula)	NCT-DPA (SVI)
1.4×10^{-5}	2.8×10^{-6}	1×10^{-6}	752	600
1.06×10^{-5}	1.61×10^{-6}	0.6×10^{-6}	1238	1200
9.11×10^{-6}	1.19×10^{-6}	0.5×10^{-6}	2354	2400
8.26×10^{-6}	0.95×10^{-6}	0.5×10^{-6}	4492	4600
6.3×10^{-6}	5.2×10^{-7}	3×10^{-7}	10933	9600

By comparing (12) and (13), one can see that the difference between the decision points of the two methods is the term $2\sigma_{pc} + 2\sigma_{pw}$. As discussed in Section II, the deviation of the spike of the correct sub-key is due to the external noise and the algorithmic noise and the deviation of the spikes of the differential traces of the wrong sub-keys is due to the external noise. Since, experimental results are obtained from the simulator output, where the external noise is negligible, σ_{pw} is zero and σ_{pc} is mainly determined by the algorithmic noise. Also, the variance, and therefore, the standard deviation of the algorithmic noise, is related to the rms value of the current signal. Since the current signal is flattened and its rms value is reduced significantly, the algorithmic noise is very small and therefore, the term of $2\sigma_{pc} + 2\sigma_{pw}$ is negligible. This point justifies the similarity of the numbers in the last two columns of **Table 2** and demonstrates the validity of (8).

5.2. Verifying the Assumption Made in Deriving (9)

In deriving (9), we assumed that $i_{pc} - i_{pw}$ is proportional to the rms value of the current signal. In order to verify this assumption, the difference between i_{pc} and i_{pw} was drawn versus the rms value of the current signal. As shown in **Figure 8**, this relationship was contrasted with a linear function and the comparison demonstrated that this relationship is linear and the assumption made in Section II is valid.

The slope of the line in **Figure 8** is equal to the parameter k_1 in (9). This slope is 0.2 and close to the value of k_1 calculated from the DPA characteristics of the unprotected ATmega16 (see (10)).

NCT-DPA obtained in this section for the example circuit was based on simulation results where the external noise was negligible. In the next section, we present more realistic NCT-DPA results by running the experiments considering the external noise.

6. NCT-DPA in the Presence of Noise

In this section the relationship between NCT-DPA and the level of current attenuation in the presence of external

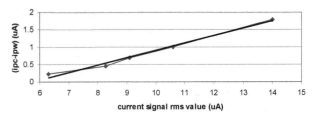

Figure 8. The difference between i_{pc} and i_{pw} versus the rms value of the current signal.

noise is investigated. First, a formula will be derived for the signal to noise ratio in DPA attacks. Then NCT-DPA is examined for a flattened current in the example circuit with a low level of attenuation in the presence of noise.

6.1. Signal to Noise Ratio in DPA Attacks

Signal to noise ratio is defined as the ratio of the power of signal to the power of noise. If $P_{exp.signal}$ is the part of the power exploited for the DPA attack and P_{noise} is the power of the noise, the signal to noise ratio (SNR) is:

$$\text{SNR} = \frac{P_{exp.signal}}{P_{noise}}. \tag{14}$$

Since we are only interested in the dynamic part of the power, the power can be translated to the variance of the signal and SNR becomes:

$$\text{SNR} = \frac{Var(\text{exp. signal})}{Var(\text{noise})} \tag{15}$$

where, Var(exp. signal) is the variance of the exploitable signal and Var(noise) is the variance of noise. As mentioned earlier, the main components of noise are the external noise and the algorithmic noise. These two terms are independent and their variances will add up. Hence, (15) can be rewritten as [9] (p. 73):

$$\text{SNR} = \frac{Var(\text{exp. signal})}{Var(\text{ext.}) + Var(\text{alg.})} \tag{16}$$

where Var(ext.) and Var(alg.) are the variances of the external noise and the algorithmic noise respectively.

We assume that an n-bit word is processed in a cryptographic algorithm and the variance of the current signal is Var(signal). If the number of current traces used for a DPA attack is large enough and the random ciphertext allows the transitions of all n bits of the word, then the deviation of the current signal belongs to n bit transitions. Since the variations of different bits are random and independent, then the variance for each bit can be estimated as:

$$Var(1\,\text{bit}) = \frac{Var(\text{signal})}{n}. \tag{17}$$

If the information of the m bits of n-bit word is exploited for breaking the security in a DPA attack, the variance of the exploitable signal can be estimated as:

$$Var\left(\text{exp. signal}\right) = m \cdot Var\left(1\ \text{bit}\right) = \frac{m}{n} \cdot Var\left(\text{signal}\right) \quad (18)$$

The variance of the algorithmic noise, *i.e.* the variance of the non-exploited bits, is:

$$Var\left(\text{alg.}\right) = \left(\frac{n-m}{n}\right) Var\left(\text{signal}\right). \quad (19)$$

Substituting (18) and (19) in (16), we obtain:

$$SNR = \frac{\frac{m}{n} \cdot Var\left(\text{signal}\right)}{Var\left(\text{ext.}\right) + \left(\frac{n-m}{n}\right) Var\left(\text{signal}\right)}. \quad (20)$$

For the DPA attack used in this research, where the variations of 1 bit of the 6-bit word are exploited (*i.e.* $m = 1$ and $n = 6$), the SNR can be estimated as:

$$SNR = \frac{\frac{1}{6} \cdot Var\left(\text{signal}\right)_{1}}{Var\left(\text{ext.}\right) + \left(\frac{5}{6}\right) Var\left(\text{signal}\right)}. \quad (21)$$

6.2. NCT-DPA of the Example Circuit in the Presence of Noise

A set of current traces collected at the supply pin of the ATmega16 microcontroller was imported into the Cadence environment. By applying the current injection feedback, the current traces were flattened. The considered current flattening situation had a flattened current with 79 µA peak-to-peak and 1.4×10^{-5} A rms value, and 98.35% reduction in rms value (see **Table 1**).

Running a DPA attack over the output of this flattened current set showed that the DPA attack was successful with less than 600 current traces (**Table 1**). These traces were collected from the simulator where there was no external noise. In order to see the effect of the external noise on the success of DPA attack on the protected microcontroller (with the current flattening circuit), a set of simulations were run by adding different levels of noise to the output of the simulator. The added noise was a random current noise with the frequency of 8 MHz, *i.e.*, the first harmonic of the clock signal of ATmega16. One should note that most of the power of the external noise is generally concentrated at the clock frequency and its harmonics [9]. DPA attacks were performed and NCT-DPA values were derived. The results are shown in **Figure 9**.

As an alternative to the experimental method, one can calculate NCT-DPA by using (8) along with the characteristics of the flattened current and the noise. For finding the maximum spike values, a DPA attack with a large

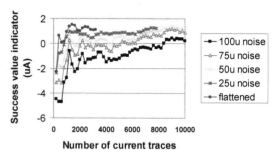

Figure 9. SVI for a flattened current and the combination of the flattened current traces and different levels of noise.

number of traces was run on the flattened current with 1.4×10^{-5} A ac rms value. When running DPA with 10,000 traces, it was observed that i_{pc} was 2.8×10^{-6} A and i_{pw} was less than 10^{-6} A. NCT-DPA was calculated by substituting these values in (8). **Table 3** shows NCT-DPA for different values of noise calculated in two ways: the experimental method and the formula.

Table 3 shows that when noise increases, the values of NCT-DPA calculated from two methods diverge. This is due to the fact that when the standard deviation of noise increases, the term $2\sigma_{pc} + 2\sigma_{pw}$ is not negligible any more (see Section V-A) and SVI no longer shows the accurate number of traces. In this case, more traces are required to remove the ambiguity between the spike of the differential trace of the correct sub-key and those of the wrong sub-keys.

6.3. A Cross-Check of the NCT-DPA Formula with a Previously Developed Relationship

Mangard *et al.* have calculated NCT-DPA by using a correlation factor and derived a rule of thumb. Their approach suggests that for small SNRs, NCT-DPA is inversely proportional to SNR [9] (p. 147):

$$N \approx \frac{k}{SNR}. \quad (22)$$

In order to compare our derived formula (8), with the relationship suggested by Mangard *et al.*, SNR can be calculated for different values of noise by using (21). Since the ac rms value of the current signal is equivalent to the standard deviation, (21) can be rewritten as:

$$SNR = \frac{\frac{1}{6}\left(i_{s}\right)^{2}}{\left(i_{\text{ext.}}\right)^{2} + \frac{5}{6} \cdot \left(i_{s}\right)^{2}}. \quad (23)$$

Using this formula, the inverse of SNR was calculated for different values of noise. The results are shown in **Table 4** along with NCT-DPA obtained from two methods. NCT-DPA is drawn versus the inverse of the SNR for both methods in **Figure 10**.

Figure 10 shows that for the numbers obtained by our

Table 3. NCT-DPA for different levels of noise using the experimental method and the formula.

Noise (pk-to-pk) (A)	Noise rms value (A)	NCT-DPA (SVI)	NCT-DPA (formula)
Flattened	1.4×10^{-5}	600	753
25×10^{-6}	7.6×10^{-6}	1200	2337
50×10^{-6}	1.52×10^{-5}	4400	5680
75×10^{-6}	2.28×10^{-5}	6200	11,072
100×10^{-6}	3.04×10^{-5}	8400	18,573

Table 4. The inverse of SNR and NCT-DPA for two methods.

Noise (rms & pk-pk) (A)	$\frac{1}{\text{SNR}}$	NCT-DPA SVI	NCT-DPA formula
flattened	5	600	753
7.6×10^{-6} (25×10^{-6})	6.75	1200	2337
1.52×10^{-5} (50×10^{-6})	12.05	4400	5680
2.28×10^{-5} (75×10^{-6})	20.9	6200	11,072
3.04×10^{-5} (100×10^{-6})	33.34	8400	18,573

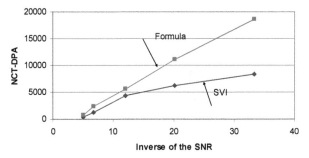

Figure 10. NCT-DPA versus the inverse of SNR.

formula, there is a linear relationship between NCT-DPA and the inverse of SNR as suggested by Mangard *et al.* (see (22)). This is another evidence for the validity of our formula. For the experimental method when noise increases, the number of current traces obtained does not show a linear relationship with SNR. One may conclude that while SVI is a reliable figure of merit for measuring NCT-DPA in the absence of noise, it does not show the accurate number of traces in the presence of large levels of noise. This confirms the conclusion made at the end of the last sub-section, *i.e.* the term $2\sigma_{pc} + 2\sigma_{pw}$ is not negligible any more and the experimental method results are not accurate.

The linear relationship depicted in **Figure 10** and suggested by our formula provides an opportunity to find an empirical value for the parameter k in (22). This parameter is the slope of the line in **Figure 10**:

$$k = \frac{18573 - 753}{33.34 - 5} = \frac{17820}{28.34} = 629 . \qquad (24)$$

We call the parameter k the *efficiency gain* of the countermeasure. This parameter can be used to estimate the NCT-DPA for the flattened currents with higher levels of attenuations (when the NCT-DPA cannot be obtained experimentally). This application is shown in the next subsection, where NCT-DPA is calculated for the current traces with different levels of attenuation.

6.4. Using Efficiency Gain for Finding NCT-DPA

In this sub-section, NCT-DPA is calculated for several sets of current traces with different levels of attenuations in the presence of the external noise measured for the setup used for collecting current traces of the ATmega16 microcontroller (Section II-C). First, using (23), SNR is calculated for these different sets, considering the measured external noise with the rms value of 2.015×10^{-4} A (Section II-C). Then using (22) and the efficiency gain k, (24), NCT-DPA is calculated for all these sets. **Table 5** summarizes the results for five sets of the flattened current traces introduced in **Table 1**.

As seen in **Table 5**, for a flattened current with a high level of attenuation, NCT-DPA is extremely large. In other words, the DPA attack does not appear feasible within the present computational performance capacities.

Using the efficiency gain to evaluate the robustness of the example circuit for the situations where experimental methods are not possible, shows the significance of the proposed formula for evaluating DPA countermeasure designs.

7. Conclusions

In this paper, a method was proposed for designing DPA countermeasures based on current attenuation. This methodology has three stages: 1) estimating the required current attenuation for a specific level of robustness against DPA attacks; 2) designing a countermeasure circuit that attenuates the current signal within the expected value suggested in the first stage [5]; and 3) investigating the efficiency of the proposed countermeasure. This methodology is based on a new formula suggested for calculating NCT-DPA using the characteristics of the current signal used in a DPA attack and the external noise of the

Table 5. NCT-DPA for different levels of current attenuation in the presence of the external noise.

Flattened current	Current signal rms value (A)	SNR	NCT-DPA
Set 1	1.4×10^{-5}	0.00079	789,395
Set 2	1.06×10^{-5}	0.00046	1,347,163
Set 3	9.11×10^{-6}	0.000345	1,822,115
Set 4	8.26×10^{-6}	0.000283	2,215,791
Set 5	6.3×10^{-6}	0.000165	3,806,614

DPA attack measurement setup. The practicality of the methodology was investigated through a case study, *i.e.*, designing a countermeasure for which DPA can not be successful with less than 10,000 current traces. In this process, the validity of the proposed formula was also investigated by comparing NCT-DPA values obtained by the formula with those obtained experimentally.

Additionally, the SNR of DPA attacks was formulated in a new format and the relationship between NCT-DPA and the level of current attenuation was investigated in the presence of external noise. Furthermore the validity of the NCT-DPA obtained by the formula was confirmed by the rule suggested by Mangard *et al*. Using our formula and obtaining the linear relationship between NCT-DPA and the inverse of SNR allowed us to define the efficiency gain of the countermeasure. It was shown that this parameter can be used to estimate the NCT-DPA for the flattened currents with higher levels of attenuations, where the NCT-DPA cannot be obtained experimentally.

In summary, the proposed formula is useful in two stages: 1) In the design stage, the designer can estimate the required level of attenuation for a predefined level of robustness; 2) in the simulation stage, where the situation is ideal and there is no external noise, the formula predicts the efficiency of a countermeasure in the presence of the external noise.

REFERENCES

[1]   P. Kocher, J. Jaffe and B. Jun, "Differential Power Analysis," *LNCS Proceedings of International Cryptology Conference*, Vol. 1666, 1999, pp. 388-397.

[2]   K. Tiri and I. Verbauwhede, "Dynamic and Differential CMOS Logic with Signal-Independent Power Consumption to Withstand Differential Power Analysis," US Patent No. 7692449, 2010.

[3]   S. Rammohan, V. Sundaresan and R. Vemuri, "Reduced Complementary Dynamic and Differential Logic: A CMOS Logic Style for DPA-Resistant Secure IC Design," *Proceedings of International Conference on VLSI Design*, Hyderabad, 4-8 January 2008, pp. 699-705.

[4]   S. Guilley, L. Sauvage, F. Flament, V. Vong, P. Hoogvorst and R. Pacalet, "Evaluation of Power Constant Dual-Rail Logics Countermeasures against DPA with Design Time Security Metrics," *IEEE Transactions on Computers*, Vol. 59, No. 9, 2010, pp. 1250-1263.

[5]   H. Vahedi, S. Gregori and R. Muresan, "On-Chip Power-Efficient Current Flattening Circuit," *Journal of Circuits, Systems, and Computers*, Vol. 18, No. 3, 2009, pp. 565-579.

[6]   S. K. Kim, "Smart Cards Having Protection Circuits Therein That Inhibit Power Analysis Attacks and Methods of Operating Same," US Patent Application, 2004/0158728, 2004.

[7]   G. B. Ratanpal, R. D. Williams and T. N. Blalock, "An On-Chip Signal Suppression Countermeasure to Power Analysis Attacks," *IEEE Transactions on Dependable and Secure Computing*, Vol. 1, No. 3, 2004, pp. 179-189.

[8]   T. S. Messerges, "Power Analysis Attacks and Countermeasures for Cryptographic Algorithms," University of Illinois, Chicago, 2000.

[9]   S. Mangard, E. Oswald and T. Popp, "Power Analysis Attacks: Revealing the Secrets of Smart Cards," Springer Science, 2007.

[10] R. Muresan and S. Gregori, "Protection Circuit against Differential Power Analysis Attacks for Smart Cards," *IEEE Transactions on Computers*, Vol. 57, No. 11, 2008, pp. 1540-1549.

[11] ATMEL Corporation, ATmega16 Data Sheet. http://www.atmel.com/dyn/resources/prod_documents/2466S.pdf

[12] H. Vahedi, S. Gregori and R. Muresan, "The Effectiveness of a Current Flattening Circuit as Countermeasure against DPA Attacks," *Microelectronics Journal*, Vol. 42, No. 1, 2011, pp. 180-187.

## 24

New Hybrid Digital Circuit Design Techniques for Reducing Subthreshold Leakage Power in Standby Mode

Manish Kumar[1], Md. Anwar Hussain[1], Sajal K. Paul[2]

[1]Department of ECE, North Eastern Regional Institute of Science & Technology, Nirjuli, Arunachal Pradesh, India
[2]Department of Electronics Engineering, Indian School of Mines, Dhanbad, Jharkhand, India

ABSTRACT

In this paper, four new hybrid digital circuit design techniques, namely, hybrid multi-threshold CMOS complete stack technique, hybrid multi-threshold CMOS partial stack technique, hybrid super cutoff complete stack technique and hybrid super cutoff partial stack technique, have been proposed to reduce the subthreshold leakage power dissipation in standby modes. Techniques available in literature are compared with our proposed hybrid circuit design techniques. Performance parameters such as subthreshold leakage power dissipation in active and standby modes, dynamic power dissipation and propagation delay, are compared using existing and proposed hybrid techniques for a two input AND gate. Reduction of subthreshold leakage power dissipation in standby mode is given more importance, in comparison with the other circuit design performance parameters. It is found that there is reduction in subthreshold leakage power dissipation in standby and active modes by 3.5× and 1.15× respectively using the proposed hybrid super cutoff complete stack technique as compared to the existing multi-threshold CMOS (MTCMOS) technique. Also a saving of 2.50× and 1.04× in subthreshold leakage power dissipation in standby and active modes respectively were observed using hybrid super cutoff complete stack technique as compared to the existing super cutoff CMOS (SCCMOS) technique. The proposed hybrid super cutoff stack technique proved to perform better in terms of subthreshold leakage power dissipation in standby mode in comparison with other techniques. Simulation results using Microwind EDA tool in 65 nm CMOS technology is provided in this paper.

Keywords: Subthreshold Leakage Power; Standby Mode; Active Mode; Propagation Delay

1. Introduction

Design of low power circuit is necessary for portable electronic devices that are powered by batteries as increased power dissipation reduces the battery lifetime. Low power dissipation by MOS transistors and its small size for greater integration capacity are the major factors behind shifting in technology from BJTs to MOSFETs. High power dissipation is one of the major challenges of integrated circuit design in deep submicron and nanoscale technologies [1-5]. The demand for higher functions with higher performance and lower power dissipation initiates the scaling of MOS transistors in every technology generations. The contribution of dynamic power in the overall power dissipation decreases with the scaling of MOS transistors. Leakage power is expected to increase 32 times per device by the year 2020 [6]. Reduction of the supply voltage, V_{DD} is considered as the most effective method to reduce the dynamic power, which is directly proportional to the square of the supply voltage, V_{DD}. In order to maintain the same performance, threshold voltage of the transistor is also reduced with

the scaling of the supply voltage. However, subthreshold leakage current increases exponentially with the reduction of the threshold voltage of the MOS transistor, making it critical for low voltage digital integrated circuit design. Scaling of transistors in every technology generations also lead to increase in the subthreshold leakage current. With rapid scaling in technology, the increase in leakage current has made leakage power a significant part in the overall power dissipation in both active and standby modes. The major components of leakage power dissipation are subthreshold leakage, gate leakage, gate induced drain leakage, and forward biased diode leakage [7]. Subthreshold leakage dominates the other leakage components in deep submicron and nanoscale technologies.

Threshold voltage of transistors used in design of digital circuits should be adjusted for maximum saving in the leakage power dissipation. Circuit techniques play a very important role to control the subthreshold leakage power dissipation in both active and standby modes. Already some techniques, such as Multi-threshold CMOS

(MTCMOS) technique [8,9], Super cutoff CMOS technique [10], Stack technique [11-13] and Sleepy stack technique [14] are available in literature to control the subthreshold leakage power dissipation in deep submitcron and nanoscale technologies. Each technique has its own advantages and disadvantages. Depending upon the requirement and application, chip designers can choose the appropriate circuit design technique.

In this paper, four new digital circuit design techniques namely, hybrid multi-threshold CMOS complete stack technique, hybrid multi-threshold CMOS partial stack technique, hybrid super cutoff complete stack technique and hybrid super cutoff partial stack technique are presented. These techniques are applied to a two input AND gate to evaluate their performance. It is found that the proposed techniques give improved performance in terms of reduced subthreshold leakage power dissipation in standby mode as compared with the other techniques available in the literature [8-14].

2. Subthreshold Leakage Power Dissipation

Subthreshold or weak inversion conduction current is the current flow between source and drain region in a MOS transistor, even when gate voltage, V_{GS} is below the threshold voltage, V_{TH} of the MOS transistor. It is due to the minority carrier drift through the channel from the drain to the source region in weak inversion region. **Figure 1** shows the flow of subthreshold leakage current in an nMOS transistor, when V_{GS} is less than V_{TH} of the transistor. **Figure 2** [15] shows the variation of minority carrier concentration along the length of the channel for an n-channel MOSFET biased in the weak inversion region. This figure shows that the concentration of minority carriers in weak inversion region is small, but not zero. Subthreshold leakage power dominates the other leakage power components because of the necessity to use low threshold voltage transistors to maintain the desired performance of the device. This leakage power should be minimized through new and improved circuit design techniques. This leakage power dissipation is undesirable in digital circuit design.

According to BSIM4 MOSFET model, the equation governing this subthreshold leakage current can be expressed as [16]

$$I_{SUB} = I_0 e^{\frac{V_{GS}-V_{THO}-\eta V_{DS}+\gamma V_{BS}}{nV_T}} \left(1-e^{\frac{-V_{DS}}{V_T}}\right) \quad (1)$$

where,

$$I_0 = \mu C_{ox}\left(\frac{W}{L}\right)V_T^2 e^{1.8} \text{ and } V_T = \frac{KT}{q} \quad (2)$$

Here V_{GS}, V_{DS} and V_{BS} are the gate to source, drain to source, and bulk to source voltages respectively, μ de-

notes the carrier mobility, C_{ox} is the gate oxide capacitance per unit area, W and L denote the channel width and channel length of the transistor, K is the Boltzmann constant, T is the absolute temperature, q is the electrical charge of an electron, V_T is the thermal voltage, V_{TH0} is the zero biased threshold voltage, γ is body effect coefficient, η denotes the drain induced barrier lowering coefficient, and n is the subthreshold swing coefficient. Equation (1) reveals that the subthreshold leakage current is a strong function of the threshold voltage and the voltages of all the four terminals of the MOS transistor.

The Berlkeley Short-Channel IGFET model [17] is used for the calculation of the threshold voltage of a MOS transistor and is expressed as:

$$V_{TH} = V_{FB} + \varphi_s + K_1\left(\varphi_s\right)^{1/2} - K_2\varphi_s - \eta V_{DD} \quad (3)$$

where V_{FB} is the flatband voltage, φ_s is two times the Fermi potential, K_1, and K_2 terms represent the non-uniform doping effect, and η denotes the drain induced barrier lowering coefficient.

3. Circuit Design Methodology Adopted for Reducing Subthreshold Leakage Power in Standby Mode

Subthreshold leakage power reduction in standby mode is significant in burst mode type circuits, where compu-

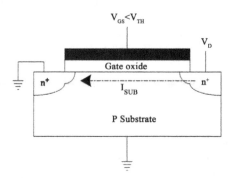

Figure 1. Subthreshold leakage current in an nMOS transistor.

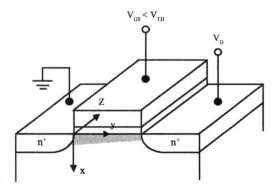

Figure 2. Variation of minority carrier concentration in an nMOS transistor in weak inversion.

tation occurs only during short burst intervals, and the system is in standby mode for the majority of the time [18]. The wastage of useful battery power during long standby period is highly undesirable. New circuit techniques must be devised to control the subthreshold leakage power dissipation in standby mode for burst mode applications. Portable battery operated devices that remain in standby mode for most of the times are greatly affected by standby subthreshold leakage power loss. Existing circuit design techniques must therefore be modified in such a way that it curbs the draining of battery current when it is not operational. **Table 1** [19] shows the dependence of subthreshold leakage current on MOS device parameters. Increasing the threshold voltage of the MOS transistor is an effective way to reduce subthreshold leakage power dissipation.

Stack effect or Self-Reverse bias effect is the phenomenon where subthreshold leakage current decreases due to two or more series connected turned off transistors. Stacking of transistor is done by replacing transistor of width W with two series connected transistors of width W/2. **Figure 3** shows the natural stacking of nMOS transistors in a two input NAND gate. When both nMOS transistors Q_1 and Q_2 are turned off, then the intermediate node voltage, V_Q raises to a positive value due to the presence of a small drain current.

Table 1. Dependence of subthreshold leakage current on MOS transistor parameters.

Transistor parameter	Dependence of subthreshold leakage
Transistor width (W)	Directly proportional
Transistor length (L)	Inversely proportional
Temperature (T)	Exponential increase
Transistor threshold voltage (V_{TH})	Increases by an order of magnitude with 100 mV decrease
Input voltage (V_{GS})	Exponential increase

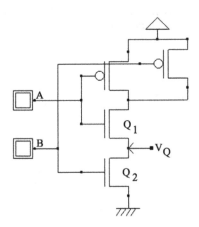

Figure 3. Natural stacking of nMOS transistors in a two input NAND gate.

Positive potential $(V_Q > 0\text{V})$ at the intermediate node between two turned off stacked transistors has following effects [19,20]:

1) V_{GS} of Q_1 becomes negative;

2) V_{BS} of Q_1 becomes negative, causing an increase in V_{TH} of Q_1 due to an increase in the body effect of Q_1;

3) V_{DS} of Q_1 decreases, resulting in less drain induced barrier lowering.

From Equation (1), it is observed that a negative V_{GS}, an increase in the body effect (negative V_{BS}), and a reduction in V_{DS} (less drain induced barrier lowering) reduce the subthreshold leakage current exponentially in standby mode.

4. Proposed Hybrid Circuit Techniques

In this section, we propose four new digital circuit techniques namely, hybrid MTCMOS complete stack technique, hybrid MTCMOS partial stack technique, hybrid super cutoff complete stack technique and hybrid super cutoff partial stack technique, for the reduction of subthreshold leakage power dissipation in standby modes. First two techniques are grouped as hybrid MTCMOS stack technique and last two techniques as hybrid super cutoff stack technique. Proposed techniques are discussed as follows.

4.1. Hybrid Multi-Threshold CMOS Stack Technique

This technique combines the advantages of both MTCMOS and Stack techniques. This proposed hybrid technique is further classified, as given above, into two types depending on the stacking of transistors.

4.1.1. Hybrid Multi-Threshold CMOS Complete Stack Technique

The proposed logic circuit for hybrid MTCMOS complete stack technique is shown in **Figure 4**. In this technique, a high threshold voltage pMOS transistor (sleep pMOS transistor) is inserted between V_{DD} and the pull up network and a high threshold voltage nMOS transistor (sleep nMOS transistor) is inserted between the pull down network and GND. Then stacking of all transistors (high V_{TH} sleep pMOS, high V_{TH} sleep nMOS and low V_{TH} transistors of the logic circuit) are done by replacing each transistor of width W with two series connected transistors of width W/2. During standby mode, the sleep signal is active high, making the stacked sleep transistors in cutoff state. So, the logic circuit is disconnected from V_{DD} and GND. This reduces the subthreshold leakage power dissipation significantly by utilizing stacking effect in both high V_{TH} sleep nMOS and sleep pMOS transistors during their cutoff states. The high V_{TH} nMOS and pMOS stacked sleep transistors are turned on during normal or active circuit operation, when the sleep signal is active low.

4.1.2. Hybrid MTCMOS Partial Stack Technique

The proposed logic circuit for hybrid MTCMOS partial stack technique is shown in **Figure 5**. In this technique, a high V_{TH} pMOS transistor (sleep pMOS transistor) is inserted between V_{DD} and the pull up network and a high V_{TH} nMOS transistor (sleep nMOS transistor) is inserted between the pull down network and GND. Then stacking of only high V_{TH} sleep pMOS and high V_{TH} sleep nMOS transistors are done. In this technique, stacking of low V_{TH} nMOS and pMOS transistors of the logic circuit is not performed. Here, only partial stacking of high V_{TH} sleep pMOS and sleep nMOS transistors are done to reduce the overall circuit propagation delay in active mode. During standby mode (when sleep signal is active high), the stacked high V_{TH} sleep pMOS and sleep nMOS transistors are turned off, thereby, reducing significant sub-threshold leakage power dissipation. In active mode, the stacked sleep transistors are turned on. The circuit propagation delay using this technique in active mode is slightly reduced as compared to the previous technique because of partial stacking of transistors (stacking of only sleep pMOS and sleep nMOS transistors).

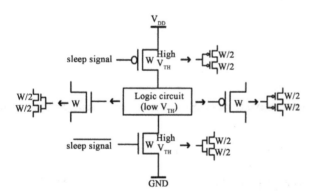

Figure 4. Logic circuit using hybrid MTCMOS complete stack technique.

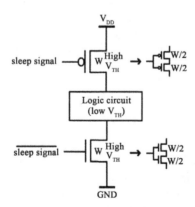

Figure 5. Logic circuit using hybrid MTCMOS partial stack technique.

4.2. Hybrid Super Cutoff Stack Technique

This hybrid technique combines the advantages of both Super cutoff CMOS (SCCMOS) and Stack techniques. The proposed hybrid technique can further be classified into two types, namely hybrid super cutoff complete stack technique and hybrid super cutoff partial stack technique, depending on the stacking of transistors.

4.2.1. Hybrid Super Cutoff Complete Stack Technique

This technique is similar to hybrid MTCMOS complete stack technique. The only difference lies in the use of low V_{TH} sleep pMOS and low V_{TH} sleep nMOS transistors. **Figure 6** shows the logic circuit using this hybrid technique. In this technique, positive and negative gate voltages are used to completely turnoff sleep pMOS and sleep nMOS transistors respectively in standby mode. During standby state (when sleep signal is active high), the subthreshold leakage power dissipation reduces exponentially because of the use of negative and positive gate voltages to nMOS and pMOS sleep transistors respectively and also due to the stacking effect in series connected cutoff stacked sleep transistors. In active mode, these sleep transistors having low V_{TH} are turned on and thus provide low resistance input-output path. In active mode, the circuit propagation delay using this technique is reduced as compared to the hybrid multi-threshold CMOS stack technique because of the use of low V_{TH} sleep transistors.

4.2.2. Hybrid Super Cutoff Partial Stack Technique

This hybrid technique is similar to hybrid MTCMOS partial stack technique. The difference lies in the use of low V_{TH} sleep nMOS and pMOS transistors. **Figure 7** shows the logic circuit using this technique. During standby mode, the subthreshold leakage power dissipation reduces exponentially because of use of negative and positive gate voltages to nMOS and pMOS sleep transistors respectively and also due to stacking effect in series connected cutoff stacked sleep transistors. The major

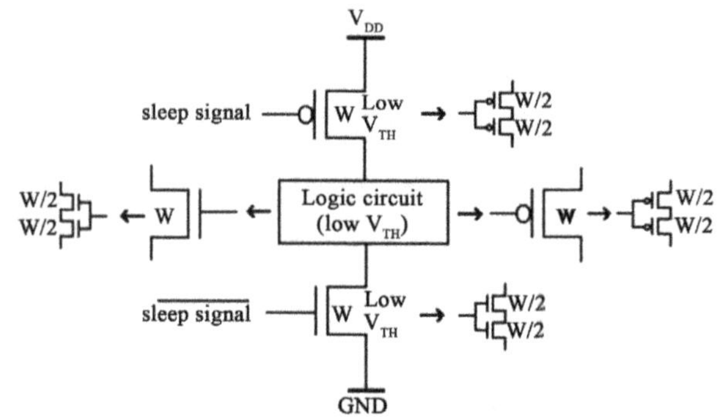

Figure 6. Logic circuit using hybrid super cutoff complete stack technique.

advantage in using this technique is further reduction in the overall circuit propagation delay in active mode as compared with the hybrid super cutoff complete stack technique because of the use of only partial stacking of sleep pMOS and sleep nMOS transistors.

5. Result and Discussion

To compare the performance, the proposed techniques are applied to a two input AND gate. The performance parameters such as subthreshold leakage power dissipation in active and standby modes, dynamic power dissipation and propagation delay of a two input AND gate were analysed in 65 nm technology using existing [10-16] and proposed hybrid techniques. Layouts of a two input logic AND gate using various techniques were simulated using Microwind EDA tool at a temperature of 27°C and V_{DD} of 0.7 V. The threshold voltage of high V_{TH} transistor was taken as two times of V_{TH} of normal transistor of the logic circuit. The threshold voltage of normal nMOS and pMOS transistors (low V_{TH}) were taken as 0.20 V and −0.20 V respectively. **Figures 8** and **9** show the

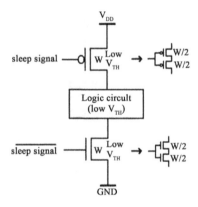

Figure 7. Logic circuit using hybrid super cutoff partial stack technique.

simulated layout diagrams of a two input AND gate using hybrid super cutoff complete stack and hybrid super cutoff partial stack techniques respectively. **Figure 10** shows the output waveform of a two input AND gate in presence of a sleep signal.

Subthreshold leakage power dissipation was measured by combining all possible input vectors. The voltage magnitude of input vector should always be less than the threshold voltage of the normal transistor of the logic circuit. Sleep nMOS and sleep pMOS transistors were turned off during measurement of subthreshold leakage power dissipation in standby mode while for its measurement in active mode, all sleep nMOS and sleep pMOS transistors were turned on. Subthreshold leakage power dissipation in active and standby modes for a two input AND gate for each input combination were measured for 50 ns time interval.

Dynamic power dissipation was measured by applying input pulse signals of same frequency with a fixed delay between them. Two input pulse signals of V_{DD} of 0.7 V and frequency of 250 MHz were applied to a two input AND gate. All sleep nMOS and sleep pMOS transistors were turned on during measurement of dynamic power dissipation. The dynamic power dissipation was measured for a two input AND gate for 50 ns time interval.

Propagation delay of the logic circuit was measured from the trigger input edge reaching 50% of V_{DD} to the circuit output edge reaching 50% of V_{DD}.

Table 2 shows various performance parameters measurement of a two input AND gate using existing [8-14] and proposed hybrid techniques.

Subthreshold leakage power dissipation in active and standby modes of a two input AND gate are compared using existing [10-16] and proposed techniques in **Figure 11**. Subthreshold leakage power dissipation of a two input AND gate in standby mode in 65 nm technology is

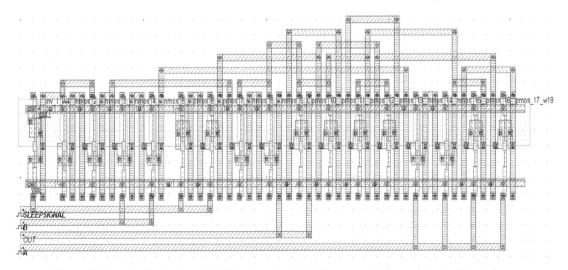

Figure 8. Layout of a two input AND gate using hybrid super cutoff complete stack technique.

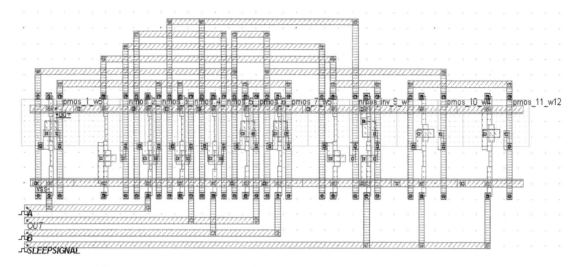

Figure 9. Layout of a two input AND gate using hybrid super cutoff partial stack technique.

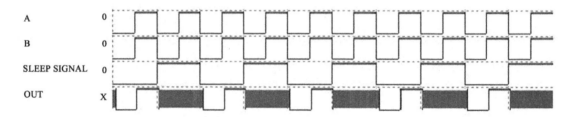

Figure 10. Output waveform of a two input AND gate in presence of a sleep signal.

Table 2. Performance parameter measurements of a two input AND gate.

Reference	Technique	Subthreshold leakage power (in nW)		Dynamic power (in µW)	Propagation delay (in sec.)
		Active mode	Standby mode		
[8-9]	MTCMOS	186.00	7.00	0.87	14.2×10^{-12}
[10]	Super cutoff CMOS	168.00	5.00	0.78	21.2×10^{-13}
[11-13]	Stack	110.00	18.00	0.98	22.1×10^{-12}
[14]	Sleepy stack	172.00	19.00	1.12	18.7×10^{-12}
Proposed	Hybrid MTCMOS complete stack	169.00	03.00	1.68	32.1×10^{-12}
Proposed	Hybrid MTCMOS partial stack	157.00	03.40	1.45	19.1×10^{-12}
Proposed	Hybrid Super cutoff complete stack	161.00	02.00	1.52	41.2×10^{-13}
Proposed	Hybrid super cutoff partial stack	147.00	02.45	1.36	31.8×10^{-13}

better using the proposed hybrid super cutoff stack technique. The proposed hybrid super cutoff stack technique proved to perform better in terms of subthreshold leakage power dissipation in standby mode in comparison with other techniques. Results show that the subthreshold leakage power dissipation in standby and active modes are reduced by 3.5× and 1.15× using the proposed hybrid super cutoff complete stack technique as compared to the existing multi-threshold CMOS (MTCMOS) technique. Also a saving of 2.5× and 1.04× in subthreshold leakage power dissipation in standby and active modes

are observed using hybrid super cutoff complete stack technique as compared to the existing super cutoff CMOS (SCCMOS) technique. It is also observed that the propagation delay reduces sharply in comparison to MTCMOS technique; however dynamic power dissipation increases slightly vis-à-vis super cutoff CMOS technique. Although dynamic power dissipation is slightly higher, the proposed technique is very much effective for the applications, specially, where the reduction of subthreshold leakage power dissipation in standby mode is warranted for.

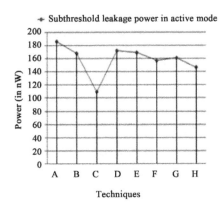 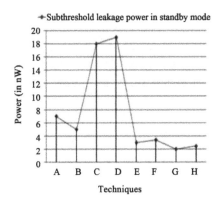

A:MTCMOS   B:Super cut off CMOS   C:Stack   D:Sleepy stack   E:Hybrid MTCMOS complete stack

F:Hybrid MTCMOS partial stack   G:Hybrid Super cut off complete stack   H:Hybrid super cut off partial stack

Figure 11. Subthreshold leakage power in active and standby modes.

6. Conclusion

Subthreshold leakage power reduction in standby mode is very much essential for burst mode type circuits, where computation occurs only during short burst intervals, and the system is in standby mode for the majority of the time. The wastage of useful battery power during long standby period is highly undesirable. Portable electronic appliances such as cell phones and pagers are used in active mode for a very short time interval. These appliances drain their useful battery power for a very long standby period. Similarly, the leakage of battery power in portable laptop during standby mode is highly undesirable. Subthreshold leakage reduction techniques during the standby mode can significantly reduce the leakage in burst mode applications. The proposed hybrid super cutoff stack technique proved to perform better in terms of subthreshold leakage power dissipation in standby mode in comparison with other techniques. It is found that there is reduction in subthreshold leakage power dissipation in standby and active modes by 3.5× and 1.15× respectively using the proposed hybrid super cutoff complete stack technique as compared to the existing multi-threshold CMOS (MTCMOS) technique. Also a saving of 2.50× and 1.04× in subthreshold leakage power dissipation in standby and active modes respectively were observed using hybrid super cutoff complete stack technique as compared to the existing super cutoff CMOS (SCCMOS) technique for a two input AND gate in 65 nm technology. The proposed hybrid super cutoff stack technique proved to perform better in terms of lower subthreshold leakage power dissipation in standby mode in comparison with other existing techniques.

REFERENCES

[1]   J. Rabaey, "Low Power Design Essentials: Integrated Circuits and Systems," Springer-Verlag, Berlin, 2009.

[2]   S. Dasgupta, A. A. P. Sarab and D. Datta, "Nanoscale Device Architecture to Reduce Leakage Current through Quantum-Mechanical Simulation," *Journal of Vacuum Science & Technology B*: *Microelectronics and Nanometer Structures*, Vol. 24, No. 3, 1906, pp. 1384-1397.

[3]   M. Kumar, Md. A. Hussain and S. K. Paul, "Performance of a Two Input Nand Gate Using Subthreshold Leakage Control Techniques," *Journal of Electron Devices*, Vol. 14, 2012, pp. 1161-1169.

[4]   M. Kumar, Md. A. Hussain and L. K. Singh, "Design of a Low Power High Speed ALU in 45 nm Using GDI Technique and Its Performance Comparison," *Communications in Computer and Information Science*, Vol. 142, 2011, pp. 458-463.

[5]   M. Kumar, "Realization of a Low Power High Performance IC Design Technique for Wireless Portable Communication Devices Used in Underground Mines," *Special Issues on IP Multimedia Communications* (1), *International Journal of Computer Application*, 2011, pp. 52-54.

[6]   S. Borkar, "Design Challenges of Technology Scaling," *IEEE Micro*, Vol. 19, No. 4, 1999, pp. 23-29.

[7]   A. Keshavarzi, K. Roy and C. Hawkins, "Intrinsic Leakage in Low Power Deep Submicron CMOS ICs," *Proceedings of the International Test Conference*, Washington DC, 1-6 November 1997, pp. 146-155.

[8]   S. Mutoh, T. Douseki, Y. Matsuya, *et al.*, "1 V Power Supply High-Speed Digital Circuit Technology with Multithreshold Voltage CMOS," *IEEE Journal of Solid-State Circuits*, Vol. 30, No. 8, 1995, pp. 847-854.

[9]   M. Anis, S. Areibi and M. Elmasry, "Design and Optimization of Multi-Threshold CMOS (MTCMOS) Circuits," *IEEE Transactions on Computer-Aided Design of Integrated Circuits and Systems*, Vol. 22, No. 10, 2003, pp.

1324-1342.

[10] H. Kawaguchi, K. Nose and T. Sakurai, "A Super Cutoff CMOS (SCCMOS) Scheme for 0.5 V Supply Voltage with Picoampere Standby Current," *IEEE Journal of Solid-State Circuits*, Vol. 35, No. 10, 2000, pp. 1498-1501.

[11] M. Johnson, D. Somasekhar, L. Y. Chiou and K. Roy, "Leakage Control with Efficient Use of Transistor Stacks in Single Threshold CMOS," *IEEE Transactions on Very Large Scale Integration Systems*, Vol. 10, No. 1, 2002, pp. 1-5.

[12] T. G. Reddy and K. Suganthi, "Super Stack Technique to Reduce Leakage Power for Sub 0.5 V Supply Voltage in VLSI Circuits," *Proceedings of International Conference on Sustainable Energy and Intelligent Systems*, Chennai, 20-22 July 2011, pp. 585-588.

[13] V. Neema, S. S. Chouhan and S. Tokekar, "Novel Circuit Technique for Reduction of Active Drain Current in Series/Parallel PMOS Transistors Stack," *Proceedings of International Conference on Electronic Devices, Systems and Applications*, Kuala Lumpur, 11-14 April 2010, pp. 368-372.

[14] J. C. Park and V. J. Mooney, "Sleepy Stack Leakage Reduction," *IEEE Transactions on Very Large Scale Integration Systems*, Vol. 14, No. 11, 2006, pp. 1250-1263.

[15] K. Roy, S. Mukhopadhyay and H. M. Meimand, "Leakage Current Mechanisms and Leakage Reduction Techniques in Deep-Submicrometer CMOS Circuits," *Proceedings of the IEEE*, Vol. 91, No. 2, 2003, pp.305-327.

[16] A. Chandrakasan, W. J. Bowhill and F. Fox, "Design of High-Performance Microprocessor Circuits," IEEE Press, New York, 2001.

[17] B. J. Sheu, D. L. Scharfetter, P. K. Ko and M. C. Jeng, "BSIM: Berkeley Short Channel IGFET Model for MOS Transistors," *IEEE Journal of Solid-State Circuits*, Vol. 22, No. 4, 1987, pp. 558-566.

[18] M. Anis and M. Elmasry, "Multi-Threshold CMOS Digital Circuits: Managing Leakage Power," Kluwer Academic Publishers, Norwell, 2010.

[19] B. S. Deepaksubramanyan and Adrian Nunez, "Analysis of Subthreshold Leakage Reduction in CMOS Digital Circuits," *Proceedings of the 13th NASA VLSI Symposium*, Idaho, 5-8 August 2007, pp. 1-8.

[20] N. S. Kim, Ann Arbor, T. Austin, *et al.*, "Leakage Current: Moore's Law Meets Static Power," *IEEE Computer*, Vol. 36, No. 12, 2003, pp. 68-75.

25

Performance Evaluation of Efficient XOR Structures in Quantum-Dot Cellular Automata (QCA)

Mohammad Rafiq Beigh[*], Mohammad Mustafa, Firdous Ahmad
Department of Electronics & Instrumentation Technology, University of Kashmir, Srinagar, India

ABSTRACT

Quantum-dot cellular automaton (QCA) is an emerging, promising, future generation nanoelectronic computational architecture that encodes binary information as electronic charge configuration of a cell. It is a digital logic architecture that uses single electrons in arrays of quantum dots to perform binary operations. Fundamental unit in building of QCA circuits is a QCA cell. A QCA cell is an elementary building block which can be used to build basic gates and logic devices in QCA architectures. This paper evaluates the performance of various implementations of QCA based XOR gates and proposes various novel layouts with better performance parameters. We presented the various QCA circuit design methodology for XOR gate. These layouts show less number of crossovers and lesser cell count as compared to the conventional layouts already present in the literature. These design topologies have special functions in communication based circuit applications. They are particularly useful in phase detectors in digital circuits, arithmetic operations and error detection & correction circuits. The comparison of various circuit designs is also given. The proposed designs can be effectively used to realize more complex circuits. The simulations in the present work have been carried out using QCADesigner tool.

Keywords: Nanoelectronics; Quantum Cellular Automata (QCA); Majority Logic; Combinational Logic; XOR Gate; QCA Designer

1. Introduction

Quantum-dot cellular automata (QCA) is an emerging nanoelectronic technology that offers a revolutionary approach to computing at nano level [1]. A very extensive research and development in the field device technology for the past several decades made it possible for designers and processing engineers rapidly and consistently reduce semiconductor device size and operating current. But the incessant development in device fabrication on the nanometer scale is limited not only by process technology, but also by fundamental problems arising from scaling, such as quantum-mechanical effects and severe power dissipation. In MOS devices the gate tunneling current increases with the future size going down to deep submicron device geometry process. As a result the device and circuit characteristics drastically are deviated from the designer's expectations of making it better suited from application point of view. Further, in several studies it is predicted that these device technologies are

approaching to its physical limits [2-4]. Any physical phenomenon that has two separate states can be used to express a logic variable in two valid logic states such as electronic spin. Quantum effect is preferred to utilize in representing logic rather than any other method. Quantum logic devices are presented under this consideration and one of these is known as Quantum-dot Cellular Automata [5,6]. QCA is an emerging paradigm which allows operating frequencies in the range of THz and device integration densities about 900 times than the current end of CMOS scaling limits. It has been predicted as one of the future nanotechnologies in Semiconductor Industries Association's International Technology Roadmap for Semiconductors (ITRS) [7]. QCA based circuits have an advantage of high speed, high integrity and low power consumption [8,9]. Also QCA circuits have an advantage of high parallel processing [10,11]. Recent work showed that QCA can achieve high density, fast switching speed, and room temperature operation [12,13]. In recent years various QCA based combinational circuit designs have been proposed [14-19] but comparatively less

---

[*]Corresponding author.

study efforts have been made with its application in the field of communication. We present here different layouts of QCA based XOR structures that can be used in design and development of specific communication circuits, like parity generators & checkers, error detection & correction circuits and LFSRs. These designs are efficient in terms of cell count, complexity and latency as compared to the already proposed designs. These designs follow the conventional design approach but due to the technology differences, they are modified for the best performance in QCA.

In this paper we propose the seven novel implementations of the QCA based XOR gate and presented the simulation results of these individual designs. A detail comparison with regard to various characteristics of these designs is also presented. The paper has been organized in five sections. The first and second section provides the necessary introduction and review of QCA fundamentals. The third section presents the conventional XOR implementations. The various novel QCA XOR topologies have been presented in the fourth section. The advantages of the proposed structures have been summed up as conclusion in the fifth section.

2. QCA Fundamentals

In this section, we briefly describe the preliminaries of QCA and computation mechanism using QCA cells.

2.1. Basic QCA Cell

A QCA cell is a structure comprised of four quantum-dots arranged in a square pattern as shown in **Figure 1**. These quantum-dots are sites in which electrons are able to tunnel between them but cannot leave the cell.

QCA information processing is based on the Columbic interactions between many identical QCA cells. Each QCA cell is constructed using four electronic sites or dots coupled through quantum mechanical tunneling barriers. The electronic sites represent locations that a mobile electron can occupy. The cells contain two mobile electrons (or holes) which repel each other as a result of their mutual Columbic interaction, and, in the ground state, tend to occupy the diagonal sites of the cell. Therefore the cell has two degenerate ground states. These lead to two polarizations of a QCA cell, denoted as $P = +1$ and $P = -1$ respectively. Binary information can be encoded in the polarization of electrons in each QCA cell. Thus, logic 0 and logic 1 are encoded in polarization $P = -1$ and $P = +1$ respectively. **Figure 1** also shows the two possible polarizations of a QCA cell. Binary computation requires interaction among bits, in these devices, among the cells. When a second cell is placed near the first cell, the coulomb interaction between the cells removes the degeneracy and determines the ground state of the first

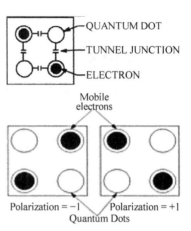

Figure 1. QCA cell and polarizations of QCA cell.

cell. The interaction between the QCA cells is nonlinear that is with a small perturbation from a neighboring cell clicks it into essentially aligned configuration either with $P = +1$ or $P = -1$ as will be the appropriate.

2.2. QCA Wires

In a QCA wire, the binary signal propagates from input to output because of the electrostatic interactions between cells. The propagation in a 90° QCA wire is shown in **Figure 2(a)**. Other than the 90° QCA wire, a 45° QCA wire can also be used as shown **Figure 2(b)**. In this case, the propagation of the binary signal alternates between the two polarizations [5].

2.3. QCA Majority Gate and Inverter

The fundamental QCA logical circuit is the three-input majority gate that appears in **Figure 3** [5]. The majority gate produces an output that reflects the majority of the in A puts.

The QCA majority gate has four terminal cells out of which three are representing input terminals and the remaining one represents the output cell [5]. Assuming that the three inputs are A, B and C, the logic function of the majority gate is

$$M(A,B,C) = AB + BC + CA$$

The two different structures of QCA inverter is shown in **Figure 4**. An inverter is usually formed by placing the cells with only their corners touching. The electrostatic interaction is inverted, because the quantum dots corresponding to different polarizations are misaligned between the cells [20]. The second inverter is built by neighboring QCA cells on the diagonal, which causes Coulomb forces to place the two electrons in opposing wells of the cell with respect to the source.

The AND and OR logic is realized by fixing the polarization of one of the inputs of the majority gate to either $P = -1$ (logic "0") or $P = 1$ (logic "1") as shown in

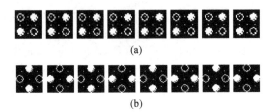

(a)

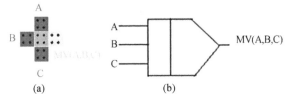

(b)

Figure 2. (a) QCA wire (90°); (b) QCA wire (45°).

(a)   (b)

Figure 3. (a) QCA majority gate; (b) Schematic majority gate representation.

(a)   (b)

Figure 4. QCA inverters.

Figure 5.

The NAND function is realized by connecting AND gate (MG) followed by an inverter. By using this 2 cell inverter, the area required and complexity can be minimized. The layout and schematic is shown in **Figure 6**.

2.4. QCA Clocking

The QCA circuits require a clock, not only to synchronize and control information flow but also to provide the power to run the circuit since there is no external source for powering cells. The clocking of QCA can be accomplished by controlling the potential barriers between adjacent quantum-dots [21,22]. With the use of four phase clocking scheme in controlling cells, QCA processes and forwards information within cells in an arranged timing scheme. Cells can be grouped into zones so that the field influencing all the cells in the zones will be the same. **Figure 7(a)** shows the four phases of QCA clock. **Figure 7(b)** shows the four available clock signals. Each signal is phase shifted by 90° degrees. In the Switch phase, the tunneling barriers in a zone are raised. While this occurs, the electrons within the cell can be influenced by the Columbic charges of neighboring zones. Zones in the Hold phase have a high tunneling barrier and will not change state, but influence other adjacent zones. Lastly, the Release and Relax decrease the tunneling barrier so that the zone will not influence other zones. These zones can be of irregular shape, but their size must be within certain limits imposed by fabrication and dissipation concerns. Proper placement of these zones is critical to design efficiency.

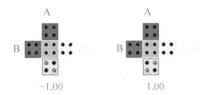

Figure 5. QCA layout of AND, OR gate.

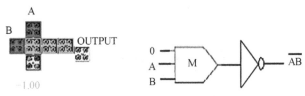

Figure 6. QCA layout of NAND gate.

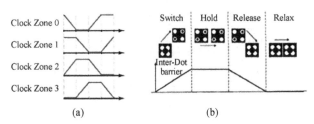

(a)   (b)

Figure 7. The four phases of the QCA clock.

This clocking method makes the design of QCA different from CMOS circuits.

Each signal is phase shifted by 90° degrees. When the clock signal is low the cells are latched. When the clock signal is high the cells are relaxed and have no polarization. In between the cells are either latching or relaxing when the clock is decreasing/increasing respectively.

3. QCA Exclusive-OR Implementations

In addition to AND, OR, NOT, NAND and NOR gates, exclusive-OR (XOR) and exclusive-NOR (XNOR) gates are also used in the design of digital circuits. These have special functions and applications. These gates are particularly useful in arithmetic operations as well as error-detection and correction circuits. XOR and XNOR gates are usually found as 2-input gates. No multiple-input XOR/XNOR gates are available since they are complex to fabricate with hardware.

The exclusive-OR (XOR) performs the following logic operation:

$$A \oplus B = A'B + AB'$$

The conventional schematic representation of XOR and two different QCA implementations for this layout is shown in **Figure 8**.

The QCA implementation for the layout shown in **Figure 8(a)** has been proposed by different authors [5,23]. This design needs either coplanar crossovers or multiple layers to implement. The design provided as a sample file with QCA Designer Version 2.0.3 [24] needs cross-

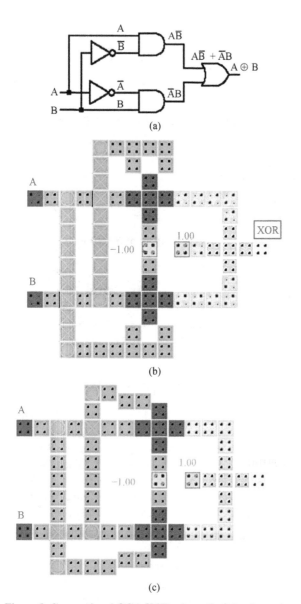

Figure 8. Conventional QCA-XOR schematic & implementation.

overs and uses three layers to implement. This design is shown in **Figure 8(b)**. We have proposed in this work seven different QCA based designs of XOR. These layouts have been designed to provide the more efficient configurations in terms of cell count, latency and complexity.

4. Proposed XOR Structures

Exclusive OR, also known as Exclusive disjunction and symbolized by XOR, is a logical operation on two operands that results in a logical value of true if and only if one of the operands, but not both, has a value of true. This forms a fundamental logic gate in many operations. An XOR gate can be trivially constructed from an XNOR gate followed by a NOT gate. We can construct an XOR

gate directly using AND, OR and NOT gates. However, this approach requires five gates of three different kinds. Logically, the exclusive OR (XOR) operation can also be implemented by the gate arrangements to follow. For instance they can also be implemented using NAND or NOR gates only.

4.1. The First Design

Every Boolean function can be build from (binary) Fredkin Gates (FGs), such that it has two inputs A, B and one output Y. The first design is based on Equation (1) which can be simplified as

$$
\begin{aligned}
Y &= (A \cdot B)' \cdot A + (A \cdot B)' \cdot B \\
Y &= (A' + B') \cdot A + (A' + B') \cdot B \\
Y &= A' \cdot A + A' \cdot B + A \cdot B' + B' \cdot B \\
Y &= A' \cdot B + A \cdot B'
\end{aligned}
\tag{1}
$$

The proposed QCA XOR gate has no crossovers and has cell count of 34 cells and an area of approximately 0.06 um^2 which is less as compared to conventional layouts. The proposed layout of this design and simulation results are shown in **Figures 9 (b)** and **(c)**.

4.2. The Second Design

The second design is based on Equation (2) which can be reduced to basic XOR equation as shown below.

$$
\begin{aligned}
Y &= (A + B) \cdot (AB)' \\
Y &= (A + B) \cdot (A' + B') \\
Y &= A(A' + B') + B(A' + B') \\
Y &= AA' + AB' + BA' + BB' \\
Y &= AB' + A'B
\end{aligned}
\tag{2}
$$

The proposed QCA XOR gate will require one crossover in order to input "A" separately out of the gate. It has cell complexity of 54 cells and an area of approximately 0.07 um^2. The proposed QCA layout of this XOR gate and simulation results are shown in **Figures 10(b)** and **(c)**.

4.3. The Third Design

The third design is based on Equation (3) which can be simplified as

$$
\begin{aligned}
Y &= \left[(A' + B) \cdot (A + B') \right]' \\
Y &= \left[(A' + B) \right]' \cdot \left[(A + B') \right]' \\
Y &= (A')' \cdot B' + A' \cdot (B')' \\
Y &= AB' + A'B
\end{aligned}
\tag{3}
$$

The QCA layout and simulation results of this design

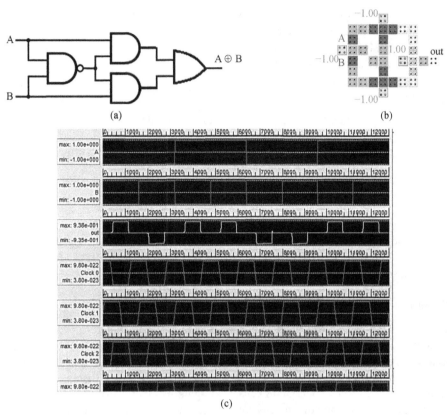

Figure 9. First proposed QCA XOR gate and simulation results.

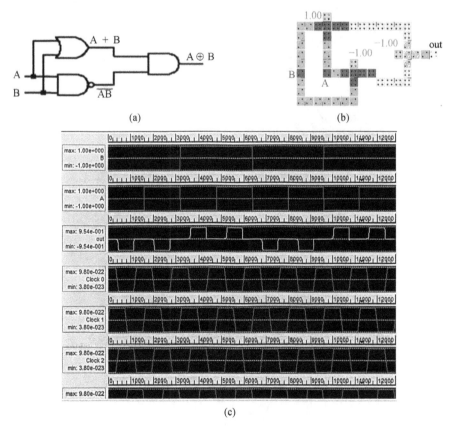

Figure 10. 2nd proposed QCA XOR gate and simulation results.

are shown in **Figures 11(b)** and **(c)** respectively. The proposed QCA XOR gate does not require any crossover. It has cell complexity of 52 cells and an area of approximately 0.08 um². It has a latency of two clock cycles.

4.4. The Fourth Design

The fourth design is based on Equation (4) which can be simplified as

$$Y = A' \cdot (A + B) + B' \cdot (A + B)$$

$$Y = (A'A + A'B) + (AB' + B'B) \qquad (4)$$

$$Y = A'B + AB'$$

The proposed QCA design has a latency of 2 clock cycles and an area of 0.09 and cell count of 52 cells. It does not require any crossover. The proposed QCA gate and its simulation results are also shown in **Figure 12**.

4.5. The Fifth Design

The fifth design is based on the gate arrangement shown in **Figure 13(a)**. It will require one crossover in order to output "out" separately out of the gate.

The proposed QCA design has a latency of 1/2 clock cycles and an area of 0.06 and has a cell count of 48 cells. The QCA layout of this gate and its simulation results are also shown in **Figure 13**.

4.6. The Sixth Design

The sixth design is based on the gate arrangement shown in **Figure 14(a)**.

The QCA layout and simulation results of this design are shown in **Figures 14(b)** and **(c)** respectively. This design has a latency of 1 clock cycle and an area of 0.07 um². It has a cell count of 54 cells.

4.7. The Seventh Design

The seventh design is based on the gate arrangement shown in **Figure 15(a)**.

The proposed QCA design has a latency of 1/2 delays and an area of 0.05 and circuit complexity of 42 cells. The proposed QCA gate and simulation results are shown in **Figures 15(b)** and **(c)** respectively.

5. Conclusions

In this paper we have proposed efficient structures of Quantum-dot Cellular Automata based XOR gates with reduced number of QCA cells and area compared to previous designs. The proposed designs have been tested and simulated using Bistable Approximation simulation engine of QCA Designer version 2.0.3. The function of the Exclusive OR gate has been verified according to the truth table. These structures were designed with mini-

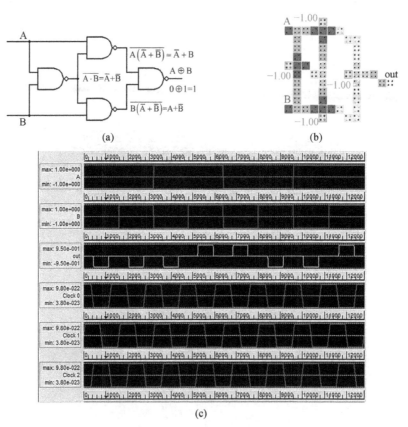

Figure 11. 3rd proposed QCA XOR gate and simulation results.

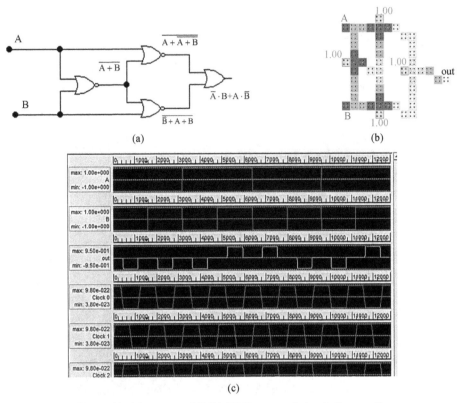

Figure 12. 4th proposed QCA XOR gate and simulation results.

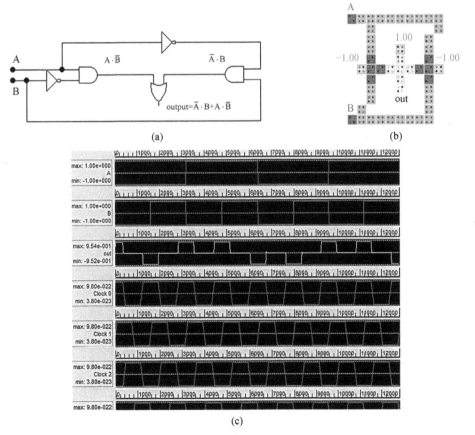

Figure 13. 5th proposed QCA XOR gate and simulation results.

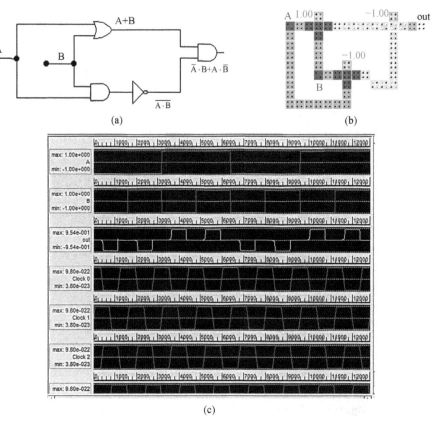

(c)

Figure 14. 6th proposed QCA XOR gate and simulation results.

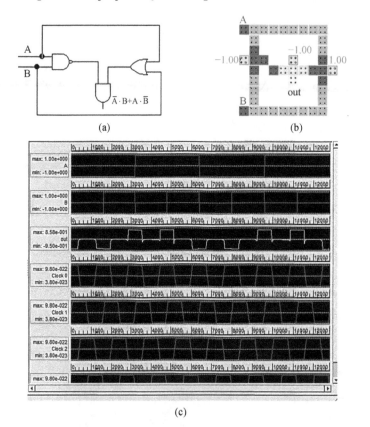

(c)

Figure 15. 7th proposed QCA XOR gate and simulation results.

Table 1. Comparison of logical structures.

EXOR Logic Structures		Complexity (Cell Count)	Area (um^2)	Latency (Clocking Cycles)
Conventional Structures	**Figure 8(b)**	84	0.08	1
	Figure 8(c)	64	0.07	1
Proposed Structures	First Design (**Figure 9**)	34	0.06	1
	Second Design (**Figure 10**)	54	0.07	1
	Third Design (**Figure 11**)	52	0.08	2
	Fourth Design (**Figure 12**)	52	0.09	2
	Fifth Design (**Figure 13**)	48	0.06	1/2
	Sixth Design (**Figure 14**)	54	0.07	1
	Seventh Design (**Figure 15**)	42	0.05	1/2

mum number of cells by using cell minimization techniques. The area and complexity are the major issues in QCA circuit design. The proposed technique can be used to minimize area and complexity.

Table 1 gives the comparison of proposed designs with that of conventional designs as shown in **Figure 8**. It is evident from **Table 1** that the proposed designs are efficient in terms of cell count, area and cross-overs (number of layers).

The proposed layouts can be easily used to design complex circuits based on XOR operation like parity generator and checker circuits, PN sequence generators, Linear Block Code circuits and Linear Feedback Shift Registers.

REFERENCES

[1] C. S. Lent, P. D. Tougaw, W. Porod and G. H. Bernstein, "Quantum Cellular Automata," *Nanotechnology*, Vol. 4, No. 1, 1993, pp. 49-57.

[2] Y. Kim, "Challenges for Nanoscale MOSFETs and Emerging Nanoelectronics," *Transaction on Electrical and Electronic Materials*, Vol. 11, No. 3, 2010, pp. 93-105.

[3] Y. Taur, "CMOS Design near the Limit of Scaling," *IBM Journal of Research & Development*, Vol. 46, No. 2, 2002, pp. 213-222.

[4] D. J. Frank, "Power-Constrained CMOS Scaling Limits," *IBM Journal of Research & Development*, Vol. 46, No. 2, 2002, pp. 235-244.

[5] P. D. Tougaw and C. S. Lent, "Logical Devices Implemented Using Quantum Cellular Automata," *Journal of Applied Physics*, Vol. 75, No. 3, 1994, pp. 1818-1825.

[6] A. O. Orlov, I. Amlani, G. H. Bernstein, C. S. Lent and G. L. Snider, "Realization of a Functional Cell for Quantum-Dot Cellular Automata," *Science*, Vol. 277, No. 5328, 1997, pp. 928-930.

[7] International Technology Roadmap for Semiconductors

(ITRS), 2004.
http://www.itrs.net/Links/2004Update/2004Update.htm

[8] C. G. Smith, "Computation without Current," *Science*, Vol. 284, No. 5412, 1999, pp. 274-274.

[9] J. Timler and C. S. Lent, "Power Gain and Dissipation in Quantum-Dot Cellular Automata," *Journal of Applied Physics*, Vol. 91, No. 2, 2002, pp. 823-831.

[10] D. A. Antonelli, *et al.*, "Quantum-Dot Cellular Automata (QCA) Circuit Partitioning: Problem Modeling and Solutions," *Proceedings of the 41st ACM/IEEE Design Automata Conference*, 2004, pp. 363-368.

[11] M. T. Niemier and P. M. Kogge, "Exploring and Exploiting Wire-Level Pipelining in Emerging Technologies," *ACM SIGARCH Computer Architecture News*, Vol. 29, No. 2, 2001, pp. 166-177.

[12] B. Isaksen and C. S. Lent, "Molecular Quantum-Dot Cellular Automata," *Proceedings of the Third IEEE Conference on Nanotechnology*, Vol. 2, 2003, pp. 5-8.

[13] C. S. Lent and B. Isaksen, "Clocked Molecular Quantum-Dot Cellular Automata," *IEEE Transactions on Electron Devices*, Vol. 50, No. 9, 2003, pp. 1890-1896.

[14] M. Z. Moghadam and K. Navi, "Ultra-Area-Efficient Reversible Multiplier," *Microelectronics Journal*, Vol. 43, No. 6, 2012, pp. 377-385.

[15] K. Navi, H. H. Sajedi, R. F. Mirzaee, M. H. Moaiyeri, A. Jalali and O. Kavehei, "High-Speed Full Adder Based on Minority Function and Bridge Style for Nanoscale," *Integration, the VLSI Journal*, Vol. 44, No. 3, 2011, pp. 155-162.

[16] M. M. Arjmand, M. Soryani, K. Navi and M. A. Tehrani, "A Novel Ternary-to-Binary Converter in Quantum-Dot Cellular Automata," *IEEE Computer Society Annual Symposium on VLSI (ISVLSI)*, Amherst, 19-21 August 2012, pp. 147-152.

[17] M. Hayati and A. Rezaei, "Design and Optimization of

Full Comparator Based on Quantum-Dot Cellular Automata," *ETRI Journal*, Vol. 34, No. 2, 2012, pp. 284-287.

[18] S. Karthigai Lakshmi and G. Athisha, "Design and Analysis of Subtractors Using Nanotechnology Based QCA," *European Journal of Scientific Research*, Vol. 53, No. 4, 2011, pp. 524-532.

[19] L. Lu, W. Q. Liu, M. O'Neill and E. E. Swartzlander, "QCA Systolic Array Design," *IEEE Transactions on Computers*, December 2011.

[20] W. J. Townsend and J. A. Abraham, "Complex Gate Implementations for Quantum Dot Cellular Automata," *Proceedings of the 4th IEEE Conference of Nanotechnology*, Munich, 17-19 August 2004, pp. 625-627.

[21] G. Snider, A. Orlov, C. S. Lent, G. Bernstein, M. Lieberman and T. Fehlner, "Implementation of Quantum-Dot Cellular Automata," *Proceedings of the ICONN*, 2006, pp. 544-547.

[22] G. Toth and C. S. Lent, "Quasiadiabatic Switching for Metal-Island Quantum Dot Cellular Automata," *Journal of Applied Physics*, Vol. 85, No. 5, 1999, pp. 2977-2984.

[23] K. Kim, K. Wu and R. Karri, "The Robust QCA Adder Designs Using Composable QCA Building Blocks," *IEEE Transactions on Computer-Aided Design of Integrated Circuits and System*, Vol. 26, No. 1, 2007, pp. 176-183.

[24] K. Walus, T. J. Dysart, G. A. Jullien and R. A. Budiman, "QCA Designer—A Rapid Design and Simulation Tool for Quantum Dot Cellular Automata," *IEEE Transactions on Nanotechnology*, Vol. 3, No. 1, 2004, pp. 26-31.

## 26

Graph Modeling for Static Timing Analysis at Transistor Level in Nano-Scale CMOS Circuits[*]

Abdoul Rjoub[1#], Almotasem Bellah Alajlouni[2], Hassan Almanasrah[1]

[1]Computer Engineering Department, Jordan University of Science and Technology, Irbid, Jordan
[2]Information Technology Department, Balqa' Applied University, Irbid, Jordan

ABSTRACT

The development and the revolution of nanotechnology require more and effective methods to accurately estimating the timing analysis for any CMOS transistor level circuit. Many researches attempted to resolve the timing analysis, but the best method found till the moment is the Static Timing Analysis (STA). It is considered the best solution because of its accuracy and fast run time. Transistor level models are mandatory required for the best estimating methods, since these take into consideration all analysis scenarios to overcome problems of multiple-input switching, false paths and high stacks that are found in classic CMOS gates. In this paper, transistor level graph model is proposed to describe the behavior of CMOS circuits under predictive Nanotechnology SPICE parameters. This model represents the transistor in the CMOS circuit as nodes in the graph regardless of its positions in the gates to accurately estimating the timing analysis rather than inaccurate estimating which caused by the false paths at the gate level. Accurate static timing analysis is estimated using the model proposed in this paper. Building on the proposed model and the graph theory concepts, new algorithms are proposed and simulated to compute transistor timing analysis using RC model. Simulation results show the validity of the proposed graph model and its algorithms by using predictive Nano-Technology SPICE parameters for the tested technology. An important and effective extension has been achieved in this paper for a one that was published in international conference.

Keywords: Critical Path Estimation; Graph Models; MOSFETs; Sequential Circuits; Transistor Level; Static Timing Analysis

1. Introduction

The revolution from the micro-technology to nano-technology and the growing demand on high performance VLSI chips drive industry companies like Intel and IBM to have their own internal tools. These tools are used to estimate CMOS circuit static timing analysis at transistor level in order to design VLSI chips with the best performance [1].

Static Timing Analysis (STA) technique is commonly used in VLSI design. It is characterized as very fast analysis compared to dynamic circuit simulation like (HSPICE, Montecito...), that's because it does not require any test vectors. It calculates approximately the gate delay using look-up table or linear equations. However, existing delay models become less accurate in nanometer circuits, because of the growing interactions between nodes [2].

The optimization objectives for designing VLSI circuits are the power dissipation, area cost, and circuit delay [3]. The hot research field concentrates on how much delay could be increased for the circuit to save more power and area; this is done by finding the accurate timing analysis of the CMOS circuits and adding some delay to the non-critical path nodes in order to improve the circuit power dissipation without degrading the circuit performance.

From a timing view, critical path nodes are the nodes, which have delay cannot be increased. On the other hand, non-critical path nodes are the nodes which their delay can be increased. This amount of increase is called the slack time, thus the slack time for critical path nodes equal zero and the noncritical path nodes have positive values for their slacks [4]. To find the slack time for every element in CMOS circuit, all timing parameters for

---

[*]This paper is an extended version of Graph modeling for Static Timing Analysis at transistor level in nano-scale CMOS circuits, published in MELECON12, pp. 80-83, date March 2012, ISSN 2158-8473.
[#]Corresponding author.

that circuit should be calculated. These parameters are circuit frequency, delay, arrival, and required times for every node in the circuit.

At transistor level, the slack time for transistors in any CMOS circuit is the maximum value of delay which can be increased without violating the circuit performance [3], thus the optimum decrease in the area or in power can be calculated exactly to fill and exploit the slack time of the non-critical path transistors [5].

Various approaches have been suggested in the past for estimating the slack time. One of the techniques which designed for slack time calculation in combinational circuits is Zero-Slack Algorithm (ZSA) [6]. It's an improved version of an efficient technique proposed in [7,8]. The main drawback of this technique is that it does not give accurate estimation for the circuit critical path or sub-critical paths. This is because the estimation is done at gate level rather than transistor level. Also, this technique does not calculate the delay of the gates simultaneously. It is using pre-defined look-up table to store the delay of gates, so any change in the circuit transistors parameters needs to update this look-up table. Also, this technique just targets the combinational circuits and ignores the sequential circuits.

The potential slack-time technique [3] was proposed as a very effective metric that measures the combinational circuit performance. In this technique, the delay of gates is calculated by using linear equation. But, this technique cannot be applied on large circuits (thousands of transistors) [9]. Also the circuits must be converted from the transistor level to the gate level. The second drawback of this technique is that it does not calculate a delay of transistors' interconnection, which is becomes important in new technologies. Finally, the potential slack-time technique just targets the combinational circuit and ignores the sequential circuits.

The most important timing parameters for any circuit are the delay parameters of the circuit. A variety approaches and techniques were used in the past to estimate the delay timing for optimization purposes. In [10,11], they used simple linear-resistor delay models for transistors in order to optimize the design. In [12], they also use an RC-model to estimate the delay, and then they solve the resulting non-linear equations by an iterative relaxation technique to optimize the design. In [13], the delay modeling is based on pre-characterization of the effective transition-resistances model. Such methods are time and space consuming and incorporate interpolation errors, also they are old and don't accurate for nano-technology parameters because of the development from Micro to Nano dimensions. Additionally, they target only the combinational circuits.

All the approaches that are mentioned have two problems: firstly, the circuits must be converted from transistor level to the gate level, where some circuits for example (memory cells, some full adders) are difficult to convert. Secondly, the gate delay calculation [14], this is because the extracted gates are limited to a few fixed structures and transistor sizes, where it is not feasible to create a delay model for every gate [14]. One way to overcome these problems is by building a transistor graph model. In this model, each transistor is presented individually, by this way; results should be more accurate and more precious, which it is the main target of this paper.

Circuit transformation from gate level to a graph model, which has vertices and edges to represent the gates and the connections, is straightforward. While, by going more deep, transform the same circuit to a graph from the transistor level instead of gate level is very complicated. That's because the vertices of the graph aren't gates, they are PMOS and NMOS transistors and the edges are the connection between the transistors terminals either source or drain or gate.

In VLSI circuit design, the delay time, silicon area and power dissipation are the essential parameters to optimize the performance of digital circuit [9]. It is known that the relation between the performance from one side as well as the silicon area and power dissipation from other side is reversed [15]. Thus, any increase in the frequency causes an increase in the power dissipation. As a result, it becomes a demand to look for new techniques that increase the operation without any scarifying the power dissipation. This could be happened if different low power design techniques are suggested and applied at transistor level [15].

In this work, clear and explained methods to find the critical time, frequency (CLOCK time), the slack and timing constraints at transistor level are proposed in order to find an effective way for estimating timing analysis of any circuit, and building a tool with clear algorithms and methods for researchers to perform static timing analysis job.

The Graph transformation and the timing analyzer in the tool incorporate accurate analytical models and equations to describe the behavior of the transistors at Nano dimensions in the circuit, the delay and capacitance equations for a transistor, which is built in the timing analyzer tool, are extracted from BSIM 4.1 which addresses the MOSFET transistors at nano-technology [16].

In this paper, a Graph model transformation algorithm, which is built inside a tool, is introduced to find the critical path of any CMOS circuit and the timing analysis using the timing analyzer. The timing analyzer depends on the transformation of the CMOS transistors in any circuit to a Graph model. Thus, based on this timing analyzer, the critical and CLOCK time are calculated depending on delay time of transistors, which are involved in the critical path, the sequential elements in the circuit also are analyzed to calculate their timing parameters. The proposed algorithm calculates also the slack and arrival times for each transistor in the circuit. It is also capable to show the effects of changing the sizing of the transistors that are located in the non-critical path in saving the leakage power for the circuit.

The paper is organized as followed. Background of timing parameters is shown in Section 2. Section 3 discusses the characteristics of the proposed graphs and algorithm in details. In Section 4, an example based on bench mark was run based on the proposed algorithm. Finally, Section 5 shows the conclusion.

2. Background and Definitions

From the 1990s, static timing analysis (STA) became the dominant simulation method for VLSI designs. STA used at the bottom layer of many optimization tools used for VLSI simulations and design. STA differs from the input vector simulation; it is easier and has greater simulation speed with almost the same accuracy [17].

In Static Timing Analysis (STA), the modeling of the delay time has always focused on models that represent gates as black boxes, without calculating the accurate internal waveforms. The STA calculates the gate delay approximately using look-up table and equations include the transistors sizes, the load capacitance and input ramps [2]. Most models in literature fall into this category. However, even the most advanced cells libraries do not have universal high accuracy for all types of gates.

Clearly, a modeling and analysis approach that is accurate within a few percent of SPICE is required for all gate types and arcs. This approach should also be fast enough for practical timing and noise analysis on multi-million gate designs. One way to overcome this problem is to move down to the transistor level and model each transistor individually which is the main target of this work. In order to have accurate results, the delay time is calculated using accurate equations in terms of transistor size, load capacitance and the SPICE parameters based on Nano-scale technology.

The maximum operating speed of a circuit which is the critical time of that circuit is limited by the signal propagation delay along the critical path. Thus the critical time of a sequential circuit is the global CLOCK of that circuit, clock is calculated by the summation of all transistors delay time along the critical path of the combinational sub circuits, with sequential elements setup and clock-to-Q timings.

Each transistor has three practical capacitances: the gate C_g, the drain C_d and the source C_s capacitances. C_d and C_s are not depending on state of transistor and its values are constant for all transistor states. C_d and C_s are calculated by BSIM4 Equations (1) and (2) respectively in terms of transistor size and the SPICE parameters [16].

$$C_d = \left[AD \times CJD \times \left(1 + \frac{VJ}{PB}\right)^{-MJD} \right] + \left[PD \times CJSWD \times \left(1 + \frac{VJ}{PB}\right)^{-MJSWD} \right] \quad (1)$$

$$C_s = \left[AS \times CJS \times \left(1 + \frac{VJ}{PB}\right)^{-MJS} \right] + \left[PS \times CJSWS \times \left(1 + \frac{VJ}{PB}\right)^{-MJSWS} \right] \quad (2)$$

Where: AD, AS, PD and PS are area of the drain, area of the source, periphery of the drain and periphery of the source respectively. These parameters which represent sizes of a transistor are obtained from the circuit netlist file. The other parameters are SPICE parameters and depend on the technology that is used to build the circuit. These parameters are obtained from the technology model-card.

Calculation of C_g is more complicated because it depends on transistor state. This capacitance consists of two series capacitances; the gate oxide capacitance C_o and the depletion capacitance C_{dep} as given by Equation (3). C_o depends on area of a transistor channel (WL) and gate oxide thickness T_{ox} and it does not depend on transistor's state of operation as shown in Equation (4), where W and L are the transistor channel width and length respectively.

$$C_g = \frac{C_o C_{dep}}{C_o + C_{dep}} \quad (3)$$

$$C_o = \left(\frac{\varepsilon_{ox}}{T_{ox}}\right) WL \quad (4)$$

C_{dep} depends essentially on transistor's state of operation because it is changing with value of V_{gs} as shown in Equation (4), where X_{dep} is the depletion layer and given by Equation (4).

$$C_{dep} = \left(\frac{\varepsilon_{si}}{X_{dep}}\right) WL \quad (5)$$

$$X_{dep} = 10^{-3} T_{ox} \exp\left[\left(\frac{N_{dep}}{2\times10^{16}}\right)^{-0.25} \cdot \frac{V_{gs} - V_{bs} - V_{FB}}{T_{ox}}\right] \quad (6)$$

Where:
N_{dep} is channel doping concentration;

V_{gs} is voltage difference between the transistor source and gate;

V_{bs} is voltage difference between the transistor source and bulk;

V_{FB} is flat band voltage of the transistor.

In saturation state the value of C_{dep} is precious and affects on value of C_g, while in linear state the value of C_{dep} is very large where X_{dep} goes to zero, where in this case value of C_{dep} can be ignored [16], and as a result $C_g \approx C_o$. Thus, two C_g values are calculated; one when the transistor in saturation state by Equation (3) and another when the transistor in linear state by Equation (4) all of these equations are obtained from BSIM4 [16].

The delay time of a transistor is dependant largely on the load capacitance of its drain, supply voltage, type and slope of driving signals. Load capacitance equals summation of its drain capacitance, capacitance of wires that connects its drain with other transistors in the circuit, and the capacitances of the other transistors that are connected with its drain. The capacitance of the wires depends on the material of the wires, its thickness, width and length.

The transistor's load capacitance is used to calculate the delay time. To calculate the delay time, RC model are used in term of transistor size and the SPICE parameters [16]. The sizes of a transistor are obtained from the circuit netlist file, while the SPICE parameters are obtained from the technology model-card. The Equations (7) and (8) are used to calculate falling and rising delay times for the CMOS transistor, respectively. The fall time is related to the NMOS, while the rise time is related to the PMOS transistor. The falling time delay is given by [16]:

$$
t_f = \frac{2C_L T_{ox} L}{\mu_n \varepsilon_{ox} W V_{DD}\left(1 - \frac{V_{thn}}{V_{DD}}\right)}
$$
$$
\times \left[\frac{\left(\frac{V_{thn}}{V_{DD}} - 0.1\right)}{\left(1 - \frac{V_{thn}}{V_{DD}}\right)} + \frac{1}{2}\ln\left(19 - 20\frac{V_{thn}}{V_{DD}}\right)\right] \quad (7)
$$

Where:

C_L is the transistor load capacitance;

T_{ox} is the gate oxide thickness;

L is the transistor channel length;

μ_n is effective surface mobility of the electrons in the channel;

ε_{ox} is the permittivity of silicon oxide;

W is the transistor channel width;

V_{DD} is the supply voltages;

V_{thn} is the NMOS transistor threshold voltages.

The rising delay time is given by [16]:

$$
t_r = \frac{2C_L T_{ox} L}{\mu_p \varepsilon_{ox} W V_{DD}\left(1 - \frac{V_{thp}}{V_{DD}}\right)}
$$
$$
\times \left[\frac{\left(\frac{V_{thp}}{V_{DD}} - 0.1\right)}{\left(1 - \frac{V_{thp}}{V_{DD}}\right)} + \frac{1}{2}\ln\left(19 - 20\frac{V_{thp}}{V_{DD}}\right)\right] \quad (8)
$$

Where:

μ_p is effective surface mobility of the holes in the channel;

V_{thp} is the PMOS transistor threshold voltages.

The effective surface mobility is technology parameter equals 0.032, 0.0128 for electrons and holes respectively. V_{th} is a core parameter in the delay equations, and it is related to the thickness of the gate oxide.

In real circuits, the task of calculating the minimum clock period of sequential circuit is computed by finding the longest combinational path between any two flip-flops of the circuit and summing setup-time, flip-flop delay to it with neglecting the clock skew and jitter [18]. The sequential elements value is changed according to the input value with respect to the change at the edge of the CLOCK, any flip-flop is sensitive either for rising or falling edges of clock [4]. Any sequential elements have the following timing parameters [19]: Propagation delay ($t_{Clk\text{-}Q}$), Contamination delay (t_{cd}), Setup time (t_s), and Hold time (t_h).

3. Proposed Graph Models and Algorithm

In this paper, the simulator transforms the CMOS circuit from transistor level into a Graph model G (V, E). This graph is cyclic graph for sequential circuits. Many papers [20-22] talked about acyclic graph for combinational circuits. This paper, additionally work at transistor level with nano dimensions, it targets the sequential and combinational circuits, which is very dominant in CMOS circuits. In addition, there is no more research papers in the literature deal with time analysis for sequential circuits, those papers also do not deal with nano-scale SPICE parameters [20-22].

Because of the importance of the capacitances which affects the transistor delay time, a capacitance graph will be built to estimate every transistor capacitances, which is used in the timing analyzer.

In this paper, two graphs are proposed; the first graph is Load Capacitance Graph (G_c), which is proposed to calculate the load capacitance and the delay of each transistor in the circuit. The another graph is Timing Analysis Graph (G_T), which is proposed to present propagation of signals in the circuit and to calculate the circuit timing constraints such as arrival, required and slack times, as shown in **Figure 1**.

3.1. Load Capacitance Graph (G_c)

The G_c is direct graph consist from set of vertices V_c and set of edges E_c, where every vertex v in V_c represents a transistor and has its type and index. Every edge e in E_c represents wire connection between two transistors, and has a weight related to its capacitance. In order to build G_c, the flowing procedure is proposed.

- Every transistor in the circuit is represented by vertex in V_c.
- If the drain of transistor (A) is connected to the source of transistor (B), then a direct edge should be added from vertex A to vertex B in G_c.
- If the drain of transistor (A) is connected to the gate of transistor (B), then a direct edge should be added from vertex (A) to vertex (B) in G_c.
- If the drain of transistor (A) is connected to the drain of transistor (B), then two direct edges should be added: The first one from vertex A to Vertex B, and another one from Vertex B to vertex A.

To manipulate this procedure the *GCG* algorithm is proposed, this algorithm reads HSPICE Netlist file as ASCII Code, then it calculates C_g, C_d and C_s capacitances for all transistors in the circuit by using BSIM4 equations, and finally, it generates the G_c graph. A transistor dimensions are read from the circuit Netlist file, while the technology parameters are extracted from technology model-card (technology file). **Figure 2** shows the *GCG* algorithm

pseudo code.

Applying this algorithm onto 2 Input AND gate that is shown in **Figure 3**, will be generated G_c that is shown in **Figure 4**.

As mention before, the purpose of G_c graph is to calculate the load capacitance C_L for each vertex in G_c. This could be achieved by tracing the outgoing edges form the vertex in G_c, and summing weights of these outgoing edges with capacitances of destination vertices. **Figure 5** shows LCC algorithm which is proposed to calculate the C_L for each vertex in V_c.

In this algorithm, each vertex v in V_c has variable vC_L to store load capacitance value, the drain capacitance of v (vC_{drain}) is stored in vC_L at the beginning (Line 2), and then the all outgoing edges of v are traced in order to find the destination vertices. Then the outgoing edges weights and terminal capacitances of destination vertices are added to vC_L. Giving an example, if such edge e connects v with source of other vertex w (Line 11), then the weight of e (eC) and the source capacitance of w (wC_{source}) are added to vC_L (Line 12), The same scenario is done if e connects v with drain of w (Line 13), which in this case (wC_{drain}) and (eC) are added to vC_L (Line 13).

As shown in **Figure 5**, the algorithm has different scenarios if e connects v with gate of w (Line 4), because the transistor have two values for gate capacitance as mention previously, one when the transistor in linear state ($C_{\text{gate\_on}}$) and the other when the transistor in saturation state ($C_{\text{gate\_off}}$). In this case, the algorithm checks the w; if v and w have same type (ex. N type) (Line 5), then ($wC_{\text{gate\_off}}$) and (eC) are added to vC_L because the transistor w is explicitly must be in saturation state (Line 6), otherwise if v and w have different types (Line 8), then ($wC_{\text{gate\_on}}$) and (eC) are added to vC_L, where the transistor w must be in linear state in this case (Line 9).

After Appling this algorithm on G_c, the purpose of G_c is gained and the C_L is calculated for every transistor in the input circuit. **Table 1** shows C_L for 2_input AND gate.

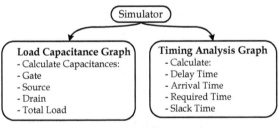

Figure 1. Simulator block diagram.

GCG Algorithm

L1: INPUT: Netlist file.
L2: OUTPUT: G_c graph
L3: BEGIN
L4: READ Netlist and model-card files.
L5: CALCULATE Capacitances $C_{\text{Gate\_off}}$ $C_{\text{Gate\_on}}$, C_{Drain}, C_{Source} for each transistor in circuit.
L6: GENERATE set of vertices V_c
L7: GENERATE set of edges E_c **AS**
{

    e (v_{drain}, w_{source}), where drain of transistor v is connected to source of transistor w.

    e (v_{drain}, w_{gate}), where drain of transistor v is connected to gate of transistor w.

    e (v_{drain}, w_{drain}) **AND** e_c(w_{drain}, v_{drain}), where drain of transistor v is connected to drain of transistor w.

}
L8: END.

Figure 2. *GCG* algorithm of G_c graph generation.

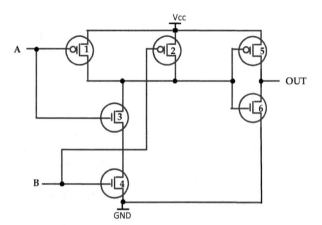

Figure 3. Conventional CMOS AND gate.

Table 1. Total capacitances for 2_Input AND gate.

Index	C_{Gate}	C_{Source}	C_{Drain}	C_{Load}
M6	1.34E−16	1.76E−16	1.96E−16	3.26E−15
M5	4.53E−16	4.93E−16	5.61E−16	3.26E−15
M4	1.34E−16	1.76E−16	1.96E−16	3.72E−16
M3	1.34E−16	1.76E−16	1.96E−16	1.77E−15
M2	4.53E−16	4.93E−16	5.61E−16	1.45E−15
M1	4.53E−16	4.93E−16	5.61E−16	1.45E−15

At the end of Capacitance Graph creation, C_L is already found and calculated for every transistor (vertex) in the circuit. There is no difference here between combinational or sequential because the rules are clear and the feedback existence doesn't affect the algorithm. In capacitance calculation, the algorithm ignores the linear capacitances for transistor's gates, thus for simplicity it uses the saturation and cut-off capacitances.

3.2. Timing Analysis Graph (G_T)

Timing Analysis Graph (G_T) is responsible for estimating the timing analysis for any CMOS circuit to deliver a static timing analysis, and exploiting the slack time for power and area optimization. Timing Graph has also transistors represented by vertices and wire connections represented by edges $G_T (V, E)$, the CMOS circuit is transformed from its view to Graph model to show the propagation of signal from the inputs to the outputs through the circuit itself.

The function of Timing Analysis Graph (G_T) is to present the paths of signals in the circuit. The path is a sequence of distinct transistors, which begins with one of the inputs, and ends with one of the outputs, where at certain input; all of these transistors are turned on. The delay path is the summation of each transistor's delay in that path. The signal goes in transistor from its gate or source and moves out from its drain. In most cases, the signal moves through the circuit in alternating sequence from drain of PMOS transistor to the gate of NMOS transistor and from drain of NMOS transistor to the gate of PMOS and so on. While in other cases, the signal goes through the circuit in constant sequence from drain of PMOS transistor to source of PMOS transistor and from drain of NMOS transistor to source of NMOS.

The timing analysis graph $G_T = (V_T, E_T)$ is a spanning sub-Graph of G_C, where all the vertices of V_C are presented in V_T, and E_T is a subset of E_C, in order to generate G_T from G_c, the flowing procedure is followed:

All incoming edges to the drain terminals are removed.

All incoming edges to the gate terminal that come from the similar vertex type are removed.

To identify the starting points of the paths, an extra set of vertices V_{IN} is added to G_T in order to represent the

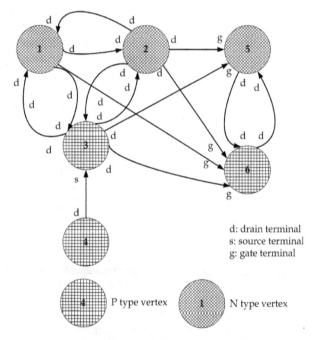

d: drain terminal
s: source terminal
g: gate terminal

P type vertex   N type vertex

Figure 4. G_c of 2Input AND gate shown in Figure 3.

LCC Algorithm
L1: FO R EACH v ∈ Vc
L2:   vC$_L$ ← vC$_{drain}$
L3:   FOR ALL w ∈ Γ + (v) where Γ + (v) = { w|(v,w) ∈ Ec }
L4:   IF e(v$_{drain}$, w$_{gate}$)
L5:   IF (type of v = type of w)
L6:   THEN
L7:   vC$_L$ ← vC$_L$ + wC$_{gate\_off}$ +eC
L8:   ELSE
L9:   vC$_L$ ← vC$_L$ + wC$_{gate\_on}$ +eC
L10:   END IF
L11:   ELSE IF e(v$_{drain}$, w$_{source}$) THEN
L12:   vC$_L$ ← vC$_L$ + wC$_{source}$ +eC
L13:   ELSE IF e(v$_{drain}$, w$_{drain}$) THEN
L14:   vC$_L$ ← vC$_L$ + wC$_{drain}$ +eC
L15:   ENDIF
L16:   END FOR
L17: END FOR

Figure 5. LCC algorithm for C_L calculation.

circuit input terminals where all paths are started from. Also, a new set of vertices V_{out} is added to identify the end points of the path. $V_{feedback}$ vertices is used to represent the feedback in sequential circuits, which returns from flip-flops output. **Figure 6** shows *GTG* algorithm, which is proposed to generate G_T.

By the end of Timing Graph G_T creation, timing analysis of the circuit are ready, this happens step by step starting with copying G_c and removing the unnecessary edges from it as shown at L4-L9. At L10-L13, input, output, and feedback vertices are created and linked with the inputs or the outputs or flip-flops of transistors connected with as in the original circuit, as shown at L13-L21. Then the propagation delay for every transistor is calculated by the tool depending on the delay equations at BSIM as shown at L22-L24.

At L25-L27, all flip-flops timing parameters like t_{C-Q}, t_{setup}, and t_{hold} times are calculated depending on the delay of transistors in the flip-flops itself. These timing parameters are formed by the delay of specific transistors in

the flip-flop, some transistors affects only setup time, some affects the t_{C-Q} and setup.

Depending on the delay for transistors in the combinational sub-circuits and using the Timing Graph G_T, critical time and critical path are found, as shown at L32-L33. Finally at L34-L36, transistors slack times are computed. The **Figure 7** show G_T graph of AND gate that is shown in **Figure 3**.

Each vertex in the G_T has a weight associated with the delay of the corresponding transistor. Therefore, to calculate vertices' weights (delay), RC model are used, the falling time equation is used to calculate the weights of NMOS vertices, and the rising time equation is used to calculate the weights of PMOS vertices. While the weights of the input and output vertices are set to zero because they haven't delay.

The arrival time of a vertex $a(v)$ is defined as the delay of the longest path between that vertex and any of input vertices in the graph. The arrival time of the input vertices $a(V_{IN})$ are zero. The arrival time for the flip-flop block is the summation of the arrival time of previous transistors and their delay. The arrival time of any vertex v in G_T $a(v)$ is calculated by using the well Known recursion formula:

$$a(v) = \max_{w \in FI(v)} \left(a(w) + \text{delay}(w) \right) \qquad (9)$$

Where $FI(v)$ is the set of fan-ins of vertex v.

The *required time* is defined as the delay of the longest path between that vertex fan-out and any of output vertices in the graph.

The *required time* of the output vertices are the critical time. The required time for a flip-flop is the flip-flop setup time subtracted from the CLOCK of the circuit. The *required time* of any vertex v is calculated by using the well known recursion formula as shown in (10).

GTG Algorithm

```
L1:   INPUT : Gc, Netlist file.
L2:   O UTPUT: GT.
L3:   BEG IN
L4:   F OR EVERY V IN Vc.
L5:       REMOVE E  IF
L6:           {
L7:               E (Wdrain,Vdrain)  where W ∈ Vc
OR
L8:               Ec (Wdrain,Vgate) where W ∈ Vc AND Wtype=Vtype
L9:           }
L10:  GENERA TE set of vertices VIN
L11:  GENERA TE set of vertices VOUT
L12:  GENERA TE set of vertices Vfeedback
L13:  FOR EVERY V connected circuit's input, output or feedback
L14:      GENERATE set of edges ET  AS
L15:          {
L16:              ET (W, Vgate)  where W ∈ VIN
L17:              ET (Vdrain, W) where W ∈ VOUT
L18:              ET (W, Vgate) where W ∈ Vfeedback
L19:              ET (Vdrain, W) where W ∈ Vfeedback
L20:          }
L21:      END FOR

L22:      FOR EVERY V ∈ VT
L23:          CALCULATE delay time    Vdelay
L24:      END FOR

L25:      FOR EVERY V ∈ Flip-Flops  in GT
L26:          CALCULATE  Flip-Flops  timing parameters
L27:      END FOR

L28:      FOR EVERY V ∈ VT
L29:          CALCULATE Arrival Time
L30:          CALCULATE Required Time
L31:      END FOR
L32:      FIND critical path
L33:      CALCULATE critical time
L34:      FOR EVERY V ∈ VT
L35:          CALCULATE Stack Time
L36:      END FOR
```

Figure 6. *GTG* algorithm for G_T generate.

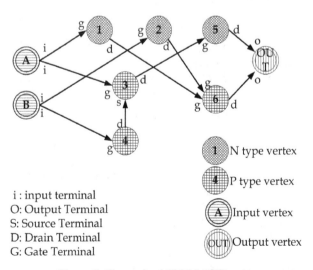

i : input terminal
O: Output Terminal
S: Source Terminal
D: Drain Terminal
G: Gate Terminal

1 N type vertex

4 P type vertex

A Input vertex

OUT Output vertex

Figure 7. *G_T* graph of CMOS AND gate.

$$r(v) = \max_{w \in FO(v)} \left(r(w) + \text{delay}(w) \right) \quad (10)$$

Where $FO(v)$ is the set of fan-outs of vertex v.

For all w vertices are fan out of v, the required time for flip-flop as block is:

$$RT(ff) = \text{CLOCK} - ff_{\text{setup}} \quad (11)$$

The critical delay D_{critical} which is the delay of the longest path in G_T equals to the maximum arrival time between all output vertices.

$$D_{\text{critical}} = \max_{w \in V_{IN}} \left(r(w) \right) \quad (12)$$

The slack time of a vertex $s(v)$ is defined as the period of time that can be added to vertex delay without affecting the graph critical delay. The slack time of vertex v is the time deference between the critical delay and the delay of the longest path that this vertex v involved in. In order to calculate the slack time, the following equation is used:

$$ST(v) = RT(v) - \left(AT(v) + \text{delay}(v) \right) \quad (13)$$

Flip-flops slack time shows up in two places, thus every flip-flop as a block has a slack time in its input and output. The slack input is also shown up at high or low values, which produced from the NMOS and PMOS transistors inside the flip-flop, thus every flip-flop vertex have:

Slack time at D input when D signal transits from high to low:

$$ST_{LD}(ff) = RT_L(ff) - AT_L(ff) \quad (14)$$

Slack time at D input when D signal transits from low to high:

$$ST_{HD}(ff) = RT_H(ff) - AT_H(ff) \quad (15)$$

Slack time at Q output when Q signal transits from high to low:

$$ST_{LQ}(ff) = ST(v) \quad (16)$$

where v is fan-out(ff) and v is PMOS transistor either there is feed back or not.

Slack time at Q output when Q signal transits from low to high:

$$STHQ(ff) = ST(v) \quad (17)$$

where v is fan-out(ff) and v is NMOS transistor either there is feed back or not.

Slack time is a positive value, and the slack time of any vertex that joins the critical path must be zero. **Table 2** illustrates the arrival time, the required time, and the slack time for AND gate as example as shown above.

In this example, each vertex has its own delay, vertices M3, M4, and M5 are located in the critical path and the delay of critical path is 5.136e–012 Sec This value is the

Table 2. Total timing analysis for AND circuit.

Index	Arrival Time	Delay Time	Finished Time	Slack Time
M6	1.20E−12	3.70E−12	5.14E−12	2.29E−13
M5	2.44E−12	2.70E−12	5.136+12	0.00E+00
M4	0.00E+00	4.23E−13	4.23E−13	0.00E+00
M3	4.23E−13	2.02E−12	2.44E−12	0.00E+00
M2	0.00E+00	1.20E−12	1.43E−12	2.29E−13
M1	0.00E+00	1.20E−12	1.43E−12	2.29E−13

maximum arrival time for the output vertices according to our assumptions based on a specific width.

Figure 8 shows a sequential circuit that contains 18 transistors, which forms the combinational sub-circuit. Also, it contains 1 flip-flop, which contains 26 CMOS transistors, two inputs, one output, and one feedback from the flip-flop.

In real circuits, flip-flops actually are consisted from 26 CMOS transistors. In this work, flip-flops are analyzed first at transistor level, and then they will be converted to a block entity, which has its new timing parameters. **Figure 9** shows the Timing graph GT for the test circuit shown in **Figure 3** which has been produced from the simulation.

The timing analysis for the combinational sub-circuit of the test circuit is shown in **Table 3**, where t_d is the delay time of any transistor, t_s is the slack time, t_{arr} is arrival time, and t_{req} is the required time. The table shows that transistors 1, 2, 13, and 16 have arrival time at zero, this because these are connected directly to the input which also have arrival time equal zero. In **Table 1** transistors 11 and 12 have arrival time equal to the flip-flop t_{C-Q} delay because these are connected to the flip-flop output which is feedback in the circuit.

Table 4 shows the flip-flop timing parameters, the table shows slack time high and low at the input (setup) and the output (C-Q) of the flip-flop, also the arrival time high and low and the required time also are shown, mainly the setup and C-Q times for the flip-flops also are shown, also from **Figure 9** flip-flop 1 is located at the critical path either in its setup or C-to-Q times, so it is also colored by red.

4. Simulation Results

To test the proposed algorithms, C++ program was written, the program reads CMOS circuit netlist file which is SPICE3 format. The technology parameters that used in the calculations are extracted from the technology model card. This technology is 22 ηm predictive SPICE technology which is suggested by Nano scale Integration and Modeling (NIMO) Group [23]. The program reads the transistors dimensions from the netlist file, builds the graphs and calculates the arrival time, the required and

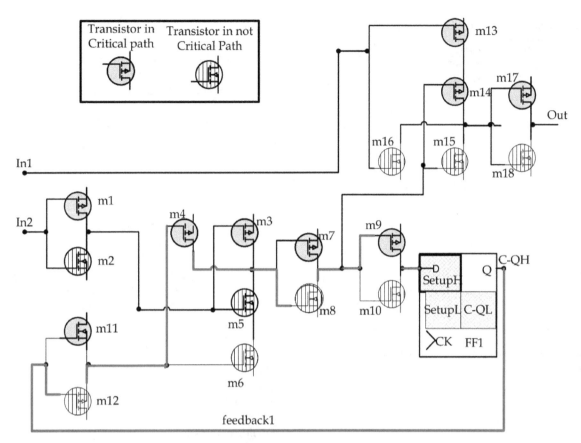

Figure 8. Simple sequential circuit example.

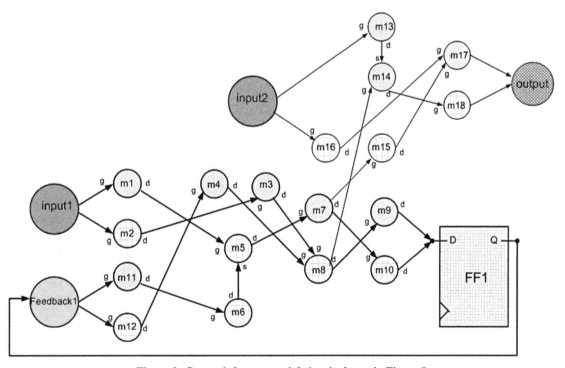

Figure 9. G_T graph for sequential circuit shown in Figure 8.

slack times for all transistors in the circuit [24].

The program was tested on several popular circuits with different sizes (inverter, OR, AND, XOR, half adder, full adder, 4 bit, 8 bit, 12 bit carry ripple adder and 4 bit

Table 3. Timing parameters for combinational sub-circuit.

I	t_d (s)	t_{arr} (s)	t_{req} (s) e−11	t_s (s)
1	7.385e−13	0.000e+00	0.7941	7.202e−12
2	1.377e−12	0.000e+00	0.8125	6.748e−12
3	1.203e−12	1.377e−12	0.9328	6.748e−12
4	1.203e−12	8.125e−12	0.9328	0.000e+00
5	2.015e−12	6.423e−12	0.9956	1.518e−12
6	4.232e−13	5.999e−12	0.7941	1.518e−12
7	8.496e−13	8.437e−12	1.081	1.518e−12
8	1.892e−12	9.328e−01	1.122	0.000e+00
9	1.114e−12	1.122e−11	1.233	0.000e+00
10	1.529e−12	9.287e−12	1.233	1.518e−12
11	7.385e−13	5.261e−12	0.7518	1.518e−12
12	1.377e−12	6.748e−12	0.8125	0.000e+00
13	8.736e−13	0.000e+00	1.608	1.520e−11
14	9.010e−13	1.122e−11	1.698	4.859e−12
15	1.600e−12	9.287e−12	1.799	7.099e−12
16	1.600e−12	0.000e+00	1.799	1.638e−11
17	2.698e−12	1.089e−11	2.068	7.099e−12
18	3.703e−12	1.212e−11	2.068	4.859e−12

Table 4. Timing parameters in second for sequential sub-circuit.

C-QH Delay	C-QL Delay	Setup Delay $_H$	Setup Delay $_L$
6.75E−12	5.26E−12	6.71E−12	8.35E−12
C-QH SlackT	C-QL SlackT	Setup SlackT $_H$	Setup SlackT $_L$
0.00E+00	1.52E−12	1.64E−12	1.52E−12
Req. Time $_H$	Req. Time $_L$	Arraiv. Time $_H$	Arraiv. Time $_L$
1.40E−11	1.23E−11	1.23E−11	1.08E−11

parallel multiplier). The simulation results show that the proposed algorithms are valid for all test cases because it does not get in any dead lock situation and return accurate results. To illustrate the program results a traditional full adder circuit is chosen as a study case.

Full Adder Circuit

The conventional Full Adder of 28 transistors is used as an example; the Full Adder has 3 inputs, and 2 outputs. It is attended to use the minimum length (22 nm) in order to reduce the size of transistor and to increase the speed of transistor, and also to reduce dynamic power dissipation. The transistors' channel widths are selected carefully for each transistor depending on the position of that transistor in the circuit; to balance between the circuit falling and rising times, this circuit is shown in **Figure 8**. The load capacitance and timing analysis for each transistor in the circuit is shown in **Table 3**, where t_d is the delay time of any transistor, t_{arr} is arrival time, and t_{req} is the required time, t_s is the slack time.

From **Table 5**, the arrival time equals zero for transistors 1, 5, 6, 8, 10, 13, 16, 17, 18, 19, 20 and 26 because these transistors are connected to the circuit's inputs. Also, the required time equals zero for transistors 11, 12, 27 and 28 because these transistors are connected the circuit's outputs as illustrated in **Figure 8**. The transistors 1, 2, 3, 6, 15 and 27 have zero slack time because they are located in the circuit critical paths, these transistors make path from the circuit's input to the circuit's output.

Table 5. Transistors timing analysis in the full adder circuit.

I	T	C_{Load}	t_d (s)	t_{arr} (s)	t_{req} (s)	t_s (s)
1	P	2.11E−15	1.82E−12	0	1.82E−12	0
2	P	1.06E−15	9.11E−13	1.82E−12	2.73E−12	0
3	P	1.78E−15	1.54E−12	2.73E−12	4.24E−12	0
4	N	2.24E−15	2.65E−12	6.75E−13	4.73E−12	1.41E−12
5	N	5.68E−16	6.75E−13	0	2.08E−12	1.41E−12
6	P	2.11E−15	1.82E−12	0	1.82E−12	0
7	P	1.78E−15	1.54E−12	1.82E−12	4.27E−12	9.11E−13
8	N	5.68E−16	6.75E−13	0	2.08E−12	1.41E−12
9	N	2.24E−15	2.65E−12	4.42E−13	4.73E−12	1.64E−12
10	N	3.72E−16	4.42E−13	0	2.08E−12	1.64E−12
11	P	3.12E−15	3.67E−12	3.33E−12	9.95E−12	2.96E−12
12	N	3.12E−15	3.70E−12	4.27E−12	9.95E−12	1.98E−12
13	P	2.31E−15	2.34E−12	0	2.88E−12	5.45E−13
14	P	1.50E−15	1.52E−12	3.33E−12	6.25E−12	1.41E−12
15	N	1.70E−15	2.01E−12	4.27E−12	6.29E−12	0
16	N	7.65E−16	9.07E−13	0	4.27E−12	3.37E−12
17	N	7.65E−16	9.07E−13	0	4.27E−12	3.37E−12
18	P	2.31E−15	2.34E−12	0	2.88E−12	5.45E−13
19	N	7.65E−16	9.07E−13	0	4.27E−12	3.37E−12
20	P	2.31E−15	2.34E−12	0	2.88E−12	5.45E−13
21	P	9.13E−16	9.24E−13	2.34E−12	3.81E−12	5.45E−13
22	P	9.13E−16	9.24E−13	3.26E−12	4.73E−12	5.45E−13
23	P	1.50E−15	1.52E−12	4.19E−12	6.25E−12	5.45E−13
24	N	1.70E−15	2.01E−12	8.84E−13	6.29E−12	3.39E−12
25	N	3.72E−16	4.42E−13	4.42E−13	4.27E−12	3.39E−12
26	N	3.72E−16	4.42E−13	0	3.83E−12	3.39E−12
27	P	3.12E−15	3.67E−12	6.29E−12	9.95E−12	0
28	N	3.12E−15	3.70E−12	5.70E−12	9.95E−12	5.45E−13

The purpose of this Graph model and algorithms which is built inside a tool is to find the critical path of any CMOS circuit and to calculate slack time in order to optimize the design. Powerful of this model is its capability to show the effects of changing parameter of the transistors located in the non-critical path like size to optimize the silicon area, or transistor V_{th} to optimize leakage power dissipation. During this optimization process the circuit delay slack times recalculated for every transistor after every change in the circuit in order to find the optimal design. To illustrate that greedy search algorithm is applied on the case study circuit in order to optimize leakage power dissipation. In each iterate during the search, V_{th} of one transistor that located in non-critical path is change to high and the delay and slack times are recalculated to all transistors. **Figure 10** shows and example of one-bit conventional Full Adder of 24 transistors before the optimization using the proposed tech-

nique, while **Figure 11** shows the same design after the optimization process where the leakage power is reduced 45% which is the optimal result by using to value of V_{th}.

The same optimization process was applied on several popular circuits with different sizes (inverter, OR, AND, XOR, full adder, 4 bit, 8 bit, 12 bit carry ripple adder and 4 bit parallel multiplier) **Table 6** show results of power reduction and number of iteration that required for optimization in these circuits by using PC with Intel CPU at 3.00 GHz frequency.

The simulation results from **Table 6** show that the proposed algorithms are valid for all test cases because it does not get in any dead lock situation and work effectively during the optimization process. Although the number of iterations increased exponentially with increasing number of the circuits' transistors, the time required for optimization is acceptable and extremely fast compared to the traditional models for timing at transistor level.

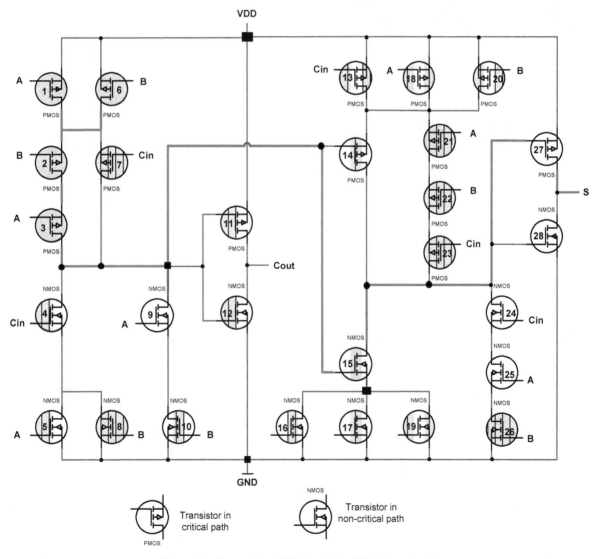

Figure 10. Conventional 28_transistor full adder circuit.

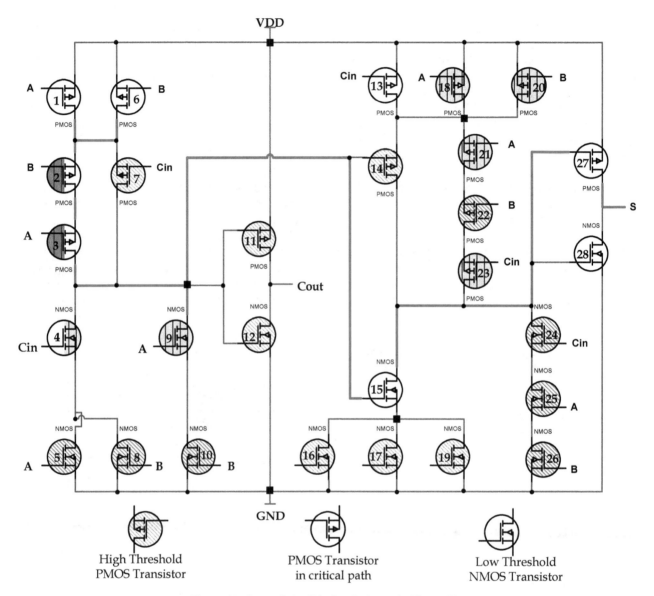

Figure 11. G_T graph for FA circuit shown in Figure 10.

Table 6. Leakage power reduction and in tested circuits.

The circuit	Number of transistor	Number of iteration	Time	Leakage power reduction
inverter	2	1	2.1e−6 second	10%
OR	4	12	4.8e−5 second	15%
AND	4	12	4.8e−5 second	16%
XOR	10	90	9.1e−4 second	22%
full adder	28	6156	0.17 second	45%
4 bit CR adder	112	12,432	1.3 second	71.2%
8 bit CR adder	224	49,952	1.68e+1 second	75.2%
12 bit CR adder	336	112,560	3.79e+1 second	77.2%
4 bit parallel multiplier	440	84,990,400	3.73e+3 second	79%

5. Conclusion

In this paper, the methodology and algorithm used for delivering Static Timing Analysis for CMOS circuit at transistor level based on the transformed graph are shown; these were applied to solve timing problems with the exploitation of time for area and power optimization. This new methodology is based on accurate timing equations for nanometer CMOS transistors and more fast and accurate when compared to the traditional models for timing, we have introduced the principles of timing analysis resulting with the slack component. It has been shown in this paper that slack time provides a very important metric which give an opportunity to optimize circuit area and power performances. In terms of timing arrival, required slack times are found for every transistor, thus setup, Clock to Q timings are found for every sequential element. The simulation results show that the proposed algorithms are valid for all test cases because it does not get in any dead lock situation and work effectively during the optimization process.

REFERENCES

[1] K. Bard, B. Dewey, M.-T. Hsu, T. Mitchell, K. Moody, V. Rao, R. Rose, J. Soreff and S. Washburn, "Transistor-Level Tools for High-End Processor Custom Circuit Design at IBM," *IEEE Proceedings of the Journal*, Vol. 95, No. 3, 2007, pp. 530 -554.

[2] Z. T. Li and S. M. Chen, "Transistor Level Timing Analysis Considering Multiple Inputs Simultaneous Switching," *IEEE Proceedings of 10th Computer-Aided Design and Computer Graphics*, Beijing, October 2007, pp. 315-320.

[3] C. H. Chen, X. J. Yang and M. Sarrafzadeh, "Potential Slack: An Effective Metric of Combinational Circuit Performance," *IEEE International Conference on Computer-Aided Design*, San Jose, 5-9 November 2000, pp. 198-201.

[4] M. Naresh and S. Sachin, "Timing Analysis and Optimization of Sequential Circuits," Kluwer Acadimic Publisher Group, 1999.

[5] F. Sill and F. G. D. Timmermann, "Total Leakage Power Optimization with Improved Mixed Gates," *Proceedings of the 18th Symposium on Integrated Circuits and System Design*, Florianolpolis, 4-7 September 2005, pp. 154-159.

[6] R. Nair, C. L. Berman, P. S. Hauge and E. J. Yoffa, "Generation of Performance Constraints for Layout," *IEEE Transactions on Computer-Aided Design*, Vol. 8, No. 8, 1989, pp. 860-874.

[7] T. Gao, P. M. Vaidya and C. L. Liu, "A New Performance Driven Placement Algorithm," *Proceedings of IEEE International Conference on Computer Aided Design*, Santa Clara, 11-14 November 1991, pp. 44-47.

[8] H. Youssef and E. Shragowitz, "Timing Constraints for Correct Performance," *IEEE Proceedings of International Conference on Computer Aided Design*, Santa Clara, 11-15 November 1990, pp. 24-27.

[9] S. Dutta, S. Nag and K. Roy, "ASAP: A Transistor Sizing Tool for Speed, Area, and Power Optimization of Static CMOS Circuits," *International Symposium of Circuits and Systems*, London, 30 May-2 June 1994, pp. 61-64.

[10] H.-Y. Song, K. Nepal, R. I. Bahar and J. Grodstein "Timing Analysis for Full-Custom Circuits Using Symbolic DC Formulations," *IEEE Transactions on Computer-Aided Design Integral Circuits Systems*, Vol. 25, No. 9, 2006, pp. 1815-1830.

[11] K. S. Hedlund, "Aesop: A Tool for Automated Transistor Sizing," *Proceedings of the 24th ACM/IEEE conference on Design automation*, Miami Beach, 28 June-1 July 1987, pp. 114-120.

[12] U. Seckin and C.-K. K. Yang, "A Comprehensive Delay Model for CMOS CML Circuits," *IEEE Transactions on Circuits and Systems I*, Vol. 55, No. 9, 2008, pp. 2608-2618.

[13] B. Rich.man, J. Hansen and K. Cameron, "A Deterministic Algorithm for Automatic CMOS Transistor Sizing," *IEEE Proceedings of Conference on Custom Integmted Circuits Conference*, Portland, 4-7 May 1987, pp. 421-424.

[14] S. Raja, F. Varadi, M. Becer and J. Geada, "Transistor Level Gate Modeling for Accurate and Fast Timing, Noise, and Power Analysis," *Proceedings of Design Automation Conference*, Anaheim, 8-13 June 2008.

[15] R. Rogenmoser and Kaeslin, "The Impact of Transistor Sizing on Power Efficiency in Submicron CMOS Circuits," *IEEE Journal of Solid-State Circuits and systems*, Vol. 32, No. 7, 1997, pp. 1142-1145.

[16] W. Yang and M. Dunga, Eds., "BSIM4.6.1 MOSFET Model, User Manual," 2008. http://www.devices.eecs.berkely.edy/~bsim3/bsim4.html

[17] D. Blaauw, K. Chopra, A. Srivastava and L. Scheffer, "Statistical Timing Analysis: From Basic Principles to State of the Art," *IEEE Transactions on Computer-Aided Design of Integrated Circuits and Systems*, Vol. 27, No. 4, 2008, pp. 589-607.

[18] A. Jain and D. Blaauw, "Slack Borrowing in Flip-Flop Based Sequential Circuits," *Proceedings of the 15th ACM/IEEE Great Lakes Symposium on VLSI*, Chicago, 17-19 April 2005, pp. 96-101.

[19] A. Dendouga, N. Bouguechal, S. Barra and O. Manck, "Timing Characterization and Layout of a Low Power Differential C2MOS Flip-Flop in 0.35 μm Technology," *2nd International Conference on Electrical Engineering Design and Technologies*, Hammamet, 8-10 November 2008, pp. 1-4.

[20] P. Y. Calland, A. Mignotte, O. Peyran, Y. Robert and F. Vivien, "Retiming DAG's (Direct Acyclic Graph)," *IEEE Transaction on Computer-Aided Design Integrated Circuits and Systems*, Vol. 17, No. 12, 1998, pp. 1319-1325.

[21] K. Choi and A. Chatterjee, "PA-ZSA (Power Aware Zero Slack Algorithm): A Graph Based Timing Analysis for Ultra Low-Power CMOS VLSI," *Proceedings of the*

Power and Timing Modeling, Optimization and Simulation, Seville, 11-13 September 2002, pp. 178-187.

[22] C.-P. R. Liu and J. A. Abraham, "Transistor Level Synthesis for Static CMOS Combinational Circuits," *Ninth Great Lakes Symposium on VLSI*, Austin, 4-6 March 1999, pp. 172-175,

[23] Nanoscale Integration and Modeling (NIMO) Group, Pre-

dictive Technology Model (PTM), 2008. http://www.eas.asu.edu/~ptm/

[24] A. Rjoub and A. B. Alajlouni, "Graph Modeling for Static Timing Analysis at Transistor Level in Nano-Scale CMOS Circuits," *IEEE Proceedings of the* 16*th Mediterranean Electrotechnical*, Yasmine Hammamet, 25-28 March 2012, pp. 80-83.

## 27

A Reconfigurable Network-on-Chip Datapath for Application Specific Computing

Joshua Weber, **Erdal Oruklu**

Department of Electrical and Computer Engineering, Illinois Institute of Technology, Chicago, USA

ABSTRACT

This paper introduces a new datapath architecture for reconfigurable processors. The proposed datapath is based on Network-on-Chip approach and facilitates tight coupling of all functional units. Reconfigurable functional elements can be dynamically allocated for application specific optimizations, enabling polymorphic computing. Using a modified network simulator, performance of several NoC topologies and parameters are investigated with standard benchmark programs, including fine grain and coarse grain computations. Simulation results highlight the flexibility and scalability of the proposed polymorphic NoC processor for a wide range of application domains.

Keywords: Reconfigurable Computing; Network-on-Chip; Network Simulators; Polymorphic Computing

1. Introduction

Technological advances in Field Programmable Gate Arrays (FPGA) and performance improvement of reconfigurable systems are making a large impact on signal processing and computer processing. In addition, System-on-Chip (SoC) methodology facilitates tightly placement of reconfigurable arrays with embedded general-purpose processors. In the past reconfigurable hardware has been used as a prototyping platform to aid in time to market development of application specific integrated circuits (ASIC). Increasingly, it is being shown that utilizing reconfigurable features in the field is producing designs with higher performance, lower cost, lower power, decreased design time, and increased flexibility.

Application-specific instruction set processors (ASIP) use extensions to standard processor instruction sets to achieve significant performance gains within various application domains. It has been shown that this approach will be a primary driver for future processor improvements [1]. *Polymorphic processors* [2,3] attempt to retain the flexibility advantages of general-purpose processors while providing the same advantages inherent in ASIPs and custom hardware logic. Polymorphism is a term borrowed from computer science, which is the ability for an object to utilize a common interface and yet execute custom type-specific actions based on the input type. Polymorphic computing provides the same functionality to a computer processor; creating a common programming interface, but allowing the execution of the algorithm to be application specific. Hence, the goal of a polymorphic processor is a general-purpose processor that can be reconfigured easily to accommodate application specific optimizations as needed.

This work presents a novel and unique polymorphic processor design. Integration of reconfigurable elements into a traditional general-purpose processor is achieved through replacement of the processor datapath with a network-on-chip (NoC) design. This NoC enables a higher level of fine-grained flexibility in the operation of the processor. The flexibility of the *polymorphic NoC* (Poly-NoC) processor can be leveraged in many ways to achieve noticeable performance gains. A cycle-accurate simulator is produced to demonstrate the performance gains achievable by the PolyNoC architecture.

2. Related Work

Reconfigurable computing has been the subject of much research [4] and it has been shown that reconfigurable computing can provide a significant improvement in performance over standard general-purpose processors [5,6]. Reconfigurable architectures offer a reduction in size and cost, improved time to market, and increased flexibility. All of which are especially important for embedded systems. The majority of systems focus on the integration of a general purpose processor with a reconfigurable resource array (most often an FPGA). The goal of polymorphic processor is to integrate these two units into a common design methodology and run-time control system.

An overview of the current trends and types of architectures has been studied and is shown in **Figure 1** [7]. In **Figure 1(a)**, the reconfigurable array is communicating with the general purpose processor through the I/O data bus. In **Figures 1(b)** and **(c)**, reconfigurable array is moved closer to the processor to decrease the communication cost. In **Figure 1(d)**, the reconfigurable unit is coupled within the processor as a configurable functional unit. With the increasing size and complexity of programmable fabrics and the use of soft core processor, a processor core can also be embedded inside the reconfigurable fabric as shown in **Figure 1(e)**.

These approaches have all been applied in very different application domains. Research has been performed to accelerate cryptographic systems [8], Euclidean distance transformation [9], matrix multiplication [10], and multimedia applications for imaging [11] and video processing [12]. In addition research has been performed into creation of polymorphic processors, which can be reconfigured and applied to multiple application domains [2,3, 13-15].

A common problem for all polymorphic processors is the integration of design flow for both software and reconfigurable hardware. Some work has been performed in auto generation of hardware design targeted at reconfigurable polymorphic processors [16-18]. Most of these approaches use the standard C language to capture program functionality and then through compiler optimization extract sections to be targeted at reconfigurable resources.

3. Reconfigurable Datapath Design

The proposed PolyNoC processor attempts to closely integrate a general-purpose processor with reconfigurable elements. This tight coupling produces a polymorphic reconfigurable processor, which can be reconfigured and extended in real time to include application specific optimizations. Enabling the ability to tailor the processor architecture to the specific application at run time is an important feature of this design.

Prior approaches at integration of reconfigurable elements to general-purpose processor have had various types of implementation ranging from simple attachment as a peripheral to tighter coupling to the memory system or co-processor usage. The PolyNoC processor approaches the design goals by integrating the reconfigurable elements into the foundation of the processor architecture. Unlike previous designs, the datapath of the processor is replaced with a network-on-chip (NoC). Instead of traditional direct wire communication with pipeline registers, the PolyNoC processor utilizes a NoC for all element-

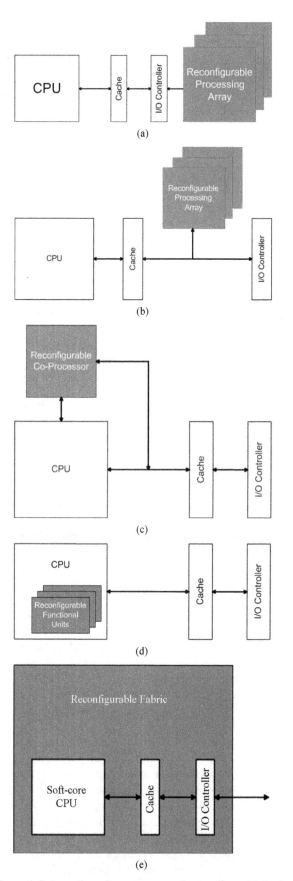

Figure 1. Integration of processors and reconfigurable logic.

to-element communication. The use of a NoC provides many advantages to the design and enables the PolyNoC processor to achieve its main goal of real time reconfigurability.

The NoC provides a flexible interconnect and allows new functional computation elements to be added and subtracted in real time. Furthermore, the NoC relieves the designer from strict constraints on placement and ordering of functional elements, as the NoC will provide element-to-element communication regardless of each elements placement. However, the NoC also place many constrains on the overall processor operation. In particular, the latency penalty from the NoC needs to be overcome by the additional advantages provided by the PolyNoC processor, namely the ability to reconfigure the processor to have application specific optimizations.

4. PolyNoC Processor Architecture

The PolyNoC processor architecture can be seen in **Figure 2**. It consists of a standard instruction and data cache connected to a instruction fetch and decode unit. Next, the instruction is passed to a packetizer. The packetizer wraps the instruction into a NoC packet and then transmits it through the NoC. The packetizer also keeps track of all instruction executions and issues new instructions. The NoC delivers instruction packets to functional units. Each instruction slowly progresses from functional unit to functional unit, stopping to get a subset of execution done.

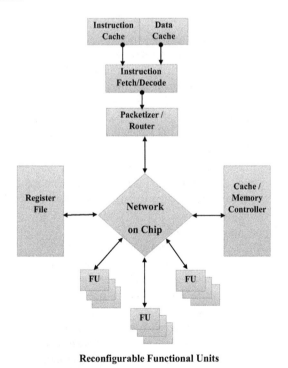

Figure 2. Network-on-chip datapath for polymorphic processors.

Rather than starting from scratch when designing the processor, an existing processor architecture has been adopted and extended. This enables the PolyNoC processor to focus on architectural issues, without dealing with the many contributing factors from compiler and instruction set changes. In addition, the use of a common target processor allows the PolyNoC processor to utilize all existing software and compiler tools available for the target processor. For these reasons, the PolyNoC processor is designed to execute SPARC code and emulate a SPARC processor [19]. Specifically the PolyNoC processor is based upon the LEON3 SPARC processor.

The base level of functional units represents roughly the stages of execution of the SPARC processor the design is modeled on. These base functional units consist of the register file, memory controller, ALU, and FPU. Each functional unit performs computations that are roughly equivalent to the pipeline stages of a LEON3 SPARC processor, the target processor being extended into the PolyNoC. As such, much of the implementation of the basic functional units can remain unchanged from a target general-purpose processor. Only modifications to the input and output communications are necessary.

Besides base functional units, additional functional units can be added to the system. These are represented by blocks of reconfigurable functional units, which can be configured depending on the current application. For example, they can be used to instantiate additional core units such as additional FPU functional elements. By instantiating additional FPU elements, the processor can be tailored to execute a floating-point heavy application. The reconfigurable functional blocks can also be configured to implement custom user logic. By enabling custom logic, the processor can execute new custom instructions. These instructions and logic can be heavily optimized and designed to support a specific application, enabling a great deal of performance increase.

5. Functional Units

5.1. Packetizer

The packetizer, as shown in **Figure 3**, functions as the primary control of instruction execution. It feeds a program counter (PC) value to the instruction cache unit and accepts the incoming instructions for execution. In order to overcome the increase in execution time caused by the NoC latency and to leverage the flexibility advantages of the NoC datapath, the packetizer allows for multiple instruction issues and out-of-order completion. To accomplish this, the packetizer must track the issuing and completion of all instructions and control the update of the PC.

The packetizer allows for an unlimited number of instructions in flight. This is constrained by the amount of

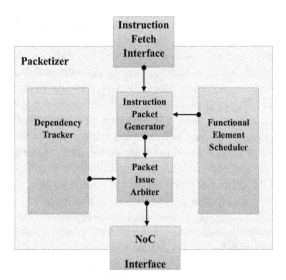

Figure 3. Packetizer block diagram.

instruction level parallelism present in the program. Before issuing any instruction, it is checked for data dependency. This dependency check is performed by the built in dependency tracker detailed in the Section 5.1.1. The dependency tracker analyses 1) data dependency among in-flight instructions and 2) control oriented dependencies from branch instructions. Once the dependency tracker declares the instruction as dependency free, it will be issued for execution and dependency tracker is updated with dependencies of the newly issued instruction.

In order to issue an instruction for execution, it needs to be packetized and transmitted to the NoC. The packetizer decodes the instruction to determine the list of necessary functional elements. For example, a basic ADD instruction will need to visit the register file to obtain input register operands, then the ALU unit for execution of the operation, then return to the register file to write the results into the output register and finally return to the packetizer to update execution completion status. Once an instruction is decoded, the functional element destinations are fed into the functional element scheduler, as detailed in Section 5.1.2. The functional element scheduler will return a network id for each functional element required.

A NoC packet is created to hold the necessary instruction contents. The critical data is the instruction itself and the destination list of functional elements. All of this data are wrapped into a NoC data packet, encoded with the destination of the first functional element and transmitted into the NoC. As instructions are completed they return to the packetizer. The packetizer checks the status of the packet to ensure it was correctly executed. Any instruction that failed execution will return as a trap condition (the packetizer will update the PC to a trap handler). If the instruction was a branch instruction, the new PC

value will be included. As a final step, the packetizer will pass the completed instruction to the dependency tracker to remove any dependencies caused by this packet.

5.1.1. Dependency Tracker

The dependency tracker is responsible for determining if a new instruction is dependency free from all currently executing instructions. The tracker accomplishes this task by maintaining an internal list of all data and control dependencies of currently executing instructions. When a new instruction is to be executed, it compares the necessary registers to the dependency lists and determines if it can be executed.

The dependency lists are implemented as simple bit flags. Two 32 bit registers are created to track status of the instruction registers, eight global, eight local, eight input and eight output integer registers and 32 floating point registers. Each bit indicates if a data dependency exists for that register. As each instruction begins execution, it is registered with the dependency tracker. At this time all destination registers being written by the instruction are flagged in the tracking register. When a new instruction is to be executed, all source registers are compared with the tracking registers. If bits corresponding to all source registers are clear, the instruction is free from data dependencies. The final step occurs when an instruction completes execution. In this case the bits corresponding to the destination register are cleared from the tracking list to indicate that there is no longer a data dependency for those registers.

In addition to tracking data dependencies, the dependency tracker also tracks control dependencies. Unlike a traditional datapath, it is difficult to signal flush operations for instructions in flight. As such, no branch prediction is used and all branching cases cause a control dependency. When a control instruction is in-flight all future instructions hold off on execution until resolution of the branch instruction. The dependency tracker provides this tracking for the packetizer to control instruction issuing. In addition, as the register windows are affected by a SAVE or RESTORE instruction, they too exhibit a control dependency. All instruction must await completion before execution.

The dependency tracker is critical to the overall operation of the PolyNoC processor. Together with the packetizer it enables a multiple issue instruction datapath. Since, the NoC datapath imparts latency penalties to execution compared to a traditional processor, a large mitigating factor provided by the PolyNoC processor is the ability to extract instruction level parallelism from the instruction stream. The dependency tracker is crucial for this ability. It checks each subsequent instruction for dependencies. If the instruction is found to be free of dependencies then it is executed at the same time as the prior instruction. This behavior helps to keep the execution elements fully utilized and provides significant benefits to overall execution time.

5.1.2. Functional Element Scheduler

The functional element scheduler provides addressing and scheduling of functional elements to the packetizer. It maintains a list of all functional elements, their NoC addresses, and the functional element type. For simple cases with only one instance of each functional element, it simply returns the address of the element when a request is made for an element of that type. For cases when more than one element of a type has been created, it performs scheduling. The current PolyNoC processor performs scheduling through a *round robin scheduling* algorithm. This schedules all functional elements equally and distributes instruction load evenly. It also benefits from a very simple implementation and critically requires no signaling from any functional element. For these reasons, it was chosen as the scheduling algorithm for the PolyNoC processor. Further performance gains can be made through more advanced and intelligent scheduling algorithms since the round robin algorithm does not take into account current status of functional elements.

5.2. Register File

The register file implements and provides access to all processor registers. It implements the register definitions according to the SPARC architecture [19]. It defines a set of overlapping windows general-purpose instruction registers. These overlapping windows provide functionality to pass parameters between subroutine calls. The execution of SAVE and RESTORE instructions allow the adjustment to a new register window, which contains shared output and input registers for different window values.

The register file further implements 32 floating-point general-purpose registers. These registers are usable by all floating-point instructions. In addition to general-purpose registers, the register file also implements the SPARC control and status registers. These control and status registers provide access to configuration and status of a SPARC processor and are necessary for compliance with SPARC execution model. Some status registers are critical in execution, for example the processor state register (PSR) holds the contents of the condition codes. The register file also supports the execution of the SAVE and RESTORE instructions, shifting the register window up or down. All of these options combine to make a fully compliant SPARC register set.

5.3. Memory Controller

The memory controller enables access to external addressed memory. This supports both reading and writing of external memory. The basic functionality of the memory controller is simple and its implementation is straightforward. The SPARC standard defines the primary external memory bus to use the AMBA AHB bus protocol. Therefore, the PolyNoC processor and the memory controller implements an AMBA AHB master controller for accessing the bus.

In addition to providing access to the external memory space, small amount of configuration memory space must also be implemented within the memory controller. This memory space provides plug-n-play capabilities for the AHB bus, enabling AHB bus slaves to be added and configuration options and memory address locations stored. This configuration space is crucial to the memory controller master controller and used to generate chip selects and initiate access to AHB slaves.

5.4. Arithmetic Logic Unit

The ALU performs all integer arithmetic and logic computations for instructions. In addition to execution of basic instructions, the ALU also computes memory addresses and branch and jump targets. The ALU must be robust enough to support arithmetic and logic operations for all data types as required by the SPARC instruction set. ALU performance can have a significant impact on over all processor performance but from the standpoint of the operation of the PolyNoC processor, it does not present any new challenges.

5.5. Floating-Point Unit

Like the ALU, the FPU performs all arithmetic and logic computations for floating point operations. This implements all basic computations on standard IEEE-754 floating-point numbers. The implementation can vary widely and have performance impacts on the PolyNoC processor. A potential advantage of the PolyNoC processor is the ability to incorporate multiple or even different FPU implementations allowing for design choices that are not feasible with a traditional general purpose processor.

6. NoC Interconnect

The network-on-chip (NoC) interconnect links all functional elements together and enables communication among them. Any instruction will traverse the NoC multiple times during execution. For the basic SPARC instruction with just the core functional elements, it will require 3 to 5 trips through the NoC to complete execution of each instruction (similar to pipeline stages). Therefore, performance of the NoC links is very important to the overall performance of the PolyNoC processor.

The NoC should also be able to provide a scalable architecture with a dynamic layout. The PolyNoC processor's main advantages are in flexibility and reconfiguration. The greatest performance gains are obtained by real time reconfiguration of the number and type of functional elements. The NoC must be able to support to addition and subtraction of functional elements with no impact to overall NoC performance. In addition, due to the heavy dependency on latency, the NoC needs to scale well. As additional functional elements are added and the total number of nodes within the NoC increases, the average latency for travel over the NoC should not grow rapidly. If the NoC latency increases too quickly, any performance gain from additional functional elements can be lost due to the penalties from increased execution time.

The NoC also needs to be able to support a flexible packet type and size. Each NoC packet will need to encapsulate an instruction and all necessary information for execution of that instruction. Data carried by the packets will vary between each instruction. To save on overall packet size, the packet should allow for a flexible packet size to shrink or grow according to the demands of the individual instruction. Packet structure should have a minimum amount of overhead when encapsulating an instruction and data. Minimizing this overhead reduces the overall packet size and lower the overall bandwidth requirements for interconnect links.

The traffic generation for the PolyNoC processor is dependent on instruction execution. As a result, the traffic load is reduced compared to other NoC systems. The execution of instructions tends to be limited by the computational time of the functional elements. This stark limit on the number of instructions currently executing makes for a low overall bandwidth requirement. The low bandwidth requirement provides one of the main NoC design techniques to improve performance. The PolyNoC processor can run the NoC communications on a *separate and higher frequency clock* then the functional elements. Since latency is a critical NoC parameter, the higher NoC clock allows compensating for the NoC delay. The latency figure is computed based on the NoC clock. When running the NoC at a higher clock frequency, the overall NoC delay is drastically reduced. In many cases, it seems reasonable to run the NoC clock at 4 or 8 times the functional element clock. This provides the ability to have up to 4 or 8 clock cycles of latency for NoC transmission within a single functional element execution clock cycle, potentially hiding all latency penalties during execution.

The PolyNoC processor presents a very unique set of requirements for a NoC. In addition, the traffic generation is the result of instruction execution. This type of traffic load is uncommon and has not been studied in depth. For these reasons, it is difficult to approach the design of the NoC from theoretical statistical approach, as is often applied during NoC research. Instead, this work has focused on an experimental approach. A simulator for NoC design exploration has been created and various NoC design parameters have been modified and tested to determine the impact on NoC performance.

7. NoC Architecture Exploration

This section presents an exploration of the architectural and topology issues impacting the performance of the PolyNoC processor [3]. The Network Simulator 2 (ns-2) [20] is utilized as a network simulation platform. Ns-2 is extended to simulate the execution of the PolyNoC processor. With this simulation platform, instruction trace data from real world benchmark programs can be run through the simulator and it provides an excellent research tool for the study of the PolyNoC processor.

The ns-2 simulator is a discrete event simulator targeting networking research. It has been used in a wide variety of networking research including simulation of NoC architecture and protocols. It provides support for a wide range of networking techniques, in addition to robust access to the underlying framework to allow for custom modification and extension of the simulator. Ns-2 is implemented in C++ with an interface layer based upon OTcl. All major simulation objects are created as discrete objects in C++. It provides very fine grained access to all objects within a network, packet structure, link parameters, routing agents, network node modeling, and support for modeling of all layers of the OSI stack. Beyond the extensive list of built in networking objects, ns-2 provides the ability to extend the platform to incorporate new designs and techniques. This extensibility is heavily utilized for modeling the PolyNoC network execution.

Ns-2 was modified and extended to support simulation of a processor executing with a NoC datapath. To facilitate this, a new custom set of applications, agents, nodes, and packets were added to the ns-2 simulator. All functional units within the processor are represented in the ns-2 simulator as an application. These applications then communicate with each other using the ns-2 node network simulation.

Using the ns-2 simulator, four main network topologies were studied and compared as shown in **Figure 4**. These topologies consist of Ring, Modified Ring, 2D Mesh, and Crossbar architectures. The ring architecture provides a simple baseline implementation. Due to the fact that a processor datapath is highly sequential, it is very similar to the flow of data through a traditional datapath. The modified ring structure attempts to provide a more robust scalability than the standard ring. In this architecture similar functional units are placed in parallel on the ring structure. This incurs a minor increase in link cost, but provides the same total delay over the ring regardless of number of functional units instantiated. The

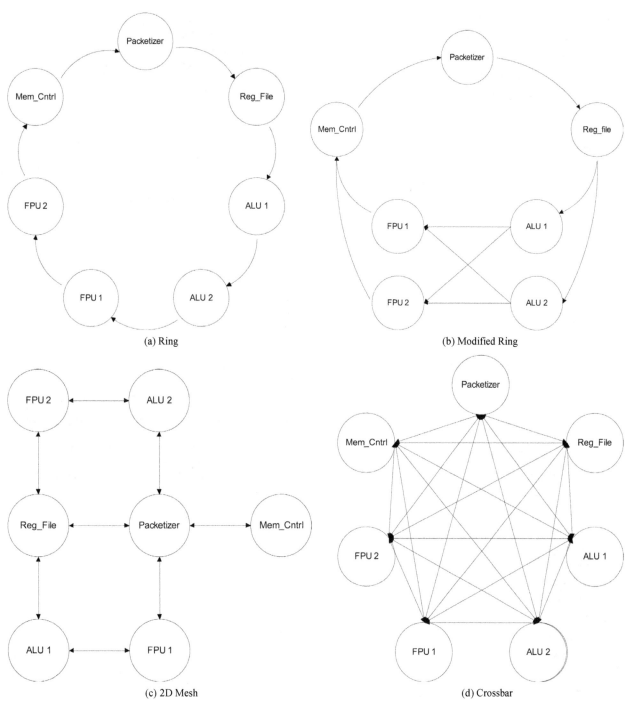

(a) Ring

(b) Modified Ring

(c) 2D Mesh

(d) Crossbar

Figure 4. NoC topologies investigated.

next architecture studied is the standard 2D mesh architecture. The architecture is a rectangular layout with bi-directional links between neighboring nodes. The final architecture explored is a crossbar. The crossbar architecture is an extreme architecture in which every node has a link to every other node. This shrinks all communications to only a single hop away, but comes with a very sharp increase in link cost as the network scales in nodes. **Figure 5** shows an example ns-2 script for evaluating the performance of a simple PolyNoC processor architecture (*i.e.*, ring topology with only basic functional elements).

In addition to exploration of the various topologies, the impact of increasing the number of functional units was also explored. The increase in the number of functional units and the ease of integration to the processor design is fundamental to a polymorphic processor. Increasing the number of computational functional units (both ALU

```
# This will simulate the CRC32 Algorithm
# with 1 ALU, 1 FPU, 1 RegFile, 1 MemCntrl
set FileName "CRC32_Ring_1_1_1_1"
# Select the benchmark to run
set Benchmark_Select_Num 4
# Link speed
set link_speed 6.4Gb
# Instruction Window Size
set inst_win_size 16
puts "Now starting execution of $FileName"


# Use only the needed packet headers.
remove-all-packet-headers
add-packet-header IP RTP NoC


# Create a new simulator object
set ns [new Simulator]
#Define a 'finish' procedure
proc finish {} {
        global ns nf FileName Benchmark_Select_Num
                    link_speed inst_win_size
        $ns flush-trace
    # Print details of the execution to the screen
    # for reference
    puts "Executed file $FileName"
    puts "Benchmark selected was $Benchmark_Select_Num"
    puts "Link Speed was $link_speed"
    puts "Instruction Window Size was $inst_win_size"
        exit 0
}
#Create five nodes
set n1 [$ns node]
set n2 [$ns node]
set n3 [$ns node]
set n4 [$ns node]
set n5 [$ns node]


#Create links between the nodes
$ns duplex-link $n1 $n2 $link_speed 0ms DropTail
$ns duplex-link $n2 $n3 $link_speed 0ms DropTail
$ns duplex-link $n3 $n4 $link_speed 0ms DropTail
$ns duplex-link $n1 $n5 $link_speed 0ms DropTail


# Attach NoC Agents to all nodes
set noc1 [new Agent/NoC]
$ns attach-agent $n1 $noc1
set noc2 [new Agent/NoC]
$ns attach-agent $n2 $noc2
```

```
set noc3 [new Agent/NoC]
$ns attach-agent $n3 $noc3
set noc4 [new Agent/NoC]
$ns attach-agent $n4 $noc4
set noc5 [new Agent/NoC]
$ns attach-agent $n5 $noc5


#Attach a NoC Packetizer to node 1.
set packetizer [new Application/NoC/Packetizer]
$packetizer attach-agent $noc1


#Attach a PE application to nodes 2-5.
set reg_file [new Application/NoC/PE]
$reg_file set process_time_ 0.00000001
$reg_file attach-agent $noc2
set alu [new Application/NoC/PE]
$alu attach-agent $noc3
set fpu [new Application/NoC/PE]
$fpu attach-agent $noc4
set mem_cntrl [new Application/NoC/PE]
$mem_cntrl set process_time_ 0.00000004
$mem_cntrl attach-agent $noc5


$packetizer set benchmark_select_ $Benchmark_Select_Num
$packetizer set inst_window_ $inst_win_size
$packetizer loadtrace
puts "We are done Loading the Trace"

$packetizer scheduler add-packetizer [$packetizer get-addr]
            [$packetizer get-port]
$packetizer scheduler add-reg_file [$reg_file get-addr]
            [$reg_file get-port]
$packetizer scheduler add-alu [$alu get-addr] [$alu get-port]
$packetizer scheduler add-fpu [$fpu get-addr] [$fpu get-port]
$packetizer scheduler add-mem_cntrl [$mem_cntrl get-addr]
            [$mem_cntrl get-port]
puts "We are done setting the processing element address."

$ns compute-routes

$packetizer sim-trace

#Call the finish procedure after 5 seconds of simulation time
$ns at 1.0 "finish_stats"
$ns at 1.0 "finish"

proc finish_stats {} {
        global reg_file alu fpu mem_cntrl
        set reg_util [$reg_file get-util]
        puts "Reg File utilization is $reg_util"
        set alu_util [$alu get-util]
        puts "ALU File utilization is $alu_util"
        set fpu_util [$fpu get-util]
        puts "FPU utilization is $fpu_util"
        set mem_util [$mem_cntrl get-util]
        puts "Mem control utilization is $mem_util"
}

#Run the simulation
$ns run
```

Figure 5. Sample ns-2 script for instantiating a PolyNoC processor architecture (ring topology).

and FPU) directly impacts the overall performance.

8. Simulation Results

For performance analysis, benchmark programs have been compiled for execution on the PolyNoC processor simulator. The benchmarks come from the well-known Mi-Bench benchmark suite [21]. MiBench provides a set of commercially representative embedded systems programs. Extracted from this set and used are the CRC32, FFT, IFFT, ADPCM.encode, ADPCM.decode, and BasicMath benchmark. This set of benchmarks provides a varied application load to get an initial impression on the performance of the proposed processor design.

- CRC32-Performs a 32-bit Cyclical Redundancy Check on input data. CRC checks are often used as error checking during data transmission.
- FFT/IFFT-Performs a fast Fourier transform or an inverse fast Fourier transform on an input data array. The FFT is used for frequency analysis during signal processing in a very wide range of application domains.
- ADPCM encode/decode-Adaptive Differential Pulse Code Modulation is a variation of the more common Pulse Code Modulation (PCM). This variation takes in 16-bit linear PCM samples and converts them to 4-bit samples providing significant compression. This algorithm is executed over samples of speech.
- BasicMath-Performs common mathematical computations that very frequently do not have hardware implementations. In this benchmark cubic function solving, integer square roots and angular conversion are computed.

Benchmark programs are first run on the TSIM LEON3 SPARC simulator. As the benchmarks are executed, a trace of all executed instructions is captured. This provides a cycle accurate, in-order instruction trace of the benchmark when it is executed on a commercially available SPARC processor. The instruction trace is then used as input to the ns-2 based simulator. The use of this trace provides an accurate traffic model of the execution of the PolyNoC processor. Trace based traffic model accurately represents the transmission of instruction packets into the NoC by the packetizer unit. This allows for very basic modeling of the instruction execution time, without being concerned with the full simulation of SPARC processor, significantly easing the implementation and execution time of the simulator.

The total execution time for all benchmarks can be seen in **Tables 1-4**. Table results show the total number of cycles to execute each benchmark with four different topologies. The total cycle count is an accurate measure of the performance of the processor. A higher performing processor will be able to execute more instructions in less

Table 1. Ring execution time (clock cycles).

Benchmark	1ALU 1FPU	2ALU 2FPU	ALU1 FPU2	ALU2 FPU2
FFT	6,126,842	4,852,776	6,085,547	5,012,044
IFFT	6,268,858	4,997,153	6,170,402	5,229,513
CRC32	55,454,286	56,015,776	37,911,220	39,543,279
BasicMath	55,457,834	55,999,913	48,527,041	48,667,159
ADPCM. decode	131,658,428	137,093,837	108,790,756	114,671,543
ADPCM. encode	137,409,561	141,663,042	108,037,207	112,377,209

Table 2. Modified ring execution time (clock cycles).

Benchmark	1ALU 1FPU	2ALU 2FPU	ALU1 FPU2	ALU2 FPU2
FFT	6,126,842	4,881,443	5,916,996	4,683,730
IFFT	6,268,858	5,024,278	6,001,722	4,737,821
CRC32	55,454,286	55,454,286	38,905,161	38,905,161
BasicMath	55,457,834	54,029,474	45,804,379	44,455,720
ADPCM. decode	131,658,428	131,658,428	100,332,329	100,332,329
ADPCM. encode	137,409,561	137,409,561	100,499,675	100,499,675

Table 3. 2D Mesh execution time (clock cycles).

Benchmark	1ALU 1FPU	2ALU 2FPU	ALU1 FPU2	ALU2 FPU2
FFT	5,767,886	4,351,394	5,495,290	4,082,665
IFFT	5,925,990	4,508,450	5,605,831	4,250,474
CRC32	51,971,730	51,971,730	33,941,356	33,941,356
BasicMath	51,937,483	50,494,185	41,226,881	39,269,764
ADPCM. decode	118,765,944	118,765,944	84,968,305	84,968,305
ADPCM. encode	129,321,184	129,321,184	88,790,061	88,790,061

Table 4. Crossbar execution time (clock cycles).

Benchmark	1ALU 1FPU	2ALU 2FPU	ALU1 FPU2	ALU2 FPU2
FFT	5,718,123	4,341,824	5,385,672	3,984,087
IFFT	5,876,096	4,498,707	5,500,106	4,099,194
CRC32	52,295,414	52,295,414	31,817,863	31,817,863
BasicMath	50,968,786	49,225,920	39,486,512	37,229,961
ADPCM. decode	118,781,718	118,781,718	85,392,11	82,539,211
ADPCM. encode	129,750,238	129,750,238	85,654,074	85,654,074

time. All the values presented were obtained using an instruction window size of 16, with an assumed NoC clock rate 8 times the datapath clock. It is reasonable assume the NoC clock can run at a higher rate then the functional elements datapath clock. This prevents the PolyNoC processor from becoming NoC bound wherein instruction execution time is limited by the NoC latency and the increase from additional functional units provides no performance gains.

Results show that all architectures exhibit scalability, and increased performance as the number of functional units increase. It can be seen that they all perform similar when only a single functional unit of each type is used. The advantages only become significant as the number of functional units increase. As the number of functional units is increased modestly from one to two ALUs/FPUs, significant performance improvements are achieved. It is important to note that a PolyNoC processor would allow this performance boost to be selectively applied during run time as reconfigurable elements are configured to act as additional functional units. The applications that are heavily FPU operation oriented benefit most from additional FPU elements, similarly ALU oriented benchmarks get more performance from an increase in number of ALU elements.

The ring architecture is simple and has very low resource cost however, its performance is lacking. The performance increase from additional function units is cannibalized by increased packet delay through the network. When more functional units are added, the latency of the overall NoC transmission increases due to the need to traverse the additional intermediate nodes. The additional penalty from NoC latency counteracts any performance gains from more functional elements, and in some cases actually lowers the overall performance of the PolyNoC processor. The modified ring architecture helps to mitigate the additional penalty from extra functional elements by eliminating the growth of delay when adding more functional units. In this case, the additional units do not increase the latency from NoC transmission. However, it still exhibits a similar weakness in overall structure; the ring based architecture delay is too high and prevents optimal processor execution either for the original ring or modified ring. On the other hand, the 2D Mesh architecture looks very promising as a candidate for NoC architecture. The max number of nodes compared to delay grows at a polynomial rate, producing a slow increase in delay relative to increase in total number of functional elements. Furthermore, for small mesh sizes, a large portion of communication occurs exclusively between neighboring nodes, allowing for an optimal 1 cycle delay time. This enables minimal latency. Near neighbor effect can also be maximized by careful layout of the 2D mesh. The mesh structure should be laid out such that node that frequently communicate with each other. For example, majority of instructions transits to the ALU after visiting the register file. Finally, the Crossbar architecture represents a reference point for comparison. It provides a connection from every node to every other node and it allows for a constant delay time of 1 clock for all packet transmissions. This can be seen as an upper limit to performance gains independent of architectural choices. This reference point is a valid comparison for

the other topologies. With all packet delays at an optimal 1 cycle delay, it achieves the highest PolyNoC performance. The overall performance is now limited by the performance of the functional elements, and the overall parallelism that can be extracted from the instruction stream.

Both the performance and the hardware resource consumption of the architectures can be seen in **Figure 6**. This figure presents the cost of each architecture based on the total number of individual point to point unidirectional links. Results indicate the superior performance of the 2D Mesh architecture. With much lower total cost, it is able to achieve a performance that is only slightly reduced from the upper limit set by the Crossbar implementation.

In conclusion, the 2D mesh structure is able to outperform all other topologies studied. It is able to scale well with additional functional units. As the more units are added, the additional latency in NoC transmission is controlled and overall system performance goes up. In general, the performance of the 2D mesh is fairly close to the theoretical maximum demonstrated through the crossbar architecture. 2D mesh structure also performs best at cost scaling. The link cost for point to point links grows very slowly compared to other implementation, while still providing large gains in total PolyNoC performance.

The final PolyNoC processor design with incorporation of optimal parameters can be seen in **Figure 7**. It shows the detailed layout of the NoC architecture and the placement of reconfigurable arrays and basic functional units. From the topology results, it is clear that the 2D mesh architecture provides the optimal balance of performance and cost. For these reasons it is chosen as the basis of the NoC architecture. This design provides a basic 4 × 4 mesh layout. This is a relatively small layout which could easily be scaled to larger size. 4 × 4 layout provides space for all basic units and a total of 11 reconfigurable arrays for application specific functional units. The design makes use of 2-input, 3-input, and 4-input switches as the backbone of the communication infrastructure. Each switch is interfaced to a single functional unit. Functional units can be a basic unit supporting the execution of the standard SPARC ISA, or a reconfigurable unit supporting the creation of new application specific instruction.

9. Conclusion

In this work, a new reconfigurable processor architecture has been introduced. Traditional fixed pipeline based datapath is replaced with a reconfigurable NoC based communications channel. Functional elements can communicate with others elements and they can be added and reconfigured dynamically enabling polymorphic operations. Several NoC topologies were explored to find the

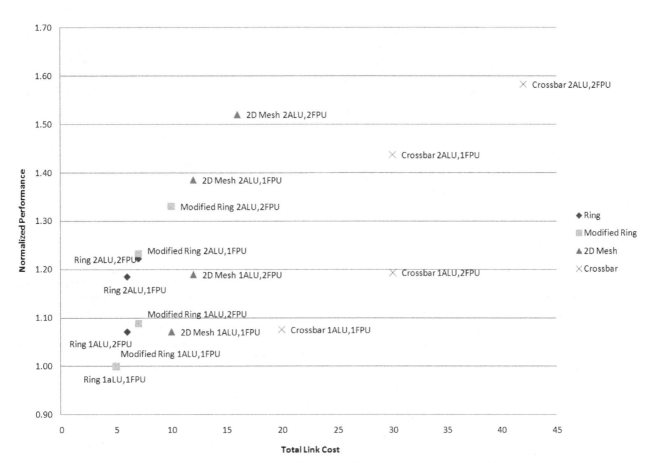

Figure 6. Cost vs performance analysis of different NoC topologies and number of functional units.

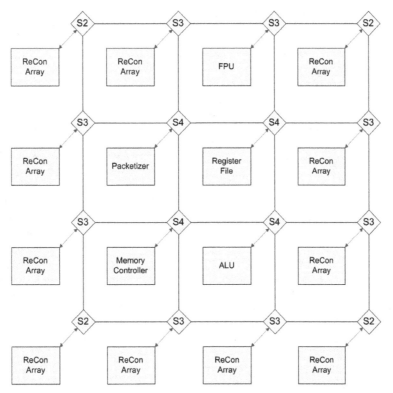

Figure 7. 4 × 4 2D mesh architecture.

optimal organization for a NoC based datapath. Industry standard MiBench benchmarks were used to study the execution of the PolyNoC processor. Results demonstrate that the PolyNoC processor provides significant advantages in flexibility of design. It is able to support both very large stream based optimizations (*i.e.*, computation of ADPCM block based encoding), while also performing very fine grained, highly coupled custom instruction group optimizations, (*i.e.*, optimization of the CRC32 hash update loop). Therefore, PolyNoC processor allows easy incorporation of reconfigurable arrays, both coarse and fine grained, for application specific optimizations.

REFERENCES

[1] "International Technology Roadmap for Semiconductors," 2009.
http://www.itrs.net/Links/2009ITRS/Home2009.htm

[2] D. Hentrich, E. Oruklu and J. Saniie, "Polymorphic Computing: Definition, Trends, and a New Agent-Based Architecture," *Circuits and Systems*, Vol. 2, No. 4, 2011, pp. 358-364.

[3] J. Weber, E. Oruklu and J. Saniie, "Architectural Topologies for NoC Datapath Polymorphic Processors," *IEEE International Conference on Electro/Information Technology*, Mankato, 15-17 May 2011, pp. 1-6.

[4] K. Compton and S. Hauck, "Reconfigurable Computing: A Survey of Systems and Software," *ACM Computing Surveys*, Vol. 34, No. 2, 2002, pp. 171-210.

[5] Z. Guo, W. Najjar, F. Vahid and K. Vissers, "A Quantitative Analysis of the Speedup Factors of FPGAs over Processors," *FPGA Proceedings of the ACM/SIGDA 12th International Symposium on Field Programmable Gate Arrays*, New York, 2004, pp. 162-170.

[6] K. Underwood, "FPGAs vs CPUs: Trends in Peak Floating-Point Performance," *FPGA Proceedings of the ACM/SIGDA 12th International Symposium on Field Programmable Gate Arrays*, New York, 2004, pp. 171-180.

[7] T. Todman, G. Constantinides, S. Wilton, O. Mencer, W. Luk and P. Cheung, "Reconfigurable Computing: Architectures and Design Methods," *IEEE Proceedings of Computers and Digital Techniques*, Vol. 152, No. 2, 2005, pp. 193-207.

[8] R. Cheung, N. Telle, W. Luk and P. Cheung, "Customizable Elliptic Curve Cryptosystems," *IEEE Transactions on Very Large Scale Integration Systems*, Vol. 13, No. 9, 2005, pp. 1048-1059.

[9] P. Baglietto, M. Maresca and M. Migliardi, "Euclidean Distance Transform on Polymorphic Processor Array," *CAMP Proceedings of Computer Architectures for Machine Perception*, Como, 18-20 September 1995, pp. 288-293.

[10] G. Kuzmanov and W. van Oijen, "Floating-Point Matrix Multiplication in a Polymorphic Processor," *ICFPT International Conference on Field-Programmable Technology*, Kitakyushu, 12-15 December 2007, pp. 249-252.

[11] S. Chai, S. Chiricescu, R. Essick, B. Lucas, P. May, K. Moat, J. Norris, M. Schuette and A. Lopez-Lagunas, "Streaming Processors for Next Generation Mobile Imaging Applications," *Communications Magazine*, Vol. 43, No. 12, 2005, pp. 81-89.

[12] H. Hubert and B. Stabernack, "Profiling-Based Hardware/Software Coexploration for the Design of Video Coding Architectures," *IEEE Transactions on Circuits and Systems for Video Technology*, Vol. 19, No. 11, 2009, pp. 1680-1691.

[13] C. Rupp, M. Landguth, T. Garverick, E. Gomersall, H. Holt, J. Arnold and M. Gokhale, "The Napa Adaptive Processing Architecture," *IEEE Symposium on Proceedings of FPGAs for Custom Computing Machines*, 17 April 1998, pp. 28-37.

[14] S. Vassiliadis, S. Wong, G. Gaydadjiev, K. Bertels, G. Kuzmanov and E. Panainte, "The Molen Polymorphic Processor," *IEEE Transactions on Computers*, Vol. 53, No. 11, 2004, pp. 1363-1375.

[15] N. Vassiliadis, G. Theodoridis and S. Nikolaidis, "The Arise Approach for Extending Embedded Processors with Arbitrary Hardware Accelerators," *IEEE Transactions on Very Large Scale Integration Systems*, Vol. 17, No. 2, 2009, pp. 221-233.

[16] M. Gokhale and J. Stone, "NAPA C: Compiling for a Hybrid Risc/Fpga Architecture," *IEEE Symposium on Proceedings of FPGAs for Custom Computing Machines*, 17 April 1998, pp. 126-135.

[17] J. Cong, G. Han and Z. Zhang, "Architecture and Compiler Optimizations for Data Bandwidth Improvement in Configurable Processors," *IEEE Transactions on Very Large Scale Integration Systems*, Vol. 14, No. 9, 2006, pp. 986-997.

[18] S. Gupta, N. Dutt, R. Gupta and A. Nicolau, "SPARK: A High-Level Synthesis Framework for Applying Parallelizing Compiler transformations," *Proceedings of the 16th International Conference on VLSI Design*, New Delhi, 4-8 January 2003, pp. 461-466.

[19] The SPARC Architecture Manual, Version 8, Sun Microsystems, 1992. http://www.sparc.org/standards/V8.pdf

[20] Ns-2, The Network Simulator.
http://nsnam.isi.edu/nsnam/index.php/Main_Page

[21] M. Guthaus, J. Ringenberg, D. Ernst, T. Austin, T. Mudge and R. Brown, "Mibench: A Free, Commercially Representative Embedded Benchmark Suite," *IEEE International Workshop on Workload Characterization*, December 2001, pp. 3-14.

Permissions

The contributors of this book come from diverse backgrounds, making this book a truly international effort. This book will bring forth new frontiers with its revolutionizing research information and detailed analysis of the nascent developments around the world.

We would like to thank all the contributing authors for lending their expertise to make the book truly unique. They have played a crucial role in the development of this book. Without their invaluable contributions this book wouldn't have been possible. They have made vital efforts to compile up to date information on the varied aspects of this subject to make this book a valuable addition to the collection of many professionals and students.

This book was conceptualized with the vision of imparting up-to-date information and advanced data in this field. To ensure the same, a matchless editorial board was set up. Every individual on the board went through rigorous rounds of assessment to prove their worth. After which they invested a large part of their time researching and compiling the most relevant data for our readers. Conferences and sessions were held from time to time between the editorial board and the contributing authors to present the data in the most comprehensible form. The editorial team has worked tirelessly to provide valuable and valid information to help people across the globe.

Every chapter published in this book has been scrutinized by our experts. Their significance has been extensively debated. The topics covered herein carry significant findings which will fuel the growth of the discipline. They may even be implemented as practical applications or may be referred to as a beginning point for another development. Chapters in this book were first published by Scientific Research Publishing Inc.; hereby published with permission under the Creative Commons Attribution License or equivalent.

The editorial board has been involved in producing this book since its inception. They have spent rigorous hours researching and exploring the diverse topics which have resulted in the successful publishing of this book. They have passed on their knowledge of decades through this book. To expedite this challenging task, the publisher supported the team at every step. A small team of assistant editors was also appointed to further simplify the editing procedure and attain best results for the readers.

Our editorial team has been hand-picked from every corner of the world. Their multi-ethnicity adds dynamic inputs to the discussions which result in innovative outcomes. These outcomes are then further discussed with the researchers and contributors who give their valuable feedback and opinion regarding the same. The feedback is then collaborated with the researches and they are edited in a comprehensive manner to aid the understanding of the subject.

Apart from the editorial board, the designing team has also invested a significant amount of their time in understanding the subject and creating the most relevant covers. They scrutinized every image to scout for the most suitable representation of the subject and create an appropriate cover for the book.

The publishing team has been involved in this book since its early stages. They were actively engaged in every process, be it collecting the data, connecting with the contributors or procuring relevant information. The team has been an ardent support to the editorial, designing and production team. Their endless efforts to recruit the best for this project, has resulted in the accomplishment of this book. They are a veteran in the field of academics and their pool of knowledge is as vast as their experience in printing. Their expertise and guidance has proved useful at every step. Their uncompromising quality standards have made this book an exceptional effort. Their encouragement from time to time has been an inspiration for everyone.

The publisher and the editorial board hope that this book will prove to be a valuable piece of knowledge for researchers, students, practitioners and scholars across the globe.

List of Contributors

Yosuke Sugiura, Arata Kawamura and Youji Iiguni
Graduate School of Engineering Science, Osaka University, Osaka, Japan

Asha Shendge and Naoto Nagaoka
Department of Electrical and Electronics Engineering, Doshisha University, Kyoto, Japan

Geoffrey O. Asiegbu and Kamarul Hawari
Faculty of Electrical and Electronics Engineering, University Malaysia Pahang, Kuantan, Malaysia

Ahmed M. A. Haidar
School of Electrical, Computer and Telecommunications Engineering, University of Wollongong, Wollongong, Australia

Sonia Zouari, Houda Daoud, Mourad Loulou and Nouri Masmoudi
Information Technologies and Electronics Laboratory National Engineering School of Sfax, Sfax, Tunisia

Patrick Loumeau
Electronics and Communications Department, Telecom ParisTech, Paris, France

Dinesh Prasad and Data Ram Bhaskar
Department of Electronics and Communication Engineering, Faculty of Engineering and Technology, Jamia Millia Islamia, New Delhi, India

Mayank Srivastava
Department of Electronics and Communication Engineering, Amity School of Engineering and Technology, Amity University, Noida, India

Somchai Srisakultiew
Department of Computer Engineering, Faculty of Engineering and Architecture, Rajamangala University of Technology, Isan, Nakhonratsima, Thailand
Department of Teacher Training in Electrical Engineering, Faculty of Technical Education, King Mongkut's University of Technology North Bangkok, Bangkok, Thailand

Montree Siripruchyanun
Department of Teacher Training in Electrical Engineering, Faculty of Technical Education, King Mongkut's University of Technology North Bangkok, Bangkok, Thailand

Lars Q. English and Mauro David Lifschitz
Department of Physics and Astronomy, Dickinson College, Carlisle, USA

Sunil Acharya
a.t.Q Services LLC, Carlisle, USA

Kim Fung Tsang, Yi Shen and Kwok Tai Chui
Department of Electronic Engineering, City University of Hong Kong, Hong Kong, China

Wah Ching Lee
Department of Electronic & Information Engineering, The Hong Kong Polytechnic University, Hong Kong, China
Department of Electronic Engineering, City University of Hong Kong, Hong Kong, China

Mihai Grigore Timis, Alexandru Valachi, Alexandru Barleanu and Andrei Stan
Automatic Control and Computer Engineering Faculty, Technical University Gh.Asachi, Iasi, Romania

R. Rezaei
Department of Electronic Engineering, Bahcesehir University, Istanbul, Turkey

A. Ahmadpour
Department of Electronic Engineering, Islamic Azad University (Lahijan Branch), Lahijan, Iran
Department of Electronic Engineering, Islamic Azad University (Science and Research Branch), Tehran, Iran

M. N. Moghaddasi
Department of Electronic Engineering, Islamic Azad University (Science and Research Branch), Tehran, Iran

Kanhaiya Lal Pushkar
Department of Electronics and Communication Engineering, Maharaja Agrasen Institute of Technology, New Delhi, India

Davood Fathi and Baback Beig Mohammadi
School of Electrical and Computer Engineering, Tarbiat Modares University (TMU), Tehran, Iran

Xinwei Niu and Jeffrey Fan
Department of Electrical and Computer Engineering, Florida International University, Miami, USA

Sanjeev Rai and Ram Awadh Mishra
Department of Electronics & Communication Engineering, Motilal Nehru National Institute of Technology Allahabad, Allahabad, India

Sudarshan Tiwari
National Institute of Technology, Raipur, India

Akira Sogami, Yosuke Sugiura, Arata Kawamura and Youji Iiguni
Department of Systems Innovation, Graduate School of Engineering Science, Osaka University, Toyonaka, Japan

Soolmaz Abbasalizadeh, Samad Sheikhaei and Behjat Forouzandeh
School of Electrical and Computer Engineering, University of Tehran, Tehran, Iran

Hassan Jassim
Department of Electrical Engineering, College of Engineering, Babylon University, Babylon, Iraq

Kasim Karam Abdalla
Department of Electrical Engineering, Engineering Colloge, University of Babylon, Hilla, Iraq

Li Ke, Peter Wilson and Reuben Wilcock
Electronics and Computer Science, University of Southampton, Southampton, UK

Yasuhisa Omura and Yukio Iida
Department of Electric, Electronics and Informatics, Kansai University, Suita, Japan

Angel Parra-Cerrada, Vicente González-Posadas, José Luis Jiménez-Martín and Alvaro Blanco
Department Ingeniería Audiovisual y Comunicaciones, Universidad Politécnica de Madrid, Madrid, Spain

Haleh Vahedi
The Edwards S. Rogers Sr. Department of Electrical and Computer Engineering, University of Toronto, Toronto, Canada

Radu Muresan and Stefano Gregori
School of Engineering, University of Guelph, Guelph, Canada

Manish Kumar and Md. Anwar Hussain
Department of ECE, North Eastern Regional Institute of Science & Technology, Nirjuli, Arunachal Pradesh, India

Sajal K. Paul
Department of Electronics Engineering, Indian School of Mines, Dhanbad, Jharkhand, India

Mohammad Rafiq Beigh, Mohammad Mustafa and Firdous Ahmad
Department of Electronics & Instrumentation Technology, University of Kashmir, Srinagar, India

Abdoul Rjoub and Hassan Almanasrah
Computer Engineering Department, Jordan University of Science and Technology, Irbid, Jordan

Almotasem Bellah Alajlouni
Information Technology Department, Balqa' Applied University, Irbid, Jordan

Joshua Weber and Erdal Oruklu
Department of Electrical and Computer Engineering, Illinois Institute of Technology, Chicago, USA

Printed in the USA
CPSIA information can be obtained
at www.ICGtesting.com
JSHW052021301024
72690JS00004B/125